# THE CATTLEMEN

Books by Mari Sandoz
published by the UNP

THE BEAVER MEN (BB 658)
THE BUFFALO HUNTERS (BB 659)
THE CATTLEMEN (BB 660)
THE CHRISTMAS OF THE PHONOGRAPH RECORDS
CRAZY HORSE (BB 110)
HOSTILES AND FRIENDLIES
LOVE SONG TO THE PLAINS (BB 349)
MISS MORISSA (BB 739)
OLD JULES (BB 100)
SANDHILL SUNDAYS AND OTHER RECOLLECTIONS
SLOGUM HOUSE (BB 756)
SON OF THE GAMBLIN' MAN (BB 626)

# THE CATTLEMEN

## FROM THE RIO GRANDE
## ACROSS THE FAR MARIAS

BY

## MARI SANDOZ

**UNIVERSITY OF NEBRASKA PRESS**
**Lincoln and London**

*First Bison Book printing: 1978*

Most recent printing indicated by first digit below:
3    4    5    6    7    8    9    10

**Library of Congress Cataloging in Publication Data**

Sandoz, Mari, 1896–1966.
The cattlemen from the Rio Grande across the far Marias.

Reprint of the ed. published by Hastings House, New York, in series:
American procession series.
Bibliography: p. 503
1. The West—History—1848–1950. 2. Ranch life—The West—History.
3. Cattle trade—The West. 4. Frontier and pioneer life—The West. I. Title.
[F594.S255    1978]    978    77–14078
ISBN 0–8032–5882–8 pbk.

Bison Book edition published by arrangement with Hastings House, Publishers,
Inc.

Manufactured in the United States of America

To the old-time hard-bitten, hard-driven cowmen, the greatest believers in next year, and the year after that—

# CONTENTS

# ACKNOWLEDGMENTS

ACKNOWLEDGMENT for assistance is due: the Nebraska State Historical Society for almost thirty years of gracious help, from Myrtle D. Berry and Donald F. Danker in more recent years; Ina Aulls, the Western History Division, Denver Public Library; the Colorado State Historical Society; Lola M. Homsher, Wyoming State Archives and Historical Department; Gene M. Gressley, Library, University of Wyoming; Illerna Friend, Barker Texas History Center, University of Texas; C. Boone McClure and the Jack Hughes' of the Panhandle Plains Historical Museum; Oklahoma Historical Society; Kansas State Historical Society; War Records and Indian Records, National Archives; American History Room, and Map and Newspaper Divisions, New York Public Library; Sylvester Vigilante, New York Historical Society; Senator D. J. Cole and Pat Hooper, Nebraska; J. C. Eaton, Denbigh, North Dakota, and many, many others, including my five brothers and sisters running cattle in the sandhills of Nebraska. They and many others keep me aware of the problems facing the rancher with no oil wells, no bank stock, just cattle.

M. S.

# FOREWORD

On all the Great Plains, reaching like a thumb down from Canada deep into the country of the Rio Grande, the one enduring figure has been the man who works with cattle. He came with the first Spanish cows, saw them multiply thick as the buffaloes on the prairie. He watched the Stone Age Indian turn into a mounted rifleman, the hide hunters sweep the buffalo away, and the starving Indians finally depart for the reservations. He had to see the newly freed range vanish before the homesteader, perhaps permanently, at least to be paid for in hard cash.

The first rancher I can remember was a tall man riding past our home on the upper Niobrara River. He sat his saddle so the fringe of his gauntlets barely stirred in the long easy trot, his horse a fine star-faced, well-coupled black, spirited but not shying from the small girl who ran from her grandmother's grasp to see. That rancher, I know now, was not very different from the old Texas cowmen of the 1850's, not in saddle, use of rope, or in the slant of his eye over the range— not even very different in these things from the early vaquero. Although my first glimpse of the rancher was back in the homestead period, when much of the higher Plains region was still free grass, government land, he could be riding through my home region today, with the same saddle and coiled rope. Even if he was in a range jeep or a light plane his eye would still slant in the same way over the grass and the stock.

Some people consider our rancher, next to the farmer (without whom we would all starve), as the most important man of our meat-rich nation. Many who are concerned with the problems of mankind upon the earth point to the population explosions in the low-protein regions, and during such meat-hungry times as wars. It is true that in the buffalo days the Plains Indian had little difficulty spacing his children so no woman was encumbered by more than one child too young to flee on his own legs from an enemy attack or a buffalo stampede. Now, on a poor man's starchy diet, our Indian population seems to be increasing at something like the appalling rate of the protein-starved peoples of Asia.

But to most of the world the cattleman and his cowboys, good and bad, are not known for the significance of their beef production. Instead they are the dramatic, the romantic figures of a West, a Wild West that is largely imaginary. To some of the rest of us, however, the rancher is the encompassing, the continuous and enduring symbol of modern man on the Great Plains. His number has grown vast and varied through the long years since the first Spanish cows trailed their dust eastward from the Pecos, and his stories have become as numerous as the Longhorns that burgeoned in the new land. I have tried, through a few selected individuals and incidents, to show something of the nature and the contrasts, something of the conflicts and the achievements of the cattlemen as a whole. I have tried to take the reader to a high ridge, where all but the nearest arroyos and canyons are hidden, where the cactus and the sage blend into the greening sweep of prairie that reaches far into the hazy horizon of May.

MARI SANDOZ

# BOOK I

*THE RELUCTANT IMMIGRANT*

## FIRST COW UPON
## THE PLAINS

SHE came first in a mirage, behind a long string of glorious although worn and impatient horsemen, moving out of the heat and shimmer of the west. By comparison she and the rest of the cattle herd seemed without significance, a little like the great humpbacked wild cows of the Plains, but smaller, longer of horn, and almost lost in the plume of dust raised by the riders up ahead. Like every mirage, this one, too, was actual somewhere, a great expedition crossing the high gray tableland between the river of the Pecos and the far curving of cap rock that fell eastward, cut by many snake-head canyons from whose red rock the east-flowing streams were born.

The Indian runners and their signaling had spread warning of these pale-faced, black-bearded men riding their big horses and carrying sharp and dangerous weapons of iron, and the noise-making fire sticks that had helped destroy whole Indian pueblo cities. Many of these white men were protected against arrow and spear heads of stone by their hard clothing that shone like silver and one, the leader, rode in a garment yellow as the late winter sun on ice, like the glistening yellow pebbles sometimes found in streams and in the mountains—the *oro,* the gold that the pale faces sought and demanded, demanded in whole cities.

These things the runners told, advising the other In•
dians to scatter or retreat to the canyons, but none of them
seemed to mention what was to be more important here
than any fire stick or improbable city of gold—the tame and
manageable cows that followed behind the bearded men.

This second season on the trail Coronado had cut his
cattle herd to 500 head, those in front still the stronger
young cows, their leader a long-bodied, well-horned four-
year-old, her coat the color of sun on heat-bleached earth,
the dark spots on face and rump like leaf shadows, here
where no leafed plant seemed to grow. The cattle she led
were of many colors, from white through yellows, reds,
browns, and blacks, spotted, mottled, and brindled, too,
grown and yearlings, all dusty soon after their swim across
the Pecos.

These cattle with Coronado were brought out of Mexico not for breeding but for eating, both young and old, a
walking commissary, their skins to furnish material for the
coarse shoes and the riatas, for the sacks and pouches and the
hundred leathern things of the expedition on the trail.

Now they were well east of the Pecos and the Spaniards rode harder, aiming for a swift and, it was hoped, a
short journey. Far behind them the cows were urged along
by the Indians, ally and captive. Here and there the spotted
lead cow and the rest managed to grab a few mouthfuls of
vagrant grass in some low spot, around some dried water
hole, the cattle bawling less as they grew leaner, the dust settling upon them until they were more and more the color
of the dead upland.

For days east of the Pecos there seemed not a rock, not
one bit of rising ground, not a tree or shrub or anything to
guide the eye across the heated, mirage-hung plain; no sign
of water, not even a sight of the Indians who spied out the
progress of these men of bloodshed. So faint was the trail of
the entire expedition that a man sent back to pick up a
piece of lost baggage had to pile up cow dung and a few
whitened bones so he could find his returning way over the

baked earth. It became increasingly difficult to hold the thirsting horses, even with the bloodied Spanish bits. The hoarse bawling of the cattle was lost as their tongues swelled and hung out. For all the angry threats and sword blows from their masters, the herders let the cattle break into hard, awkward gallops at the least smell of water, caught from far off, the lead cow a true daughter of the arid uplands of Spain, missing nothing. And when the herd reached the few gray water holes, the cattle could not be held back but plunged in, trampling those in front into the mud, or drinking too much of the alkali waters and sickening, perhaps staggering off to die alone.

Finally the land began to change as subtilely as the haze upon it, with shy little clumps of shaggy or varnished blooming plants—yellow, perhaps, or cactus red, and finally the strips of blue flowers, blue as narrow lakes, or fallen sky. Here and there a deep gash cut the dead earth, perhaps with red-streaked canyon walls, and a clump of dusty cottonwoods or scrub oak at the bottom. Sometimes there were trails now, narrow as two hands, radiating from the dry water holes and the canyons, the paths of the humpbacked cows, the Indians said.

Now the droppings of these buffaloes grew plentiful, and very well cured for hot evening fires. They found places where Indians had fled, and came upon some in skin shelters, with meat drying, their burden-bearing dogs standing to bark at the cattle herd, or the silent ones coming to run among them, nipping at their heels, sending them into a scattering stampede. But they did not run far, gathering in a green pocket to feed, cropping swiftly as they had learned to do whenever there was grass. Plainly there had been early water and grass here, perhaps back in March, enough so the cattle of Coronado could have lived well. There were curious holes that the Indian guides called buffalo wallows, dry as cracking stone now, but also filled with water once.

The eighth day from the Pecos the Spaniards heard a far roaring for an hour or so and then, when their cattle were much disturbed, trying to run that way, the whole expedition was suddenly surrounded by a dark and moving herd of monsters that browsed in their swift walk, every direction black with the grunting, snuffling, great-bodied buffaloes. Coronado's men tried to push past the tossing, shaggy heads, but while those down-wind ran off in thunderous speed, their thin, plume-ended tails up, those coming through ahead moved straight on, blocking the way as though the Spaniards did not exist.

There was trouble with the cattle herd now, suddenly lonesome for even these strange relatives. The roaring and fighting of the wild buffalo bulls excited them, too, set up a bellowing, particularly among the male yearlings that had escaped the butcher's knife and were now growing into ambitious young bulls. A thinly-covered wildness was suddenly laid bare among these cattle, particularly in those that had been gathered from the early stock gone free in the northern settlements of Mexico.

After the first herd the Spaniards were never far from buffaloes or the nomadic Indians who slipped up in small parties to kill the less wary with bow and lance or to stampede a few over some canyon wall with whooping, flapping robes or perhaps with fire. By now the expedition had reached the great cap rock that ran into the horizon both north and southward, the bluff line cut by many canyons like the claw marks of some gigantic bear reaching for his prey. Deep in one of these wide gashes, between the red and purplish canyon walls, flowed a clear, glistening stream, through bottoms that were green and flowery and spacious enough for all the Spanish stock for weeks.

There was a little skirmish with warriors from the Indian village in the canyon but Coronado whipped them easily and settled there for several days to rehabilitate his worn men and stock. But the cattle had to be watched carefully against the curious and thieving Indians who drove off several head while the herders dozed.

One afternoon a great dark cloud came rolling out of the arid west, with a terrifying roar of wind and crashing thunder. Indians and whites, too, fled up the canyon walls as the sky opened, the hailstones large as nuts, some large as Spanish oranges, and driven by the powerful wind into every overhang of rock, chopping into the soft layerings. The lightning was a constant flashing of yellow, and rose and violet, the thunder shaking the bleeding red walls. The terrified horses plunged and fought their picket ropes until most were free and bolting up the steep sides of the canyon to escape the fury trapped and echoing there. A few of the officers' horses were shielded a little by the bucklers and helmets that the slaves managed to hold over them, but hardly one of the rest escaped some injury from the storm or the panic. The soldier tents were swept away, even the armor dented.

Although farther back in the narrowing, more protective canyon, the meat animals had stampeded, too, with many sheep killed, and the foolish cattle running far through the branching canyons and breaks, some broken or dead from plunges over precipices and into deep arroyos, the herd altogether so scattered that none could be certain all the live ones were eventually found.

From there Coronado turned southward, now and then crossing deep-cut springs and small streams that perhaps died in the sand farther on, rarely with water enough to satisfy the large herds still left to him. Forage, too, was short and more cattle became hoof-worn, even the spotted lead cow. Worse, Coronado could hear no word of the golden cities from the Indians anywhere, although one man remembered white travelers who had been through here; not like these riders in iron and gold, with the herd of spotted cattle following, but three white men and one black, walking, all poor and very, very hungry, years ago.

Ah, yes, the lost Cabeza de Vaca, The Head of a Cow, who, with his fellows, had wandered seven years through the wilderness afoot. It was he who had brought them much news of the rich and wondrous cities that lay beside a great river. Coronado heard the old Indian's story with concern. If De Vaca passed here, then the golden cities must be back north, farther north even than the Canyon of the Storm. But the men of the army were sullen and hungry, the corn all gone, and only meat left, buffalo or the gaunted sheep and stringy cattle. Even the horses were rough-coated and bony, a disgrace to any well-born Spaniard. The general was determined to go on, but he must move faster, lighter. He selected around thirty horsemen, half-a-dozen strong foot soldiers, one of the blue-robed friars, an untrusted guide, and some Indians, and so struck northward for Quivira. Reluctantly the army and the rest, the herdsmen, too, saw him go and then did as ordered—started back across the burning plain of summer to the Pecos and the corn-growing pueblos of the upper Rio Grande. They went reluctantly, many looking northward to where their general and the more fortunate ones had vanished into the hazy, shimmering horizon, this time surely on the trail of the golden Quivira.

As had happened before, a footsore cow could be forgotten this hurried, unhappy morning. In a gnarled and thorny thicket of mesquite and cactus back from the waters of the Colorado of the South, the spotted lead cow stood hidden, motionless. Once she was drawn to follow the herd she had led so long, but she was very lamed and had escaped the butchers only because there was plenty of fat and tender buffalo for their gleaming knives. Perhaps she lifted her head to bawl her concern, but even the smell of the departing herd was gone with the shifting wind. She snorted the dust from her dewed nostrils and the moment of loneliness dropped from her, as all things would drop from her in their ripening time, the ticks that were so much a part of her Spanish kind, and the calf she bore.

After a while a cud ran up her throat and slowly her jaw began to move from side to side, her eyes closing, her tawny hide like the sun on the dusty, drouth-faded prairies

she had crossed, her head and flanks spotted as with leaf
shadows there among the thorns and cactus.

It is assumed that there were few if any survivals
from the cattle that escaped the herd Coronado brought to
Texas, but those he left behind exhausted in northern Mexico propagated very fast, so fast that twenty-five years later
they had increased to wild herds numbering in the thousands. They and the earlier stock that had strayed from the
northern Mexican settlements found America even more
compatible than their old homeland. In 1555 seventy or
eighty bulls were brought from these far reaches to Mexico
City for the bullfights, some of them twenty years old, *cimarrones,* outlaws that had never seen a man, at least no white
man.

Naturally the region that grew millions of buffaloes
could be expected to prove a fine seed bed for the much more
adaptable and varied horned immigrant from Spain, one so
much a part of those peoples that Cortes called his splendid
palace Cuernavaca—Cow's Horn. But Mexico had problems far south of the Rio Grande, including a serious uprising, silver mine booms, and new settlements to be built and
controlled. Finally, forty years after Coronado's journey, a
whole rash of explorers and colonizers, official or surrepti-
tious, started north, some to seek out Quivira or at least gold,
more to spy on the French said to be encroaching from the
regions beyond the Mississippi.

Then in 1598 Juan de Onate put 7,000 head of livestock and a million dollars into a self-supporting colony in
New Mexico, the first on what was to become United States
ground. Hard behind him came the Franciscans and Jesuits,
to plant their missions that were economic and defensive institutions as well as spiritual. Thousands of Indians were
gathered to these as neophytes and grounded not only in the
Faith but in the arts and crafts of the vineyard and the pasture as well. They were taught to grow and handle cattle on
the choice ranges of the padres, to ride that new creature, the

horse, like centaurs in their herdings and so become the first vaqueros—developing the equipment and the techniques for a whole new life and livelihood.

From Coronado on animals escaped the traveling herds and strayed from the unfenced pasturages. Often they were scattered by Indians who hunted them for the sport of killing the curious creatures and, where there were no buffaloes, for meat and to trail along with the village, a wondrous servant to the Indians who knew the stubborn resistance of even the buffalo calf to the lead thong or the herder's urgings. These spotted cattle of the white man were more manageable than even the pack dogs.

The escaped cows learned to follow the shrinking waters of the summer heat as the buffaloes did, saving themselves by their cunning from all but the whipping of winter storms. Before these they drifted southward, humped up and shivering, while the buffaloes faced the northers and grew thick and matted wool on their heads and forequarters against the cold. The great drouth of the middle 1660's was severe enough to drive the game, particularly the buffalo herds, from vast stretches of their customary range. The hunting Indians of the region found it easier and more exciting to fall upon the tamed Indians who grew corn and beans, melons and fruits in large fields and gardens, as well as cattle for the missions. They swept off the mission horses and, mounted, rode wild as the wind, stampeding the herds of the padres in every direction. They started regular raids across the Rio Grande to drive off the horses and cattle of the Mexicans. In the flight back an occasional wild-eyed cow broke for the brush or sneaked away to hunt out her home pasture, or her calf that had been killed because it could not keep up. These were seldom pursued, their number augmented by occasional stampedes of small herds, perhaps by the smell of a cougar hunting in the night or by thunder and wind and hail. These cattle took to the breaks and the brush, hiding by day, grazing in the night and early morning —soon as wild as the spotted and black cattle reported very early in the Texas country, perhaps descendants of those lost by the first explorers, even if not from the lead cow of Coronado and others of his herd.

All these years the pueblo Indians of the New Mexico region had suffered inhuman treatment from the Spaniards—the soldiers, colonists, and the secular authorities. Many lived in rank slavery despite the orders of the king and the protests of the missionaries. Finally the only thing the Indians had lacked—a leader—appeared, and in 1680 the whole pueblo region was suddenly aflame. Great herds of cattle were whooped away as the Spaniards were driven out, the missions emptied and destroyed, the tame Indians scattered. Then, when there was little left in the pueblo country worth the raiding, the tamer Indians of west Texas suffered almost continuous attack from the wilder tribes. Finally, in desperation, the victims sent delegations under baptized natives to the Spaniards, asking them to return to their old region, to bring back the trade, and the protection.

Although the first little missions in Texas seem to have been established down on the Rio Grande by refugees from those farther up, they probably had some cattle. The first herd of any importance into Texas, however, seems to have been the seed stock brought by Alonso de Leon and his missionaries in 1689. He was sent against the French who had been pushing into east Texas. Some say that at every river from the Rio Grande to the Louisiana border he turned loose a bull and a cow, a stallion and a mare. Certainly the first missions established on the Neches River in 1690 had a seed herd of 200 cattle, which the Indians scattered as fast as they multiplied, and faster. Most of the wild game seemed to vanish, too, and in three years the missionaries were reduced to eating crows. By then the French menace had lessened and the missions and the scattered stock were all abandoned. These cattle became the breeders of the great wild herds that increased so fast it was almost an explosion in the hospitable brushy river bottoms. It was 1716 before the

Spanish established permanent missions and colonies in Texas and long before that cattle and horses were running loose by the thousands in the Neches region, with wild cattle thick in the brush of the Trinity River bottoms, too—cattle that were fast and very fat. There were black bulls among them, as black and glistening as court satin—Castilian bulls grown larger, rangier, their legs and horns both lengthening, it seemed.

The new missions were strung from the region of the French threat westward to the upper San Antonio River, the latter soon the center of settlement. When the Indians once more harried the padres out of the eastern missions they also moved to the San Antonio.

Gradually stock raising became almost the only civilian occupation despite the government's attempts to compel farming. The most prolific ranches in Texas were, however, around the Goliad missions, farther down the San Antonio River. By 1770 the Mission of Espiritu Santo claimed to have 40,000 cattle, branded and unmarked, between the Guadalupe and the lower San Antonio. It was assumed, without anybody trying to prove it, that the unbranded could be gathered in a roundup of those with brands, in contrast to the uncontrollable *cimarrones,* the true wild ones.

As long as Louisiana was French, export of cattle and hides was banned to that region and with Mexican markets much too far, the herds were worth very little. At Espiritu Santo and Rosario bulls were prized mostly for the fiestas. There were no matadors or bull rings but there were always the "Days of the Bulls," with bull-tailing, bull-roping, and riding. If an animal was to be castrated, it was more exciting and more dangerous to wait until he was grown and then run him down and rope him as a wild one on the prairie. This method produced many new *cimarrones,* bulls that took up with the cattle born to the brush.

In 1767 horned cattle had been seen west of the Brazos, wild and roaming in large herds over the plains far from any settlement. Hunting wild bulls was by then the established sport and a Frenchman crossing Texas was taken on such a hunt. He observed that only the slowest could be run down, the swiftest, wildest always escaped, to pass on their excellence. In 1777 another Frenchman found "Castilian" cattle and mustang horses on the Brazos River and on the Colorado, too, not far from Coronado's camp of two hundred and thirty-six years ago in incredible numbers. They were hunted as the other wild creatures, the buffalo, the cougar and the javelina and could be even more dangerous.

Back in 1757 the Spaniards had founded a mission and presidio up on the San Saba River for the Lipan Apaches, as a barrier against the French coming down from the north with their friends, the Wichita Indians of the Red River country. The Lipans were also to act as protection for the San Antonio region against the other, the raiding bands of the Apaches. The next year a large force of Comanches, Wichitas, and their allies destroyed the San Saba mission, killing several people, including two of the friars, and scattering the tame cattle herds. The captain at the presidio was sent out with 500 troops, some cannon, and about 500 Indian allies to punish the raiders. At the Red River he found the Indians fortified, with a ditch around the stockade and a French flag flying on the wind. Inside, it was said, some French traders directed the defense. Perhaps this was a story to cover the humiliation by the savages. Anyway, most of the 1,000 Spaniards and allies charged the stockade and not only were whipped back but lost their baggage and cannon.

After this failure the raids spread to the San Antonio settlements. There were times when the Comanches left hardly a horse gentle enough for any except the vaqueros to ride, and sometimes even those venturesome men were afraid to get far out on the range. Then, by secret treaty, the French ceded Louisiana to Spain in 1762, and the Texas settlements expected quieter times.

But by now the hostile Indians had all the advisors

they needed from former mission workers, and the government no longer pushed the colonization or protection of
Texas as a political or military outpost. So after 1770 ranching along the San Antonio River withered as under the hot
winds from the Staked Plains, although the wild cattle kept
spreading. During the next seven, eight years the vast herds
down at Espiritu Santo were rounded up only three times.
The Comanches, Apaches, and Lipan Apaches, too, slaughtered tame herds in unbelievable numbers, both for meat
wherever buffalo was scarce, which was generally over most
of the cattle territory because buffaloes disliked the scrub
timber stretches and the ˙brushy bottoms that cattle preferred. But most of the slaughter was pure sport and devil-
try. In this the Lipans, the pretended friends for whom the
mission up on the San Saba had been built, were the worst.

In 1777 they were living near the presidio of San
Antonio de Bexar ostensibly for protection from the hostile
tribes but this put them right among the tame herds, the
ones that didn't have to be driven, or dragged, from the
brush. While professing friendship, their young men ran off
cattle and horses and blamed it all on the outside raiders, denying that increasing numbers of wild Indians were hidden right in the Lipan camps. San Antonians charged that it
was the Lipans themselves who killed and ran off 22,000
head of tame cattle at one time. They had even learned to
make their own gunpowder from some traitorous mission
workers who gave away the secret so precious on the frontier.
Guns one might steal, but not a consistent supply of powder
and ball, particularly powder.

In 1776 De Mézières, a Frenchman working for
Spain, had been sent to Texas to punish the Apaches of the
east, including the Lipans, and to make Spanish allies of the
tribes of the north, those who had long been friendly with
the French traders. He was to go to the villages up on the
Red River, get 1,000 allies, who would be paid by the missions for all the captives they could bring in, to be turned
into neophytes. He did get the cannons lost in the attack

twenty years before, but nothing much besides this came of his expedition.

By 1790 the Texas missions hardly functioned as missions any more, and four years later they were secularized, the schools, farms, ranches, and other mission ventures closed, the chapels to become parish churches or stand empty to the wind and the rattlesnakes who liked the feel of stone around them at least part of the year. The mission lands were divided among the Spanish colonists and the tame Indians, which didn't mean much, in the light of the Spaniards' treatment of the subject Indians in the past. Still, most of them could do what most of the cattle did, scatter to the brush.

It was fitting, considering the long deification of the cow, that the first seed cattle to reach Texas should have been brought in by missionaries, by men of God. Through the wild herds that their stock fathered, they left a permanent mark upon the region, an imprint that was to spread as the cattle climbed the ladder of east-flowing streams on their march northward, eventually to become numerous enough to feed the meat hungry of the country, and many back across the sea, to change the lives and beliefs of many men, and much of the nation. Already, in 1800, Texas was characterized by her wild cattle, by her great and fabulous herds.

With the Spanish knife seldom set against the young male and never, obviously, in the wild herds, there was much natural selection, with the young scrub driven out everywhere, his blood given no perpetuity. But that left large numbers of bulls to fight for supremacy, or for banishment from the herds, perhaps even death. As with most other wild ruminants, the males usually kept apart except in the breeding season. Some, particularly the ponderous old sires, kept entirely to themselves all winter, feeding alone, chewing their placid cud on some sun-warmed slope alone. Others gathered in small, loose bunches scattered over the bottoms, none turning a head toward the cows, who usually kept their distance, most of them heavy with the coming spring calves.

But finally the grass started, grew up tall enough for good cropping with the forward jerk of the bovine head, to make up for the missing upper teeth in front. The faded winter hair was rubbed off on rock and oak and mesquite, baring a sleek and glossy new coat. The little bunches of cows had calves bucking and playing around them, the yearlings, bulls and heifers, were restless.

Even before this the bulls in their little herds began to lift their noses to the wind, stretching their dewlapped throats far out, working their nostrils this way and that, testing the whiff of some far spring blooming, or the stink of carrion from winter storms, from early lightning, or perhaps death in a bog. But now there was something else, too.

Afternoons cattle gathered around the shrinking water of the small creeks, many withdrawing to their sandy bed, perhaps leaving only a few moist threads on the surface and scattered water holes. High above an eagle might be circling slowly, and off against a yellowish little bank a dog coyote could be waiting, too smart to get his soft pads near the clumps of gray-green prickly pear cactus farther down the slope, or to risk the sharp and spreading horns of the cows scattered over the bottoms after watering. He waited. If nothing better came up, perhaps a late cow might leave the water holes for a little while and then he could smell out the dusty placenta afterward. At the best there might be a good bullfight, with a possible cripple or a gored one left behind. The coyote settled to his haunches, his red tongue lolling lazily in the warm afternoon, and finally he stretched out to sleep, but alert.

Several times there was a low roaring on the wind, so far off it was barely to be felt instead of heard, perhaps a big blue-roan bull somewhere pawing dust upon himself in wrath, or a black one, six, seven years old, his shining coat touched with patches of red-gold along the belly as he showered the earth over himself, his neck powerful with the great bulge behind the head, the big dewlaps flapping from throat to knees as he tossed his thick and pointed horns. Lately he had begun to hang around the water holes instead of hastily sucking up his fill of water and then marching back to his pasturage, away from the herd of cows and young stuff that loitered sociably around the slopes until the sun began to settle.

Suddenly the black bull started toward the rise and the watering beyond. He stalked in pompous anger, on the prod, making impatient grunts and rumblings to himself, his heavy horns, with the forward tilt of the fighter, swayed with the rhythm of his angry walk. In mounting fury, like the approach of a desert cloudburst, his rumblings grew louder, settled to a steady, rolling sort of "Uh-h-uhh-uhh-hh," with pauses between the grunting roars, and pausing in his entire march as well, as though challenged. Then he lifted his head and a deep, subterranean thunder vibrated in his chest, rising to a high, defiant bellow, "Mu-uhh, mu-uhh—" neck outstretched, mouth open, trumpeting to all the wild country.

So he marched down the slope to the water holes, past the resting but watchful cows, the curious young stock. The bull drank deeply but slowly, even though he had not been to water for two, perhaps three days. Then he turned and walked in dignity to a cut bank and suddenly butted his shoulder against it, his powerfully muscled forequarters bulging, his flanks seeming even lither as he curled up the earth and sod before his thrust. Several other bulls drifted in with the little herds, drinking, scattering out over the worn bottoms or standing in the drying creek bed, to switch tails at the flies awhile and chew the cud. Most of the cattle settled down on the worn benchland dotted with cow chips, the cows groaning a little, comfortably, as they let their forequarters down. The yearlings were restless, or sleeping flat in the sun, the young calves shying in exaggerated terror at any convenient weed or thorn or ground squirrel or grackle—

running, bucking, kicking their heels, or suddenly uneasy or hungry and blatting for their mothers.

The big black bull paid little attention to any of this or to the other bulls. They knew their rank and territory long ago. They glanced at the black's excitement, calm as the old cows. Bulls didn't cut out herds of she-stuff as the mustang stallion who watered here with his mares, fighting away all other males so long as his youth would last. Bulls, promiscuous, were free of jealousy other than the one of territorial rank. The others here were free to follow any cows that favored them, so long as they acknowledged who was boss here, and kept away from his choice of the moment, stayed out of his way generally.

Today the black bull wasn't satisfied by a simple challenge thrown on the wind. He kept getting more truculent, fighting the sod, starting over again with a kind of private bellowing deep in his chest, to himself, and pawing dirt from an old bull scrape in the soft earth. He hooked a horn into the ground, deeper and deeper. Then he thrust in the other horn and went down on one knee, still bellowing, head down, eyes bulging, and goring the earth to the bowels. Finally he rose, shook himself, and rubbed a shoulder against the edge of the bull hole as his powerful lungs sprayed the flying earth from before him.

A fat young heifer came down the cowpath near the bull's hole. He lifted his head to smell her, but only for a nose-curling instant, letting her go on past, her arrogant walk tamed by the rejection. But another bull, a tawny brindle with white and smoke upon him, got up and walked slowly to meet her at the first water hole and stood beside her, testing the smell of her. With water dripping from her jaw, she turned a backward look to the bull roaring up on the knoll and then she started down through the brush, the brindle right after her, but without too much hurry while in sight of the bellowing lord on the rise.

Over in the bull scrape the black was covered with yellowish earth, his horns tipped with wet clay as he thrust them into the ground as into a great and powerful enemy. He worked up a fine fighting fury, sending his threats and his challenges to the sky and to the echoing bluffs on the far side of the little creek in quick, rib-jerking bursts of bellowing that rose high and hoarsely shrill to carry far over the prairie. Suddenly he stopped, his head turned. From back over the rise came a faint and distant rumble and a bellow, twice, three times.

The resting cattle stirred. Overhead the eagle still soared, a bit of black curved hair far, far up. The coyote rose, sniffing eagerly forward without taking a step. Only the other bulls seemed unconcerned. One did lift his head, barely pausing in the rhythm of his chewing. He swallowed, and then his jaw began moving again.

The faint *uh-hing* came nearer, a deep and throaty rumble, but without the marching measure of the black's to the water holes. The trumpeting bellow came nearer and nearer until suddenly a bull broke the rise, running down the slope, switching his hindquarters this way and that as he tried to follow the zigzag of the cowpath until he broke from it in his momentum. He was a furious and magnificent specimen, a little heavier than the black, a dusty pecan dun with the golden line down his back, his sides and belly light-splotched. His horns were thick and yellowish, well-sharpened for their bloody work by long whetting on the ground but spreading, fitted to the side thrust, not forward-tipped for the head-on lunge to throat or belly.

At a hundred yards the dun stopped, pawed the earth, giving a higher, wilder bellow for every one of the black's. He charged upon a scrubby thorn, broke it, tossed it over his back. His sharp eyes spied out the coyote and he charged him, but the sly animal just side-stepped around the tall cactus clump. Plainly this was only a feint, too, for the bull had already turned, head lifted, tail arched, looking toward the black as upon an interloper, as one who had just come into the territory long owned by the dun. Purposefully now he marched toward the bull hole, eyes bulging, lower

lip curled away from the foolish little teeth. The black
climbed out, running heavily to meet the challenger. Some
distance apart they stopped, roaring challenges, feinting
thrusts this way and that, trying to out-maneuver each other
under the noisy fury and the rising dust, their heavy little
charges shaking loose the earth still clinging to their powerful shoulders.

Slowly they circled each other, dusty heads down,
eyes rolling, seeking an opening. Once they both stopped,
facing, heads down, tongues out, rumbling, and now the
other cattle were suddenly up, some running in to see, but
turning aside well out of the way, moving impatiently, making low, sympathetic mooings. More cattle strung in over the
rise. A couple of driven-out scrubs edged up, but were ignored. The fat heifer and her bull came slowly out of the
clump of brush, side by side, very close, but drawn to the
impending fight.

Now the rumbling stopped. One bull lunged and
then the other, taking a side swipe with a dusty horn, but
met only by side-stepping, parrying, the answering thrust.
Then they both lunged together, the crack of skull on skull
a thunderous report. With foreheads locked, the bulls pushed
mightily this way and that, the black yielding a bit before
the weight of the dun, his hind hoofs struggling for solid
footing, tearing up the earth as he was thrust back, their
shoulder muscles standing out hard as dusty metal, the massive necks pushed up in humps almost like the buffaloes of
the high regions. Then the black's hoofs caught and the dun
went back, back, until suddenly he twisted his head to free
a horn, drive it into a black shoulder. He was blocked with
the crack of horn on horn, and then with a quick motion
caught the blackish brisket, tore it to hang down, the dust
clotted red.

Now the black worked with blood fury, trying one
side twist after another, working to unbalance this opponent,
drive an up-turned horn into a shoulder, a rib, the belly. So
they thrust and parried, and swerved this way and that, with

their heads tight as though sealed, hoofs digging. Curious calves were drawn up to see, and scuttled back as the fight suddenly swerved their way, scared by the bawl, and the panting, the sharp and desperate scrabble of the hoofs.

Now and then the bulls backed apart and then rushed together again, apart and together, the sharp reports echoing over the creek, the dust rising like smoke, the ground torn. Foam flew, their tongues hung out, their breath rasping, tearing. Once the black's horn raked the dun shoulder, cutting to the blood, but he had to pivot against the heavy drive to his belly, and was caught in the brisket again. Now there was a strong smell of blood on the dusty air and a bellow rose from the wild cows, heads down, angry tongues out, eyes bulging, the younger cattle pushing up closer. The coyote thrust his nose around the cactus, sniffing impatiently.

By now it was plain that the fight was more than a test of strength. Neither bull dared to turn and flee. Instead, they fought it out head to head, swerving, twisting, thrusting, glancing, butting together, their throats almost silent with the straining, all but the panting, tearing breath in the dust. The sun lowered, a flock of wild turkeys came flying over toward their roosting trees along the far bluffs. The cattle stirred uneasily, hungry, looking off toward their range, yet still held. Both the bulls were reaching exhaustion, their heads still coming together, but without the sharp crack of bone, the twisting struggle slowing, hesitant.

Here and there an old cow struck out over the rise, and stopped when there was a sudden confusion of hoofs and grunting in the fight of the bulls, and a low rending bawl of pain. Then, in a swift scrabble and turn, one of the bulls, the dun, was running with a bulging of gut bursting from his torn belly, the panting black hard on his rump, trying to hook him between the legs, but too worn out. Once the dun stumbled but pawed himself up with desperate hoofs, and ran again, the black, with ragged skin flapping, still after him when they disappeared over the evening rise.

As the sun rose next morning an eagle was circling lower, followed by several buzzards in more awkward spiraling, dropping fast beyond the rise somewhere. The coyote was gone and on the whole slope of the little creek there was only the dusty black bull, lying flat, ragged, torn, with hide loose at the shoulder and the brisket, one thick, powerful horn brown-coated in dried blood and gut.

After a while three vaqueros came up along the drying creek. When they saw the bull just rising to escape to the brush, they spread out, riatas down. The black was cramped and lame but he tried to run a little before a loop settled over his horns.

"It is a good way to do, this watching for the fights in the spring," one of the dark-faced men said.

"It is the best way to get good bulls—the winners of the fights, before they can run fast again," another said a little sourly. But they did not look sour. They sat their horses admiring the black.

# CHAPTER II

## NOBLE ANCESTRY

T HE men who captured the full-grown fighting black bull from the wild herds of Texas couldn't have known how much their catch resembled the ancient cattle of Europe and Asia, and how long the close tie between man and his kind had existed. Fossil remains of cattle from the middle Pliocene, perhaps three to four million years ago, were first found along northwestern India. This great beast, one of whose species was a direct ancestor of the ox, apparently lived in the forest but grazed in the open glades, something like the early Texas cattle along the Trinity, the San Antonio, and the Brazos—hidden in the timber and the brush by day, but feeding outside at night. Pliocene cattle, however, seemed to browse on twigs and shoots instead of grass. The female was hornless but the bull carried a horn spread between six and seven feet. In Europe the mid-Pliocene ox, slenderer of limb than the Asiatic, has been found in central Italy and southern France.

By the early Pleistocene several bovine types were living in south Asia. At that time, around a million years ago, Europe had three recognizable forms of the ox. The urus stood six feet at the shoulder and roamed the forests the same time that early man lived there. But the urus, not very hardy for all his size, retreated farther south before the great encroaching ice fields than the horse or the sheep of his time, or early Paleolithic man, the early toolmaker. When this first glaciation withdrew, nearly half a million years ago, the great African-Asiatic animals returned to Europe— among them the elephant, rhino, and hippopotamus as well as the urus and a primitive Asiatic bison. Of these the urus, the *Bos primigenius*, was perhaps one of the easier victims to man's crude weapons.

Around one hundred thousand years later, say almost four hundred thousand years ago, the second glaciation swept down over Europe, and with more severity, too, but this time the cattle were apparently heavily haired, something like the Scottish Highland stock of today. At least the cattle stayed, and when forage failed they were surely easy hunting. With the tendency toward domestication that the cow shared with the horse and the dog, occasional ones perhaps became approachable very early.

Twenty-five thousand years later the weather warmed, meadows appeared, and forests sprang up again. A fighting breed of cattle, one that could stand off the lion of southern Europe, spread rapidly. The next invasion of ice, which lasted another twenty-five thousand years, was less severe, but the cattle had the hairy mammoth and the woolly rhino to compete with for the shrinking forage. They did this so efficiently that when the icecap once more crept back northward, cattle and bison became the dominant great beasts of Europe, with man and his growing use of weapons their greatest enemy. The next hundred thousand years were the era of early man and his increasing ascendancy over the animals. This period ended the middle Paleolithic, reaching from the Heidelberg man through the Neanderthalers. At their caves in the cliffs, these Neanderthal men had watched the game in the valley below, with perhaps the first domestic animal, the tamed wolf or dog beside them. Perhaps the men planned traps for the wild cattle as they did for the wild horse, with surrounds and occasional stampedes over the cliffs, probably using fire—methods improved by their successors, the Cro-Magnons, and followed by man with limited weapons everywhere, including the Indians of Texas when the Spaniards came with iron and powder. Apparently early man cooked his beef in hot water fifty thousand years ago, and even earlier than that he had learned to crack the bones for the marrow. Like any other carnivorous creature in nature, the Cro-Magnon ate the visceral organs and fat of his newly killed cow first as the American Indian did of the buffalo or the wolf of a Texas calf.

The urus, the wild ox of the Cro-Magnon, was an imposing animal, long in the leg, swift and powerful, superior in stature, speed, and strength to his neighbor, the bison, and with much greater horn spread. One horn of a *Bos primigenius,* converted into a drinking goblet measuring six and a half feet in length, was reported in Alsace-Lorraine until around 1800, the historic drinking horn of the Strasbourg Ox. While this was from a much later specimen than any the Cro-Magnons saw, many skeletons of bulls of their time measuring six feet or more at the shoulder have been unearthed—truly fitting creatures to dominate the ritualistic life of Cro-Magnon man.

Paleolithic man not only lived off these cattle but by the latter period, perhaps twenty to twenty-five thousand years ago, he was paying them his finest tribute in magnificent paintings. There are around thirty-five known caves in Spain, over forty in France with walls painted by Old Stone Age man, giving cattle a prominent place in his magicoreligious cults. Perhaps the finest of such paintings and, judging by their excellence, certainly not the first, are those in Lascaux Cave in southern France. Here, in limestone hollowed out by water, is the flowering of the second of the two capital events* of man's history—his discovery and proficiency in art in a great and apparently sudden outburst, explosion. It is interesting that much of this flowering is concerned with cattle. The main chamber of the Lascaux Cave is called Hall

* The first was toolmaking.

of Bulls because of their domination of the high-ceilinged
space that would hold 100 people easily. At the entrance a
unicorn initiates the monumental animal dance of bulls,
horses, and deer around the walls, the largest portrayals those
of the cattle, the horses smaller, the deer comparatively very
small. The bulls vary in size from around ten feet tall above
the knee to over eighteen feet in length. Many of the cattle,
both bulls and cows, have the forward-turned horns as some
of the early Texas stock apparently had, the color varying—
black, small-spotted or brockled, brown or almost Hereford
red, some with darker lower legs, some with the whole face
or the lower part dark. One brockle-faced bull has a lowish
hump, like many of the blacks of Texas had.

In the smaller chambers and galleries that lie beyond
the Hall of Bulls at Lascaux there are more pictures of horses
than of cattle, but often the latter dominate by size or position. There is a huge cow leaping over other animals; one,
red with a black head, is nine and a quarter feet long. Other
large cows are blackish, brown, or red. Of the red cows,
great and small, some have delicate heads and fancifully
curved horns, much like those found in some early photographs of Texas cattle around twenty thousand years later,
cattle that descended from the Spanish stock that the friars
brought.

Lascaux Cave must have served Old Stone Age man
much as Chartres Cathedral, for instance, served man of the
Middle Ages. Here where he pictured the mysteries as he
tried to understand and engage them, through creatures
upon whose magical favor he existed, the main chamber is
not one dominated by the horse or even the great rhino, but
by cattle—the Hall of the Bulls.

Cattle—bulls, cows, or calves—run through much of
ancient mythology and religion but it was in Egypt that the
cult of cattle apparently reached its highest development.
Towering above all the other Egyptian gods was Osiris,

sometimes said to have been born of a cow. The sacred bull Apis was regarded as the image of the soul of Osiris, with a second bull-god figure, Mnevis, supposed to contain the actual soul of the highest god, with many lesser cattle figures running through Egyptian mythology. Such deification of the bovine was the natural, almost the inevitable result in any society that placed cattle at the top of its wealth symbols, locally or nationally, for any considerable time.

From prehistoric days Egypt concentrated on the breeding of two animals, the greyhound and a polled, a hornless cattle. In the rock tombs of Deir, dating before 2500 B.C., are many pictures showing the handling of cattle. The tomb of Huy, who was in charge of Tutankhamen's royal herds, portrays his men branding King Tut's cattle, while the tomb of Auta, of the Fifth Dynasty, before 2625 B.C., shows a bull branded 113 on the left rump.

Around 1000 B.C. the priesthood that ruled Egypt and the temples owned all the towns, vineyards, orchards, the shipping facilities, and half a million cattle, reminding one of the beginnings made by the missions of Texas and Father Kino's cattle empire in the southwest and California. The Egyptian god Amon alone owned more than 400,000 cattle. The Old Testament, by its repeated use of cattle in the symbolism, illustrates the importance of the cow in Jewish history and the deep identification with her kind, by such stories as the casting of the golden idol when Moses was late coming home from Sinai. The idol might have been the king of beasts, or the ruler of the skies, but instead, out of a deep mystical memory of the people, it was a calf, the golden calf. "And they rose up early on the morrow, and offered burnt offerings—"

And so it was almost into the twentieth century, even in America, even the burnt offerings.

In India, where the cow made her first known appearance, she is still in a measure a sacred creature on the streets and the roadways. In Sanskrit the word for soldier meant "one who fights about cows." Curiously, most of the fighting, and the bloodshed, in Texas and farther north on the prairies of the Great Plains was over the cow.

Cattle have a much shorter history of domestication by man than as figures in his religious rites and activities. There seems no evidence of any bovine domestication in Europe at the time of the great Lascaux paintings. The earliest remains of a domestic cow have been found between the eastern end of the Mediterranean and the arid plains of Persia and Arabia. Here the ox became the real foundation of agriculture, where the fertile, watered earth of the ancient world drew vigorous pastoral tribes to push in from mountain and desert to build the historic cultures of such peoples as the Sumerians; the Babylonians, apparently originators of the zodiac with its sign of Taurus, the bull; the Assyrians; Chaldeans; Medes and Persians. Apparently it was the mountain and desert men who domesticated cattle along with the other far-walkers: donkeys, sheep, goats, camels, and horses; the farmers who tamed the less wandering creatures: pigs, chickens, geese, and so on.

About eight thousand to ten thousand years ago migrations of New Stone Age man pressing into Europe from western Asia brought domestic cattle among their other animals. Some time after 6000 B.C. the lake dwellers of Switzerland had two kinds of domestic ox, the urus and a Celtic shorthorn. In northern Iran, where these immigrants probably originated, the cattle remains found seem to be of Celtic shorthorns, but there is some belief that the cattle brought west by the people who became lake dwellers may have had zebu blood from India and were therefore distant relatives of the modern Santa Gertrudis, the Brangus, and similar cattle developed in the twentieth century in America by crosses with Brahma blood.

Many students of prehistory consider planned food production man's first great economic revolution. While Old Stone Age man ate the flesh of the urus, his successor, New Stone Age man, counted his wealth in cows. Further, he discovered that the tractable creature, the ox, could be harnessed to help roll stones too large to drag and possibly from that transferred the rolling principle to relays of load-bearing logs and finally some genius, perhaps too lazy to keep transferring the logs on up ahead, cut off pieces and with heated rocks burned holes through the middle for an axle and he had the wheel. No civilization that lacked the patient bovine creature, not even the highly developed Mayan cities or the Andean cultures, developed the wheel to move burdens. Wheeled toys have been reported from pre-Columbian strata in Mexico and some Mayan archaeologists think some of the pottery was made on the wheel, but understanding its principle came to very little with no strong tractable creature to pull the wheel.

As man tamed the cow and the horse he learned to control breeding, a science well developed for the horse at least four thousand years ago in the Euphrates Valley if not elsewhere. Breeding for improved stock sprang up everywhere from eastern Asia to England and Spain. By 630 B.C. Andalusian cattle were a hardy lot, some used as work oxen but mostly bred for beef. They were descended quite directly from *Bos primigenius,* substantially horned, great in stature and strength, and well adapted to the hot, dry summers. It was this blood that fitted so well into Spanish America. The last known urus, a cow, died in 1627, long after the Spanish cattle had carried a good measure of the blood across the soil of Texas.

The first cattle brought to the western world were not from Spain. In 982, over five hundred years before Columbus landed his Andalusian bull and some heifers at Hispaniola, Erik the Red put a nondescript assortment of northern domestic animals, including cattle, ashore on Greenland. In 1004 the real colonizer of the mainland, Karlsefni, brought the first cattle to Nova Scotia. When the Norsemen moved farther south they took the cattle along and remained, some stories say, until after Columbus landed in the West Indies.

When a sickness struck the people all died, and their cattle, although winter-hardened Viking stock, disappeared, as did the English cattle left by the starved-out colonists of Virginia later. Cattle were found alive in 1598 on barren Sable Island off the southern tip of Nova Scotia but Spanish cattle, with the gaunt old wrecks of Spanish ships on the shore. These southern cattle, certainly unaccustomed to the rigorous winters of the region, were still there in 1633, increased to 800 head. They were the same stock, apparently, as the cows of Coronado and the mission herds that produced the wild cattle of Texas from which the Longhorn was developing—the only bovine brought to America that could live without man, either at Sable Island or on the brushy, timbered bottoms of the Trinity.

Not until the Anglos, the English speakers from the United States began to penetrate the Texas region did the cow have much value beyond the local use of meat, leather, and tallow, and for sport. It is true that from 1763 to 1800, while Louisiana was once more Spanish, herds as high as 2,000 head were driven from the old mission ranges on the San Antonio River to stock Louisiana territory. The government claimed all unbranded herds and issued permits to kill or drive away cattle at four bits, four Spanish *reals,* a head. This was considered a license for early-day cattle rustling by some and brought much wrangling between the government and the citizens of San Antonio, who claimed many of the *orejanos,* the unmarked ones.

These problems, like many others of Texas history, were solved by events far away. Spain turned Louisiana back to France under Napoleon. Jefferson, the man to see an opportunity and to grasp it, consummated the Louisiana Purchase December, 1803, and put the aggressive Anglo-Americans hard up against the Texas border. They didn't remain on their side of the line long, had, in fact, been slipping into Texas for some time, seeking adventure, escape from the sheriff, or were lured by the hope of fast wealth, particularly in cattle. As early as 1800 Philip Nolan had led a party into Texas, ostensibly for mustangs. Although Spanish soldiers overtook and killed him, nobody was deterred. Early in 1807 Zebulon M. Pike was arrested while seeking the headwaters of the Red River and dragged off to prison in New Mexico. The publicity of this reminded more Anglos, and many who didn't need reminding, of the region below the Red, and the accounts of the rich bottom lands with vast herds of wild cattle to stock them, free for the taking. There were frequent civilian invasions from the eastern border. In 1812-13 one expedition got far enough to capture the town of San Antonio and was later slaughtered. Two more, in 1819-20, proclaimed the independence of Texas, but failed, too. Then in 1821 Mexico won independence from Spain and Texas became a part of the new republic.

Now a fever for Texas swept the United States, with rushes of homeseekers setting out from Illinois, Kentucky, Tennessee, Missouri, and particularly from the Gulf states. Some of the newcomers brought their own seed cattle, others bought a start in Texas or below the Rio Grande. If there were energetic young men in the family, as was usual, they could catch a good start for a ranch from the wild herds out beyond the settlements. It was work, but the cattle were free and acclimated, important because often the outside stock seemed to sicken and die in the easy climate. The cattle that lived matured and multiplied very rapidly, almost doubling their number in two years. Heifers often calved in eighteen months, and stock could be driven overland to New Orleans cheaply, or shipped there from the coast, or to the West Indies and Cuba.

Most alert, perhaps, of all the adventurers coming in were the Connecticut Yankee stock, such as the Austins. Moses Austin, a St. Louis banker who lost his fortune in the panic of 1819, had secured permission from the Spanish Government in 1820 to settle 300 families in Texas. He died, but his son Stephen established the colony called Austin in 1821, with 5,600 settlers. By 1828 the population was

20,000, with stock raising, based on the Spanish cattle, the principal activity, in spite of the raiding Indians and the thieving Mexican soldiery, as hated by the Mexican revolutionaries running ranches in Texas as by the Americans. The troops requisitioned cattle and mules without payment and then failed to protect the herds against the Indians. There was trouble, too, about brands and strays and other minor matters with the gringos, the greenhorns, as the Mexicans called the Anglos. Mexico, hoping to colonize the state rapidly, had offered land grants to farmers and ten times as much acreage to the cattle grower. In 1826 a man who had his colonizing contract declared void organized a little rebellion. It failed, but it made the Mexicans headshy about the gringos and in 1830 immigration from the United States was outlawed. This couldn't be enforced, not with so much of the border still wilderness, but it helped to keep the settlements boiling and led to the massacre of the Americans at the Alamo, which was the old Mission San Antonio de Valero, established in 1718. Then came the victory at San Jacinto, a battle won by a group of early Anglo settlers who were to leave their mark on Texas, some of their names to be known over the cattle country as far as the Yellowstone and beyond. Like the list of *Mayflower* immigrants, the roster of those at San Jacinto grew and grew.

By the time the Texans became Texians, as the citizens of the new Republic of Texas liked to be called, the longhorned cattle of the region were rapidly being recognized as Longhorns, a fixed breed. The Longhorn, in addition to his predominantly Spanish blood, carried a mixture of strains brought in by the Anglo settlers: some Missouri stock, noted as work oxen; a little of the nondescript Arkansawers, and some blood from the swamp runners of Louisiana —a bit of French stock crossed on the local Spanish, smaller and spike-horned, perhaps from the region of the transplanted Acadians. One Texan who had some knowledge of the swamp cattle on the Louisiana side, knowledge earned by popping the brush to catch the wild ones, was James Bowie, who achieved fame for his knife, his search for the lost Bowie mine, and his death at the Alamo.

The degree of this outside blood in the Texas stock varied, as did the Texas blood itself by locality, partly due to different origins and partly perhaps to a few isolated breeding areas.

The early Spanish explorers hadn't described their cattle very carefully. Onate, in 1595, agreed to take 1,000 head of "cattle," *ganado mayor,* and 100 head of "black cattle," *ganado prieto,* the stock of the fighting bulls, into New Mexico. Much of the seed brought to Texas, California, and the Southwest after Onate seems to have been blacks, and during the seventeenth and eighteenth centuries breeding black cattle was much encouraged in Mexico. In early 1800 "black cattle" was almost a generic term, like "white faces." Some of these were solid in color but the more characteristic were perhaps those called linebacks, black with a shading or an actual stripe of white, dun, or brown from nape to tail, sometimes with the cross at the shoulders, the lobo stripe, like that of the zebra dun mustang. Sometimes these linebacks were lighter or spotted toward the belly. Occasionally there were reds, browns, and blues. Often the blacks and the variations among them had sunburned faces, brownish, and lighter around the eyes and muzzle—mealy-nosed, as the Texans called it—like the Moorish stock still seen in the bull rings, with horns set close together at the root and curved forward to kill, not too different from the horns of some of the cattle pictured in the Hall of Bulls at Lascaux. The Texas stock was quick, restless, keen of eye and nose. A wounded bull might hunt an enemy down by scent, trailing him. The early stock had long horns compared to the New England and Missouri cattle brought in, but probably never equaled the horns of those grown later in Texas.

These "black cattle" were usually what was meant

by the Spanish; the undifferentiated "cattle" of Onate were called Mexican. The Mexicans were broader, heavier-horned, and many-colored.

"They used to come all shapes an' colors," an old trail driver of the sixties liked to say. "Yeh, all colors, 'ceptin' Hereford red, or green—" Then he would work his tobacco from one jaw to the other, his wind-leaned, skeptical old mouth twisting as he did it. With his cud settled, he always added, "—Come to think on it, I seen one right nigh to green once. One a them grulla blues, with the hair yellow along in the spring, an' slippin'—"

The crossing of these many-colored Mexicans and the black Spanish with the small infusion of immigrant stock that the Anglo-Americans brought produced the Longhorn, heavier and rangier, the horns lengthening in a sort of throwback to the urus, often snaking out eight, nine feet from tip to tip. Perhaps this horn growth and the longer legs resulted from the same circumstance that stretched out the bones of the men who grew up over much of Texas, and over most of the later cattle country, too—the sharply tilted Plains, which were leached of their iodine by the swift run-off water.

When the American colonists began to spread over Texas, they found wild cattle scattered from the Rio Grande to the Red River along Indian Territory, and from the Louisiana line to the uppermost breaks of the Brazos on the west. This wild stock gathered in small bunches, staying in the cover of the oak, mesquite, or other scrub timber during the day, and came out on the prairie only toward dusk, grazing against the wind to catch the first scent of danger. A rider could go fifty or sixty miles a day across the region and seldom see one head except perhaps some careless young stock badly hidden. The Longhorns were watchful as wild turkeys, keen-nosed as deer, and made wary of any rider from far off by the first little hunting.

Back in the mid 1830's the San Marcos River region

was found stocked with wild cattle brought in by Partilleas, who had established his ranch there thirty years before and was driven out by the Comanches. In 1851, after Texas joined the Union, Captain Ware, pushing through westward with a herd, decided to winter on the San Marcos, near the old ranch. He lost many cattle, tolled off into the brush by the wild stock—smaller than common, all brown, and wilder than any deer.

By this time the Longhorn was established as a true pioneer, a fitting partner for the pioneering men who were edging out upon the Great Plains. The Longhorn cow, the leader of her bunch as the buffalo cow was in her herd or the mare among the mustangs, was tough as rawhide and as land-fixed and dug-in as any hoe man, and even harder to drive off her accustomed range. But she could move fast enough if the rains failed and the creeks and water holes dried up. Sticking her wet nose into the wind, she followed it to other holes or other creeks, and when they were gone, too, she pursued the smell of moisture under the dry stream beds up to the canyon springs or down to surfacing water. If necessary she could cross dry tablelands to other watersheds, even those she had never seen before, even if they required two, three days of hard, dry travel.

The Longhorn cow was, next to the buffalo out on the open plains, the first to know when snows and blizzards, the blue northers, were due. Smelling a storm, she fed hard and then headed for the breaks and thickets and browsed on dead leaves on the winter brush until the sun cleared off the wind-blown ridges. For defense she depended on her horns and hoofs, and the sharpness of her feral senses and instincts, once more as acute as when she was truly wild blood. She fattened when there was grass, gaunted down when the pasture was gone. She fought off the screwworm fly and healed her bruises, rubbed her shedding hair off on rock and bank, on stubby oak and mesquite, until her coat gleamed like silk. She shed her ticks, escaped the heel flies the best she could, and rubbed their ripening warbles from her back when she failed. She adjusted her increase to what the range would carry, bore her calf in sheltered seclusion, and taught him to lie as still as the shadows which his mottled hide often imitated—so still that the sharp-eyed predator detected no movement, not even the blink of an eyelid. She fought for her calf with coyote, wolf, cougar, and man. She organized relays of calf watchers so they were protected during the far march of the cows to water. Long before the cattlemen discovered it she knew that the steer was often better at calf watching, and more inclined to it, than any cow. She bore calves for many, many years, weaned each in time to make room for the next. When the day for dying finally came she took herself off into some remote spot and died in decent privacy.

She was a character, in a region of characters, deserving the idolatry that man had bestowed upon her so long. She was the creature to whom many men had dedicated their lives and to whom there would be many, many more dedications.

# CHAPTER III

# *THE COW WALKS AGAIN*

THE ancestors of the Longhorn had walked westward out of Asia, across Europe, and up the American continent to Texas. Now, as wild cattle they were once more bawling their protest before the push and angry shout of man, but this time was different. This time they were not going to seek out a new home with man, or to feed the hungry on a long march. This time the herds were to be traded for gold, for money in the saddlebags or, if the trail wasn't through too heavy timber and swamp miles, perhaps hidden in the false bottom of an oxcart piled high with trail gear to deceive the alert thieves in the land that had no law beyond that of powder and ball and the cold knife between the ribs.

In the past it had usually been breeding stock, largely she stuff, with some selected bulls, that man had taken with him. Even the meat herds were mostly sturdy cows, the bulls less tractable and trail-worthy, the steer, with the Spaniard's aversion to the cutting knife too rare to count.

But the herds that the American trail drivers gathered were usually steers and yearling or two-year-old bulls because they sold better, the steers often five, six years old, with a long, steady trail stride. Some were from the swamp-

lands, where almost every mouthful of the rank grass was
pulled from watery roots; others, wilder, came from the
brushy bottoms and had to be cut from their protection at
dawn while out grazing. Sometimes they could be driven off
with some tamer decoys but often they had to be roped and
thrown, perhaps chased into the thorny thickets, tearing
both man and horse. When the steer went down, the brush
popper had to be off and, jerking the short hogtie rope, the
piggin' string, from around his waist, tie the steer down until he was too stiff to run and could be gathered into the little
herd that was the morning's catch.

Some of the captives were driven to the Gulf ports
and forced into boats for the Louisiana cities. Even some
good steamships between Galveston and New Orleans and
Mobile carried cattle when there was no better cargo,
crowding as many as possible between decks, the entire ship
scrubbed afterward. The company generally bought the
stock and sold them at the Louisiana ports because the usual
freight rates were too high for profit and the rate level must
not be disturbed. Cuba could use beef, too, and now and
then some reached there, but it had to be cheap, very little
above the shipping charges.

The cheapest transportation was overland, on the
rangy steer's own tough shanks. Often these early drives
had no fixed destination, the drivers realizing they might
have to change their direction a dozen times through path-
less forests and marshes and over great swollen rivers. They
traveled light, every man carrying his own grub outfit, with
such tin utensils as he thought he needed to cook his meat
over a fire perhaps built of half-dried cow chips. Some carried little except coffee beans to be pounded in a little skin
pouch with a rock. That and their tobacco, either eating or
dipping—gumming tobacco as some called their snuff. Always they carried guns, very necessary against any Longhorn
that showed fight as well as against thieves, predators, and
rattlesnakes, which were plentiful and very big in the watery
regions.

The first non-Spanish drovers to New Orleans were three, four French ranchers over east in the Trinity River country, beyond contact with the original colonists. Some of the early herds from the Anglos in Texas did reach New Orleans before the Mexican revolution, and the number increased steadily after that as the early beef bonanza drew more and more immigrants to Texas, until that city was the Texian's best market. Many herds were driven to Shreveport or Vidalia and other river ports, and flatboated down from there. Unhappily, steers that sold for $10 in north Texas near the Red River loading points brought $45 in New Orleans. Many drove straight through, particularly from the southern ranges, the main route hitting the Trinity River at Liberty then east across the Sabine and on to the Mississippi, with few bridges and many streams to be forded, ferried, or swum. "Stands" a day's drive apart were established on the main-traveled routes, offering meals and pens for the night. Even so the powerful Texas stock sometimes broke out in a wild stampede on both the southern and the northern routes. One herd surged over the pen fence at a plantation near Shreveport, tromped the carriage house and all the fine vehicles into the ground, and ran over the slave quarters, killing a whole Negro family. The steers rounded up alive after the run didn't come near paying for the damages.

These herds for the southern markets, often only a few hundred head, were usually caught from the brush— mostly wild, stubborn bulls instead of the more desirable steers, both for meat and for trailing. A quicker way to get stock that was more tractable although not necessarily with a higher percentage of steers, was to raid the herds of the Mexican ranchers. The raiders were mostly wild, bold-spirited recruits from the States, many of them GTT's, Gone to Texas, suggesting a certain urgency in the departure. Others were from the American settlers who had fought in the Texas army for freedom. Nearly all were young and became known as "cowboys"—a term that was soon a fighting word if spoken without a smile. These raiders thought no more of killing a Mexican than of shooting an Indian down or of cutting a rattlesnake to pieces with a doubled rawhide rope. They gathered up herds along the Guadalupe and San Antonio rivers, often from Mexicans who had fought beside them on the Texas side, but all Mexicans were the same to them now.

The great hunting ground of these cowboys lay between the Nueces and the Rio Grande and often across into Mexico, their raids generally planned for moonlit nights. Twelve, fifteen cowboys swept off herds varying from 200 to 600 head, keeping them on a steady run that they could hold for twenty, twenty-four hours, dropping any stock that didn't keep up. After that they slowed to a trot or even a walk, giving the cattle and the horses and riders a little respite while they waited for the men who had stayed behind to discourage or to ambush pursuit. This was before the brush, particularly the mesquite, had moved in over the region, spread by the undigested seeds in the cattle droppings. In the open country, with travel easier and grass plentiful, the worn herd could be managed like the domestic cattle many of them were, driven along slowly enough for grazing and watering—actually letting them put on meat. Some of these herds reached the New Orleans market but the majority went to stock the coastal ranches. Goliad, of early mission stock tradition, became a kind of trading center. Here eventually Mexicans counterraided, and for many years there was no peace or security on this Bloody Border.

The only precaution in these raiding times that the Anglo rancher could take was to keep his cattle wild—so chased, whooped, and dogged that they scattered at the sight of any rider, Mexican or Indian. In addition the Texians, in the wild, open region without law, felt they must work up a reputation for relentless pursuit. In 1839 Andrew Sowell and other rangers under Paint Caldwell chased raiding Mexicans out on Prickly Pear Prairie, north of the Nueces River. Here the nopal, the prickly-pear cactus, had grown up higher than a rider's head in great spiny gray-green tangles and piles, standing, sprawling over the dead growths, many of the great cactus hands with red and purple knots of fruit that looked like the swollen finger joints left after frost amputation. The ground, when visible at all, was hot as a gray stovelid just before it turns red, mottled gray so the coils of the great rattlesnakes were almost invisible.

The horses of the pursuing rangers gave out and they had to turn back, leading their worn animals, picking their booted way very carefully. From the time they entered the burning cactus prairie until they got back out, they were never beyond the sound of the whirring rattlesnakes. Some of the Mexicans captured later said that several of their band were bitten while fleeing across the prairie, the victims buried the best they could manage.

Another time out on this great cactus tangle Sowell noticed a herd of mustangs run from a little clump of brush and trees. Looking for water, he rode over that way. As he approached, his horse, although accustomed to the region and its inhabitants, plunged and reared back from a terrible stench and the blood-freezing whirr of great rattles. A snake about nine feet long and as thick as the thigh of a man had been run over by the mustangs. Back broken and infuriated at his immobility, the rattler was striking out with the great wedge of head, armor-scaled like some dragon, the crooked white fangs long as the worst thorns of the monte. And all around him was the sickening stink that every creature of the brush country knew so well.

The Mexican war of 1846 had disturbed the growing movement of beef on the hoof; its end, with Texas in the Union, accelerated it. Substantial northern outlets for Texas cattle were known as early as 1842, when a herd of 1,500 head seems to have reached Missouri. Four years later Edward Piper of Ohio drove 1,000 head up from Texas to be fattened there, the first of what was to become a steadily increasing stream of range cattle to the cornlands, enough to double and redouble the corn acreages in many regions. Cattle from two 1853 drives were fed in Illinois, one from Indian Territory, the other trailed home from Texas by Tom Ponting. Part of both herds seem to have reached New York City alive. These Longhorns, really moderately horned, judging by the pictures in the magazines, running loose on the street caused great excitement, and, with another depression settling over the East, a new crop of emigrants to Texas, with many GTT's among them.

Illinois soon became an active feeding center for Texas and Indian Territory cattle, with Independence, Westport, and Kansas City the largest markets. During 1853-55, 100,000 southwestern beef cattle reached Kansas City, an estimated two thirds of these from Texas. Apparently Texans did not let their southern sympathies interfere with business. When a drove of 2,000 cattle went through Dallas for the north, to feed "our abolition neighbors," the *Dallas Herald* said, "we hope that this southern diet will agree with them," overlooking the northern origins of many of the ranchers.

St. Louis became the great market, and many Midwestern cattle were fattened and killed there, the meat shipped down the river to New Orleans. Cattle from the Cherokee Nation also reached the city. An attempt to feed some Longhorns with corn at the market was a failure; they ran away from it. In 1854 the St. Louis *Intelligencer* said, "Texas cattle are about the nearest to 'wild animals' of any now driven to market. We have seen some buffaloes that were more civilized."

But for some years there was an urgent demand for beef in expanding California, particularly after the gold strike. Ironically, in 1833 California had 424,000 head of cattle. The next year the missions were secularized and the padres started a massive slaughter of their herds for the hides and tallow. Contractors worked on a fifty-fifty basis and often only the hides were saved.

In addition to the missions there were several hundred rancheros in California at the time, their cattle of no more value than those of the missions. It was an era of aristocratic existence: the dons with their elegant flat hats, slashed, gilt-laced trousers, embroidered jackets, red sashes, and serapes; the women in their silken gowns and delicate shoes of satin or kid, the married wearing the high combs, and out-of-doors, the mantilla. Mission-trained Indians did the work, prepared all the tallow and hides for the Boston ships waiting in the harbors, ships that had brought luxuries and fineries all the way around South America. One of the youths carrying the dried hides into the surf to the conveying boats was Richard Dana, working out the time he described in his *Two Years Before the Mast*.

Although the butchery of mission stock was sudden it was apparently well organized. Six men armed with long Spanish knives rode at full speed through the herds, giving each head of cattle a blow at the back of the neck so it fell dead. Behind them the skinners ran in, and the butchers, who took the best cuts for solid beef and jerky. They were followed by swarms of Indian women who gathered the tallow into leathern hampers, to be tried out in large iron or copper kettles and, cooled a little, poured into skin *botas* containing an average of 500 pounds each.

There are apparently no records of the number of hides shipped by the missions and the rancheros in that bloody year of 1834. The port of Los Angeles received 100,000 hides, 250,000 pounds of tallow, and several cargoes of soap from the butchery. Evidently the buzzards and wolves got the flesh—the wolves, the worms, and the stinking winds.

At the time of secularization the twenty-one missions owned 396,400 head of cattle. By 1842 this had dropped to 29,020 head. Then the 49ers came to eat up everything in sight. Prices climbed like an eagle on the wind. There were rumors of $200 steers and 75-cent mine candles containing a nickel's worth of tallow. Texans headed their herds westward.

It was not an easy prospect to face, and the trail hands slung rifle scabbards to their saddles and prepared to fight their way through the Comanche and Apache country and any trouble beyond. There were, of course, the trails of the military, the stagecoaches, and emigrants, but all these moved faster than a trail herd and required much less grass and water. At the best it was a long, long whooping way to California, with vast stretches fit only for desert camels. Even the iron-hard hoofs of the Longhorns were worn sore on the stony reaches, their horns banging in the wild, tangled charges upon shrinking water holes, perhaps to find only alkali-crusted mud, cracked and stinking. Farther west they struck the routes of earlier herds from New Mexico and Arizona to the coast and the Texans made it through, past some flats that were snow-white with the bleached bones of the mission slaughter, and past the newer bones of meat gone to feed the hungry gold seekers, the stink of carrion and death still about them. Now and then a critter or two left the herd to bellow in anger and terror over the bones, eyes bulging, tongue out, others drawn to join in.

From the beginning there were Indian raids against the Texas missions, some energetic and persistent enough to drive the missionaries out. Ever since the settlers first pushed in, there was a skirmishing against the Indians, one that lasted longer and with more intensity than anywhere else on the Great Plains, with more depredations and killing, more captives taken. Originally the missions had encouraged the taking of captives to be turned into neophytes by paying the tame Indians for bringing them in. Later the Indians kept right on capturing anyone worth ransom—Mexicans and whites, the ransom usually paid by individuals or by the government. Sometimes captives were taken by the Texas Indians as the northern tribes did occasionally—to add to their people. It was during such a raid that the small girl Cynthia Ann Parker was captured, with some others, after the massacre of Parker's Fort in 1836. In 1840, at San

Antonio, twelve Comanche chiefs brought a party of sixty-five Indians to a council with a dozen Texas leaders to bargain for the freeing of thirteen white captives. The Indians, suspicious in the stronghold of the whites, had brought only one of the captives along, the rest to be delivered later, when the good faith of the Texans was clear. Some of the settlers proposed that the chiefs be held as hostages. Upon this the Indians made a break for freedom. Thirty-three were killed, thirty-two captured, and seven white men died in the fighting. But many, many more whites were killed in revenge raids for this. Thirty years later young men were still avenging their dead relatives upon whites who had never heard of the Massacre of San Antonio.

There were friendly Indians, individuals and tribes, during these years, mostly enemies of the Comanches and Apaches or individuals like Caddo Jake, who taught the young Charlie Goodnight that a boy could stagger home under the carcass of a new-killed deer if it was gutted and everything useless thrown away. But too many Indians recalled the Spanish torture and mutilations upon their people and the later massacre of their chiefs. In revenge they committed depredations and atrocities unequaled anywhere else.

The Texans struck back but the Indians had vast hiding territory in the wild plains and the Cross Timbers, those parallel strips of scrub trees and brush that ran southward out of Indian Territory and across much of central Texas. It was seldom that any Indian was caught and, as happened elsewhere, those caught were often not the depredators and so more wrongs were left to avenge. When the early ranchers moved into the region of Jacksboro they were struck by the Comanches, several killed, horses swept away, one rancher lanced almost to pieces. More and more atrocity stories came out. In west Parker County the Sherman family was attacked; the father, ill-fitted for the Texas frontier, didn't even have a gun for hunting game. The Indians, so it was reported, drove the family into the rain, attacked Mrs. Sherman, shot her with arrows, and then stripped the house and swung out through Loving Valley and the Keechi Creek region, their herd of stolen horses growing as they whooped them off westward.

The small ranchers scattered through the region immediately raised a posse and followed the Indians through the western Cross Timbers and out upon the open prairie, gaining on them, encumbered as they were with the stolen horses. But the Indians got into a migrating buffalo herd who not only hid the trail but held up the pursuers. Without food or blankets or a change of horses the posse gave up. The reports of twenty-three killed in the Indian raids brought out the Rangers under Sul Ross. They struck the camp and among the captured Comanches was the chief's wife, the Cynthia Ann Parker carried away at Parker's Fort twenty-four years ago. She was sent to her relatives but died, apparently of a broken heart, far from her chieftain husband and her son Quanah, called Quanah Parker because among the Plains Indians a man became a member of his wife's family, the children taking the mother's name when surnames were first thrust upon them.

This punishment of the Comanches by the Ross expedition was only a temporary defeat for the tribe that had well-defined trails over the same Staked Plains that tested Coronado so severely back in 1541. Their raiding trails reached from beyond the Canadian River in Indian Territory down through Texas and across the Rio Grande to the good horse herds of north Mexico, and anyone who settled near these routes was in trouble.

By now ranchers were pushing hard into the Comanche hunting lands. Back in 1855 Kit Carter had headed up the Brazos with his wife and one child, following the precious water to a spot he had seen and admired. Few white men knew of the hidden bend or that it was the favorite shelter and camp ground for many Indians. They did not give it up easily and Carter had many chances to try his rifle against them as they raided his herds and attacked his home and his rapidly increasing family. Carter's Bend was thirty miles from the nearest neighbor but Mrs. Carter was fitted for the life. She was the sister of Sul Ross, most famous Indian fighter of Texas, and no Indians, rustlers, or tragedy managed to shake the Carters loose from their spot on the Brazos. It was a long haul. Nine years after the Ross expedition that brought back Cynthia Ann Parker, one of the Carter sons, working out from Graham with eleven other cowboys, was surrounded by perhaps fifty Indians. The cowboys opened fire with their pistols but the Indians charged with their arrows and some long-range rifles. The white men managed to hold them off all day. One was killed there and six wounded, two mortally. The Carter boy died that night of an arrow in the side.

Still the frontier was moved farther out, thrust out. As under the Mexican Government, the Republic of Texas offered a settler 177 acres of land for farming; for ranching he was allowed a total of around 4,440 acres, a square league. With an enlarged family more could sometimes be added, up to a total of eleven square leagues at small cost. Through the various land scrips the settler could buy up a section, 640 acres, at fifty cents an acre. In the annexation agreement Texas was permitted to keep all her government land, to dispose of as she pleased. Land frauds were common, as they had been under the Mexican Government and the Republic.

The settlements creeping up the streams scared out not only the shyer game but some of the early frontiersmen who might be gone like a quail flushing far ahead of the gun. It was in those years that men like Kit Carter, Richard King, Dudley Snyder, the Olives, the Lovings, Charlie Goodnight, and scores of others started into cattle. They needed not only seed stock, theirs for the rounding up, but lots of range, still free farther on. They also needed a readiness to fight Indians and other raiders, and the will to search out markets, always to search out and fight for markets.

By now everyone knew that the Texas Longhorn took

rivers like an otter and that his long, swinging stride could carry him almost anywhere that a market could be scared up. Although the competition and the middleman still cut into the profits at Shreveport, particularly with the depression of the middle and late 1850's, it is perhaps true that more cattle passed through there than anywhere else in those years. Shreveport was close, and several trailers made two drives a year. They could start out as late as September, when branding and other ranch work was done and the steers fat. The drive could be a slow one, with a plain wagon road all the way. At the port the cattle were loaded on barges, forty, fifty steers to each, and towed down the Red and on to New Orleans. This avoided the early spring start necessary for the longer, more uncertain northeastern drives, with the dangerous spring crossing of the Brazos, perhaps, and certainly the Red.

Saddle ponies for ranch work and the trails cost around seven, eight dollars, some good ones with Mexican brands, wet stock, accepted without questions. Costing so little, the horses were usually turned out in the fall, perhaps even chased off, to keep the raiding Indians, who would get them anyway, from coming to the ranches. The remuda of a trail herd was often mostly mustangs, perhaps new to rope and saddle—a wild circling of grays, blacks, duns, sorrels, and bays inside the rope corral every morning, their manes a cloud about their heads, the long tails streaming. Usually they were sold when the drive was done.

By 1859 cattle were moving steadily to Missouri and farther northeast. Many took the Old Beef Trail, as it was called, almost from the start. A herd of say 500 big steers might leave the Waco region early in June, cross the Trinity at Dallas and the Red at Rabbit's Ford, where the trail wagon was ferried over for a dollar. From there they went through the Indian Nation, crossed the Blue at Nail's Mill, and on to the Boggy and the Canadian, the Arkansas at old Fort Gibson and then over into Missouri, perhaps to Neosha and Honey Springs, perhaps on to Springfield, a little town, but a place where cattle might bring around $50 a head, at first. The drive was leisurely, taking around two and a half months, the steers holding their weight well. By this time thousands of cattle were trailed to Missouri and farther into the Midwest, many to Chicago and beyond. Truly it seemed that the grasses of the great western prairies could grow meat enough to feed all the nation. But the meat of a four- , five- , even six-year-old steer that had walked from Texas to the Hudson could be mighty tough, and no denying.

Nor was there any denying that after a Texas herd passed, the local cattle began to die, and no amount of dosing and drenching could save even a poor farmer's lone milk cow.

But these did not seem serious problems to the adventuresome business of trail driving, very adventurous to those who had never eaten the dust of the drags or been nearer to ranch work than the romantic pictures of this new hero, the cowboy, in *Harper's Weekly* or *Leslie's*. They did not exist at all as problems to the young men and boys who, disappointed in the California gold fields, stopped off on the way home to become Texas trail drivers. Most herds had boys along now, some very young but usually from ranches, boys equal to a man's work and responsibility before there was enough down on their cheeks to catch a little dust.

Not that all of even the responsible boys could resist an occasional range bullfight. In the spring and early summer boys and some men, too, liked to sneak out and drive a couple of good fighters together, not wild brush poppers but more manageable ranch bulls who would put on a real battle. Grudges between some of them grew up, so it took careful watching to keep them from killing each other and spoiling the fun.

Gradually these fights grew into regular Sunday contests over much of the ranch country, the bulls brought together at a good central watering place, with perhaps everybody except the owners knowing about it and going to

slouch over the saddle horn and watch. Sometimes bull
calves with fine roaring voices, big, powerful, and full of
meanness, were hidden out from the cutting knife, to grow
up for the fights. There was much far gathering to these contests and high betting until the owners discovered how their
best herd sires were spending their strength.

But serious times were coming, as everyone knew
even in the wilds of Texas, and trailers hurried their herds
together. Early in April, 1861, Jesse Day with two young
sons started his Longhorns across the Brazos at Waco. Usually
if there were steers in a bunch, one of these led, as the bell-
wether led sheep, even into the slaughterhouse, except that
the good wether was allowed to escape to bring others to the
knife. Eventually some trailers took their good lead steers
back to Texas, to use again. But the steers of Day's herd
were all new and they balked at the first stream they faced,
the Brazos in roaring flood. He plunged his horse into the
boiling current to toll the leaders to follow while the boys
crowded the rear with yihoos and whipping. But the water
was so deep and wild that the man and horse were swept under and away.

"Let 'em go!" the elder of the sons shouted. Together
they spurred down along the river. They found the father
after a while, washed up, and took the body back to a nearby
town to bury. Then, fiercely determined now, they gathered
up their herd and pushed it into the river and on northward,
to blaze their own trail to Kansas City. At the Missouri
border they were halted by angry farmers armed with squirrel guns and pitchforks, shouting threats against the Texas
herds that brought a sickness to kill their cattle. The boys
had to go around, hunting out rougher country with fewer
farmers. Finally they reached St. Louis, sold the stock, and
bought horses that they drove down to Louisiana for the
sugar plantations. When they got back to Austin they went
up the trail to fetch the body of Jesse Day home, and then
gathered another herd. But it was too late to go far, with the
feared, and anticipated, fighting against the Yankees started.

There were few slaves in the cattle country and with the men gone to war, no one could gather up a herd in a region that had no fences to hold more than a couple of wrangling horses. The Union sympathizers, fairly numerous in north Texas, hurried to safer territory across the Red, their cattle running loose, too.

With no one to pursue her, the Texas cow spread and burgeoned like the bluebonnets of the April plains. Starting with an estimated four million, the Longhorn increased so the herds spread out toward the buffalo ranges and deep into the Timbers, unbranded, unmarked, unaccustomed even to the sight of a rider. As was usual in any new region, there were almost no old men in Texas, and the few herds gathered were mostly the work of boys too young for the gray uniform. Many stories were told of these young cowmen. One of them, W. D. H. Saunders, a rawboned seventeen, with half-a-dozen others about his age headed for New Orleans with 1,100 steers—meat that the Rebels needed desperately. They swam the Colorado, Brazos, Trinity, Neches, and the Sabine to the Mississippi. There they heard that New Orleans was in the hands of Union troops. After chewing this over for an evening, they decided to swing around north, planning to sell the herd at Mobile, beyond the Mississippi, with no way of ferrying the steers across the stream a mile wide here and around forty feet deep. Young Saunders hunched his awkward shoulders as he slouched wearily in the saddle and looked at a river such as he had never seen, the far side only a dim line beyond the swirling water, brown-gray, almost like the flanks of their lead steer already shying angrily from the first sniff at the stinking floodwaters.

"We got 'er to do. We can't let them damnyankees get one over on us," he said, rubbing the soft curling of young beard on his chin, but doubtful.

The trail-gaunted young cowboys beside him nodded. They took down their ropes, fell in around the resting herd, took it back from the river a way, and started the steers running straight for the water, crowding them, whooping, yell-

ing, popping the ropes on the bounding flanks, pushing
them hard on the tail of Saunders' horse as he put the animal
into the water, and went half under. But the horse came up,
swimming strong. The young cowboy shook the water from
his face and looked back. The lead steers were being
crowded over the bank, eyes rolling in panic, many trying to
hold back, feet braced at the water's edge against the press
of stock behind, others working to turn back into the rushing herd, their horns a thorny thicket pointing in every
direction.

"Crowd 'em! Crowd 'em!" he yelled, knowing nobody
could hear.

Then suddenly the mouse-gray steer jumped far in,
came up swimming. Several others in the lead took to the
water behind him, their horns up, strung out, kept from
crowding too close by some of the cowboys to avoid raising
the waves too high. The leaders hesitated again when they
neared the current, very swift, rushing past in a foam-
streaked swelling full of floating trash and branches and now
and then a small tree. For a whole minute it seemed a spin
was inevitable, the lead steers to turn back and start a mill,
here in the middle of the Mississippi, where the entire herd
and perhaps some of the riders would be lost. Horrified,
young Saunders dropped back and drew his laboring horse
in on the upstream side of the faltering lead steer until the
animal saw him. Then he struck confidently ahead, pointing his quirt to the far, far bank as he had directed the herd
all the way. He had to hope, and for a while he listened to
the wild churning behind him. When he dared look back,
the river was full of cattle still swimming, some drifting
downstream but not too far, their horns looking truly like
the rockers of half a thousand granny chairs floating across
the boiling flood, the riders whooping along beside them
and behind.

It was a long, long mile, and the noses were barely
above the water the last 100 yards, but they made it, the cattle crawling out the far side, standing panting, and reluctant

to set one foot ahead of the other to make room for those climbing out behind. When they were all out only 100 had failed to make it—refused the river entirely.

It was a story to cheer the home folks back in Texas, whether their sympathies were still with Indiana or Ohio or Vermont or heatedly with the South. The story of the boys grew and spread all over the cow country for generations.

Some experienced cowmen didn't do nearly so well. Dudley Snyder, who delivered thousands of Texas steers to the Confederacy after the Mississippi River was lost to the Yankee gunboats, had two work oxen, trained swimmers. On land they drew his grub and tackle wagon, at streams he unyoked them and put them in the lead of the herd. They never faltered, not even in roaring floodtime, and the herd, accustomed to seeing them ahead all the miles of the trail, followed them confidently. Too valuable to sell for beef, they pulled the old wagon back to Texas each time.

The vast unbranded herds of cattle attracted hideouts from both the North and the South, particularly draft dodgers, bounty jumpers, deserters, and plain outlaws. Many gathered up little herds in the Western Cross Timbers and similar regions, even though it was understood among most of the Texas cattlemen that unbranded calves and young stuff were to belong with the brand of the older stock. When the Texans dragged home from the war they were faced with more than Indians to fight. They found the cattle thieves thick on the northwest border and well dug in, with brands established and the guns to defend them. Early in the war the ranchers of the Keechi, with Jim Loving as leader, had formed a loose sort of protective association to fight these rustlers moving in, and to brand up the calves of the war widows, but this became impossible as more and more men went to fill the shrinking ranks of the Confederacy.

Almost no she stuff had been sold during the war years and outside of the rustlers there had been no cattle enemies except the very rare Indian raider. The Comanches, angry that they had been driven from their reservation lands in Texas and the region across the Red, had refused to join the Confederacy as some tamer Indians did. They had promised to raid the border but no Indians were very interested in gathering wild cattle from the thorny brush and breaks when the herd-minded buffalo was still plentiful out on the open prairie, and much easier to crawl up to. So the Texas cattle had multiplied until at least 6,000,000 were running free in 1865, and that in spite of the drouth of 1863-64, when the Brazos that drowned Jesse Day and other hard-bitten trailers went so dry it was said a man could ride its bed for 300 miles through the Palo Pinto region without wetting a fetlock of his horse. Vast stretches of post oak died, crops failed, and corn for the horses of the rangers who tried, with their depleted ranks to hold off the rustlers, had to be bullwhacked in from east Texas.

But now the rains were back and the men returning from the war, those who would return. They found the rustlers, the mavierickers as they called themselves, already trailing large herds North, cattle that had been held ready for the moment of peace to open the routes. True, their herds were unmarked stock and, by custom, classed as mavericks, free for the taking as soon as no longer running with the cow. Even the term maverick was a new and curious one, from Samuel Maverick, the already legendary figure sometimes said to own more cattle than anyone else in Texas, although apparently he never claimed more than the 400 head he brought in to the mainland from an island in 1853 and sold out completely three years later, at range delivery, still only an estimated 400 head.

All over the impoverished, devastated South seed stock was desperately needed, even more than the meat they lacked so long. But Confederate money was worthless and even good young cows at $3 to $5 found no buyers. There was a great beef shortage in the north, too, where the breeding stock was dangerously low. A good-grade, matured beef animal, worth around $5 in Texas brought $50 in the

North. It was this harvest the maverickers reaped now, making up their herds from the gentler stock. The returning Texans, shorthanded, and without a cent of northern currency, learned to round up their cattle against bluffs or other barriers, roped and branded the wild stuff in the open, developing tricks and short cuts on top of those learned from the Indian and Mexican vaqueros of the old mission herds.

A stimulating element in this, like a shot of redeye to the swill-barrel johnnies of the frontier towns was the race of the new railroads heading west, like long fingers reaching up the main streams. In the North the Union Pacific had already crossed into Nebraska and was pushing up the Platte into the buffalo plains. Other railroads were creeping across Missouri, and to reach this market the old Shawnee Trail across southeast Kansas into Missouri, grown deep in grass during the war, was cropped cleaner than a barroom floor, the water holes and riverbanks chopped into bottomless mud by thousands of sharp and eager hoofs. Once more the farmers hurried out to guard the border against the disease their cattle had not suffered once during the war years with no Texas cattle on the trail. Most of them had been guerrillas in the war and Union men, to whom any Texan was a bloody Johnny Reb. At the first death of a milk cow near the trail they were out with guns, axes and scythes, pitchforks and bull whips.

"Can't you see our herd is clean and healthy?" the southerners tried to argue.

"They carry poison wherever they go!" a Missourian shouted in reply, waving his Long Tom, his thumb on the hammer.

"Just tromping over the grass, they makes it poison!" another added.

After some shooting and a horsewhipping or two, and several stampedes that spread the cattle and with them the fever, Baxter Springs, Kansas, became the end of the trail. But there, without pasture or shipping facilities, the herds had to be sold to any Kansan who would take them off the owner's hands. Some sent their cattle on to Kansas City and St. Joseph by the fort-to-fort road and the railroad or steamboats for the eastern corn country. Many were bought by Iowa farmers, until their cattle came down with the fever. By then east Kansas stock, too, was dying of this Texas sickness, and so Baxter's day was done.

The summer of 1865 the drive had been small but the next year an estimated 250,000 cattle crossed the Red into Indian Territory for Missouri or Kansas. The first drives ran into trouble with the Five Civilized Tribes of the Territory. These Indians raised cattle, too, and demanded ten cents a head toll for the grass the herds ate going through. Some drovers paid it, a legal charge; others traded cattle for their passage; a few drew guns and bluffed or bulled it through, although the Indian Act of 1834 penalized drovers $1 a head for cattle driven across any Indian lands without the owner's consent. Others swung around east into Arkansas, risking attack from the farmers and the raiding thieves hidden out in the rough breaks of the Ozarks. One of these trailers was Captain E. B. Millett, who made it to the Mississippi but by then his herd was too gaunted to sell in the glutted market. He crossed into Illinois, bought winter feed for his cattle, and lost money. Many other herds were started north without specific destination and most of them ended disastrously, the cattle scattered over southeast Kansas, hunting feed, unsold. But the owners went home to gather up more herds for next spring—even Millett. It was like a call, a sacred call that could not be denied.

R. D. Hunter, a Scotsman who had sickened in the Colorado mines, started toward Texas that 1866 for cattle. At the Red he bought a herd of 400 at $25 apiece. On the way to Sedalia, Missouri, the sheriff took the herd over and arrested Hunter, along with the bosses of around 10,000 head more. Hunter got the sheriff to take him to the county seat for a talk with the authorities. As soon as the two men were out of sight, the trail bosses headed the herds west for Indian Territory thirty-five miles off, without stopping for rest or grass. At the county seat it seems Hunter had a sociable drink with the sheriff, enough to get him drunk, and then slipped away to overtake the herds. After a few days recuperating in the Territory, they struck westward for about 150 miles, then north to hit the Kaw River near Atchison. They ran into settler trouble there, too, but got across the river to St. Joseph and shipped the stock to Illinois at a profit.

The obvious route to avoid the farmers and settlers was to swing clear around west but the Comanches were still more dangerous, even for the old cowmen, thorny as the brush of Texas, and tough as the *bois d'arc,* the osage orange of the Red River bottoms. The drovers now were all kinds, from youths like Saunders and his companions who had swum their herd over the mile-wide Mississippi, hound-gutted Confederates, experienced stockmen who had been fighting Indians and Mexican raiders for years, army mule skinners, and professional Indian fighters, to the riffraff of the southern river towns, gamblers, con men and hide-outs from the law and just plain murderers. They were all looking for a new cattle route north.

Jesse Chisholm, a half-breed Cherokee hunter and trader, had built a post near the Wichita Indian village on the Arkansas River up in Kansas. Some time later he organized a trading expedition to the tribes down in the Washita River region of southwest Indian Territory not far from Texas. For three years he made regular trips back up to his post with bull trains of buffalo robes and furs, sometimes driving small herds of cattle, and returning loaded with trade goods. Soon white men and Indians were using his trail up through the Territory to the Wichita site. Then in 1866 Joseph G. McCoy, from Illinois, saw some of the big Texas herds and listened to the troubles encountered in marketing the season's quarter million head of cattle, with little except violent receptions, the year a calamity to most drovers.

McCoy hunted up the officials of the Kansas Pacific

Railroad heading west, eventually to Denver, and proposed
that they build shipping pens and other facilities for handling the Longhorns at some Kansas frontier station. He
spoke of the hauling this would bring to the road, the large
trail pay rolls to be spent in the town, and touched on the
troubles of the trailers with Indians stampeding the herds,
sweeping off their horses, and from the violent farmers and
the bands of "no-counts"—discharged and jobless soldiers
ranging the prairies, stealing, pillaging and murdering. But
mostly McCoy stressed the money ready for the taking.

With arrangements made for carload deliveries of cattle to Quincy and Chicago, McCoy went out to find a suitable
railhead along the KP, and met Colonel John Jacob Myers,
an enthusiastic Texan who blandly promised 1,000,000 cattle
to come up the Chisholm trail and north to any station Mc-
Coy selected. Meaning exactly what he said, Myers worked
out an extension from Chisholm's place on the Washita to
the Red River and south to his home town of Lockhart, then
spread the word that McCoy would maintain an honest
market up at the new town of Abilene, Kansas. By then it
was almost midsummer of 1867, too late to increase the drive
to Kansas very much that year, but early enough to draw
those already on the road or about ready to start—35,000
head. It was a cholera summer and the plague that struck
the troops guarding the Kansas Pacific trackworkers through
the state sickened, even killed, many cowboys on the trail.
R. D. Hunter, who had run into trouble with the sheriff in
Missouri last year, drove 1,200 head straight through to
Omaha before he heard of Abilene. The railroad records
list Myers' own cattle as the first Texas herd to reach the new
market although several others claimed the honor. Among
these was C. C. Slaughter, said to have shipped the first cattle out of Abilene. Many favored him because C. C. was the
first native cattle king of Texas. His father, who had dealt
in early wild Spanish cattle, had been Sam Houston's right-
hand bower and the first man to be married in the Republic, C.C. the first child born of the marriage.

But no matter who was first. The world's greatest cow path, the Chisholm Trail, was started, although Chisholm's road was only the middle section, and the trail was not widely known by that name until it no longer led to Abilene. By then the trail had moved westward, kept moving westward before the push of the granger, the despised hoe man.

# BOOK II

*INDIVIDUAL RANCH SPREADS*

# CHAPTER I

# SOME DEDICATED MEN

**M**ANY an early Texan lived almost as wholly from his cow as the Plains Indian from his buffalo. She was meat, fat, soap, and candlelight to him, and her skin had even more uses than the buffalo's. Although it was less commonly the white man's dwelling, she often did provide his shelter and the cover for his wagon bows, the door to his first dugout, and perhaps the floor and the rugs. Early ranch and settler shacks were often lined with rawhide against the blue northers and the scorpions, centipedes, and rattlesnakes. Rawhide made the woven bottom of the Texan's springless bed and his chairs, stools, cradles, trunks, valises, baskets, buckets, dough pans, and even the settler's churn, although some thought it gave the butter a peculiar flavor.

Cowskin furnished the rancher his winter coat, his carriage and wagon robes, often his bedcovers as rawhide made his poncho and his chaps, his *chaparejos,* to protect him against brush and thorns and rain and cold. In addition to the regular leathern uses, rawhide often took the place of iron, cotton, wood, and even silver or paper. It was the rawhide riata in place of the surveyor's chain that measured off the Spanish land grants. The horses were hobbled with strips of rawhide instead of iron, and sometimes shod with it, as were

the oxen. In a pinch rawhide served as slates, blackboards,
playing cards, and faro table tops. Portraits and holy pictures were embossed or burned on it. When the horrifying
cholera epidemic of 1849-50 swept up along all the western
trails to the edge of swift water, and reached San Antonio,
too, there were so many dead in the town and the fear of infection was so great that the corpses were simply rolled into
cowhides and buried. To the Texan the cow was all the
things the buffalo was to the hunting Indian, except perhaps
the center of his highest religious ritual that the buffalo
occupied in the sundance of many Plains tribes, and perhaps that could come, too.

The restrictions in trade and money during the war
made Texas even more surely the Rawhide State. The trail
drivers used the skin of the cow as thread and twine, pins,
nails, washers, screws, bolts, as well as iron and cloth. While
hackamores and picket ropes were usually horsehair, the
lariat was rawhide, of four, even eight long, even strands,
round-braided into graceful length, stretched and oiled until
the throw rope was just stiff enough to sing out like a fiddle
string and just the right weight for deft and accurate aim.
While the Texas Ranger was turning to the Colt
six-shooter, California vaqueros still lassoed and dragged
horse-stealing Indians to death rather than shot them, as the
early Spaniards of Texas had also done. Once duels were
fought by horsemen with leather riatas, each man trying to
dodge the rival's loop while trying to rope him, jerk him off,
drag him to pieces behind a spurring run through the cactus. Sometimes more or less friendly chapping contests decided who was to escort the very occasional girl home from a
ranch country dance. Even the winner would be stiff for a
week from the spanking his saddle-leaned buttocks took
from the rawhide chap leg wielded against him. A particularly keen rivalry between Negro or Mexican bullwhackers
or cow hands was sometimes settled by bull whips at a certain number of steps, the experts snaking the whips out in

powerful, stinging, flesh-cutting lashes that sounded like sharp pistol shots but carried farther on the wind. To admit defeat short of blindness or collapse was shameful beyond a man's gut. Sometimes the welted faces were carried with a little of the show-off of the German officer's sword-cut cheek. Even in Texas the welts were proof of a little extra Texas dash and sand, an ability to ride life to a finish even as it had to be lived in the San Saba country.

Perhaps it was true that the Texan of 1867 needed to be tough as whang leather and hard as a flint hide, with the darkness of defeat and ruin on all the South and, except in the vast increases among the Longhorns, as heavily upon Texas. In addition to all the rustlers there was the Reconstruction Act of March, 1867, passed by the Radicals over President Johnson's veto. By this the South was turned over to the carpetbaggers pouring in all the past winter and to the local citizens not "disfranchised for participation in the rebellion" called scalawags.

McCoy's promise of good facilities and a sure and fair cattle market at Abilene started a booming of hope from the Red River to the Gulf and out beyond the Cross Timbers. But he had no control over the depression in the East. The first trainload of Longhorns sold very poorly in Chicago and the second shipment, around 900 head, found no market at all and had to be taken to Albany, New York. Apparently it wasn't that no one wanted meat, even trail and railway-gaunted meat, and from cattle rumored diseased enough to sicken any cow that touched the ground the Longhorns walked on. There just wasn't much money around. Newspapers reported long queues of the unemployed being fed in the Tombs at New York City, and not with beef or even beef soup.

Surely these postwar years seemed enough to discourage anyone, but to many men of Texas the cow had been a way of life for a long time—dedicated men, dedicated to the cow with all their property, their time, even their lives.

One who was already an old-time cattleman by 1867 was Richard King, a New York Irishman. At ten he had stowed away on a schooner for Mobile. Discovered, he was made cabin boy and was on the steamer back in 1842 when the chief of the Seminoles and his principal warriors were lured on board for counciling and then told they were prisoners. Later, with a partner, King operated twenty-six small steamboats on the shifting, treacherous Rio Grande. Much of this time Captain King was also a cattleman. As early as 1852 he selected the Santa Gertrudis country of south Texas for a ranch, and bought the land as he could, land of many and sometimes doubtful titles: Spanish, Mexican, Texan, and United States. Some of it he had to buy twice. But it was coastal plain and seemed worth the effort. There was green-gray prickly pear, with the great flat ten-inch tongues or hands, reaching up to eight, ten feet. Most of the scattered trees of the sandy region had been brought in by the Longhorns dropping the seeds as they roamed the region. The most prolific were the mesquite and live oak, both able to exist without rain, both low, twisted, and often in clusters or *mottes* penetrable only to small animals or a determined man on foot. The oaks favored the coast, particularly the sandy belt, the mesquite spreading farther west on the black loam and clay as well as the sand. Willows came in too, and the huisache, the wild persimmon, the ebony and the brazil bush—all gnarled and thorny, mostly four, five feet high, seldom much above the mounted cowboy. This was the wild brush that the Longhorn favored, and therefore the cowman.

By 1867 King had bought out one partner for $50,000 and dissolved the agreement with another. He hoped to own all the land between the Nueces and the Rio Grande and, further, to control a strip of land three miles wide from Brownsville to the railroad in Kansas for a cattle trail. The King Ranch already contained a good portion of this land the captain coveted, and the Chisholm Trail promised to serve as a cattle highway when beef prices came back. In the meantime he started to fence his range with wooden planks, another typical King dream. But his cattle were flourishing and he had great plans for improved stock. For this the scrub bulls must be kept out, away from good blood.

In the meantime the glutted markets forced the Texas ranchers to set up hide and tallow factories, to reap something from the great herds, make a little northern money. King was one of the first to try the slaughtering sheds and pens set up along the coast at such places as Fulton and Brazoria. Here cattle scarcely worth the rustler's trouble were harvested for the hide, worth more than the whole cow alive. Some were mossy old steers with horns eight or nine feet across, rough, wavy horns so heavy they threatened to tip the steer's thin rump up into the sky. Here New England buyers gathered hides for their tanneries, tallow for candles and soap. Sometimes hoofs and horns went to glue and comb manufacturers and hair for plaster and padding. Only the meat was worthless, left to rot or to feed the hordes and clouds of gorging scavengers—the small skittering animals and the larger, the foxes and coyotes, the buzzards and magpies, with the flies gathering thick over everything, in clouds around the long sheds and the factories as thick as the stink. At Brazoria Negroes were hired to take what was wanted of the carcasses and then slid the rest down the chutes into the river, where fish fought obscenely over them, great catfish, evil-whiskered mouths slashing and crushing, the fish leaping clear of the water in the struggle. A factory down at the bottom of the Brazos attracted whole schools of fighting sharks.

This waste of meat distressed Richard King, who had known the hungry and saw this all as profit lost besides. He tried preserving the flesh of newly-killed Longhorns by injecting brine into the veins. The process failed but he brought in several thousand hogs to fatten on the meat. Many got away into the brushy country, where descendants of the King pigs were killed and eaten by cowboys for many years.

The factories weren't the only places where cowhides were taken. Mexicans scoured the country, hamstringing the fleeing Longhorns with machetes, stripping off the hides. Some fired the grass to herd the cattle together in unburned strips and pockets. After blue northers the cattle that had drifted into bunches and piles along the coast drew out everybody, even boys and some women, to skin the dead and the dying. Only the slaughter of the buffalo up along the regions of the railroad exceeded the hide taking here.

Yet even in this time so sorrowful for the cattlemen Richard King was laying plans for better cattle, with more meat and with an immunity to the disease the North called the Texas fever but which no Texan intended to admit existed. For this better, this immune stock King was working out better range methods, more efficient handling and care. His methods, all his methods, would be his own, and if there were those who objected, he intended to be too high, too big to reach, for anybody, or any power to reach. He was a dedicated man.

There were other men with determination in the cow business. Soon after the Mexican War James Olive had moved his family from Louisiana to Williamson County, Texas, and started in cattle. He and his wife were quiet, religious, churchgoing, but there was trouble between the father and the eldest son, young I. P., called Print, for Prentice. In Texas this grew like the thorns, with the son's taste for bad companions, hard liquor, cards, and gun play and the mother still shielding him as she had from birth, keeping his actions hidden from the father when she could, standing before him with her broad skirts outspread between him and the son when his misconduct was discovered. Finally Print was drawn into the war, wounded, and, recovered, made a mule skinner and captured at Vicksburg. Paroled in an exchange of prisoners, he was appointed to garrison duty at Galveston. Here, in idleness, he found drinking and gambling even more attractive and more available, as well as several shooting scrapes that involved no one that an Olive could possibly have termed a damnyankee.

When the war ended, Print went into stock raising near home. Pleased at what looked like a sober settling down at last, the father and two of the other sons bought more stock. Print and the other three had their farms separate but they ran a ranch farther west on a large tract of state land together, each with his own brand. Under Print's hard riding, hard cussing, they built reservoirs to catch any water that fell, dug wells, and later put up windmills. Their cattle grew into thousands. For a while they neighbored with the ranchers around them, particularly with the Snyders, J. W. and Dudley, also of Williamson County. It had been Dudley who trailed beef to the Confederacy, swimming his herds behind the two oxen who drew his trail wagon but led the steers across the swollen rivers. Dudley Snyder was known as a good man to tie to, and Print Olive missed few tricks.

In 1866 Print had bossed the general roundup of the region, really only a great cow hunt for stock branded before the war, the unmarked, the mavericks, to be divided among the ranches represented. At night the men gambled in the light of brush fires with the unbranded stock, a top critter worth $5 in chips, down to a yearling valued at fifty cents. The Moore boy who was along watching for his father's strays kept the fires going for two bits a night. Print Olive furnished the grub: coffee, corn meal, salt, whisky, and all the beef a man could eat—so long as it wasn't Olive beef. But that was customary.

By the 1870's many were complaining about the Olives, not aloud, but among themselves. Their stock was shrinking while the Olive herds, particularly Print's, more than doubled every year. There were some complaints at the courthouse but nothing came of them except that a couple of the bellyachers seemed to quit the country. At least, as Print said, nobody saw them around any more. Then there were rumors of trouble with a new settler, a young

man called Deets Phreme, who went into cattle. One spring
day Print Olive, his brother Ira, and some hired help starting on a cattle drive ran into Phreme and a couple of his
hands. It seemed that the Olives accused him of killing
their cattle and pistol-whipped him until his face and head
were cut and swollen, knocked him down, and told him if
they caught him on the range again he would be shot.

Old-timers warned him to go, get out, but Phreme
was determined to stay. He had a legal right here. He was
still as stubborn when he heard the Olive version of the encounter, saying they had found some of their brands in the
Phreme herd and while the men cut out their stock, Print
and the settler had words. Later Phreme and his hired man
had shot at young Bob Olive, Print's brother, tried to bushwhack the youth.

Plainly they were setting the young settler up for a
target, the old-timers said.

A few days later Print Olive managed to meet Phreme
out on the prairie. "Did you shoot at my brother Bob?" he
demanded.

"No, I didn't," the settler replied, "but I sure as hell
would like to take a pop at you!"

The two men fired almost the same instant and fell
together in the stinking powder smoke, both badly
wounded. Phreme died soon afterward and Print Olive
was several years really recovering. This time he was tried
for murder and acquitted. "Easier to move men than cattle,"
he was reported to have said after the celebration.

Now the rumors about the Olives were more open,
some perhaps spread by them to scare the settlers from the
range they claimed, and harder to hold with so many pushing into the San Gabriel and Brushy Creek region. This man
or that one vanished, and while few in Texas reported their
comings and goings, some were settlers or little ranchers
who left families without so much as a pone or a spoonful of
hominy grits.

Maverickers, as well as out-and-out rustlers, and anybody that Print Olive decided fit these terms, were given fair warning to keep off the Olive range, claimed by the only right possible on public lands—the guns to hold them. Cattle prices were coming up again and large rustling outfits followed the rise like the eagle's shadow follows him on the ground below. Some of the ranchers had been hiring tough, gun-fingered cowboys, men who didn't care whose cattle they burnt with the ranch brand or whose milk cow they whooped off into the passing herd. In return the little outfits and the settlers stole back as much as they dared, and a little extra for their trouble.

Here and there suspected rustlers drew together in gangs for self-protection by lies, perjury, intimidation, and murder. Not that these methods were unfamiliar in a country largely unorganized, and where many a man even in high position was traveling under a name that never belonged to his father.

An old man called Pea Eye because his eyes were squushed together, although apparently large enough to see one of these gangs stealing cattle, appeared in court as a witness against them. Not long afterward his faithful ox team drew him into his home yard, down in the bottom of the wagon dead, full of buckshot. It seems nothing was done about that, except that one man was found hanging to a pecan tree and another vanished. Some of this was not far from the Olives, grown into a powerful clan of farmers, ranchers, and even peace officers, as peace officers went on the frontier.

The pointed complaint that stock was still vanishing in the Olive region Print Olive switched as handily as a spinning bronc switches ends. "We mean to kill any man found skinning our cattle or running off our horses." He said this half-tipsy in a bar but even those on fair terms with the Olives stood away a little, silent, remembering some of the things told of this fierce-eyed, gaunt-gutted man.

In a little while everybody knew that Print Olive meant what he said. The *Austin Statesman* reported the

death of Turk Turner and James H. Crow over near
McDade, adding:

> Two beeves had been killed and skinned and in the
> absence of the parties who did it, the carcasses were dis-
> covered and watch kept to see who would return to carry
> away the beef and hides. Finally the above parties re-
> turned with a wagon and after having loaded up and
> started away they were fired upon by unknown parties
> and both killed.

It seemed the bodies were found by Crow's young
son sent to look for his father after school. The dead men
were several hundred yards apart, the team tied to a tree.
Later it came out that there was more than the *Statesman*
printed. Turner and Crow had been wrapped tightly in the
fresh hides of the cattle they killed, while still alive, and left
on the prairie to suffer the slow and horrible Spanish "Death
of the Skins" as the burning sun drew the green hides tight
and hard as iron about the men. The brands had been
turned up conspicuously for everyone to see—brands of the
Olives.

There was alarm in the region, the women afraid,
their eyes filmed with the horror of what had happened to
Turner and Crow when their own men rode away, for the
skins drew as tightly about the innocent as the guilty.
Turk had been regarded as a desperado but Old Man Crow,
though he had son in the pen, had been considered honest.
Besides, there was a courthouse and law here against rustlers.

Although Crow's son accused the Olives of the murder, nothing came of it. They were still on close terms with
two of the region's most prominent citizens, Dudley and
J. W. Snyder. The Snyders had a newly-purchased herd over
on the Olive range. Young Moore, who as a boy had kept the
fires burning for the roundup gambling back in 1866, was
hired to keep an eye on the stock and was boarding with the
Olives.

Early in August the brothers, Print, Jay Thomas, and

Ira, with four cowhands, including two Negroes, were branding a new herd. Although they were working the stock at the ranch, at night the men stretched out on the prairie beyond the corrals to sleep, their guns ready, apparently expecting a raid on the cattle. Around one o'clock, when the moon was well hazed, they were awakened by shots, men setting fire to the ranch buildings and shooting at anyone seen moving out on the dusky prairie. All the Olive outfit except young Moore were well armed. They fired from behind banks and bushes in the rising flames from the ranch house. There seemed to be fifteen, perhaps twenty in the attacking mob, some scattered in a wide circle around the ranch, others closer up, apparently with shotguns. In that first stiff fire in the light of the burning ranch Thomas was hit with several blasts of buckshot. Dying, he thrust his rifle into young Moore's hand and motioned to him to unbuckle the cartridge belt. Print was struck in the hip and crawled painfully for better cover, growling his curses against the men who killed his brother. One of the Negroes was dead, too, the other badly wounded. Inside the corral the cattle were milling hard from the shots fired into them and in terror of the flames rising high from the burning logs of the ranch house, sparks, and rolling smoke over them. As they surged against the poles of the corral, the attackers jerked the gates back and the big steers stampeded for the breaks, almost running over the defenders scattered behind the shadowy clumps and banks.

The fire of the buildings died rapidly and the lowering moon was lost in the smoke that filled the valley. In the darkness the fight became a watchful preparation for dawn, but with the first graying that might show a known face, the attackers slipped away. The ranch hands got Print stretched out to ease his wound a little and covered the half-naked body of Thomas. Then they discovered from the wounded Negro, who had been the first to awaken, that the place had been robbed of seven or eight hundred dollars Print kept on hand as down payment on cattle delivered.

But plainly this was not just a robbery; it was a plan for extermination. Many blamed the Turner and Crow killings. Crow's son, who had served time, promised vengeance. It was known that he headed a lot of toughs and desperados, probably the mob that attacked the Olive ranch. But immediately another gang loudly claimed the honor in saloons and the country post offices. Not even Print seemed certain who the attackers had been, with a dozen enemy outfits long itching for a showdown. In addition the Olives still had the trial for the murder of Turner and Crow before them. When court convened, the Olive forces camped at one side of Georgetown, the county seat, with an estimated forty armed men ready to drag the jury out to the trees down along the San Gabriel if the verdict went against them. On the other side of town it seems another camp had gathered, sixty men against the Olives, determined to uphold the law of Texas, here so close to Austin, to stop this bloodshed practically on the capitol steps.

All through the trial the town was divided into these two armed forces, the main street a barren and dusty sort of dare line between the waiting belligerents. But in the end the Olives were turned loose and without bloodshed.

By now more dead men had been turning up. Two were found hanging by their picket ropes near the Williamson County line, with plenty of money still on them, so it wasn't robbery. Later in the summer another dead man was found in the timber, stripped naked except for a hickory shirt and a blanket over him. "Almost like he was ambushed in bed, like Thomas Olive was," some said.

The law-abiding people of the region were furious as a bull at the smell of blood. Here, within a twenty-five-mile distance, ten or twelve men had been killed during the past few months, and more farther out. Newspapers agreed in their protests, pointing out that more men had been killed in Texas the last year than she lost during all the lamented war. The editor of the *Austin Statesman* suggested a remedy, "— instead of hanging, have horse thieves and robbers surgically rendered incapable of crime and of the procreation of knavery."

As Print recovered enough to get around in his buggy, the bold attack and the death of one of their brothers stirred the Olives to a revenging fury, particularly young Bob, and the eldest, I. P., Print, his small eyes always burning in one rage or another. The women of the region pitied his wife, even those who envied her the wealth of her husband's ways. She had been an orphan reared by her grandfather, and was now the mother of a growing family, including a son who roused his father's anger and contempt as Print himself had infuriated his religious father. It was said that both Print's wife and his parents begged for a quieter life, for peace for the children. But families counted very little in these days of cow feuds, and Print and young Bob were laying for the killers of Thomas. Then one day two Negroes stopped in at the home ranch and asked Mrs. Olive for a drink of water. Although Negroes outside of the army were not allowed to carry guns, Print saw they had pistols strapped to their saddles. He ran to the house for his rifle, for once not beside him. With it across his arm he got between the Negroes at the well and their horses. When they started to leave, he pulled down on them, ordered them to halt, to explain their business.

Oh, they were just out hunting stolen horses and needed a little water this hot day, one of them answered amiably.

"Then why was you asking my wife where her husband's at?" Print roared. "Don't make a move!"

Scared, one of the men jumped for the horses and was shot dead on the spot. The other surrendered and was driven off the place with a bull whip, so it was rumored, perhaps to explain the deep red and swelling cuts on his dark face and the bloody shirt slashed from his crusted back. Within a month Print Olive was tried for the murder of the Negro and acquitted.

"Just another of them biggety Lincoln Niggers

gettin' an Olive ticket to hell," a sympathetic southerner said, and counted the dead Negroes credited to Print and to his brother Bob on his fingers, moving to the second hand and grinning. But no one counted the white men openly.

Even those friendly to the Olives were getting uneasy about Print. He was drinking more, brawling more, too, perhaps with the Union vets who had returned to Williamson County but often with long-time associates as well, until one or the other of the more peaceful brothers or a trusted ranch hand had to coax him out of the bar. Not even his brothers were spared Print's violent tongue now. And there were so many ways to get even with a rancher, ways that didn't involve actually facing his gun. He had cattle to be stolen, scattered, or destroyed, range ready for the lucifer or even flint and steel. He needed some who passed as friends in the emergencies common in the wilds, not only in prairie fires, stampedes, or attacks but in accidents and sickness. Even in ordinary times he needed someone to offer a pleasant word not forced by the fear of a low-slung gun, particularly a man with children, with a growing boy. There were rumors that even Print Olive's wife dared a little gentle urging for a move to new, less-crowded range.

Perhaps the wildest section of all Texas was the Big Bend country of the Rio Grande. Most of it was barren earth and rock, the stream squeezed into a deep canyon by the dark and rugged mountains, like a great hard-knuckled fist thrusting the river toward Mexico. In the entire region it seemed that nothing could ever be found except by the eagle or the buzzard. Yet even here at least one man had dedicated himself to the cow. Milton Faver was from the outside, too, although few who knew him had any idea of his origins, but no one doubted that he was the first cattle king of the Big Bend, with vaqueros to work his cattle and a trooping of Mexican farm hands for his fields and gardens and his famous peach orchards. His wife was a beautiful Mexican, fitted to her courtly, educated husband who spoke

French, German, Spanish, and English fluently. It was said he came to the region in 1854, and that while he brought no cattle with him he tolled a comfortable number to swim the Rio Grande and burned his little F brand on them. Others said Faver was from England, had come to Mexico and started in cattle by trading with the Indians and then moved to Texas in 1857. Another account was that he came much later, straight from the North somewhere for his health, and that the start in cattle came with his beautiful wife.

He established the famous Cibolo Springs Ranch, later a freight stop for his ox trains on the Chihuahua–San Antonio line. The ranch, in the Chinati Mountains, was good tillable land, irrigated from living springs that had watered the cultivations of prehistoric Indians there. Faver's peaches were famous, and his peach brandy, too, particularly at the roundups. He made it in his fifty-gallon copper still, with enough extra to trade to the Indians but never delivered until they were safely far away from the ranch.

As the herds of Milton Faver, Don Milton as his Mexican neighbors called him, increased, he built new ranches for cattle and for sheep, the first of the latter in the region of the wolf and the eagle. At Cibolo he built a fort against Indians and bandits, the walls twenty feet high, with tall lookout towers and portholes. The commander at Fort Davis furnished him with a cannon and some troops who took their orders from old Don Milton. But during the wartime shortage of men the soldiers were withdrawn from such frontier stations as Davis. Indians raided the region as they pleased, and while Faver's Mexican help fought well, he lost all his cattle except thirty, forty calves in the corrals at Cibolo. With these and what he got through persistent and careful trading he built up a new herd, much of the stock from the Indians who liked Mexican spurs, bridles, and so on, preferably silver-mounted, and knew where to find plenty of cattle for the taking.

Sometimes even the friendly Indians raided Faver's

stock, particularly the sheep, with their astonishing panic that the Indians found so amusing. The raiders killed Faver's brother-in-law, who was foreman at the sheep ranch, and stole the man's wife and sons. They were never traced although some reported them up in Indian Territory a long time later.

Still Don Milton Faver stayed on, to dominate the wild Big Bend country for thirty years. His trade grew; he increased his string of freight wagons with their fast-walking Mexican oxen and set up five freight stations. Each had a good adobe house and a little irrigated farm so the station keeper could grow his frijoles, his chili, and corn, with his Mexican peaches ripening golden and red in the sun. Thousands of Faver's cattle roamed free and unbranded, not even with the small F, and when Don Milton died he was buried on top of the mountain behind his house at Cibolo. His origin and his past were as deep a mystery as ever, as much as the man's nature.

Charlie Goodnight was another man who made his whole life out of cattle. At nine he had ridden bareback from Illinois to Texas. It wasn't as far a piece as to Oregon in 1845, but it was a long, dreary overlanding for the family, with no good prospects and without solidarity, for Charlie's father was dead and the stepfather acknowledged as a pretty poor stick. Still, the boy got a fine bow to his growing legs all those miles, and soon there was another, a more acceptable stepfather. In 1856 the twenty-year-old Charlie Goodnight formed a partnership with his stepbrother, Wes Sheek, to run cattle on shares. At that time most of the ranchers penned their stock at night against Indians, the occasional rustlers, and against the persistent urge to go wild. Soon the herds were too large for corraling and after a year Goodnight and Sheek trailed their stock to Palo Pinto County, where the fall mesquite grass was like a golden buffalo robe spread over the earth and where the Comanches came riding with the full moon. Scouting the Indians led Charlie Goodnight into the Rangers. By the end of the war his herd was estimated at around 8,000 head but he knew they might not be able to collect more than 1,000, with the roundup diffi- culties in the Cross Timbers country and with the neighbors, near and far, who had stayed home branding diligently.

The protective association formed by the early.cattle- men of the region, to serve until law and order arrived, had disintegrated long ago and little unmarked stock within reach of a hot iron went unbranded. The Comanches were a constant threat and Goodnight and some other discouraged Cross Timbers cowmen went looking for new range, freer from Indians, the running iron, and the growing crop of carpetbaggers reaching out from Austin. The others headed across the Rio Grande into Mexico where a whole party of Rebel officers had gone. But Goodnight valued markets too much. He gathered up what he could of his remaining cattle, added a wild bunch of around 250 head he cut off at a water- ing place, and with a few cowboys to help, he moved 1,000 head farther up the Brazos, twelve miles from a settlement. He was freer of the maverickers for a while but he ran into immediate trouble with the Indians.

The buffaloes, never very fond of timbered, brushy or rough country, were probably always scarce up and down central Texas. They had become even scarcer after the Civilized Tribes were crowded into eastern Indian Terri- tory, forcing the local Indians west and south, making more hungry people to feed. Before the cattle came in these In- dians had to venture out among their enemies on the open plains for their meat. Then the white men brought their spotted cows, drivable stock, and the even more attractive American horses, meaning larger, non-mustang horses and much more valuable to keep and to trade to the New Mexi- cans, the *comancheros*, who dealt in stolen stock from the Indians. The young braves took to this with whoops of joy, waving blankets to stampede them flying off west into the wild country.

Goodnight had gone back to gather up another herd

of around 1,200 to 1,500 cattle. He started for his new ranch shorthanded and was attacked by Indians who killed a wily old frontiersman he had along and swept away all the cow horses except those the night herders were riding. After that it was one raid after another in the region; many people killed and around 10,000 head of cattle run off.

Trail drivers had discovered early that herds of more than 1,800 to 2,500 were too difficult to water, to handle in stampedes, and to protect against raiders. Most stories of great trail herds of 5,000, even 10,000 and 15,000 head, came from liars while talking to a tenderfoot who didn't know that fighting a grizzly barehanded was a feat. They simply threw in another grizzly, even two. However, many reliable men were certain that in 1866 a party of around 100 Indians started west from the San Saba region with a herd of 10,000 cattle they had stolen from the ranchers. How they got across the waterless Staked Plains to the Pecos, or if they went that way, wasn't known, but the cattle disappeared and some of them, some of Goodnight's, were found in New Mexico later.

By the next spring Goodnight was prepared to move again. With his partner he gathered up a beef herd to trail to New Mexico and Colorado—2,000 big steers and fat dry cows. But the Indians stampeded them, fought off the trail hands, and swept the whole lot away. Thoroughly disgusted at last, Charlie Goodnight gave up ranching in Texas. Too many Indians and no use begging for help from that Reconstruction gathering of scalawags and carpetbaggers down at Austin. In addition there was the news of glutted markets up in Kansas and farther east. But the mining regions of the Rockies seemed to have some money left. Besides, George Reynolds had taken a small herd no farther than New Mexico the summer after the war and found that steers worth at the most $8 or $10 in Texas brought $60 up there. Not only that, but his sister went along on the drive. Of course he could start from Fort Davis in the Big Bend country, on the other side of the Pecos, with no Staked Plains to cross and almost none of the Comanche country.

Even so, it was no Natchez promenade with ruffled parasols and crinolines for a lady, Goodnight was told.

No, but Sallie Reynolds could sit a saddle longer than most of the hard-bottom cowhands of the country. Besides, that drive was nothing compared to one from the Brazos. It would take real time, money, and sand to swing down an unknown trail through waterless country to get around the Comanches, or most of them. Yet Charlie Goodnight, an old cowman at thirty, insisted he was heading for Colorado and going around the south to do it. He gathered up little herds of loose, unmarked cattle here and there. Some objected to this, particularly the Jacksboro Unionists, who had left Texas for the safety of south Kansas during the war and then come tearing back to their old stomping grounds to get a crack at the cattle before the Texans were out of their grays. Thieves, Goodnight called them, and they paid him back in the same coin a time or two, until it seemed the bad blood between them would break into gun play, especially now that Goodnight was preparing to quit the country with cattle he had run out of their herds, claiming they belonged to him but with no brand to prove it.

Old Charlie, as some called him now, was convinced by his wartime experience with the Rangers, and since, that any crossing of the Indian country of northwest Texas was to be avoided. To those who pointed out that the Comanches surely preferred fat young buffalo to trail beef, there was the reply that they preferred anything they could trade to the *comancheros* who were selling the stolen stock to the new ranchers starting up in New Mexico, the trailers to California, or to the Denver traders for the mines.

Goodnight also knew something of the country he would have to cross on the southern swing and the turn westward to the Pecos and up its briny, forbidding canyon and beyond. The reputation of the stretch to the Pecos was bad

ever since the first cattle came to Texas with Coronado. The
other two ranchers who were to go with Charlie Goodnight
to Colorado got scared out just chewing it over. In the end
the old rancher Oliver Loving, who had tried to talk Goodnight against it, too, asked to go along.

Oliver Loving, father of Jim of the Keechi region,
was the most experienced cowman on the cattle fringes of
northwest Texas. Back in the 1850's he ran a small, remote
supply store on a military trail, with a few slaves and a good
ranch herd. On the side he bought most of the minor lots of
cattle then produced in the Cross Timbers and trailed them
to Shreveport or New Orleans. In 1858 he and another man
pointed a herd northward, swung around the larger settlements to avoid trouble, turned eastward, swam a dozen
streams, and marketed the cattle in Illinois. In 1860, with
John Dawson, he headed 1,000 steers to the new gold camps
of the Rockies by striking the Arkansas River below the
Great Bend and following the stream up past Pueblo, where
they wintered. In the spring Loving peddled the stock in
Denver for good money but the Civil War broke out and the
authorities refused to let him return to Texas. Only his
friendship with Kit Carson, Lucien Maxwell, and other old-
timers got him away, to help feed the Confederacy, as the
Denverites had feared.

After the war he enlarged his roundups with Bose
Ikard as his right-hand man. Bose was a former slave from
the Ikard ranch, a good bronco buster, exceptional night
herder, good with the skillets when necessary—an all-around
ranch and trail hand, tough and lasting as rawhide, one of
the most devoted men any rancher ever had.

Goodnight had planned his drive in the hope that
there was some nice money loose for beef in Colorado and
certainly there would be grass to hold any stock not readily
salable. Now another and, by his planned route a more immediate, hope came up—the hope of selling beef to fill Indian contracts in New Mexico on the way. There was even a
chance of cornering a little of the often-exorbitant prices

that some Indian contractors seemed to get. True, the agent for the Mescalero Apaches at Fort Sumner was already charged with graft in cattle dealings, but there were other agents around the post for other tribes, and the government was advertising for steers to be delivered there.

So, in 1866, trailing a mixed herd of 2,000 steers, cows, and calves, with eighteen hands, mostly armed, they set out, the fifty-four-year-old tough and range-hardened Loving in charge of the herd, Goodnight scouting ahead. But neither of them had ever been over the route which had stretches that few except the Comanches raiding into Mexico for horses even attempted. Those Indians preferred to make the run early in the spring or in the fall, when there was some hope of finding water holes not dry mud baked iron hard.

# CHAPTER II

PULLING FOR NEW GRASS

IN THE early years of the cattle drives most of the larger
herds that marched north in the swinging walk of the
Longhorn were steers, with some dry cows, all headed directly for the slaughter pens or perhaps by way of the fattening grasses of Indian Territory or Kansas or the broadening
corn regions of the Middle West. But almost from the start
there were herds with young she-stuff, the seed for new
ranches. These were usually headed for the opening ranges
of the north and the west, yet they had to cross the same Indian barriers as the beef herds, the Civilized Tribes demanding toll in cattle and, even before the war, in money.
West of them were the reservations of the Southern
Cheyennes and the Arapahoes, and of the Kiowas and Comanches, who still claimed vast hunting grounds in northwest Texas, where the Southern or Texas herd of buffaloes
ranged. It was usually to these regions that the raiding Indians escaped with their loot and certainly no drover could
hope to get a trail herd of cattle up through there. Besides,
there was the Kansas summer quarantine, June to November, on cattle brought in from Texas. This one might avoid
but if not, there was the expense of holding the herd to
fall.

Goodnight and Loving gave no thought to these obstacles now. They were headed the other way, down the old Butterfield Trail, to follow it as far as seemed handy. Goodnight, out far in front on his short-coupled black, looked over his shoulder from a rise, back toward the Texas of the Palo Pinto country and the Brazos, almost as though he were making a last mind picture of it, bidding it good-by. Then he considered the long, dusty line of their herd winding toward him out of the breaks. They were already getting trail-broken, and moving pretty well. Perhaps it was true that in Colorado a cattleman could still make a living.

He let his impatient horse out, pointing his hat at arm's length before him, signaling the direction. So Goodnight scouted the trail for water, for range and bed ground, doubling back to give his signals. Loving, behind him, knew how to get the most from the men and the herd. All but the two point riders, the best men of the outfit, shifted positions daily to relieve those on the dusty side and those riding drag —always keeping the herd strung out well and yet close enough to let them feel each other, hold them in an unbroken file to crawl like a thin, dark, thousand-segmented joint snake over the rolling prairie. It was a pretty route through the mirage region, the Phantom Hill country. By then the herd was a fine traveling unit, the leader taking his place every morning, keeping it day after day. As in most beef herds, the steers had traveling companions and when separated they raised their heads to get wind of each other, bawling until they got together. Each strong young cow gathered her own following within the herd. As in most good-sized drives, there were a few muleys, born hornless, and within a few days these bedded down together, a little apart. As usual, too, there was a loner or two who went prowling up one side of the herd and down the other, apparently searching for the never lost. Sometimes there was an outcast, hooked at everywhere, with even the muleys making the horning motion. All these, unless steadied down early, ended up with the drags, with the poor, the old, and the

very young. But the two-year-old heifers were the real
flighty ones wilful as young Texas girls, and most difficult to
settle down, to road-break. Some never settled down at all
and these it was best to eat early, if the owner could bring
himself to kill his own beef.

Then, with this mixed herd, every morning there
were the newborn calves to kill on the bed ground. There
would be hundreds of these dropped before the herd reached
Sumner in New Mexico. Every morning one of the trail
hands made a circle, disposing of the freshly dropped stock,
who couldn't keep up anyway and would only weaken the
cows. But all that day the mothers would bawl and try to
break back, and particularly that first night. If the cow had
smelled her calf, or sucked it, she might have to be yoked to
a steer, or hobbled, so strong was the Longhorn's instinct for
her young. But even with the best of care they would have
slow, difficult trailing for the Pecos route, at the best not
good for a mixed outfit.

Loving had the herd traveling very well in the heat
and dust by the time they reached the head of the Middle
Concho, where they rested and fed before starting over the
dry, horse-killing jump of around eighty miles to the Pecos,
with twelve, fifteen miles considered a good drive in the
burning sun. Then, after days without water, and the smell
of it from the river to drive the cattle wild, they would have
to pass the poison lakes marked by whitened bones long before the first Spaniard rode through that way. They had been
warned against the poison lakes, the alkali strong enough to
kill everything that drank the water, and just beyond was
the Pecos, with most of the bank very steep, the crossing a
swift, swimming current.

Goodnight and Loving watered the herd, steers,
cows, and calves, with all they would drink and filled the
canteens and the water barrels of the grub wagon to over-
flowing. Then in the afternoon they pointed the herd to follow the sloping sun out upon the pale baked earth.

They trailed late that first evening, made dry camp,

and pushed on early. While the Longhorn on the range often went without water for three days, driving dried out stock as it did men. The second night the herd was too thirsty to bed down, many trying to break back as they walked and milled all night so it took most of the men to hold them. Goodnight realized that this wouldn't do—the cattle had walked enough on the bed ground to take them most of the way to the Pecos. He got the herd started very early, knowing that the cattle would have to be pushed today, the faltering whipped up by the sleepy, worn-out cowboys under the sun that shimmered in great rippling mirage lakes ahead. The canteens dried up, the water barrels began to rattle in the wagon, and the dust rose in bitter white clouds that grayed them all. It cracked the lips under the protecting kerchiefs tied loosely enough to be drawn up over the nose, almost to the hat-brim, the dust-rimmed eyes bloodshot and burning; it stung and burned in the sweated saddle galls.

The pointers had to hold the strong leaders back while the drag riders whooped and cursed and popped their down ropes to keep the weaker stuff up. The herd bawled and then moaned for water, until many grew silent, their swollen tongues hanging out dry and dusty, eyes sunken, their ribs like some old pole fence. Often a maddened one turned to fight, as a critter drawn from a bog will, perhaps with the same desperation of death upon it. Those, too, were left to die.

The men grew as raw nerved, on the prod, worn, without sleep, and what was worse for a good cowhand, helpless to relieve the suffering of the stock. Irritable and dangerous, swift anger lurked in them as in a rattler, and with guns handy at the hip.

Loving worked with the drags now, holding them together the best his long experience could manage, fighting the alkali dust and the thirst to save as much as he could from the stock they had salvaged out of the losses of the war years and all the thieving and the Indian raids since. Goodnight had pushed on ahead into the pale, cloudless night, the second without sleep. The cook boiled up black coffee to hand to the men as they passed on the shadowy prairie, trying to make the stock follow the bells Goodnight had put on the lead steers, keep them reasonably together, help prevent the stampeding at any whiff of water that tolled them to some long-dead wallow or pond perhaps off to the side. Each time Goodnight spurred hard to overtake the leaders, to slow them, avoid a disastrous pile-up. But long before the steers reached such places they had usually slowed by themselves, with only a hopeless kind of bewilderment as they milled over the dried mud, bawling hoarsely, unwilling to leave where water had been, the weaker cows beginning to go down, too, as even the strong calves had long ago.

The men were ready to drop in the rising heat of the day, swearing thickly, their tongues stiff and swollen, as though unaccustomed to words. But mostly they were silent except for the "Hi-ah! Hi-ah!" to keep the drags moving. Finally one of the men couldn't stop his call, going on and on until he fell to mumbling, saying "Damn-damn-damn," over and over to himself, sitting his horse like a limp and leaking meal sack. At last Loving came to pull him from the saddle and push him under the bank of an arroyo, offering a little strip of shade almost wide enough to cover the man's gaunt frame. Tying the horse to a hastily driven picket in the bottom of the cut, out of sight, he left a precious half-filled canteen with him and went on. "Wait till dark, then try to follow the trail," was all Loving could suggest, without much hope, realizing that Indians were probably sniffing around the herds.

When Goodnight fell back to look over the plodding horses, the men swaying in the saddles, the stock falling all along the trail, he realized something had to be done, and fast. With the dry canteens strung to him like the gray and empty hulls of some futile fruit he set out for the river, pushing the plucky little black to stumbling, so he cursed himself for his brutality, his own tongue refusing the words.

He slowed down but almost at once he was urging the tired horse faster again, faster and faster, while he wondered at the fools that cattlemen were.

Back from the hard twenty-mile ride over the burning earth Charlie Goodnight saw it was a case of saving what he could of the dying herd or losing all. With the four men and horses that had stood up best, he let the stronger cattle, around two thirds of the herd, go as fast as they could, making no effort to trail herd them beyond pointing the leaders for the Pecos, trying to let the men take turns at a few minutes' sleep in the saddle.

But there were the poison holes this side of the river to avoid. The herd must be swung out so the first smell they got would be from the Pecos itself. The old cowman watched for it, saw it come: the lead steer suddenly lift his head, his dry tongue out stiff as a stick of dark and sandy wood. He broke into a feeble, stumbling run, then the others behind him, too, in sprawling gallops, the earth thundering hollowish as the wind carried the smell and the excitement back along the strung-out herd, the men fighting to keep them so, to avoid bunching and piling up in the swimming depths of the Pecos, stomping each other under.

In spite of all that the five worn men could do the cattle poured into the river valley in a broad, dust-gray blanket, the dried alkali rising in choking white smoke over them. The leaders went over the Pecos bank, the followers in a cascade upon them, thrusting them out and clear across the narrow roiling stream before they could stop for the desperate drink. Goodnight, ahead, turned the cattle back, and as the jam of the frenzied animals spread up and down the narrow river they blocked the current, damming it to rise halfway up the banks. Then they had to be quirted out, the leaders found and started, to keep the herd from foundering themselves. Slowly, falteringly, they backed out of the water, stopping to blow, lolling their swollen, dripping tongues, and finally started away slowly before the whoops and popping ropes of the cowboys, to stop in the grass away from the Pecos valley and the alkali water, the first grass they had tasted in days.

Here the men were set to hold them, working in relays, with plans to let them sleep, too, hoping there would be no Indian attack now while Goodnight was going back to help Oliver Loving. But worn down as the men were, they couldn't keep awake, and some of the cows broke for water again. This time they got to the alkali holes back from the river. Before they could be stopped three had finished drinking and fell in their tracks, some of the others dying later.

Back on the trail the weary Oliver Loving was still with the drags, around 500 of them able to move. The wind turned and carried the smell of water from a place where the Pecos ran between banks six to ten feet high. Nothing could stop the stampeding cattle and they poured over the bank, falling and going under, most of the horse herd, too. Many of the weak ones drowned right there, and some were swept into a quicksand bend. The cowboys worked for two days but in the end 100 head had to be left in the river although still alive, in the quicksand, and stranded under high bluffs at the water's edge, with no way to reach them. Three hundred others had been dropped on the way to the Pecos, not counting the newborn calves killed—all those bones strung out to mark the desperate trail, the graveyard of the cowman's hopes.

After several days to recruit the stock and the men, the herd was pushed up the east side of the Pecos, through country where the only living creature seemed to be the fish in the stream. Not even one prairie bird panted through the shadeless noontime, no kingfisher flashed his blue as he dove straight down, to come up with wriggling of silver in his mouth, no buzzard circled the pale and empty sky. But there were rattlesnakes, and of these one cowhand with eyes so crossed that they looked in two directions, and poor eyes at that, got seventy-two before the herd reached Sumner.

Fort Sumner was the center for around 8,500 Indians gathered to reservations, but the soil was poor, and fuel, even grass, scarce. The heat and drouth were particularly trying for the mountain Navahos who had been torn from their lovely homeland to live on the sterile plain among their traditional enemies. But it was a common misery, for all the Indians were on the edge of starvation, and Goodnight and Loving got the exceptional price of eight cents a pound on the hoof for the steers, two-year-old and up. No wonder the Texas Indians went to such trouble raiding the ranches for herds to trade to the New Mexican *comancheros*.

Of course the partners still had the cows and calves, between 700 and 800 head, but neither man had suspected there was such money in cattle these days, and both were happy even with all the cutbacks. Charlie Goodnight was suddenly less angry with Texas, less impatient for a look at Colorado ranch possibilities. He hurried back on the 700-mile trail to gather up another herd for the Indians before winter. He rode ahead, followed by a pack mule carrying the $12,000 in gold under the provisions, with three cowboys coming along behind. They traveled down the Pecos by night, sleeping hidden out during the daylight, and prepared to shoot a path through any Indians or holdup outfit who might have heard about the sale at Sumner and try an ambush.

Their real trouble came from one of the swift night storms of the arid country, the sky blazing with lightning—great, blinding forks of it crashing to the earth, the thunder shaking the ground so that the dust rose in a hazing in the rainless night. One bolt struck too close to the pack mule, and he was gone with the provisions and the gold. Goodnight had managed to get his hand on the neck rope and hung on while the mule ran, bucking and bawling like a bay steer, provisions flying in every direction. Finally the mule was worn out and Goodnight, too, scratched and skinned up. The money was safe but the food was lost and no telling how many Indians might be around, so they couldn't risk much shooting, even if there had been any game beyond an occasional catfish. Before they got through the 200-mile ride down the Pecos they would have been happy to trade a lot of the gold for a bait of even Yankee sore-thumb bread.

Up near Fort Sumner Oliver Loving put a little meat on the cows and calves the Indian agent had turned back, and then trailed them slowly to the Raton Mountains, the Arkansas River, and beyond, blazing the trail most of the way. Near Denver he sold the whole lot to John W. Iliff for his range in northeast Colorado, in the heart of a new cattle region.

Down in Texas, Goodnight collected his second herd of the summer, 1,200 head, all steers, able to travel fast and strong. But with no cows to quiet them they were a stampeding outfit, nervous all the time and very hard to handle, particularly after they were struck by a herd of migrating buffaloes, a bull herd, coming in a solid, lumbering string reaching back for miles, moving under the wild urge that drove them southward before the winter and back with the spring. Headed into the wind, the lead buffaloes hesitated at their first sight of the cattle, and Goodnight hoped his herd might have room and time to pass. They were about halfway through when the wind carried a whiff of man smell to the buffaloes and they stampeded, following their noses straight upon the trail herd in a thundering run. Goodnight and his hands tried to turn them but it was like turning the cloudburst waters from a dry wash. The stampede cut the steers in two near the middle of the herd and the snuffy old mosshorns went crazy. Those cut back by the buffaloes turned and headed for the Brazos bottoms again, the drag riders trying hard to start them into a spin. Those beyond the buffaloes had curled their tails up and fled toward the Horsehead Crossing of the Pecos, with the cowboys riding hard at their rumps. Goodnight was with these and by fast work they got the leaders to turn upon themselves and managed to hold the steers while the buffaloes poured by, between the two halves of the steer herd. For almost an hour they thundered past, the air full of their gruntings, the shaking of their running hoofs. When the steers were finally brought together again a day was killed, but not a head was missing.

There were scattered buffaloes all the way to the Middle Concho, and the line riders had to spur out here and there to drive them off, for even the wind of one of them set the tails of the steers up again. Plainly the whole buffalo country was no place for the wild Longhorn.

This time, before the dry stretch from the Concho region to the Pecos Goodnight gave his herd all the water and grass they would eat to sundown and then drove all night on the trail so well marked by his earlier passing, often by the stench of the dead. In the cool of the morning he grazed the steers again and then went on. After the first such stop they didn't eat much, for thirst, and he kept them moving all day and the next night, too—hard to handle and mighty hard on the men, but they crossed the Staked Plains to the Pecos without losing a head. The whole drive took around forty days, the cattle quiet and gentle when Goodnight made winter camp about forty miles below Sumner. Loving came in, too, and they struck a dugout into the bluffs on the east side of the river and lived there in comfort until spring, supplying beeves to the government contractors at Sumner and over at Santa Fe. Apparently they were the first Texans to establish a ranch in south New Mexico.

Loving had much to tell that snug winter in the dugout, stories of Iliff, who in 1865 had gone to the Cherokee Nation in Indian Territory and drove 1,300 cattle to New Mexico on a government contract. Last summer, two years after the massacre of the Cheyenne Indians at Sand Creek, he was furnishing beef to the Union Pacific construction gang laying the tracks toward Cheyenne, up in Wyoming, in the middle of an Indian war. Iliff said he had little real trouble.

"Seems it's the Yankee bluebellies the Indians are

after," Loving told Goodnight. He talked often of the grass
he saw up in Colorado—long and cured up seedy and golden
in the fall. He heard it was like that all the way across to the
Milk and the Marias in Montana, and with hungry Indians
sitting on reservations every few jumps up along the Missouri River all through Dakota Territory.

But in Wyoming and Montana there were still millions of the buffaloes that had stampeded Goodnight's Longhorns, eating the grass, and followed by wild Indians. It
seemed, though, that a man could make a go of ranching up
that way, as Iliff was doing in the South Platte Valley. It was
even possible to drive cattle straight through the wild Sioux
country to the mines in Montana where beef was bringing
real money. The meat they were eating up there now was
mostly trailed in from Oregon. Yet last summer, while they
were both fighting thirst and alkali down there on the Pecos,
Nelson Story had trailed a herd of 600 Longhorns from deep
in Texas up past Fort Laramie to the Montana gold fields
over the route called the Bozeman Trail. He made it, although the Sioux had closed the trail to all except heavily
escorted army trains going to the new forts being built to
guard the route. Men were picked off every few days, horses
swept off, and yet Story got through.

"He wouldn't have made it through the Comanches,"
Goodnight said sourly.

"No, guess not. Seems the Sioux prefer fat hump ribs
of buffalo to beef, anyway trail beef. Besides, they got no
place to trade the cows, no *comancheros*. I did hear they're
hell on Yankee bluebellies. Ran a whole army out of the
country summer before last, but they don't make raids
against the settlements like the Indians do down in Texas.
Iliff ain't uneasy."

"Sounds like country worth looking into," Goodnight
admitted, scratching his beard thoughtfully.

By late January they heard more of this Bozeman
Trail route to the fabulous beef prices at the Montana
mines. The Sioux and Cheyennes up there had annihilated a

whole detachment of troops under a Captain Fetterman
—eighty, ninety men massacred, they heard tell at Sumner.

By now it became a sort of race to get cattle from
Texas to where they paid out. During its first summer the
Goodnight-Loving Trail had grown into a prominent route
to good markets and to a great new range country. Some
smallish herds had plodded to California over the old Butterfield Trail long ago, usually starting early, when the
holes and wallows still might be wet and the heat was less
burning. Now the route was suddenly rediscovered as far
as the Pecos and extended north toward Wyoming. The success and profits of the Goodnight-Loving drives in 1866 multiplied in the telling, particularly the profits. True, it was a
hard route but Texas was the Rawhide State, the men of
rawhide, too. The need to believe the stories was very great
in the hard times of 1867.

Unfortunately the Comanches soon discovered the
herds crossing the vast, isolated stretches of the Pecos country—out of reach of the punishing troops and Rangers—big
bunches of cattle trained to drive well and ready to be
swept away, with good trail horses for the taking, too. The
Indians captured two herds early in 1867, attacked emigrants on the trail and Goodnight and Loving as well on
their return to the Keechi range. The two men escaped, to
buy up more cattle for New Mexican contracts and the
northern ranges. Goodnight accumulated powers of attorney
from the neighboring ranchers to gather up stock with their
brands for the trail herd, paying around $20 in gold for
the best beef steers, about $5 under the price in greenbacks.
With his Circle road brand on the herd they started, this
time into almost constant Indian trouble.

Knowing that she stuff worked or trailed had a tendency to come in heat, Goodnight always put in a number of
bulls, but the steady travel was doubly hard on them, particularly on the full-grown animals. Their testicles, banged
and bruised against their legs for several hundred miles,

swelled and became so infected that the bulls died. After they lost two on the drive to the Pecos and another, a big dun from south Texas, was swelling so he might be lost, too, Goodnight roped him and got down with the cutting knife and the tar pot to keep the flies from starting worms in the wound. It was so hard to spare these good range bulls that instead of castrating him, Goodnight pushed the dun's kernels up against his belly, cut off the entire bag, and with some unraveled manila rope and a knife point to punch holes, he sewed the wound up by whipping the edges together like the cook snubbing up a hole in a flour sack. Within a week the big dun bull was pursuing the cows again, and tromping at the heels of the leaders, hurrying them along. This became standard practice with Goodnight and others who had to trail large animals, and as a sort of restorative for an aging bull. Goodnight had some other firm convictions about herd sires. While they were an important outlay of money he always kept enough on his range to make a fine roaring, particularly evenings—enough bulls so they really chased the cows and kept the percentage of calving high.

The loss of the two good range sires from the herd on this drive was insignificant compared to the cost of the Indian raids. They stampeded the herd on Clear Fork and almost as soon as the cattle were gathered up for the trail again they struck once more. Men were hit, too, one with an arrow, the hoop-iron point of it driven almost to the barb into the bone behind the ear. With two men to hold the cowboy, Goodnight worked it out and then poulticed the wound with cold mud. The man recovered, but there were more attacks farther on, with increasing stampedes, the herd run-crazy by now, gone like fall leaves in a windstorm at almost any movement. Men were killed and wounded trying to hold the herd against a whoop and the flap of a blanket. Goodnight followed some of the stock that had been swept away but all this took time and finally Loving, uneasy over the delay, started ahead to be at Sumner for the bidding on the government contracts. With One-Arm Wilson, an experienced old cowman, he struck out.

"Now be careful. Keep well hid during the day," Goodnight advised uneasily, although he was talking to men who had been in the country a long, long time.

But Oliver Loving was in a hurry and for all his experience he let the Comanches locate them on the Pecos. They put a bullet through his wrist and one into his side. The two cattlemen managed to hold the Indians off until night. There, too badly wounded to get away, Loving made such plans as he could to keep hidden, and for his defense if the Comanches smelled him out, and sent One-Arm to get through the Comanche line for help, if possible. It took days, but by incredible cunning and endurance Wilson reached the herd and Goodnight. He was in such bad shape he could barely speak to tell what had happened. He had left Loving surrounded, wounded, with nothing to eat.

Back on the Pecos, when it seemed that Loving couldn't hold the Indians off any longer or hide any more, some Mexicans found him and took him to Sumner, where Goodnight finally traced him. The shattered wrist wasn't doing well, after all the exposure, but Loving was so anxious to locate the stock the Indians swept off and probably traded to the *comancheros* that Goodnight consented to leave him and go make the investigations himself. While he was away gangrene set in, through the neglect of the army doctor, the Texans felt, neglect because Loving was a Reb. When Goodnight returned with some of their stock rescued from the Mexicans, he found Oliver Loving dying. He got the arm amputated but it was far too late. For all the heroic courage and endurance down there alone on the Pecos, and at the hospital, the tough old cowman Oliver Loving died.

By now it was too late for the Indian contracts, and when the herd finally reached Sumner Goodnight headed it on toward Colorado. From the Raton Pass region he looked down over the mountain slopes to the great fall-yellowed grasslands of the upper Arkansas River so like the cloud-shadowed swells of a golden sea. He pointed the herd along the north-flowing creeks and up near the head of one of these, the Apishapa, Goodnight stopped. The canyon was around twenty miles long, not very deep, but with walls steep enough so it was practically inaccessible except at the two ends, which could be kept closed very handily by casual line riding. The creek, between banks lined by box elders, shyly sank out of sight during the day and ran again when the sun settled behind the canyon walls. The cowboys joked about it, glad they could laugh after the very grueling drive.

Here Goodnight established his ranch in what seemed to him a most beautiful cow country and perhaps his would be the first extensive cattle venture in southern Colorado. At least he had the world to himself again, with, so far as any of them knew, little danger from raiding Indians, probably more danger from outlaws. So they turned the cattle loose and set to cutting pines for a log cabin while Goodnight went back down to meet Joe, Oliver Loving's son, bringing up a herd. He knew Indian fighting but the herd, 3,200 head, and short around 1,000 head from Indian raids and stampedes, had been too large and so were in bad condition. Goodnight took 1,000 of the strongest and trailed them over Raton in snow, the wind sharp as ice. He got to Apishapa Christmas Eve, 1867, a hard and freezing drive behind him. It was a winter herd and not considered so dangerous to the so-called American or non-Spanish cattle among the estimated 147,000 head in the state, but large drives were nevertheless competition, and besides there would surely be summer drives, the cattlemen of Colorado realized, and they looked upon the Texan, the Johnny Reb digging in on the Apishapa with concern.

Early in the new year of 1868 Iliff came to Goodnight's ranch and bought $40,000 worth of cattle to be delivered in the Cheyenne, Wyoming, region. Some of these were to be slaughtered and shipped by the new railroad, the Union Pacific, to Chicago in iced cars, which was surely the opening of a new era.

But actually the new era opening was the day of the vast free range country from the cap rock of Texas northward to Canada. In this region the cattlemen were to attain an importance and a dedication never dreamed before, not by men like Goodnight, or Olive, or Richard King, or even by any of the new ranchers just beginning to move into the territory that would be the purest cattle state of all—Wyoming. The rest of the cow country would have other important pursuits and industries: Texas her vast plantation and farm areas; Colorado, Montana, and the Dakota territory their mines and wheat; Nebraska and Kansas as well as some of the others their corn and wheat. All these would be cattle states, but Wyoming would be the truest, the purest cow country.

# CHAPTER III

# THE MOVING TRAILS

B Y 1868 the future of the cattle business north of the Rio Grande was taking on the shape that was perhaps inevitable from the time the first mission stock went wild, or even earlier, from the day the first cow escaped Coronado's beef herd to hide in the brush, to drop her ticks and her calf as they ripened.

With the end of the Civil War, *Longhorn* meant a breed of cattle and a cowboy was no longer a raider, a thief, and a murderer, but a hard-working cowhand, often rowdy when he hit town, spurring his horse and popping his pistol, to scatter the anklers, the people afoot, send them fleeing through the dusty street like a settler's hens before the hawk's approach. He was still sometimes a thief or a killer, as his boss might very well be, but any man who wasn't a worker, hardy, tough, and full of sand, wouldn't stick with the cow business long enough to pay for his saddle. In the meantime the Longhorns were spreading northward over the grass of the prairies. They came faster than the Indian could be driven back or the railroads climb up the Platte and the Smoky Hill rivers, the hide men turn the great buffalo herds into stinking carcasses. The buffaloes would be vanishing even faster if flint hides could walk themselves the far distances to market that the Longhorns did.

100

It was once said that all the roasting meat of a Texas steer could be packed into one of his horns, but as the cattle spread out of the coastal plains and the swamps and brushy bottoms to the higher regions north and westward, they kept growing larger. Plainly, as the herds increased, some natural selection took place, aided later by the Anglo's cutting knife that spared only the best for sires. With their mixed ancestry, the cattle of Texas probably adapted themselves so well through long-dormant characteristics. Running wild and needing to fight off enemies, they returned to wilder ways and wilder dimensions much as the gentle house cat does when turned out into the brush, developing breadth of jaw and power of muscle that had vanished through thousands of years at the milk saucer and the soft cushion.

Similarly the cattle of Texas sharpened in nose and eye, lengthened in leg and wind and in the spread of horn demanded by the new life—all throwbacks to the keen senses, the standing height, and the greatness of horn found in *Bos primigenius* and their probable cousin, the Strasbourg Ox, augmented perhaps by the iodine-leached regions of Texas.

The Longhorn matured slowly, reaching a maximum weight of from 1,000 up to 1,600 pounds at eight or ten years. In 1868, 224 selected Texas steers weighed in at Abilene, Kansas, averaged 1,238 pounds, and this after half a day in the pens. How much of this was horns, grown to their best heft and spread in the steer, was not recorded.

With the movement of vast, trail-gaunted beef herds to market the demand for fatter meat grew, meat requiring more corn, corn of better feeding quality, shorter growing season, greater yield, and of vastly increased acreages. In addition there was the booming population, the millions of immigrants sent to America by the unrest and the famines in Europe. Many were laborers hoping for work, particularly on railroad construction gangs, but mostly they sought homes and land in the West, their plows and sod corn pushing as hard at the jingling spurs of the cowboy as he tromped the heels of the buffalo hunter and the Indian.

Once the cow had changed man from hunter to herdsman, now with her need for corn she was changing the agricultural pattern of much of a nation, and with her flesh much of the nation's diet and, eventually, much of the outside world's. Surely nothing short of earth, water, and air could have been more important to the life, the rise of man, than the cow. It was no wonder that her image appeared on the earliest coins, and long before that on man's religious objects and his religious places, to invoke the cow's great mysterious power. Often these showed exquisite craftsmanship, and many of these early portrayals resembled the Longhorn that was plodding the trails out of Texas to new pastures, to new meanings, new significance.

The roundups of the late sixties and early seventies were still largely cow hunts, as men went bear hunting or out for mustang, and with little more claim to the quarry until captured. The methods were also still the same—cutting off little bunches outside of the brush or breaks if possible, otherwise roping the stock one by one, hog tying them, later throwing them into little herds held somewhere in the open. Indians still slowed the mavericking. In the Palo Pinto country they kept many of the ranchers afoot much of the time. Many stories were told of outwitting the Indians. It seemed that the five Cowden boys and the three neighboring Bradfords began their mavericking afoot, barefoot, in mesquite and cactus and rattlesnake country. The eight youths had one mounted cowboy along to hold the stock and bring up the drags. Their scheme was to run around a bunch of cows and then ease them into a pen. Those they couldn't pen they got with two ketch dogs who snagged them by the nose and hung on, much as the dogs of England did in the bullbaiting except this was wild stock capturing. Jeff Cowden, the fastest, always took the lead in the runs, but in the cattle business all except Jeff made fortunes from their barefoot start. Even after the Indians were gone and Jeff Cowden had all the horses he could hope to ride, and tame enough to avoid a fight every time he hit the stirrup, he kept on working stock afoot. It was said he roped the smokestack of the first railroad engine into his region by running up alongside.

Many men with good boots high enough so they need not fear the ordinary rattler, and with good cow horses, depended on dogs for their cattle hunts. A good ketch dog was prized like a fine cow horse. Some were so well trained that on sight of a bunch of cattle they singled out the only slick ear, the only maverick in it, and held the charging, bucking critter by the nose until it was roped and tied. Now and then a mavericker tailed his fleeing quarry down. He spurred up on a flying cow, caught her tail, dallied it around his leg or the horn of his saddle, swerving his horse suddenly to jerk her down hard, bust the wind out of her as she rocked in the dust. This required a good horse, trained, and a good man, but the technique was old, thousands of years old.

Mavericking by any trick or turn was not for the shorthorns, for the tenderfoot. No outfit could afford to take chances with more than one or two green hands at a time, not even a big one with the boss an experienced moss-horner and a good Indian fighter on the side. Often the captured cattle were corraled at night at the ranch of some cowman in the outfit or perhaps at some of the pens built out in the wilds for general hire. Even then the men usually rode herd on the stock at night, for a milling in a corral was soon a stampede over the fence.

Maverickers had to travel light. Usually each man carried his own grub in a wallet—a sack with both ends sewed up and a slit for the hand down the center. Filled, this was tied behind the saddle on top of what he called his bed, seldom more than a slicker. Often there was a boy along who stayed with the trapped mavericks, tied down or kneed, or otherwise secured. He looked after the bunch of wallets, too, and usually had a string of tin cups on the rawhide hobbles swung around his pony's neck.

Soon after the war a boy from Michigan named

James H. Cook came to work for Ben Slaughter of the early cattle family. Ben had his maverickers working the Frio River, which, like many Texas streams, was often dry. The *corrida* or cow runners, ten rawhide-equipped Mexicans, bossed by John Longworth, started on their cow hunt with a bunch of decoy cattle. They took pack mules for the provisions, a rattling of cooking utensils, and practically nothing else, not even slickers. The provisions were green coffee, sow belly, corn meal, saleratus, and pepper berry, with a good supply of black navy plug tobacco and prepared cornhusks for cigarette wrappers, the Mexican's idea of a smoke, lit by the flint and steel each man carried. They camped near an old corral of strong, close-set posts standing at least seven feet above their solid footing in the ground. These walls were lashed together with long strips of green cowhide that shrank up tight, the gate posts of powerful oak with loose poles to slide in place. Staunchly built wings of poles ran out from the gate about 200 yards or more each way to help pen the wild stock.

At sunrise they started on a cow hunt with the decoy herd, Longworth leading the way through the thick growth of chaparrel and mesquite. About a mile out he left the herd in a dense clump of brush under the guard of two men and signaled the rest to follow him. Keeping as quiet as possible, they rode in single file, young Jim Cook bringing up the tail behind the dark-skinned, leather-chapped Mexicans. After a couple of miles there was a sudden crashing up ahead. Instantly every rider shot forward, bent low over his horse's neck. Jim's horse went, too, almost skinning out from under the boy, who didn't dare to try holding him back because he might never find camp again if he lost the rest. Clinging to the horn, he let the horse tear hell-bent this way and that through the brush and cactus and scrub timber, Jim dodging and ducking branches large enough to knock him from the saddle and warding off the whip of the smaller ones with his upraised arm, keeping the jagged stubs and branches out of his face and eyes but getting the sleeve ripped and cut to rags by the thorns and catclaws. He rode all over the saddle and out of it as the horse took the brush expertly, hurdling the low-bent mesquite trunks, snaking under big live-oak branches that left barely six inches for the stooping boy, switching in and out across the prickly-pear stretches growing from two to ten feet high and almost solid in places. The cactus the horse couldn't dodge he jumped, knocked down, or tore through, his breast and legs cut and torn, but he kept on, snorting in his frenzy—a true cowcatcher, as hot after the prey as a hungry coyote at the tail of a dodging rabbit.

Finally the run ended, even for the greenhorn from Michigan. Suddenly before him one of the Mexicans was stopped, outside a mesquite clump, a hand up in warning, pointing to the brush just ahead. There were cattle in it and young Jim Cook caught a faint rise of Mexican voices in a curious, coaxing, wordless song, the song of the brush, while the waiting brush horses quivered, ready to jump for any wild critter that made a break. Thin and quavering the song crept high and higher, and then sank low, gentle, soothing, the beat of it the soft throb of quiet and rest in the untamed heart.

Then the singers seemed to be closing in on the cattle from all sides, narrowing the circle about them. They moved slowly, quietly, their horses stepping delicately with barely a snapping twig to disturb the song. After a while some of the little herd started, coming toward Jim. He recognized them as of the decoys, but there were wild Longhorns with them, cattle that whirled about as soon as they saw the boy. He wanted to shrink out of sight but was motioned to stay perfectly still. There was an experienced cowcatcher on every side of the herd, stopped now, motionless as a clump of thorn. The decoy cattle, fairly calm, simply milled around through the thicket and by the time the wild ones were well mixed into them, Jim could hardly hold his horse or himself either. Finally the men began to move a little again, very quietly, singing softly, the sound coming as from the air, from everywhere as they rode carefully and slowly, around and around the cattle without seeming to, all except young Jim singing the Texas lullaby and perhaps he, too, for his horse fell into place in the slow circling and the boy was too excited to know what he did.

After an hour or so Longworth rode away out of sight of the herd, dismounted, and tightened the cinch and then returned to the circling and another man dropped out to do the same, making ready for a run or a roping, and then another, until all were ready. The horses, too, had had a breathing spell. Now Longworth turned away into the chaparral, still singing, and the Mexicans slowly closed in on the cattle, starting them after him, pointing the herd in the direction of his voice when he was lost in the brush. Everybody kept off a little from the cattle, and no one made a sudden move or sound that might start a stampede, the well-trained horses stepping carefully without toss of head or jingle of bit, not even a snort or side-jump for a rattler.

Longworth led the herd toward the corral and into the wings, the wild ones following the decoys, uneasily, suspicious, heads up, their horns seeming alert as feelers, until suddenly there was no place to go except straight ahead with the tame cattle, the men crowding them now, giving them no time to see the open country left behind. Then the Mexicans spurred forward, pushed them all through the gate, threw the heavy poles into place and lashed them there with rawhide as the wild stock, knowing now they were trapped, raced and surged around the high walls.

That this was work for experts, for artists, even the boy from Michigan realized and he intended to learn it, although he discovered that the hunts, even when so carefully planned and carried out, often failed from some sudden movement of man or horse, the flushing of a noisy turkey gobbler, or a drove of peccaries crashing off through the underbrush. Anything or nothing at all might stampede the cattle, perhaps even sweep the decoys away. At such times the swift hiss of a rope here and another there downed at least that many, not much for a day's work but something. Or perhaps, in the clearer spaces, the men tried tailing a few, then jumped off each time to make a swift tie around the feet with the piggin string, to leave the Longhorn heaving and struggling with his four feet together. If the wild maverick was up before the tailer got a knee on his neck and his nose up, the man might have to run before the charging critter through cactus and tangling brush, in serious trouble with perhaps nothing like a tree to shin up, no time for a telling shot.

For this work the men received $8 a month and found.

Some maverickers did their roping at night when the cattle left the brush to feed, but it was reckless business even under the bright Texas moon. Then after the trapping there was still the holding and the gathering to be managed. Often troublemaking old steers were necked to tame oxen, perhaps some steady work bull. Perhaps a gunny sack was slipped up over their heads, the opening tied shut around the horns, with the bottom to be cut out in a couple of days, to permit feeding. But the best remedy for the real troublemaker was still a bullet between the eyes. Often these were outlaws anyway, cattle caught sometime before, or even raised in a ranch herd and gone wild, therefore less afraid of man, wilier, often with less desire to run, more to fight.

Sometimes the eyelids of such troublemakers, such outlaws were sewed up so they had to follow the decoys to avoid thickets and cactus and other dangers. Sometimes the more ruthless cattle trappers cut a string or tendon of the knee or bound a wet rawhide thong tightly around the leg just above the hock, to dry, as the green hides dried around the men in the Spanish "Death of the Skins," shutting off circulation and movement. Sometimes the worst fighters had their horns chopped off, knocked off, or cut with a pistol bullet. Sometimes the cartilage of the nose was slit and a tie rope run through the hole, but this was more the idea of the easterners and the real outlaw soon jerked so hard the hole tore through. Besides, mutilated cattle brought very little when put on the market. That was why ranchers always mistrusted canned beef; they knew the kind of animals that sold as canners—old bulls, decrepit old cows, and the lumpy jaws, the injured, the mutilated.

However the cattle were trapped, with the fencing limited to brush and pole construction, there was seldom enough enclosed range to feed them long. They had to be started on the trail north soon or they would starve or have to be turned out to scatter back into the wild and be twice as difficult to recapture. Usually they were thrown in with the cattle of other ranchers or maverickers for the trip north. Perhaps they were sold to professional trailers, or to northern buyers who took possession on the spot. But the Texans learned a little caution about swift purchase and delivery. In 1867 a buyer down from the North had gathered up a herd from the ranchers near Waco and moved them out at once. When he was gone it was discovered that his greenbacks were counterfeit. A posse took the trail after him. The swifter of them caught him at the Red River crossing. Some said Print Olive was in the lead of the posse, although that was probably a mistake, for the Olives had their own herd on the trail. Anyway, it seemed that the buyer of cattle with counterfeit bills never made it over the river. The cattlemen took possession of the herd and sent it on to Kansas under their own man and were more willing than ever to sell a couple dollars cheaper for gold instead of greenbacks.

Because mavericking opened the cattle region to out-and-out theft, the Act of 1866 made it a misdemeanor punishable by fines and jail to drive stock from the "accustomed range" unless the drover could prove ownership. Still, with the drifting of cattle in storms and through drouthed or burned-over range, and the disappearance of water holes, there could be little real enforcement even under a well-intentioned administration in all the vast unorganized region of Texas. The already rather general practice of road branding for the drives was made a requirement in 1871.

Soon after the war young Wesley and Otho Burton had put up picket pens at their ranch north of Waco, offering to brand any trail herds coming through from south Texas without a road mark. The large herds often belonged to half-a-dozen men and carried as many brands, brands unknown north, or unrecognized. A cover brand for the whole herd facilitated collection and established ownership in case of theft, stampede, or other accident on the road. The Burtons charged fifteen cents a head to brand big steers, some from the lower country ten, fifteen years old, ten cents each for those under four. In 1871 they road branded more than 4,000 head for the King Ranch. The stock came in four well-managed herds, each one taking five, six days at the pens.

A Mexican showed Wes Burton his way of managing the tough old Longhorns. A wrinkle-horned paint steer refused to enter the big pen leading to the long branding chute. He fought off the riders, dodging them, slipping from corner to corner quick as a blue racer. Finally one of the Mexicans offered to whip some sense into the old outlaw. He grabbed up a fence rail, went afoot for the steer, and when the animal charged, he side-stepped the fury of dust and power and gave the old paint a lick across the backbone that echoed loud as a pistol shot. Then, before the steer could recover, he was pushed into the chute, running before the uplifted length of rail. The Burtons watched in admiration, but knowing it was dangerous inside the high picket corral with those horns sharp as Spanish daggers.

Sometimes the southern stuff was wilder than deer and harder to handle. One trail herd stampeded right into Waco, only a few houses then, with brush still growing in the road before them. The town baker stepped out to shoo the cattle away from his door. One of the steers lunged for him, caught him under the chin with one long horn that burst from the man's scream-torn mouth, and then dragged him 200 yards before a cowboy could shoot the steer down. The baker died, the animal was butchered and the meat given away.

"No critter's let alive after he's brought on a killing,"
the men from the saloons told any newcomers around, and
went back inside to wet their parched throats.

During the short season of 1867 at Abilene, Joseph
McCoy, the father of the town's cattle trade, had proved his
talk of saving the trailers from the abuse and violence they
got from farmers and growers of northern cattle on the eastern trail. But the eastern market had proved very poor and
yet the dust of the first trail herds of 1868 rose early and the
little cow town of Abilene was full of waiting buyers. Thousands of cattle were bought for the feed lots and pastures of
Illinois, for northern Indian contracts, and to stock the new
ranches as far away as Montana. As the herds came in they
spread farther and farther out over the prairie for feed and
water, cleaning the new grass to the roots, churning the banks
of the Smoky Hill River to bald gray mud. The town was a
roaring bonanza station, every cowboy who could get in afire
with the trail pay in his pockets and a burning thirst in him
for fun and for a wet of his dusty gullet. A great invasion of
saloonkeepers was ready for him, with their hangers-on—
gamblers, dance-hall girls, and all the other women, white,
black, and mixed, who didn't bother with any fancier approach than a tent or a shack down on the bottoms. There
were con men, robbers, and killers, not only gun and knife
men but garroters from the slums of the eastern cities, too.
And stalking through it all were the trail-herd owners and
bosses, and cowmen in to buy, most of them as dust-bitten as
the worst drag rider, for there was only one herd time—
from dawn to dawn. But with the dust scrubbed away at the
bathhouses, and the gray rime pounded from their hats, they
gathered at the Drovers Cottage or even in the all-Texan
cowboy hangouts, to talk cow. Many were quiet, soft-spoken
men, whether Texas born or from Tennessee or New England. But not all. Some were as wild and colorful as the
cattle they drove. Shanghai Pierce's voice was loud as any
brindle bull's in the springtime, and the jingle of his gold

bag was heard even farther by the small outfits with stock to sell, whether down on the Brazos or on the Smoky Hill at Abilene. He was credited with disposing of most troubles rather permanently, perhaps by gun or even the rope at a pecan tree, but for most occasions there was the clink of the gold in the bag that his old Negro companion always carried.

With this fine start, the year of 1868 still was not a profitable one for Abilene or the Texas cattle sent east, although 1,000 cars went out of Abilene in June. Soon after the first of these reached Illinois there was an appalling outbreak of Spanish, Texas, fever, with a spreading alarm through all the north country that was touched by Texas cattle or meat. The alarm was particularly felt among the owners of Shorthorn cattle. Many thought the deadly plague was shipping fever, the idea talked up big by the Abileners as they told about a shipment of around 40,000 cattle picked up in Texas by Chicago buyers and crowded upon Mississippi River steamboats at the mouth of the Red. The cattle reached grazers and feeders at Cairo thin and weak, and within a month domestic cattle all around were dying so fast that most of the region was stampeded into pushing all the stock to market, unfinished and even much breeding blood.

"Got to get 'em off our hands before they all die," the desperate feeders admitted sourly to each other.

It seemed that Illinois was so snorting mad that any man bringing in a load of Texas cattle now would have been mobbed, given a feather overcoat, and a ride on a bucking rail. It was easy enough to talk about it lightly out in Abilene until the bottom went out of the market, flooded by the dumping, and the buyers wary of all southwest cattle, with the stock still dying, when the shipments reached Chicago, the disease spreading there, too.

Then cattle began to die around the eastern shipments from Abilene, and finally it got out that some were dying around the trail herds of the town, even the milk cows at Abilene, and the scattered stock of the homesteaders. The whole region was really under quarantine between March and the end of November since 1867, some discovered but unenforced. To avoid trouble that might bring fines, even jailing, most of those losing stock near town were immediately paid for their losses, as legally entitled, the dead cattle buried by the drovers and others interested in keeping the news well-corraled. Soon, however, the new settlers along the streams crossed by the Chisholm Trail were standing at their homestead lines with their guns cocked, crowding the trail westward into buffalo country.

"Let the buffaloes do the dying," they taunted.

Some of the trailers swung around west by preference, seeking grass not tromped under thousands of sharp hoofs, some deciding to drive on through to the Union Pacific along the Platte. But the fever scare spread to the northern ranges, too, the American stock from the east and from Oregon dying, with more panic marketing and more people afraid to eat Texas meat. Even the trail drivers stopped butchering the usual strays gathered to their herds. Salt sow belly became the cowboy's staple, which he called sow bosom, mimicking the elegant people coming in who said "gentleman cow."

But fat pork, salted or smoked, although fine in a bean hole, was not for strings of dusty, waterless days. The trailers returned to fried beef, beef sliced thinner than ever and fried even longer.

In the meantime New York State, with fine herds of blooded stock, was quarantining western and northwestern cattle, and a convention on Spanish fever was called in Illinois, with delegates from all over the North and Canada but apparently none from Texas, where there was still angry insistence that their fine, healthy Longhorn cows were attacked by the envious heretical Yankees, and by growers unable to meet the competition of free grass and free-running cattle. The federal government ordered an investigation, too. Various theories were propounded. Some thought it was a shipping fever; others pointed out that frost stopped the spread of the disease and suggested that it might be a tick-borne infection. There was no denying that some cattle in from south Texas were so ticky they actually looked gray from the swollen bodies of millions of ticks.

"Hell, if them ticks was poison, why don't the critters packin' 'em around die?" The old Texans snorted over their rawhide whisky. "Or us that works with 'em?"

But there was no denying that Illinois had a disastrous disease among her cattle. Many buyers went broke, even big feeders like John T. Alexander, who lost $75,000 through the Spanish fever and much more through the panicky demands of those holding the mortgages on his extensive lands, compelling liquidation at this unfortunate time.

Of the 75,000 cattle that reached the Abilene region in 1868, one fourth had gone to Illinois in June, but after the outbreak of the fever, the herds waiting for cars in Kansas and those on the way up found no buyers. Any possible profits were eaten up by the cattle that had to be held over, with herds spread too close for grazing a hundred-mile region around Abilene, the dead smell of disaster on every wind. The town boosters did work up some sales and managed to snag a few buyers for the stock cattle to go to the growing range country farther up, but nobody wanted the beeves. The businessmen even worked up an exhibition car of buffaloes to be shunted all over the East, hoping to make buyers think about the West without remembering the fever. The buffalo exhibit drew crowds everywhere, and brought out buffalo hunters, a special train of them.

The Illinois legislature barred all Texas and southern cattle from the state unless wintered outside of the banned region, the proof of this to be a "swear paper," as the cowboys called it, an affidavit sworn to before a justice of the peace. The cowmen had a good round of drinks on that one. Hunt up J. P.'s out on the open range? Well, there were a few in the cow towns and more could be made. Even

off in Illinois some feeders knew that this was an easy spin
for any lariat, but they had a lot of grass and corn and very
little to eat it. Buyers crowded Abilene early in 1869 and the
swear papers were ready.

By now the Kansas Pacific had cut through the buffalo plains of west Kansas and headed into Colorado. The
Union Pacific had reached Utah's borders. Drovers could
find shipping points anywhere from the Missouri River to
Rock Springs, Wyoming. Yet the largest herd of the year
seems not to have gone north at all. It was larger even than
the 10,000 the Indians had swept together back on the San
Saba region and apparently whooped off up the Pecos for
the *comancheros*. Now a herd estimated at 15,000 head of
mixed stock was reported leaving the Brazos of lower Texas.
The owners were a group of Confederate veterans disgusted with carpetbag rule and the political equality of the
Negroes. But instead of heading for Mexico as those who
wanted Goodnight to join him right after the war, these were
going to California. The 200 men with many wagons and
around 1,200 horses drove the cattle in four divisions, still
far beyond good workable size. But they were going through
country tapped by the *comancheros* and when there seemed
danger of night attacks by Indians the whole drive was
bedded in one vast, spreading herd over the prairie, like a
great mass of buffaloes resting. It was a story to tell around
the campfires and the Alamo bar. But few envied the men,
and besides they would still have the problem of markets,
and every cattle owner along the whole trail would be
howling about the dirty, disease-spreading Rebs as loud as
the mobs of Missouri pukes ever had.

There was growing danger along much of the trail to
Abilene, too, but that didn't scare out many, not even the
women. George Cluck and his wife ran a ranch down on
Brushy Creek, in the troubled region near the Olives and
half-a-dozen other violent outfits. Around April 1 the Clucks
trailed out 1,000 good steers. Dudley Snyder drove a similar
herd along close enough for mutual protection. Mrs. Cluck,

with three young children and a fourth due in the fall, went along, driving a team of Indian ponies to an old hack, a camping outfit back of the seats, a spyglass and a shot gun at her hand.

They found the Red River in a roaring, rampaging flood, the whole broad valley full of herds waiting for the waters to subside. But Cluck and Snyder were out for the best of the market, which meant getting to Abilene ahead of the rush, so Cluck's men lashed old cottonwood logs to the running gears of the hack to float it and with the woman and children watching, one of the trail hands climbed into the seat and whipped the ponies off into the swirling water, splashing red. When he was across, Mrs. Cluck climbed up behind her husband on their most trusted horse, a powerful swimmer. The children were carried in the arms of expert riders. All up and down the bank men from the other outfits gathered to watch in alarm and amazement.

"Hell, they're from Williamson County—they grow 'em tough and longhorned down there," one admiring old cowhand said as he replenished his cud and started his jaw working again, now that they were all out of the boiling flood and drying off on the far side around a big fire.

Through the Territory the two trail herds moved closer together. The Indians gave them little trouble but they had to pull their guns on some white rustlers who charged out of the Wichita Mountains, demanding a big cut of the herds. The ruffians far outnumbered the sixteen trailers and some of the young drivers were very nervous. But Mrs. Cluck loaded the rifles in the hack and handed them around. "If any of you boys don't want to fight," she said, "then get in the hack here and look after the children and let me have your gun."

Even the youngest trail hand had to push his horse forward after that and get out to back up George Cluck, who was standing firm against the bearded ring of outlaws. He wouldn't give them even one damned lumpy-jawed critter, if he had one. "I got sixteen fighters as good as ever crossed the Red," he told them; "boys raised on the rattle-snakes, wildcats, and cactus of Williamson County. If any-body's honin' for a fight, let him get his prayin' done—"

The outlaws looked off over the fine herds strung out along the foothills, spreading a little now to feed. Then they looked around the cowboys, the least of them grim-faced, their hands all on their guns, ready, and behind them the hack with the small children and the woman fondling the hammer of her shotgun with her thumb.

The leader motioned with his bristled chin toward the foothills, and turned to follow his departing gang.

By the time the Cluck and Snyder herds reached the Abilene region their story had been spread around a cou-ple of days, so there were friendly and curious looks for the woman and presents for the barefoot children when they walked along the dusty streets of the cow town. But a drum-mer for a dress-goods house was angered, particularly at his seventh slug of Old Crow. "What a risk some men will take for a little money!"

" 'Tain't money. It's for the cows," a man beside him at the bar corrected. "That Mrs. Cluck, I hear say, don't want to let a single head go. Like to keep 'em all, if they could, and so she comes along."

The range country of Texas had no banks, and pack-ing large sums of money drew outlaws and Indians upon the returning trail drivers, and sometimes outlaws dobbed up to look like Indians. One year M. L. Dalton brought back $16,000 from the sale of a small herd in New Mexico, the next year $22,000, and then $6,000, in gold, which he buried with the rest somewhere on the ranch, it seemed, to be dug up as needed. In 1869 he started home from Kan-sas with $11,500 and two new wagons loaded with ranch provisions and a couple trunks of finery and geegaws for his wife and daughters. Near his ranch in Palo Pinto County he and two of his men were killed and scalped, scalped very in-expertly, some said. The attackers took the teams, wagons, and supplies, but threw away some worthless stuff, including an old shoe. In it was the money, in greenbacks—found along the trail and saved for his widow. But she couldn't bear to stay at the ranch any more, even with good help. She sold out to Jim Loving, feeling his sympathy for her because his father had died from the Indian wound he received over in the Pecos country.

Abilene had about the only real money loose in the region east of the buffalo country, and so the cow town drew a great deal of noise and lawlessness, much of it only roistering cowboys—several hundred, maybe a thousand of them trying to spend their trail pay all the same night. The gamblers were there, the bad men and various kinds of outlaws who had fled to the frontier for their own reasons, and were drawn by the smell of money or of violence even sweeter to some noses. The tracks at Abilene divided the town, with the churches, the courthouse, newspaper office, and many ordinary citizens on one side. On the south was Texas Abilene, the Lone Star district, with the stock pens, the hangouts for the trailers: saloons, dance halls, and the dance-hall girls with the scattering of shacks of the Loners at the bottoms, the Arkansaw Kittys, Weepin' Sadies, and Mex Maria. Here the Texans didn't fight the Mexicans—the greasers—but joined forces with them against the damnyankees. It was the old sectional split, with the blood of the war still very red, particularly here with many from prewar Bloody Kansas. Many Johnny Rebs had their best yells ready now that the shooting seemed over.

"If them shorthorns, them Come-Latelies had fit like this on either side, the war'd been over in six weeks," a soured old freighter said scornfully and out loud. He went around town unarmed but trailed his bull whip over his shoulder, letting the popper drag far behind him as a sort of dare to anybody spoiling for a little trouble. But although his tongue was mean as a thorn in a felt boot, nobody ever stepped on an inch of his popper, not high-heeled boot or cowhide work shoe.

Each year the cattle to Kansas and the Abilene region doubled, with 150,000 head in 1869, of which over 2,000 cars were shipped East. In 1870 the drives to Kansas totaled around 300,000 head, with the railroads suddenly in a fine rate war east of the Mississippi. There were rumors that whole trainloads of cattle were hauled from Chicago to New York for nothing, with perhaps even a little present for the shipper, so important had the business suddenly become. Good stock brought good prices and many "through" or fresh-driven Texas herds brought around $30 to $40 a head, with $50 to $60 for herds wintered north of the tick regions. The season had been a dry one, the grass rich and seedy, the cattle sleek and fat.

Before spring everybody predicted that 1871 would be the greatest year of the cattle trails, even with the growing unemployment in the East and the curtailment in meat purchases. The news of a boom in Abilene drew not only many new buyers to jam the drover hotels but swarms of hangers-on thick as buffalo gnats around the ears of a city dude come West. Not all the gamblers and gunmen drawn to the town were from the East. Ben and Billy Thompson came up from the southwest where they were known as two of the best gunmen in the region. Ben reached Abilene first. He was twenty-seven, above the average intelligence, with steady nerves and a cool eye along a gun. It was said he never shot for the love of killing, as so many here did, but threw his gun down as calmly on a man as on a rabbit or flying tin can. Born in Nova Scotia, the Thompsons grew out of boyhood down in Austin, surrounded by the patriots who had fought for Texas freedom and by many killers, including such men as the Olives and the other outlaw gangs able to stand up to them.

Ben Thompson had been a printer on an Austin paper, but gambling drew him. He was of medium height, with blue eyes, swarthy but fastidious as most gamblers were, and made friends everywhere. He started the killing early, the first apparently a Frenchman over a girl down in New Orleans. His reputation grew until he became the bad man of his Rebel regiment. Since then he served two years for shooting a man, Abilene heard, which seemed extreme for Texas, when the Olives and their kind killed people by the handful.

Released some months ago, Ben was drawn to Abilene because he was about broke, and, like hundreds of others, he hoped to pick up a little loose money bawling for its mammy. He found it. He had barely cooled his saddle when he made $2,600 at one sitting in a card game.

Billy Thompson came up with a trail herd soon after his brother. He was twenty-three, taller than Ben, slender, attractive, and friendly, but always in one scrape or another, usually with Ben handy to help him out.

In spite of his first-day luck, Ben had the gambler's weather eye that made him uneasy about the summer here. But since Billy had come up he decided to stay awhile and before the $2,600 was cut into his old friend Phil Coe hit town. Phil was a gambler but an unusual one. He was a big, loose-built man, over six foot four, with a full brown beard and generally unarmed. Not even the war got him into the habit of carrying a gun, although he had drifted from one frontier town to another ever since. This fit into Abilene's ordinance against gun packing. That this was often not enforced didn't trouble Coe, even though he carried several thousand dollars in his money belt. He put this in with Ben Thompson's gambling stake and together they opened the Bull's Head Saloon, well equipped, the faro bank the best that money could buy, and welcomed their fellow Texans.

The boom in cattle plodding northward started very early this year. All through May the Abilene prairie for fifty miles each way was spotted with trail herds cropping the grass to bald roots. From an imposing hilltop one sweep of the eye might take in 30,000 or even 50,000 cattle. The Slaughters, Reynolds, Driskills, Richard King, Shang Pierce, Print Olive—all the Texans seemed to be there except those pushing up the Goodnight-Loving Trail or cutting through to stations west of Abilene or heading on North.

Gradually there was a spread of news that the great herds around Abilene were not all waiting for cars, as many tried to believe, but for buyers, particularly after the first trainloads hit the market and sold badly, some not at all, and were once more held in not-too-hopeful or welcoming feed lots in the Illinois region by the western owners. Many herds lacking buyers in Kansas were pushed north the 300 miles to the Nebraska cow towns on speculation, hoping for government greenbacks if there was no chance of gold coins counted out on a horse blanket at the trail campfire. Many were held up around the Republican River or beyond Schuyler and Lincoln without too much hope.

Certain that Abilene would be overrun with too much loose money, the town council had hired Wild Bill Hickok as marshal for the season. He was just back from the doctor at Topeka about his eyes and glad to take the job. By the end of the first week Bill was one of the town marvels, with his golden curls flowing over his shoulders, his waistcoat embroidered in a twining of roses, his black cape lined in silken color. Many who knew him realized he was a determined enemy of the southerners, the Johnny Rebs, but his hatred seemed particularly for the Texans, jealous, it was said, of their flamboyance, the native dash of so many of them.

From the day the Bull's Head opened over on Texas Street, it was a bonanza, the trail drivers drawn to it like ants to a trickle of sorghum dropped in the sand. The Yankee saloonkeepers and dance-hall owners looked with pursed mouths toward this new place taking away so much of their trade, so much of the southern trade, about the only men with money to throw around.

There were rumors of several plans to drive out the Bull's Head. The easiest was to take Coe's liquor license away, but he stayed right on as gambler in the place, and the doors fanned as steadily as ever. Some suggested that shooting would be the best, and cause enough excitement to grow a prairie fire of thirst. Of course that meant going against Ben Thompson's gun, but Marshal Hickok had been hired for just such emergencies. Somehow he let the matter drag, perhaps really softening, as some said, or had never been what writers like Nichols tried to make him. Still, with the trade largely Texas, the situation couldn't be handled like an attack on a wolf den with spade or giant powder. A passable face had to be put on the elimination of the saloon, particularly with the town full of armed Texans, and, as the Abilene *Chronicle* said, more cutthroats and desperados in town than in any other its size on the continent. But the saloonkeepers were impatient. They couldn't wait, not with business already melting away, the cowboys of the herds still held nearby sticking around their camps, without pay until the cattle were sold.

Several opportunities for reasonable dispute arose or were made. Some claimed that Hickok had accused Coe of running crooked games and while there was no gun fight, with Coe unarmed as usual, there were threats of death to both sides and Hickok took to walking down the middle of the street out of easy range from alley lurkers. Others said that Wild Bill got a cut to help pay for his finery from crooks fleecing the cowboys. Some sentimental newcomers liked to think that Hickok's feud with Phil Coe could be over a woman.

Then there was a disagreement that promised to amount to something. It was over a picture a traveling artist slapped across the front of the Bull's Head. The picture was of an object familiar to everyone around any cow town—the full and imposing figure of a big red bull. Before the artist got more than the outlines sketched in, the eyeballers pushing up around his scaffold began to laugh a little, and to nudge each other, with a few roaring out loud. Laughing made dry throats, and the swinging doors below the scaffold fanned up more thirst.

As the crowds grew around this favorite water hole of

the Texans, the dandy, slim-fingered Wild Bill Hickok came
strolling along in the street, out beyond the horses stomping
flies at the hitch racks. He had a sawed-off shotgun across his
arm but he went on past. Apparently he saw an opportunity to carry out the main task assigned to him—the closing
of such competition as the Bull's Head, and with the law-and-
order element doing the job. The news of the picture was
spread around among the proper people. They came to look
up at the painting and denounce it as shocking, as too realis-
tic and suggestive—degrading and immoral, in fact, an insult
to the virtuous women of the town and a bad influence on
the children. The picture was not only recognizably a gentleman cow standing in plain sight along a public street, but
of a gentleman cow of entirely unnatural proportions.

"Mebby you ain't never seen one a them old Texas
herd bulls," a slow-spoken, earnest young cowboy tried to
argue reasonably.

The next news to spread around the camps was that a
delegation of good people had called on the proprietors of
the Bull's Head, going inside, of course, but making it clear
they had not come to buy. "No, no!" the leader protested to
an invitation to have a friendly one all around on the house.
"We have come, sir," he started firmly, "come to demand
that you remove the offensive picture of the—of the ah-h-
h—" stalling before all the derisive, sunburnt faces around
him.

One of his delegation filled in the words, speaking
primly. "—remove the vulgar picture of the ox."

"Ox!" one of the cowboys roared, the rest taking up
the hooting, the laughing that sent the delegation hurrying
out and up the street. "Ox, they calls it, and them com-
plainin'!"

Later it got around that a bucket of paint had been
bought by the anti-bull faction, by men whose own buildings
showed no interest in paint, not even good Yankee bluecoat
blue. Wild Bill and the rival saloonkeepers tried to save
their good crusade, now that it was beginning to work. But

when the men came with the paint bucket and a ladder they found armed guards protecting the picture, and business picking up at the Bull's Head, even though the rest of the town was almost empty, with the herds going on past, or to be held for next year down along the Arkansas or far out in Indian and buffalo country somewhere, perhaps several herds thrown together for protection, the men thrusting dugouts into some bank and holing up for the winter.

But around the Bull's Head sparks flew as from a railroad engine on a windy night. Gunplay seemed inevitable, perhaps a battle to the finish on the dusty street called Texas. At the urging of Coe the bull was painted over, but the picture got only one coat, thinned down with linseed oil, and the offending outlines of the bull left shockingly visible to any of the tender-minded coming down that way.

It was plain to everybody by now that there was much more to this fight than the amateurish picture of a red bull. Some said that half-a-dozen Texas cattlemen were involved, including Shanghai Pierce. Old Shang had always been a wild man but since his wife and baby son died he was more than ever the lone and angry wolf, riding the range with his Winchester slung to the saddle, brooking no interference. After the vigilante lynching of the Lunns and All Jaw Smith he jumped bail in Texas and spent his fury loafing around Kansas City. There he heard about the growing North-South troubles at Abilene, where his herds were headed, and that John Wesley Hardin's outfit had been attacked by the Osages on the Kansas border. It seemed an Indian had demanded a steer for the herd's passage and, when refused, shot the steer down. Young Wes killed the Indian on the spot and left his body tied to the beef carcass. It would make a lot of trouble for the herds of Pierce and everybody else coming through now, but the boy bad man wasn't the one to care about that.

It was told around that Wes Hardin, already a fugitive from justice for cold-blooded murder, showed off up at Abilene by taking the guns away from Marshal Hickok.

Then there was the story that Pierce, Driskill, and Ben Thompson had squared it with Wild Bill to let Hardin shoot his way through Kansas as he had through Texas—a special favor to young Wes, to keep him quiet about their part in the mob that strung up the mavericking Lunns.

"Yeh, they want the maverickin' stopped now, seein's they got their start in cows made," some accused.

Anyway, Old Shang Pierce wiped the Kansas City sweat from inside his brown hat that matched his uncowmanlike brown suit and got his valise packed for Abilene. "I got to check on all this talk with my own flapping ears," he said.

Down on Texas Street he was told that when Hardin came to town Ben Thompson and his gambler, Phil Coe, were still making money in the Bull's Head although the rest of Abilene was like a winter prairie-dog town. Apparently Wild Bill was more anxious than ever to drive them out, and hoped to set young Wes against them, get him to do the shooting. Perhaps Thompson and Coe tried the same trick of insinuations and talebearing to get Hardin to kill the marshal. Anyway, John Wesley Hardin ignored both sides until Wild Bill pronounced him a dangerous man with that brace of illegal pistols swinging at his slender hips, and tried to disarm him. That was when the marshal found himself looking down the two barrels and compelled to drop his arms while the Texans standing around let out a Rebel yell.

But young Wes knew better than to push his luck too far. He hit for the open country, doing a little killing on the way out, some said, but apparently the dead man was only a Mex, a southerner, and demanded no action from the law.

Now, however, Marshal Hickok had to get the owners of the Bull's Head out of town or eat dirt before all the cow country, particularly after he had been letting his young admirers brag around that their Wild Bill had killed forty-three men since the day, ten years ago, when he shot down McCanles up in Nebraska. Thompson went to visit his wife, who had apparently been hurt by a runaway in Kansas City, and left Coe to manage the place. With Ben gone and not many Texans around, Hickok finally shot Phil Coe— over a girl, some tried to say. Others told other stories. One was that Coe had joined some straggling Texans in a last night of roistering around the saloons and dance halls before they started home next morning. One of them fired a shot at a dog that ran out of the dark and tried to bite them as they turned toward the Alamo. For once Phil Coe was carrying a pistol and Hickok saw his chance. He ran around to the back door and confronted the Texans in the bright light of the Alamo's open front doors, demanding "Who fired that shot?"

With the gun still hot in his hand, Phil Coe admitted he did. "I shot at a dog."

Hickok drew his pistols and Coe fired, too. Still the poor shot, his bullet went through the marshal's coat while he caught one in the belly, jerking back a little before the impact. He fired again and missed, the men around him falling back from the poor marksmanship, their guns out. Williams, one of Hickok's assistants, came running around the dark corner to help. Bill saw him, fired twice, and killed him instantly.

Some thought that perhaps the stories of Hickok's eye troubles were true, or maybe he was nervous, with the Texans around him, and fired at Williams more by shadow than by sight. But the instant he knew what he had done he gathered up the body, carried it into the saloon, sobbing over it.

With Coe mortally wounded, and the wide Kansas prairies still full of gun-toting cowboys from below the Red River, no matter how deserted Abilene might be, everybody involved scattered and nobody remembered that the outlines of the bull, the ostensible excuse for all the trouble, were still very plain, and unnoticed.

Hickok left town in a hurry. Some said he headed East to a doctor about his eyes. Topeka, or maybe Kansas City. Others, knowing the Thompson brothers, the Hard

Case relatives of Coe, and the chute run of Texans who had seen young Wesley Hardin make small of Wild Bill by taking his guns, were certain Hickok left for his health all right.

Shanghai Pierce listened to all the stories and roared out loud enough to be heard down at the crossing of the Red when he saw the painting of the bull. He stalked unarmed, as always, through the empty streets and ordered his herds coming up the trail turned off to Ellsworth, far to the southwest.

Not even McCoy, father of Abilene, could hold the Texans now. By fall blue asters and shining goldenrod had grown up along the breaks where everything had been tromped into the ground for four years. Late geese settled down within the sound of a pistol shot of Abilene, if there had been one to disturb their night.

The town council terminated all Hickok's official. connections with Abilene and early in 1872 a group of farmers and citizens of the town sent word asking the cattlemen not to return. It was as uncalled for as horns on a hog. The end had already come, in one swift slide from the all-time peak of cattle drives to nothing. Fully 600,000 head had reached Kansas in 1871, mostly to the Abilene region, and perhaps 300,000 of these had not sold at all and would have to be wintered mostly at the drover's expense—thin-hided Texas cattle in sub zero country, and without hay or shelter.

On top of the overgrazing, a wind-driven prairie fire swept over much of the range, leaving it black as dusty velvet, to swirl up in gray clouds of soot. Finally the worst fall rain that even the Indians could remember washed over Kansas and up through Wyoming and Dakota Territory. The wind shifted to the north, turned the rain to ice and then to a blinding three-day blizzard. Even buffaloes froze to death, and the toll among the greenhorns out for hides was never really calculated. Old troopers died between army posts, and even trappers and long-time buffalo hunters were missing until the snow thawed off. The Texas cattle, poor-fleshed and weather-soft, froze by the thousands or drifted into gullies and canyons perhaps a hundred feet deep in loose, wind-swept snow. It was wholesale ruin for the drovers. Some worth $100,000 in the fall were bankrupt in May. Skinners swarmed out with the first thaws to strip the dead stock, 50,000 hides shipped out from one station alone, enough to break the market for the buffalo hunters, too. One cattle company got a herd of 3,900 head up to the sheltered, long-grassed Republican River Valley and still found only 110 of them alive in the spring. Many did worse.

So ended Abilene as a cow town, a trail town, a boom and bonanza town. The fancy saloons closed; the gamblers, the women, and the bad men drifted away, the bad men first of all. Where the great herds had tromped the earth of the corrals and the loading pens, horseweed, skunk mint, and the yellow rose of Texas, the sunflower, grew up fat from the rich earth memory of the cattle. Yet another memory remained of the boom days, the memory of the flamboyance that would always cling to the quiet town, a little like the outlines of the bull visible through the paint on the front of the old saloon.

The Santa Fe Railroad reached Newton, Kansas, July, 1871. Stockyards were built and with the old Chisholm Trail shortened and straightened out, the place became a booming cow town overnight. For one season it was the roaringest and bloodiest cow town of Kansas. Saloons, dance halls, and gambling houses sprouted on the shimmering plain. The tough district, Hide Park, was some distance out and included, as was usual, a dance hall called the Alamo. There was no town organization that first season—only a couple of justices of the peace, constables, and a sheriff with deputies. Twenty-seven places sold liquor, eight provided gambling, with eighty professional gamblers working the town, but no church or religious organization anywhere.

Once more almost the first to reach the new place

were the gunmen. Boldest, most arrogant was perhaps Art Delaney, known as Mike McCluskie, an agent of the Santa Fe Railroad hired as marshal by the saloons and gambling houses to keep the Texas cowboys under control. In August there was an election to vote $200,000 in county bonds for the Newton and Southwestern Railroad down to Wichita. A Texas gambler served as special policeman at the polls. Somehow he angered Mike McCluskie of the Santa Fe, who shot and killed him. Hugh Anderson, a friend of the dead man up with a herd of Longhorns, swore to get McCluskie on sight. He was backed up by a crack-shot Kentuckian and two Texans not bad on the bead either.

One August night, when the cattle boom was about a month old, McCluskie came into the Tuttle Dance Hall with Jim Riley, a thin, tubercular youth who followed the rail-road gunman around like a little fice dog that barked and snapped from behind his master. Mike McCluskie was warned that Anderson and his outfit were gunning for him but he lingered at the gambling tables, with Riley lounging near the door. Suddenly the door was kicked open and Anderson, his fellow avengers, and several cowpunchers stomped in. The click, rattle, and whirr of the gaming stopped. McCluskie jumped up, reaching for his gun, but Anderson fired first and the marshal turned as from a blow and dropped, mortally wounded. A peacemaker rushed in to quiet the men, but young Riley, with his beloved friend bleeding on the floor, drew his guns and began shooting. He sent the peacemaker staggering to fall dead outside. He brought Anderson and five of his men down, two of them dead, one fatally wounded, and three bad-hurt in the fight-ing. Two bystanders were hit, one to die later. Then, as sud-denly as he started the slaughter, the youth with the deadly aim coolly stepped out into the night.

The new marshal organized a posse but Riley was never seen again so far as Newton heard and some thought that was the way the town wanted it. Evidently Riley was

GN, Gone North, as people had been saying GTT, Gone to Texas, for a long time. A few years later there was talk that he might be the outlaw called Doc Middleton up in Nebraska and Dakota. Doc sometimes used the name Jim Riley and he was slim, blond, quiet spoken, but not tubercular so far as anyone knew. To be sure, the open life of the outlaw was considered very good for that disease and for several others, too, except lead colic.

The Tuttle Dance Hall massacre, with nine men shot in fewer minutes, roused the better element of Newton. They organized a town government, built a jail, and hired five policemen to keep the Texans headed straight down the chute in the future. But settlers had been swarming in everywhere along the railroads the last couple years. They brought quiet to the town, they and the growing depression in the East, with jobs scarce as Democratic chances, now that Grant was running again. Everywhere across the Newton trail settlers were measuring off homestead lines with a rag tied to a spoke of a wagon wheel and counting the turns. They broke strips of prairie and warned the Texas drovers off their sod corn and beans and setback wheat, holding them up for damages to grass and crop. Now the justices of the peace, elected men, were suddenly switching sides, turning against the voteless drovers. One of the early settlers was an advance man for the German Mennonites, a religious and frugal people who came with palmfuls of smuggled Turkey Red wheat hidden in their pockets.

Ellsworth, out west of Abilene on the Kansas Pacific, had been a cattle market before Shanghai Pierce turned his herds there from the trail to Abilene in 1871. He found no buyers there either, but less organized opposition to these Texans who brought the business than had grown up at Abilene. The comical trio of old cattlemen, big Shang Pierce and his friends Seth Mabry, the five-foot-three cattle king, and One-Armed Jim Reed pooled their unsold herds, 3,000 big steers, to be wintered together for early sale ahead of the 1872 drive. Pierce managed to sell 1,000 of his to the government before that.

The next spring the Kansas legislature pushed the tick quarantine line westward, making it illegal to drive Texas cattle not only to Abilene, now that the whole region was deserted, but soon to both Newton and Ellsworth. Angrily, McCoy pointed out that all these towns had really been illegal summer market for "through" stock, meaning straight through from the tick regions, ever since 1867.

With around 40,000 cattle wintered in the region, Ellsworth, even though sharing the drive with Newton on the Santa Fe, became the leading shipping point on the Kansas Pacific Railroad in 1872. By midsummer more than 100,000 Longhorns were grazing around the town and the fires of the cow camps dotted the night prairie like steady fireflies. Even without ready buyers the Texas herds had to be set upon the trails. Cattle, unlike a bale of cotton or coal in a mine, could not be held for a rise. After a steer reached maturity, holding meant aging past top sale, with expenses for care and grass piling up.

During the unhappy summer of 1873, 177,000 cattle were reported up the trail by July, with thousands more on the way. The seventy-six cattlemen, mostly Texans, who owned the herds included the Colonel Myers who had worked with McCoy to start the Abilene trade in such high optimism. Even without the money of a good cattle market, many gamblers were tolled to Ellsworth, including, of course, the Thompsons. Once more Ben came first, with Billy up the trail a few days later. Ben hoped to go into the saloon business but found it overcrowded. Apparently he pawned his diamond stickpin and ring, and with a little borrowing on the side, got enough cash together to set up gambling tables at Joe Brennan's saloon, known as Gamblers' Roost by the cowboys.

Cad Pierce and Neil Cain drove herds up from Austin about the time the Thompsons arrived. Cain often dealt monte at Thompson's tables and Pierce bucked the board. Here, too, the law was Union; County Sheriff Whitney, a northern veteran and old Indian fighter and Brocky Jack Norton, one of Hickok's deputies back in the old Abilene days, the city marshal. They worked for order and got it through to mid-August, without a serious gun fight. By then the herds were tapering off for the season, and the town fathers decided a small, cheaper police force would do. They fired two of the men, and three days later the town had a shooting that gave it a wild name. Some noted gamblers in at Brennan's were playing for unusually high stakes. The Thompsons were there but not playing, Ben trying to look after Billy, who was drinking too much. Cain was dealing monte and Cad Pierce, with considerable money in his pockets, wanted to bet higher stakes than Cain would take. Ben Thompson got John Sterling to cover the extra money. John, a little drunk, volunteered to cut Ben in on half the winnings. But when he won $1,000 he picked it up, put it in his pocket, and left.

From there on the stories told were many, but it seemed that Ben Thompson ran into Sterling the next afternoon and reminded him of the promise. Unarmed, he got struck in the face and so he went for Sterling with his fists but a policeman held him off with a six-shooter. Later, at Brennan's, while Ben was talking this over, a policeman and Sterling, carrying a shotgun, passed the swinging doors. One of them called in, "Get your guns, you damned Texans, and fight!"

Nobody would loan Ben a gun. Running out for his own pistol and sixteen-shot rifle, he accepted the challenge of Sterling and the policeman. "Meet me at the railroad grade and we'll have it out with no bystanders getting hit!" he called after them.

But in the meantime Billy Thompson, already pretty drunk, had got to Ben's double-barrel shotgun and let it go off, striking the sidewalk at the feet of Millett and little Seth Mabry, so Ben had to go to take the gun away from him.

Soon a real crowd was gathering against them and he gave the gun back, but reluctantly. "Now be careful, Billy," he ordered.

Sheriff Whitney heard about the disturbance and unarmed, in shirt sleeves, went out to the Thompsons, who insisted they wanted no trouble. Ben hadn't even been armed.

"Well, put up your guns now, boys," he said. "I'll see you're protected."

Together the three went back toward Brennan's saloon, walking friendly abreast. At the door a Texas cowman yelled a warning, "Look out, Ben! Here they come!"

Ben whirled, saw the policeman running up with his gun drawn. In the shooting that followed Sheriff Whitney was hit by a load of buckshot from the gun in Billy Thompson's unsteady hands.

"My God, Billy, you've shot our best friend!" Ben protested. Three days later Whitney was dead.

The Thompsons and their friends claimed it was an accident but the newspapers and the officers denied this, pointing out that Billy slipped away to his horse and fled while Ben watched with the reloaded shotgun ready. After the mayor disarmed the policeman, Sterling and the others with them, Ben finally surrendered and was released on bond. Later one of the new policemen ran into Cain and Pierce, a good friend of Billy Thompson's, on the street. Although Pierce was unarmed, the officer shot him twice, chased him into a store, and beat him over the head with the gun until his skull was broken. Alarmed, the town organized a vigilance group to rid Ellsworth of undesirable Texans and issued a warning to Lone Star men—the very men who made Ellsworth's boom, even though cattle had fallen to giveaway prices. The governor of Kansas offered a $500 reward for Billy Thompson but he was gone down the trail to Texas. Later a Ranger picked him up in Austin and sent him back to Ellsworth. There the town's women got interested in him, brought him cakes and meat pies and other presents in jail until he was released.

The railroad for which Newton was voting bonds the day her massacre started reached Wichita the summer of 1872. The town, on the old Chisholm Trail, was by many days the nearest northern rail point to the incubator, the cradle of the Longhorn. For many years Wichita had been an outpost and trading center for Indian Territory, the freighting point for the various Indian agencies and army posts. Government men and contractors were common here from back when the first bull trains plodded back and forth to the Territory, their wagons dusted from the trails through the red country. Now the town had a peculiarly varied and noisy population. Trail-gaunted cowboys hunted up barbers and bathhouses to wash away the red dust before they went on the town, to stalk through the milling of land-seekers, buckskin-breeched old scouts and plainsmen, Mexican ranchers and trail drivers with their wide flat hats and an occasional colorful serape over a shoulder. There were brightly-blanketed Indians, too, from the Territory and many, chiefly from the Civilized Tribes who had brought the first plug hats to the region, now dressed like the politicians, businessmen, or ranchers that they were. The gamblers were in town, too, some in flashy vests or the deceptively quiet frock coats, the madams plumed and silken, the dance-hall girls in flashier dress. One gambling house sent a brass band parading the crowded street to lead the customers to the door. Here and there signs appeared:

> Anything goes in Wichita. Leave your revolvers at police headquarters and get a check. Carrying concealed weapons is strictly forbidden.

There was a fiddling preacher in town. He elbowed his way from one crowded saloon to the other and sang a popular ballad with fiddle accompaniment, perhaps a song of a girl waiting for her wandering cowboy, or of a cowboy who would never return. Afterward he played a couple of hymns, preached a little hell-fire and damnation, invited

everybody to the services in the dugout schoolhouse, and
pushed his way out, his fiddle shielded under his arm. Publicly he ignored the girls who chucked him under his
bearded chin or moved up close against him, and what he
did in private was nobody's business in Wichita.

For several weeks the town was terrorized by Hurricane Bill Martin and his Texas gang, known as cattle
rustlers and dangerous men. They rode down the streets
shooting and yelling, with or without the cooperative permission of the officials, depending upon who asked to know.
Eventually vigilantes were organized here, too, and under
their pressure the marshal, afraid to move, asked an attorney
to arrest Hurricane. The man tried it, while half the town
watched, or wished later that they had been watching, well
out of gunshot, of course. Turned out to be pretty tame. Bill
gave up his gun without a peep as loud as a new-hatched
meadowlark on the prairie. With the help of the citizens
fifteen or twenty of the gang were lined up and marched
over to the police station where the judge fined the lot and
threw Hurricane into jail.

Although Wichita seemed to be booming, it was a
boom that nearly everybody realized must be short as the
tail of a January calf. The busiest spot of all was the land
office, and the settlers scattered their dugouts, soddies, and
log huts all along the streams and over the high tableland.
There were Indian scares but most of the fighting was far
to the southwest, usually against white thieves stealing the
reservation horse herds or the buffalo hunters that the
troops were supposed to hold north of the Arkansas River.
But the hide men slipped past the disinterested bluecoats
and chased the buffaloes to the Cimarron and deep into the
Panhandle, leaving only rotting carcasses where the great
herds had moved dark and fat for the fall hunts of the Indians.

The year of 1873 had started uneasily. There was the
dead smell of graft over Washington, a stink worse than
spring on the buffalo ranges, with rumors of bribery in Con-

gress by the Crédit Mobilier. Women managed to relieve the dullness of their lives a little by the scandalous stories of Henry Ward Beecher and the beautiful Mrs. Tilton. Then came Black Friday and the collapse of the nation's financial structure, banks falling like a herd of stampeding Longhorns going over the cap rock. The scare of war with Spain over the Cuban massacres was called an attempt to save Grant's administration with a war boom. But that collapsed, too. Although 405,000 cattle came up the trail during Wichita's second summer and spread out 100 or more miles through Kansas, it wasn't much like the booming 600,000 head to the Abilene region in seventy-one except that there was no market in 1873 either.

The falling cattle prices had long cast their shadow across the path of the moving herds, the foreboding shadow of general economic collapse. In spite of their uneasiness, and all their energy and initiative, many of the cattlemen went broke. The Texans saw everything they had built up since the war defeat swept away. Even Charlie Goodnight was cleaned out by the panic.

Wichita, with the well-established trade to Indian Territory and the great government contracts for Indian goods, always with big graft rake-offs all along the way, had a kind of basic stability as solid as a wide-tired freight wagon. Even some of the dance halls were run by people of education and some refinement. Not that there wasn't shooting, too, but with more money left in circulation and the busi-ness less seasonal, Wichita offered more than Abilene ever did. A Negro group sang to guitars, an armless wonder put on daily performances. There was a variety theater, a beer garden with a band, a hall with from 100 to 150 players of keno, bawdy houses with twenty, thirty women apiece, and several brightly lighted churches. In addition there were always Indians camped down at the river, usually friendly but now rather surly over broken treaties and the loss of the buffalo ranges, their relatives killed in the fights before and after the attack on Adobe Walls, followed by General Mackenzie's expedition into the Panhandle. There were raids clear up on the Smoky Hill Trail and one right over on the Medicine, later said to have been by white men painted up, ranch hands, scaring out the swarming settlers. A dozen little stockades were thrown up along the Kansas frontier, but the early winter cooled everybody, including the actual redskins.

The gloom over all the cow country deepened all winter and the early herds of 1874 ran into trouble everywhere: George W. West and his brother Sol had started very early from Lavaca County and struck burnt range in the Territory and an April blizzard that froze their horses and scattered their herd. George West, generally considered an impatient man, roared that if he had to fight the winters he'd do it up north where the grass was fattening and the railroads handier. After selling what they could gather up, he divided the profits with Sol, handing him his seventy-five cents, and made plans for a move north. Perhaps no one had told them about the grasshoppers up there, darkening the noonday sky, making the railroad tracks so slippery that the engine wheels spun, or that up at the mines in Montana a full-grown steer sold for $10.

During 1874 only 166,000 cattle were shipped from Wichita and Ellsworth, 151,618 in 1875. By then the Chisholm Trail was closed forever by the farmers, by their fields and their buckshot and by the justices of the peace and county judges who gave the farmers the damages they demanded for their crops, to be paid before the herds could move. Sometimes the trailers bulldozed their way through with guns. But that couldn't work long.

By 1876 the land around Wichita was mostly settled and the homesteaders heaping their complaints about recurrent Texas fever on top of the long protests from the breeders of blooded stock, particularly Shorthorns. Finally the legislature had to push the quarantine line westward once more, shutting out all cattle not wintered north of the fever regions of Texas from any market east of Dodge City. So now it would be the town built by the buffalo hunters who had fought the cowboys all along the fringes of the cow country from Fort Griffin to Sidney, up on the Union Pacific. But the skin men were gone from most of the region, and the wind blew sweet over the weeds grown up in the hide yards and down the practically deserted streets of Dodge.

# CHAPTER IV

# THE INDIAN SUMMER
# OF OLD DODGE

THE year 1876 was the end of an era, not only for the wandering Chisholm Trail and its cow towns but for the whole nation. Philadelphia was straining to put together the first representative world's fair of the industrial age, and even the most remote country store and cattle-trail saloon was planning to celebrate the Centennial Fourth of July with noise, and with oratory, if possible.

The nation's first hundred years ended under a sky dark as a Panhandle black blizzard. For months one federal scandal after another had blown its stinging load into the eyes of the public, the dirty tracks of the grafters plain to the very doorstep of the White House for all who could still see. The cattlemen, and the farmers, too, were angry, desperate after all the years of lagging prices and the rising monopolistic power of the railroads and meatpackers while the workingman, the beef growers' ultimate market, faced repeated pay cuts and growing unemployment. Although contributions to Hayes' campaign for the presidency seemed generous enough, the rumble from the voters scared his managers and so once more the bloody shirt of the Union dead was hauled out to stampede the voters like Longhorns before a flapping Indian blanket. Yet even this proved not enough, and Tilden was elected president by a popular majority of over a quarter million votes, with the House of Representatives going Democratic, too. But Hayes, and particularly those who had put their money on him, would not take defeat so easily. It was immediately made plain that Grant and the army would back Hayes, not the elected Tilden, come Inauguration Day, with cannon probably mounted in the circles of the street intersections, as the French planner of Washington anticipated. But the cannons would not be turned against a revolution, only against the entry of the legitimate government.

Unwilling to bring on another bloody civil strife, Tilden agreed to leave the contested election to the decision of a commission. They threw out the Democratic electoral votes of Florida and Louisiana and declared Hayes the winner.

This decision in favor of the minority Republicans was not made until midwinter, very close to Inauguration Day. It brought immediate and loud cries of "Stolen election!" and "A shameful steal of the presidency!" through the southern cattle country. Usually the Jack Texans kept quiet as a wild calf in the brush when it came to politics, but Charlie Goodnight, down there visiting and looking around for cattle, heard a drunk humming "Marching through Georgia." Galled by the presidential decision Goodnight roared out, "By God, it's another bloody march all right, but through Washington, D. C., this time. I thought I pulled out of Texas to get away from the damned carpetbaggers. Now we got them in the White House!"

When the news reached Dodge the streets were full of dirty snow instead of angry, gun-armed Texans ready to answer the jibes of the northerners, which included most of the gamblers and hangers-on around the saloons, and the bluecoats from the neighboring post. No bullets spurted dust from the windy street, no men ducked for cover. No horses along the hitch racks plunged, perhaps screaming like a woman as they were hit, and broke loose, to head for the open country, with men spurring after them, while others shot it out where they crouched. It would have been a time for bystanders to run for the washouts, with windows crashing from stray bullets, or thin walls torn, with women and children crying inside, the dead not only those who were sprawled in the streets and alley. If this steal of the election had happened in the summer, the taunts of the northerners, feeling bigger in the trickery than from any fair win, would certainly have brought blood to run in the streets of Dodge, and who could tell where else in the cow country, with troops close almost everywhere, in little knots, but only enough to aggravate, to arouse a tender pride that dared not be satisfied short of death?

One of the flamboyant bluecoats that some Texans had had to endure would never come charging against them in any fight now, nor his less famous brother take out his anger and envy by brawling and cracking southern heads up around Hays only a few years ago. George Custer had ridden out in arrogance once too often and found the Sioux up on the Little Big Horn no peaceful, unguarded winter camp like the Cheyennes that he struck down in the Washita country only a few years ago, and very near to the new cattle trail planned to Dodge City.

Another and more recently active enemy of the Texans died during the fateful year of 1876. Wild Bill Hickok would never bulldoze another man, north or south, nor draw upon an unarmed one, or one of unequal marksmanship. Many who had endured the bragging ways of his admirers took a little satisfaction in McCall's bullet up there at the new gold camp of Deadwood, particularly some who knew how Hickok had killed his men, from McCanles through Coe and Williams. But there were a few who realized that halos bright as January sundogs had surrounded all the lights he faced for a long, long time now, with the shadows of a permanent night creeping in all around him. In this even the men who despised his kind the most, the outdoor men living with the sharpened senses, particularly unbounded sight, felt a deep pity.

Yes, 1876 was the end of an era, not only the end of a hundred years but of a ten-year period that demanded the gaudiest, the most exaggerated characters to continue, if not the violent heroic times and deeds of a very bloody war, at least such heroics as could be whipped up to feed the public's voracious, wolfish hunger. The two showiest, Custer and Hickok, had not survived the year, and even the most conspicuous of Indian scouts, the tattered, rope-belted California Joe, who couldn't be separated from his jug by Custer or from his tangled red hair by the Indians, was dead, too, ended by a bullet up in the White River country of Nebraska. Violent ends to fit a violent time.

The year also brought a beginning to the cow country, the start of a long, slow revolution not visible for years. At the Centennial at Philadelphia W. S. Ikard, early rancher of Henrietta, Texas, saw his first Herefords—a handsome red cattle, with clean, curly-haired white faces and white-lined backs, the horns shortish, the eyes mild. But what interested Ikard was the blockiness, the short bones, and the width and depth of the meat on shoulder, back, and hindquarters—steak animals. And certainly good keepers.

"Can they graze?" he asked.

Their owner swore they were one of the best keepers known, slow, even-tempered, easy to handle. "Here, put your hand out," he said. And as Ikard extended his hand, the young bull sniffed inquiringly at the silver-studded leather cuff the Texan wore, tested it with a speculative tongue.

Ikard went home without the Herefords, but the white faces haunted him and he talked of them repeatedly. "Too short-legged; never make it to water from the range," some of the other Texans argued.

"Nah, never cover the ground for good grazing here," Ikard's hands agreed.

But W. S. worried the idea like a coyote returning to a bone that smelled of the marrow inside.

The year was also a new beginning for Dodge City, up the Arkansas River. There had been a scattering of cattle in there before, some in 1872 while the place was still Buffalo City, the first tent stakes barely pounded into the baked earth or the whisky barrels unloaded. Doc Barton, looking no more than nineteen at the time, had hit the place with eight trail hands, 1,000 cattle, and high hopes. He had swung out around the great buffalo herds and the Indians who were building up to the fury with which, two years later, they struck the hide men at Adobe Walls in the Texas Panhandle. Doc had reached the Arkansas far up in Colorado and followed the river and the railroad survey down. At the Dodge station the piercing headlight of the engine puffing westward out of the evening had scared his cattle, and some of his trail hands, too. Here was a railroad at last, but there were no loading pens and Doc had to take his steers clear down to Great Bend.

Since then a few settlers and small ranchers had gradually sifted into the region to supply Fort Dodge and the growing town with milk and a change from buffalo meat, later to serve as holding ranges for Texas stock until delivered at Newton, perhaps, or farther north, kept for better prices, sometimes for any price at all. At first whoopers were hired to keep the migrating buffalo herds off the range but now most of the buffaloes were gone and the Indians, except the few making trouble down around Double Mountain Fork and the Thompson canyon in Texas, had been whipped to the reservations.

Dodge City was born the daughter of the hide men, born out of their need, and matured to their joy. As the buffalo herds dwindled, their bleaching bones whitened the prairie like morning frost in November or even strips of snow, and great bone ricks grew along the railroad at Dodge. But they were poor compensation for the lost drying prairie, where thousands of hides had once been staked out, or the hide yards said to have held as many as 100,000 buffalo skins at one time, piled and baled, waiting for the strings of empty cars. At the best bones were cheap pay, and besides they did not replenish themselves with the recurring spring-time.

One business after another had moved away from Dodge, some of the gambling dens and dance halls first, then even a tailor, perhaps, or a harness shop. A few followed the shrinking buffalo herds deep into west Texas but generally they went to the mine camps of Colorado and beyond. Sometimes the owner scooped the few coins from the till into his drawstring pouch or an old tobacco sack and skipped with whatever else he could pack off before the creditors came, if they weren't hitting out somewhere in the night themselves. Every few days the wind whistled through more empty windows, somehow broken almost as soon as the owner turned down an alley.

The deserted prairie had grassed over behind the buffalo herds, deep and wonderful as it had perhaps never been before, the shy prairie plovers not rising until the rare intruder's feet were upon them. Most of the wolves were gone to fatten on the last harvest of the buffalo hide men far down in west Texas, many coyotes following as was their scavenging nature. Even the old trails of the hide wagons were grown over into yellow bands of sunflowers and gum-weed reaching toward Dodge. Around town the cockleburs and the stinking bee plant had moved in, with the horse-weed and the yellow rose of Texas, the big sunflower, growing man-high in the old freight lots, the elephant corral, and the hide yards.

On Front Street grass had pushed up through the old sidewalk and grew into the burning days of July, some still standing between the gray boards that winter. Then suddenly it seemed that the Centennial year might bring a new era to Dodge also. Perhaps the hide town had only slowed down a while, drowsed a little in an early squaw winter of

life before a fine, long Indian summer. Rumors told of a
new cattle trail well west of the latest quarantine line. Several Texans were laying out a route through the wilder
Indians in the west end of the Territory, hoping to avoid
the long stretches of sparse prairie and jack oak—stretches
with sandy stream beds and upland ponds practically waterless after the first of May. Some recalled the hard drive that
J. W. Driskill made to Dodge last year with a herd of 1,450
Longhorns. It was summer and they went without water four
days crossing Indian Territory and then, when the experienced old drover just about gave up saving his stock and
hoped only to rescue his pitifully small crew of four men, the
old lead steer had lifted his head with the dark swollen
tongue sticking from his mouth. He saw what Goodnight
saw on that terrible drive to the Pecos nine years ago. Here,
too, the worn cattle tried to break into a shuffling, stumbling
run terrible for the weary and desperate men to see, and
yet wonderful, too, for this meant there was water near. They
struck it just before sundown and worked all night to keep
the thirst-crazed cattle from killing themselves.

Somehow they got the herd through those four days
and that night of watering with the loss of only one cow,
but the faces of the men when they reached Dodge and their
stories made every hopeful trailer uneasy about trying a
western drive until more permanent water was located.

Then, the spring of 1876, with Dewees and Ellison,
the Millett brothers, Bishop, and Head and several others
already on the way north, stockyards were thrown up in addition to the old loading pens. Riders carrying words of welcome were sent out: grass fine, water plentiful, no grangers
or practically none, and drinks two for a quarter.

Few of the old-timers around Dodge dared believe
that the herds would actually stop there. "Hell, when they
get to them dry stretches they'll swing 'round west through
Colorado, or east, spite of the quarantine," a dozen merchants and saloonkeepers told their help, one way or another.

Then one day a pearly thread of haze seemed to cling

to the southwestern horizon. Later a faint sound like bawling somewhere high up floated on the wind, and a thin, dark line appeared, moving over the rolling prairie like fall ants hurrying with winter almost upon them. As the line neared and became a string of cattle heading for the crossing above the toll bridge, the crippled gatekeeper jerked off his hat and waved it toward the town, yelling, pointing. But he was probably the last one of all of Dodge to discover the fast-walking lead steers, already breaking from the pointers toward the smell of water.

So, almost overnight, the deserted Daughter of the Hide Men became the Queen of the Cowboys.

Before a month was past the herds wore the grass down in one great swath from Doan's Crossing of the Red River north to the Arkansas and the new Western or Dodge City Trail was established, with dust hanging over it like dry smoke along the sky. Most of Dodge and many hundreds drawn there by the beef bonanza were as excited as with any gold strike up around Deadwood Gulch. They saw Dodge as the new metropolis of the West. To them this was not to be a boom but permanent.

A few tried to stay calm—men like Robert Wright, who had hunted the region long before the railroad came, and Mayor Hoover, who sold the early buffalo hunters their whisky back in 1872—ran it right into their tin cups from a barrel set on pegs driven into the prairie. Such men took a lot of codding and scoff for the four years since then, magnified to forty.

"Old-timers like Bob there always think yesterday's chickens was bigger than today's geese," a homesteader just north of town said, perhaps because he hoped to sell his place for building lots in an expanding city.

But Wright knew the wealth of those buffalo years, with their vast spread of hide outfits, so recently working the region from the Republican River up at the Nebraska line down to Double Mountain and along the cap rock to

the Concho, where a scattering were still out. He knew about
the traders and their bull trains of goods following the
herds, the long strings of wagons racked high as great hay-
loads, hauling in the dried hides, the millions of dollars
harvested each season—all with almost no investment, very
little risk. Still, there was no denying that the cowboy's
sweat and dust were sweet as prairie roses compared to the
stink of the buffalo skinners. There had been stink, too, in
the drying hides staked down all over the prairie around
Dodge like great faded leaves around a giant tree, say a
catalpa, like dead leaves dark-edged and stiff, pressed close
to the earth by the coming winter.

The cowboys usually had all their trail wages when
they struck town, perhaps two, three months, or half a year
and longer if the herd owner was short of cash until he sold
the stock. Generally they never wallowed in the velvet long,
perhaps only one lurid night. So Dodge clasped them grate-
fully to her maturing bosom and consented to be their
queen. Her youth had been gaudy, with liquor, gun fights,
and the fast-growing Boot Hill Cemetery that was started
in the wild clashes of the track layers, the troops from the
post and the first hide men. There was even a time, back in
1873, when many believed that Dodge City had been ordered burned to the ground. The quiet, inoffensive Negro
servant of Major Dodge, commander out at the fort, had
been killed by members of the vigilantes, who were, the
army men complained, an outlaw gang running a hell hole
of a town. But although the troopers came, the torch was
never set to the tinder-dry shacks of Dodge. The town was
left to face the collapse of her great boom and the hope of
a bonanza in beef, perhaps not quite so profitable in hard
cash but certainly drawing a lot of fancy, overadvertised gunmen.
Not until last year, 1875, when the hide men and
their gun-packing hangers-on were mostly gone, did the law-
and-order faction of the town, the mayor and his supporters,

pass an ordinance against carrying concealed weapons. Now, as then, they were opposed by the other saloonkeepers, the gamblers, and dance-hall owners, and particularly by the merchants made wealthy by the once apparently inexhaustible buffalo. Now luck was bringing the dusty strings of Longhorns bawling over the south table. It wouldn't be like the hide days but they planned to make the most of the new opportunity, not let a few do-gooders annoy the cattle kings, their trail hands, or the buyers. There were shipping points all the way from Dodge west to the mountains ready to grab any trade driven out here. The railroad, too, favored a wide-open town. It brought business and visitors, easterners and foreigners, come to see, to feel part of a wild and romantic west. Large hunting parties with eyes beyond the buffalo and antelope were particularly welcomed, men traveling in private cars, with money to invest in railroad lands, even railroad stock.

Mayor Hoover, prominent saloonkeeper of Dodge, brought in a gun slinger to keep the cowboys in order. They ran him out. Next the mayor hired Wyatt Earp, one of the many gunmen of the West who did their killing not for fun or personal reasons but for pay, shooting on whichever side paid the best. Earp had a hand-picked force, including the Mastersons, of whom young Bat, well known for courage and marksmanship since the fight at Adobe Walls, was a talented and tireless gambler. It seemed he had been wounded in a shooting scrape over a woman down in Sweetwater, Texas, but was recovered.

Earp and his men wasted no time trying to quiet Dodge, but did aim to keep most of the noise and the shooting south of the Dead Line, drawn, as usual, at the railroad tracks. On the north side gun toting could bring arrest or even a shooting at sight, although Earp and his force took more satisfaction in buffaloing the ordinary cowboy, pistol-whipping him across the side of the head and then dragging him off to jail for the $2.50 bonus per arrest. They managed around 300 arrests a month, and split between $700 and $800 on top of their wages. This buffaloing galled the Texans particularly, and from damnyankees at that. They considered anything short of a bullet in an encounter fit only for Negroes and poor whites and did a little plotting to get even in what they considered a manly way.

Some said it was news of this that pushed young Bat Masterson to head for Deadwood Gulch, talking gold. But although he left Dodge in July and got as far as Cheyenne, the big outfitting station for the Black Hills, it seems he found such good pickings at the gaming table there that he stayed. Wyatt Earp left Dodge, too. In September he and his brother were headed for the gold fields by wagon, perhaps because the cattle season was about over, and the gambling with it. Trailers coming back from the north said the Earps had urged Bat Masterson to return to Dodge and run for county sheriff. There would be more Texans up to buck the tiger next year, pure profit on top of what Bat could rake in as sheriff.

A lot of cattle had come into the Dodge region during the summer of 1876 but what was called the season's largest single drive of Longhorns wasn't marketed there but crossed near the town and went on north. Richard King had gathered up 30,000 head from his coastal ranges and divided them into twelve herds, each with a crew of fifteen good men, fairly well paid: the trail boss at $100 a month, the cowboys $25, and the cook $30. The first herd, around 2,300 head, reached the Ellis, Kansas, region at the K.P. in early June and was pushed on to the hungry Indians at Red Cloud Agency in northwest Nebraska. By mid-June thousands of King's stock grazed along the Smoky Hill River, with several herds already well up toward the Nebraska cow town of Ogallala.

Although King avoided the thickly settled regions, there was loud complaint about these "through" herds directly from the depths of the fever-bearing regions. Northern stock began to sicken all along the route. Even lone milk cows that happened to cross King's trail died, and traders at the agencies and the army posts up North lost their stock, even those they hurried off into the White River breaks or the Pine Ridge. Angry letters were fired to the state governors and petitions were circulated for wider quarantine areas and better enforcement from the Red River to Montana.

By now even north Texans were turning dark faces southward. They rode long distances to plan resistance not only to rustlers and the *comancheros* but also for a stand against the coastal herds that carried the killing fever to the stock of north Texas.

By the end of the 1876 season the prairie that had been so deep and golden in cured winter range last year was bare as a mangy coyote's rump for eighty, a hundred miles around Dodge, even most of the cow chips on the bed grounds tromped to dust. Here and there the looser knobs and hills were blowing curls of sand across the darker ground, to lie like thin drifts of yellowish snow. Thirty thousand cattle had been shipped East from Dodge out of the 322,000 reported into west Kansas. Even though this number did not approach the Abilene region, with its 600,-000 cattle in seventy-one, or the 405,000 to Wichita and Ellsworth in seventy-three, it was a vast increase over the two years since. Besides, many herds went up through Colorado, some to feed the booming gold camps of the Black Hills. Usually they were stopped by the reservation Sioux who still claimed the Hills, but although the swooping warriors were threatening in their paint and feathers, there was usually nothing that a couple of Longhorns cut out for the hungry Indians wouldn't settle, perhaps worn-out, footsore, trail-gaunted steers tough as rawhide for the Sioux whose teeth had bitten into fat young hump rib of buffalo only a few months ago.

The real danger up around the Hills was the loss of the trail hands. Sometimes even men of long experience swapped their saddles and gear for a pick and a gold pan.

"You can't get them to dig a shovel of dirt even for a branding fire but up here they'll prairie-dog it all day into hard rock," an angry cattleman snorted as he gnawed off a fresh chew and put the plug away in his back pocket, in its saddle-worn place.

Many herds went on government contracts to the northern Indians, all on reservations now except the last remnant out with Crazy Horse and Sitting Bull in the Yellowstone country. In addition many herds of young steers or she-stuff went to northern ranches, some pushing well beyond the Platte, many deep in Wyoming, poised for a run into the Yellowstone country as soon as the troops cleaned the Indians out. Instead, Custer's foolish ambition gave the Indians their great victory.

Business in the cattle trail towns was strictly seasonal, the winter months quiet as in a hibernating dog town. Dodge was very different now from the days when the hide men came in after a couple of good fall months with thousands of dollars dragging heavy at their greasy pockets. But not all the town slept. Invitations were sent all around Texas and the Southwest, promising a good cattle market next summer and a fine welcome, with some traveling shows and play-acting brought in, even a prize fight, and everything running wide open.

Each year the gap between the Texans and the Yankees had narrowed a little, at least during the quiet times of winter. Last summer the Yankees on the streets were outnumbered many times by the southerners, the "damned Texans," or "the goddamn Johnny Rebs," although they were the men bringing in the business. Now there was the public fury over the election steal, but the North was the only market for beef, with money tighter than dried rawhide, unemployment growing, more railroad wage cuts coming, bringing threats of strikes that might spread westward, knock out the shipping points.

But the cattle had to be sold, if possible, and some

steer herds were started up the new Western Trail to beat the glutted market, gathered before they could put an ounce of spring meat on their narrow ribs. Perhaps not realizing how fast settlement was moving westward Powers, Bulkley and Company angled one of their herds off east ward from the barren trail into the quarantine region of south Kansas. The grangers swarmed upon them like angry bumblebees and only after a heavy fine and damages for haystacks and crops barely planted could they move on.

Very little grass was left to start around Dodge this spring, after the overgrazing and the sharp hoofs of last summer. But every green spear that pushed through the ground was cropped off at sight. The quarantine line, the homesteaders, and the range claimants had pushed in .to a line running just east of the Dodge town limits, with many settlers along the river westward, too, crowding into the newly established ranches. The stretches of open prairie were so limited now that the campfires were like some low-lying red-starred Milky Way in the haze of night. One June day 25,000 cattle changed hands and with so many cowboys taking their turns on the town there was a great deal of noise and dust and galloping of horses, and some popping of pistols, particularly when the crews started back to camp.

But most of the trouble rose from conflicts and ambitions among the local men or those tied in with them. Robert Gilmore, or Bobby Gill, as Dodge knew him, the brother-in-law of Billy Thompson, was up to see about Billy's defense in the shooting of Sheriff Whitney over at Ellsworth. While in Dodge and pretty drunk he made a few remarks about law enforcement. According to the Dodge City *Times* Marshal Deger grabbed him and headed him toward the cooler, kicking him along as he went. Bat Masterson, from the sheriff's office, was not fond of Deger anyway, even before he entered the race for county sheriff against him. He ran up and got an elbow clamped across the marshal's throat like a cowboy mugging a calf. In the kicking and cursing, Bobby Gill broke loose, but Deger's assistant jerked Bat's gun from his holster and put it on him to let the marshal go.

Some Texans stood around to watch. They weren't fond of Deger either but many had lost money to Bat and didn't realize that he was a friend of the Thompsons, and so of Gill, up to get Billy Thompson turned loose. They just pushed their hats back and grinned their enjoyment, not mixing in, not even when Deger whipped his gun over Bat's head until the blood flew. Some of them had been buffaloed that way last summer by Earp and the Mastersons. Now it was amusing to see it going the other way.

In the meantime Ed Masterson, assistant to Deger, did his duty and arrested Bobby Gill for disturbing the peace. Bat was fined $25, Bobby $5 and costs.

Although it was all a mix-up the Deger side strutted a little. This fining ought to lose Bat his job as deputy sheriff and take him off the ballot for sheriff. Instead, Bat bought into the Lone Star Dance Hall, a hangout for the last remnant of shaggy buffalo hunters and some of the wilder Texas cowboys that Deger was always hazing. This made Bat a bona fide citizen, a property owner, and added to his sudden reputation for sympathy with the poor drunken celebrants. Often now he had four, five of them laid out sleeping it off and cheating Deger out of the arresting fee. This was a different man from the one who collected bounty for arrests last year. Truly Dodge City seemed to change a man.

Before this the long-rumored prize fight was finally staged. Due to the opposition from the law-and-order factions and the thin-mouthed folks of the town it was staged in front of the Saratoga saloon just as the sun rose in slanting light across the prairie, the police off to bed, and the belles from below the tracks free to come out. Whitney, described as a noted fighter, was matched against Haley, the Red Bird of the South. Much of the town managed to be out to see the fight, or at least stand back at the fringe of the crowd and gather what was happening from the yells and curses.

The rest heard about it for days, or read the account in the papers. It seemed that about the forty-second round Red was plainly in pretty bad shape and by the sixty-fifth he had both ears practically chewed off, one eye broken, the other closed, one cheekbone crushed, seven teeth knocked out, his nose and jaw broken, a flap bitten from the side of his tongue, and generally bruised and battered up. It seemed that the Red Bird of the South was deserting the ring, disgusted with the fighting business.

It was a hot, flyblown summer around Dodge, with so many cattle close-packed, once nearly 100,000 head, the herds clustered like ants around a splattering of sorghum, the hungry stock kept separate only by constant herd riding, day and night, the cattle dropping flesh while the buyers haggled or weren't there at all. They were particularly scarce after the railroad strikes spread west, crippling some lines as far as Omaha and Kansas City and no telling where next, even with President Hayes calling out troops against the strikers, whom he called revolutionists, perhaps remembering how he got the presidency less than a year ago, with these same troops under Grant ready to back him against the man who was legally elected to the White House.

Talk of the troops fraternizing with the strikers brought rapid shifts and drastic action. By September the strike seemed broken. But there were still cattle waiting out at Dodge and cowboys, tired of the long delay, tore through the dusty town shooting up the place when perhaps they had no money to do anything else. Most of the officials frowned on this but the hanging signs, the false fronts of the stores kept drawing their bullets. Even the rain barrels along the street, filled long ago against the danger of fire in the drouth, burst into holes that spouted stale and stinking water.

Finally fall came and with it the end of the cowboy disturbances of 1877 and the golden hope of the season. Instead of surpassing the 322,000 cattle into the region last

year, only 201,159 head were reported, and this in spite of
the decision of the Supreme Court that found the Missouri
quarantine law against Texas cattle as such unconstitu-
tional. That meant that the Kansas blanket quarantines
were out, too, and local inspection posts had to be set up,
with veterinarians to inspect the stock for disease or suspected disease. Once more the good blooded stock of Kansas was in immediate danger. Not that the quarantine had
been stringently enforced. Still there were ways of keeping
ticky cattle out so long as men had guns and ropes and bull
whips and the chance of collecting damage for grass and
crops and gardens.

The buffalo hunters were all pretty well out of
work, and many trail drivers found $25 a month mighty
slow pay. These, in addition to the loose-end veterans, North
and South, and the newly unemployed, brought on a great
jump in horse stealing and cattle rustling. The thieves
seemed particularly drawn to the easy law and easy money
of places like Deadwood and Dodge City. Bat Masterson,
sheriff of Ford County now, and considerable unorganized
territory, too, was busy chasing these thieves, and successful
enough to increase his reputation as a dashing young man
and apprehender of outlaws, and for arrogance, too, particularly on the premises of other officers, and at the gambling
table.

Then, early in April 1878, Ed Masterson, Dodge
City's new marshal, was called out to quiet six cowboys having a noisy evening at the Lady Gay, south of the Dead Line.
The noisiest seemed to be Wagner, a cowboy hurt thrown
from a horse recently and not carrying his drinking whisky
very well. Masterson disarmed him and gave the gun to
Walker, his boss, to be checked with the bartender until
they headed for camp. Later the marshal saw Wagner on the
street but with his gun back in the holster. He tried to disarm the cowboy a second time and in the scuffle that brought
a crowd out the marshal got the pistol pushed into his belly

with a bullet. He staggered back, his hands clapped tight over a hole big as a fist. Bat and some others came running up, firing. Wagner and his boss were both hit and managed to get away in different directions while Ed Masterson drew himself up and with his clothing asmolder from the close shot, blood streaming over his boots, he walked stiff and wooden through the crowd of dark-faced Texans parting for him. It seemed he must go down every step he took, but he reached Hoover's saloon and fell inside the swinging doors. He died a little later, up in his brother Bat's room, but before anything could be done Wagner was dead, too, and although his boss was recovering it would be a long, long time before he was in the saddle again.

Bat buried his brother out at the fort because Dodge City had no respectable burial ground for man. The news item about this was used to advertise the healthy climate of this mecca of the cow. Here lead poisoning was the only fatal disease of man, and only those who lived in the midst of violence were susceptible. The *Ford County Globe* carried a eulogy of the dead marshal, with a short verse, a rhyming verse. Perhaps culture was coming to Dodge, or at least something resembling its shadow seemed to be sidling up.

This summer the Comique opened with Eddie Foy's troupe as one of its chief attractions. After a harsh difference with Bat Masterson, Foy was drawn to him, even when Bat's friend, Ben Thompson, fairly drunk, pushed backstage and, wanting to shoot out the kerosene lamp, ordered Eddie to get his goddamn head out of the way. It was a boisterous time and left Foy with enough experiences to relate and write about the rest of a natural life.

It was while Foy was in town that, as some told it, the attempt was made to collect the $1,000 bounty the Texans supposedly put on Wyatt Earp's head. Others told a different story, saying it didn't have anything to do with Earp until he pulled his gun. Several cowboys, they said, were doing a little of the usual celebrating, not aiming at anyone, just firing into the air. Earp and Bat Masterson wounded one of them, George Hoyt, who died later from the amputation of a shattered limb.

A much more exciting story was told of the incident by the Earp sympathizers and those with an eye to a good story. They said that Wyatt had stopped outside of the Comique to look around the night and listen to the singing and square dancing inside when the cowboy Hoyt rode by. He saw Earp, turned, and came back at a dead run, firing three shots from his .45 at the officer. The bullets tore through the thin wall beside Earp, across the stage, and into the boards on the far side. Foy was calling the sets, but at the first shot he dove for shelter while the girls new to Dodge screamed and had to be pulled down to the floor by the dropping cowboys. Outside, the firing picked up, windows came crashing in, bullets whistled. Hoyt had missed, shooting from the running, plunging horse, and Earp missed, too.

By then others were joining in on both sides, the gun blasts like exploding fireworks in the night. As the cowboy spurred away south, Earp dropped down to catch him against the sky and took careful aim. On the bridge the horse's hoofs slowed and a body thumped to the planks. The dying man was captured, and turned out to be one of the 4,000 on the Wanted List the Texans were said to have put out earlier in the year, with substantial rewards on their heads. Before he died, Hoyt claimed some of the cattlemen had promised to take care of the Texas warrant out for him if he got rid of Earp.

So Hoyt was dead and some of the Dodge citizens had their own stories of what happened, and their own notions on the entire situation. Either way Earp shot a man. Before long Clay Allison, a well-known and often troublesome rancher from the Cimarron, hit town. It seems he came to protest the shooting of Hoyt, an acquaintance, a friend. Afterward there were stories about this, too, stories that Allison hunted up Bat Masterson for an explanation. Seeing that the rancher had been drinking, Bat decided to wait until he sobered up. Whatever happened, on August 6 the *Dodge City Times* mentioned that Clay Allison came to town the past week and on August 30 that Bat Masterson had departed for Hot Springs, Arkansas, for medical treatment and rest.

The items were generally cited to prove that Allison really had made Bat Masterson hunt his hole. Some said the rancher had come to town with twenty-five cowboys, rifle-armed, ready for real trouble, and went through one saloon after another looking for the town policeman or the marshal to wipe them off the face of the earth as Hoyt had been wiped out.

Whatever the facts, nobody got hurt, but neither Bat nor Wyatt Earp spent much time around Dodge afterward.

By the first of September there was more serious trouble on the wind for Dodge City. Rumors had been flying most of the summer that Indians were jumping the reservations to the south and denied, confirmed, and denied again. Then, finally, a cowboy came spurring into Dodge, his lathered horse lurching down at the hitching rack, the man without his hat, his gun out, his eyes wild, yelling, "Indians! Indians hitting straight for Dodge!"

Men jumped for their horses, came running out with rifles and scabbards, stuffing extra cartridges into the saddlebags, perhaps gulped down a last slug at the bar, and were gone, too, for the bridge or the shallow river. A couple of old Indian scouts moseyed out to see what was going on, laughing aloud when they found out where the cowboy thought he had seen the Indians.

"They was looking right over the hill at me. I seen them warbonnets a-waving!"

The old scouts went back into the saloon out of the hot sun that shimmered the heat plain around Dodge. "Them Indians down there don't go wearin' their warbonnets out scoutin'," one said.

"Sure you ain't working with them Indians, maybe planning to sack the town?" someone asked. "You been pretty friendly with some of them."

"Oh, I·laid out with a squaw couple years back but a man don't need to be accused of goin' against his own kind just for that. I know them wasn't Indians, warbonnets or no, if that greenhorn seen 'em spyin'."

The first heat for scalp taking cooled when it turned out to be a thirty-mile ride in the sun and dust, but several did start out, while others got the news spread around the saloons, dance halls, the grocery stores, and to a couple of the preachers. There was a little debate about telegraphing the fort, and somebody finally did, although there was a growing contempt for any fighting the army wanted to do. "Ain't never come out for any a them earlier rumors," one of the loafers said, to nobody in particular.

Turned out all that the cowboy had seen was a couple of stray soapweeds along a ridge. So he went back down the trail as he had started, with the name of Indian Bill hung to him for life.·

Although the cowboy didn't know it, the Indians were out, hurrying north, around 290 Northern Cheyennes, mostly afoot and sick and dying, hoping to escape the starvation and fevers to which they had been brought from their healthy hunting grounds in the Yellowstone and Powder River country. The Cheyennes were determined to take their people back before all died but insisted they were going peacefully. Mounted troops easily overtook the long string of worn and footsore women and children, with only around eighty males along, counting boys and very old men, and few arms beyond the hastily made bows. So the Indians had to outwit the troops sent to drive them back, or leave them dead. They made one night escape after another. But some of them were shot, including children. Angered and desperate for horses to get the sick and wounded away fast, and for guns, the young warriors did some raiding along south Kansas. Scare headlines flashed over all the telegraph lines, in all the papers, on every rumoring wind. Hundreds of whites were killed, a whole trail herd captured, the Kansas border aflame. Turned out the only flaming was a house near Dodge and not an Indian up that far yet. The trail herd came in unaware that an Indian had jumped the reservation. Most of the whites supposedly killed turned up, too, some without knowing they had been missing. But some were killed, and some dead were plainly from white-man guns, somebody getting rid of an enemy or two while the Indians were around to be blamed.

The cattle season was about over and Dodge had time to get stirred up like Longhorns before a tornado. The town would surely be burned to the ground, women ravished, men tortured, children get their heads bashed in or dragged off to captivity. And as the alarm grew, thirst quickened and the saloons gathered in the business. Nobody seemed to remember that Dodge was supposed to have the finest collection of gunmen in the nation, well armed and equipped against any handful of sick and ragged Indians. Telegrams went to the governor's office demanding at least 100 stands of guns, with appropriate ammunition, although the governor replied with a little understandable sarcasm.

The Indians kept eluding the troops as they neared Dodge and so a big party of local citizens, cowboys, and others honing to fight Indians went out, with much big talk and many promises to show the troops how to catch Indians. They rode away in high spirits, well supplied with ammunition and drinking liquor. A Texan who had been with a civilian outfit trying to catch Comanches last summer along the breaks of the Staked Plains watched them go with curling, sun-cracked lips.

"I can see them, getting up too close, and then when the Indians begin to pop sand in their eyes, those civilians will break for home. Takes rawhide troops to stand against yelling Indians, sneaking up through the grass."

He was right about the break for home. The next

day the Dodge City expedition against the Cheyennes came whipping back, their horses dropping in their tracks, some believing that the Indians were whooping at their tails. Instead, they were slipping around Dodge as quietly as possible, to cross the Arkansas up the river and head away north, the darkness undisturbed by anyone, cowboy, Dodge Indian fighter, or federal trooper.

Most of the earlier men dedicated to the cow brought their herds of selected steers to Dodge for shipment now, or through the region on their way to Ogallala, and perhaps some lesser stock to fill government contracts, or young stuff for the northern ranches. Such men as the Slaughters, Snyders, Blockers, Reynolds, Milletts, and King followed the pattern in a general sort of way. Mifflin Kenedy, the Pennsylvania Quaker who was behind King's move to Texas long ago, and his ranch partner for a while, was now running cattle up farther in Texas. His son James, called Spike, had brought his father's herd to Dodge earlier in the summer and hung around in some mighty un-Quakerish spots. As every cowman knew, the get, the calf, didn't always resemble the sire much. Young Kenedy was in trouble most of the time for carrying a pistol or perhaps disorderly conduct. He even got into a rough-and-tumble fight with the mayor called Hound Dog Kelley perhaps because he ran a pack of hounds. The Texans had another explanation for the nickname. "Just naturally looks like a hound dog caught in a smokehouse or a chicken run—looking whipped, and that hair hanging down like lop ears."

"Naw, looks more like a dog that's just been whipped back by an old boar coon come fallin' out of a persimmon tree."

But Hound Dog Kelley had been an old army sergeant and was a mean man in a waller fight, good enough to put down the hotheaded young Spike Kenedy, who was contemptuous of physical encounter anyway. Helpless, naked without his gun, Spike brooded around Dodge awhile but along in October he vanished. Not long afterward four pistol shots were fired into one of the little shacks behind Hound Dog's saloon, the one where he usually slept. Hoofbeats were heading off north by the time Wyatt Earp and a policeman hurried in to investigate. The mayor was away sick at the hospital in Fort Dodge but two dance-hall girls had rented the house. One was not hurt but the other, Dora Hand, a singer at the Comique, the Queen of the Fairy Belles, had been killed instantly.

Spike Kenedy was suspected. Although out of town some time, he had been seen back just before the shooting. Nobody started after him until late the next afternoon. The delay proved wise or lucky. Apparently the killer had fled north, but Sheriff Bat Masterson knew where the Kenedy ranch was and started down that way with the town marshal and assistants, including Earp. Kenedy came up on them from the north and was ordered to throw up his hands. Outnumbered, he set spur to his fast horse, but one of the bullets hit him in the shoulder and another brought down the horse, pinning the rider.

Because the officers were after him, Spike assumed he had killed the mayor. He couldn't believe that it was the Queen of the Comique that he got instead.

Mifflin Kenedy hurried to Dodge and got three doctors to work saving his son's life. Sober, with the resolution and courage of his ancestry, and a boyhood among the wild Longhorns, Spike faced the removal of a piece of shattered bone in his right arm. After a long illness he was acquitted for lack of evidence and went home with the father. Later Dodge heard that Spike learned to shoot well enough with his left hand to kill a man face to face, and ended the same way, with a gun in his good hand, as befitted a Texan if not a Quaker.

There had been outbreaks of Texas fever up as far as Dakota Territory and with settlers and better cattle pushing into west Kansas a petition demanding the exclusion of all through Texas cattle brought legislative action, backed by Wright, one of the fathers of Dodge. Not even the very hard winter made the cattlemen forget the fever and early in 1879 the quarantine line was moved up to the east edge of the town's stockyards, and from there east along the river to the county line and south to Indian Territory.

The Texans were furious, some still certain that their fine, healthy cattle could not possibly spread disease. It was the inferior northern stock and range. Some of the businessmen of Dodge hurriedly planned special attractions to hold the cattle trade next summer. A cowboy band was sent all around the Southwest while at home there was worry over the Murphy Movement for Temperance. Some tried to treat this as a joke in the face of much talk for an ordinance that would close the saloons all day Sundays.

"Bound to drive us to church," one of the local followers of Bob Ingersoll complained.

"Hell, nobody's been burnt yet. You ain't seen the law against gambling and whore houses enforced, have you?"

But with so many herds already passing Dodge, they had to be cautious, particularly after another saloon killing. Usually those battles were little except a lot of lead that sent mirrors, bottles, and glass crashing, but hurt very few. Then in a fight over a woman at the Long Branch Saloon, Cock-Eyed Frank Loving, a young gambler and apparently no relative of the Lovings of Texas, exchanged shots with Richardson, a freighter with a reputation as a bad man. They started in so close that their pistols almost touched, the crowd jumping back and taking to the floor. Bullets flew, ten, eleven at least, as Richardson chased Cock-Eye around the stove and finally fell mortally wounded, still firing. Loving was barely scratched although it was Richardson who claimed several dead men to his credit and had taken to fanning his gun lately. Cock-Eyed Frank, mild and quiet, had apparently never killed a man before, just wore his gun for show.

Yet in spite of this little outbreak, Dodge had tamed down, although she still refused to honor the dry law of Kansas. With the loose money shrinking, Sheriff Bat Masterson, defeated for re-election, left the town for the Colorado mining camps. Earp was already headed for Tombstone, with Bat to join him there some time later. Other gamblers and would-be gamblers were leaving, too, some to Deadwood or Ogallala, the new queen of the cow towns. Billy Thompson was still working with trail herds and managed to stop five bullets up at Ogallala. Ben heard that a posse of citizens was waiting to hang his brother as soon as he got off the flat of his back. Outlawed up there, Ben asked Masterson to shag up that way and get Billy. Bat went and smuggled the wounded man out to Cody's place at North Platte in a wagon and finally down into Kansas.

Next year Bat was back at Dodge but only to put his gun on the side of his brother. The fight started because Jim Masterson put the run on a bartender that his partner, Peacock, wanted to keep. Bat came shooting as he hit town and got lead back. Wild bullets crashed into a drugstore, the Long Branch Saloon, Hoover's liquor store, and the corner of the town jail. Unfortunately one bullet did go through the lungs of the bartender who was the cause of the fight, and for this Bat was fined $8. Many local people were furious that Bat, an outsider now, should come in with his gun strapped down. Neighboring towns were caustic, too, but about the justice handed out. "It costs $8 to shoot a man through the lung in Dodge City—"

To the relief of many Bat took his brother to New Mexico with him, leaving the town mighty quiet. The railroad had reached down to Caldwell, over east and south of Dodge, deep in the quarantine region, but so close to Indian Territory that the ban was easily ignored. Within a few months Caldwell became the Border Queen and, with neighboring Hunnewell, brought a new movement of cattle up the grassed-over Chisholm Trail. Many of the good herds

from central and north Texas took this shorter route, risking
the quarantine to pull in a little of the rising prices, probably ready to fall before a good run of stock.

The cattlemen who turned to Caldwell knew that
these outlets, all of them were very temporary, a little like
the grab a tenderfoot on a mean horse makes at the apple.
Southern ranchers threw their boiled shirts into their valises
and headed for Washington to talk up a permanent trail,
one safe from the harassment of settlers, grafting local
politicians, and prohibitive legislation. In 1883, with cattle
prices still up and blooded stock spreading, Shorthorn
breeders of west Kansas were fondling the ears of their fat,
chunky calves. So the quarantine line was pushed out still
farther, far beyond Dodge, leaving only a narrow strip up
the Kansas-Colorado line open to trail herds. True, stock
still reached Dodge but the enforcement might come any
moment. Besides, many cattlemen scorned the petty officials
who let the quarantine be evaded for a price, and despised
themselves as bribe givers. They looked toward the new
National Stock Growers Association and the convention
planned for the fall of 1884 at St. Louis to consider permanently improved beef prices, lower freight rates, and
better packing-house practices. The chief interest of the
Texans, however, would be a National Trail of some sort.
Richard King had long believed in a trail bought and paid
for, but he knew that was hopeless. Early in 1884 his trail
boss struck the Dodge region with a big herd and added
another to travel close, making 5,600 head for the long pull
to Montana. Even with King's fine large crews, this was too
many cattle together in a possible hailstorm or tornado. But
the prices for northern-grazed stock were very good and King
ran in notorious luck.

He also ran in notorious cheek and brass, bringing
such herds from the fever coast into the quarantine region
where fortunes in blooded stock fed on the prairie.

Down in the Cherokee Strip the trails were closed
with barbed-wire fence and although the cattlemen got

troops from the War Department to cut the fences, they could do nothing about the fever quarantine. In addition, this year there was foot-and-mouth disease, with the government men out killing the infected cattle. Then the trail drivers pushing north beyond Dodge City found plowed furrows laying out a strip varying from half a mile to six stretched from the river to the Nebraska line, with a fine of $500 for crossing outside the furrows.

Range was getting mighty scarce up north, too, many saying that they had more cattle than they could handle if the state legislatures pushed through the Herd Law they threatened. That would mean keeping range cattle off the settler's unfenced grass and crops or pay damages. The presidential election coming up added another uncertainty up north. Although the Republicans talked optimistic, some recalled 1876 and were not certain they could throw out enough southern votes this year to win.

Dodge City, with the breaker bottom and the backset plow, had produced 75,000 bushels of wheat in the region and seemed very tame, particularly after the news that four men accused of robbery had been dragged out down at Medicine Lodge and left hanging in a neat row. Apparently the best Dodge could do now was an occasional spite range fire and a hard winter, nothing to compete for even the tenderfoot. The businessmen, however weren't giving up. They planned the biggest crowd roundup of all time. Their saloons were still running, but under pending action to close them, troublesome yet perhaps a little cheaper than the licenses they paid in legal days. Hoping they could stay open a while longer, former Mayor Webster raised $10,000 for a two-day bullfight the Fourth of July. The newspapers all over the nation picked it up, spread it out with big stories of the sins of Dodge as though these were still true. Moore, a Scottish attorney at Paso del Norte, Mexico, was hired to find matadors and to sell the idea that the fight was not brutal and bloody as many thought it, but to make it somehow even more exciting. The men would use no weapons ex-

cept the small darts and the skill and dexterity with which
man can evade the angry bull, making it sound very hazard-
ous and bloody.

For this "First genuine bullfight on American soil,"
meaning since it was part of the United States, Doc Barton
was chosen to pick the bulls. He knew the region since as a
soft-bearded young man he drove the first beef herd up to
Dodge in 1872. By the end of June he had twelve bulls in
the hastily built arena, out at the fairgrounds, all adequately
ugly, pawing at any approach and charging against the corral walls so the planks bent and the braces outside cracked
and buckled. People gathered to look, a few women with
parasols, but even the men keeping well back, codding Doc
and his cowboys a little.

"Going to give the bulls a few of those toadstickers,
too?" someone asked, the watchers laughing, already against
the Mexican fighters coming in, aliens, opposing fellow
citizens.

Much money was staked on the animals, with the
customary drinks all around. Once more Dodge found the
horned ruminant her mainstay as she had from the start:
the buffalo, the ox of the freighters, the Longhorn, the growing importance of the Shorthorn, and now the bull of the
arena. Posters went up everywhere, mostly of the fighters in
their fancied outfits, slapped on walls and building fronts. A
few wanted pictures of a big red Longhorn range sire somewhere, but that brought up the Bull's Head at Abilene and
the killings that caused. Too many church members here
now anyway, and no colorful characters like those of Abilene
around, no Wild Bill Hickok left, not even a Phil Coe.

The local newspaper ran stories of Mexican bullfighters, their fierceness and polished courage, their narrow
escapes, so narrow that all the men were badly wounded
many times. They all expected to die in the arena, yet they
were temperate men; none drank strong liquor and all had
regular occupations. Captain Gallardo, the chief of the matadors, was a tailor in Chihuahua but the most famous bull-

fighter of Mexico, nevertheless. Many southern cattlemen sent word they had seen him kill bulls at Paso del Norte. His two-edged Toledo blades were three feet long; one was one hundred and fifty years old, the blade of his great-grandfather, a famous bullfighter of Spain. The other four men were an inspector of public works, his artist son, and two musicians.

Visitors piled into Dodge. The railroad brought carloads of them from the east to crowd the hotels and the Pullmans and empty boxcars set off on sidings. Ranchers and even some settlers camped out on the old hide-staking, cattle-tromped bottoms, with covered wagons, tents, or merely bedrolls dropped beside the saddle, for even now petty thievery had not come to Dodge. Horse thieves, cattle rustlers, highwaymen, murderers, these were plentiful, but only settled civilization brought the petty thief, the need for locks.

Cowboys came, too, only around 500, but in white Stetsons, double-breasted flannel shirts, some in chaps, all handsomely booted and spurred, with money in the pocket. All morning of the Fourth side-lamped carriages, buggies, buckboards, and lumber wagons arrived, some with boards across the bed for seats, or perhaps a dozen children on the hay in the bottom. There were many, many horsebackers, and some men afoot, even a few women, all moving across the shimmering heat of the July prairie into Dodge.

The streets were jammed so no one could be found, few could move. The saloons boomed, gambling games ran full blast as they seldom did since the buffalo-hide days. Metropolitan correspondents came early. Some worked hard to revive the old colorful characters, real or imagined, writing of them as though they were still there. One even forgot that Wild Bill lay buried up at Deadwood for eight years and had him striding the night of Dodge, his cape thrown back to show the red-plaid lining. But there wasn't a gun anywhere except on the officers, not a shot boomed out without a swift trip to the cooler, no cannon cracker popped, and no cowboy spurred up and down the streets picking out the lights or lassoing, without partiality, the red-globed lamps down south of the tracks and the clear white one before the Methodist Church. The correspondents complained that the only profane language they heard was from an old woman in a Mother Hubbard. However, a couple of old dance-hall girls, of the Fairy Belles years ago, and hopeful before they hit town, really smoked up the air when they saw the handsome, high-busted, wasp-waisted young women imported for the entertainment at this great festival.

By now the American Society for the Prevention of Cruelty to Animals had appealed to the governor of Kansas and brought, for one bad hour, a rumor that the governor would surely stop the fight. The businessmen faced staggering losses and infuriated guests, including the cowboys, with no telling how many would suddenly sprout angry guns. Fortunately the messages and the letter to the governor met with some unaccountable delay.

But Dodge had her own dissenters. One minister prayed publicly that the town be spared this "stench in the nostrils of civilization" and worried some of the businessmen. But everything was wasted on Webster and his colleagues. It was said that the mayor received a telegram from the attorney general's office reminding him that bullfighting was against the law in the United States. He merely snorted "Hell, Dodge City ain't in the United States."

Finally the hour of the bullfight came, with no officials to stop it. The fairgrounds, forty acres along the bottoms between town and the river, had a race track and an amphitheater that seated around 4,000. A hundred-foot arena was laid out before the grandstand, the plank walls eight feet high, with eight screened escape slots for the bullfighters when pushed too hard, if it came to that, and two escape ladders. To the west was the bull corral with a chute leading into the arena, and an alleyway alongside wide enough for the horses to drag the dead bulls away.

So there was to be killing—

The seats were packed early, almost one third of the spectators women and children, the former of both kinds that Dodge afforded, with a deputy sheriff delegated to keep them separated. Somehow he managed, perhaps because he knew all the dance-hall girls and those who ran their own little business in shacks along the river. A wife or two did elbow her high-nosed way out because she had been seated too close to her husband's mistress. There was a little disturbance among the others, too, with a little hair pulling, but quickly settled, the section gay in plumed hats and fluttering laces.

Inside, opposite the leading citizens, were the cowboys and their girls, many taking the highest seats possible, with the most flamboyant companions possible. It was a gay, boisterous crowd, with joking cowmen calling to each other across the stretches of sweating spectators, their voices carrying well from long years of shouting against the wind, but lost in the growing noise of the cowboys and their roar "Bring on the bulls!"

The animals were herded in, the tips of their horns sawed off and rasped smooth, while a bullfighter in a red cape helped horsemen handle them.

Around two o'clock Webster and the promoter led the little parade of notables over the dusty, unshaded road from town, followed by Beeson's Cowboy Band, tootling and drumming fiercely, their instruments gleaming fire-hot in the bright Kansas sun. They heralded the colorful bullfighters on horses gleaming satin but soon dusty, too.

Finally the entry trumpet blew and the white-hosed bullfighters marched into the ring. Gallardo, with a green sash to set off his embroidered scarlet jacket and knee breeches and the red and gold of his cape, Rivas in yellow with red, and a white cape with horns. The other two were in red and blue, the picadors, dressed like any Mexican cowboy, rode behind them. So they marched around the arena, bowing to the officials and their ladies, the little queues under the cornered black hats bobbing, their dark faces unmoved by the hoots of the northern cowboys already too deep in celebration. Deliberately, gracefully, the bullfighters moved, their black pumps sending up little spurts of fine dust under their firm tread.

When the arena was empty, a second trumpet brought out a big, red, fierce-looking bull. As he leaped through the entrance the streamer-decorated banderillas were flung into his neck from both sides to sting and enrage him, send him charging at the outflung cape of Gallardo as he stepped out and began to play the fluttering red cloth, lead the bull to make lunges at him, luring him from his course by the live, fluttering cape, standing unmoving as the horns passed and struck at the unresisting folds that flapped over the bull's angry eyes while the crowd roared, although some who had seen the fighting of Spain waited.

The bull didn't have quite the forward set of horn of the old Castilian fighting blood brought to Texas long ago, or the force of shoulder. Besides, he was too long in the leg for the proper beauty and grace in this formal dance of the power of the bull against the feather lightness of the cape, symbolizing the bold spirit of man against the darkness, the evil.

"I think of it as a dance, not with evil—but with God," one man protested, an American, but in a crumpled white linen suit and an African explorer's hat. "A sort of wrestling with God—"

"God?—dragged in on such a killing?" a cowboy behind the man cut in as he would head an escaping cow back into the herd. "My father is a missionary and he would protest this as savage, brutal, and bloody."

The man in the white suit turned around to look the trail-gaunted youth over. "You are, perhaps, forgetting the symbolic partaking of the blood and the body of God?— pure cannibalistic survival, one way or another practiced in many religious rites," he said.

But before the cowboy could answer his neighbor

nudged his ribs, yelling, "Looks like the bull's put the run on 'im!"

It was true that the matador was fleeing for the nearest escape slot, the bull hard after him, kicking up dust, head down, right at the flying heels, the picador spurring in, another of the fighters running up with a challenging cape.

"There's where you need a good gun on you, and a fast draw," someone told the man in the white suit, leaning far forward past several spectators to say it.

Down in the arena the bull tried to butt into the narrow opening and then circled the ring, head up, eyes and ears alert, searching, and finally stood out in the center, nose up and flaring, tail switching, the banderillas flopping, their flags streaming as he pawed the earth, throwing showers of dust over his forequarters, with a roaring deep in his throat that was his challenge to a rival, to the enemy that his keen nose smelled all around him here.

Now each time Gallardo taunted the bull with his cape, the charge, the horns, came a little closer, still closer, until it seemed each time the horns passed the man's lean thigh that it must have been more than what it seemed, a caress, that the flesh must have been torn, and the stands whooped. But always the man stood unmoving, untouched.

When the matador finally slipped away again, the other three closed in. The dusty bull charged them, one after another, but no matter how swiftly and fiercely he lunged and wheeled, he could not catch them any more than the will-o'-the-wisps rising from the rotting bogs of the Arkansas. More and more darts were flung into his back, until the sticks and the fluttering streamers reached from horn to tail and drops of blood jumped down his dusty sides. The stands yelled for the kill, all except a few around the man in the white suit. Considering that the bull was fresh from a range herd, he fought hard and the matador worked with skill and agility enough, and with a deftness and courage particularly surprising in this new country, for wasn't such a spectacle more fitted to a dying era, the man in the white suit suggested.

At the end of half an hour the bull seemed tired and a cowboy was signaled in to rope him and drag him out. This stirred up the ranch hands who longed to have their kind of skill displayed, too, yelling, "Throw him, cowboy! Bust 'im flat!"

The roper tried but the bull was too strong to be pulled down and too tired and tamed to go against the rope hard enough to throw himself. Finally he had to be dragged out, bloody, dust-caked, the streamered darts shaking as the big animal pulled back until his wind was cut off. In the gate he charged the horse, grazing the unprotected ribs, and then broke back into the ring, to the whooping of his partisans, to be dragged out again.

Now the crowd kept up the roaring for a real fight to the finish, but the next bull fled the matador as his ancestors down on the Trinity once took to the brush at the sight of man. He ran frantically back and forth where he felt the gate must be, reaching his eager nose up and down, then trying to climb the plank wall and falling back, so with the hoots and the whistles of the Mexicans he was let out. The third bull had little more fight in him, and the fourth the same. But the fifth was the worst of all. In his desperate attempt to escape the thick and frightening smell of man, he got jammed into one of the escape slots, unable to go ahead or back out. A cowboy in the front row above him flapped his white hat in the bull's dusty, blinking face, then kicked him in the head with his spurred heel. Finally the bull got himself loose and fled to the cattle pen amid jeers and the piercing whistles and a tootling from the band.

Almost before he was gone the crowd was whooping for a return of the first bull. Because, contrary to the first publicity, it was later announced that Gallardo would kill the last bull of the day with his sword, the crowd wanted to see it done. So the red bull was turned back into the arena and the Toledo blade handed down to the matador with the little cape now, the muleta.

Everybody who knew anything about bullfighting realized Gallardo must incite the bull to charge again and again until the right moment for the death thrust came. The bull must run up on the sword held directly above his lowered attacking horns, the matador standing firm and unflinching for the thrust that would, it was hoped, kill the bull before he reached the man. Even those who knew nothing of this moment of chilling solemnity, this supreme moment, were suddenly quiet. The bull, angrier, fiercer now than ever, charged. Gallardo swept him past with the muleta across the blade. The great dusty red animal was much too large for the ring but he wheeled easily and charged again, his horns buried in the slipping folds of red cloth. Each time Gallardo drew him closer upon himself, closer and closer, and if the grace, the purity was not quite there, it was plain that the horns barely missed the man's thigh and a little above. Once more, not far from one of the escape places, the muleta went out and came back, this time in very close, unhurried. The bull plunged forward, to the cries of alarm as the matador seemed to stumble, then went down, to a great gasp of horror all around, some clapping their hands over their eyes to shut out the bull butting his great horns downward.

But Gallardo had thrown himself lengthwise between the horns as they rammed into the earth, and as the bull jerked back, he slid to safety behind the open wall with the movement of a snake.

The bull had brought blood from the thigh and, doubly infuriated now, he nearly tore the escape down to get at the man. Finally he backed off, but fiercely, tail switching a little, head up, bloodshot eyes rolling, poised as a panther.

Although his left thigh was grazed, the red of the trousers dark—streaked to the bloodied white hose, his clothing torn—Gallardo stepped out again, this time to try for the finish. The crowd roared for him now, even many of the cowboys as they stomped their boots and cheered his bow. The matador signaled the band to repeat the music for the kill. To its brassy beat he walked directly toward the bull, the muleta over the thin, shining steel out and aimed above where the lowered horns would be. But the bull did not come, and so Gallardo showed him the naked blade, carried it to him, and finally the animal charged but without the opening the fighter needed. The muleta swung into play and once more, twice more, the bull went past, but very close, drawn upon the man as the crowd held its breath, and then applauded. Again and again Gallardo made the approach and finally the bull came just right. The thin, swift steel pierced the vital spot at arm's length, blood gushing. The bull's momentum slowed, he stumbled, went to his knees and down almost upon his head, his horns striking the ground beside the steady, the impersonal black slippers of the fighter. He lay still, and the crowd, gone silent, burst into cheers now, in a cheering that rose up in a great spreading wave with even a few of the Mexicans crying their *"Ole! Ole!"* the people up, stamping and whooping until the rickety rows of seats threatened to collapse, and the mayor held up both hands for quiet, for a steadying.

Now the first day's bullfight at Dodge was done, the first on United States soil.

There seemed general satisfaction over the town that night. "The punishment, the tortures, and the cruelty were even less than that inflicted upon animals in the branding pen," the *Ford County Globe* reported. The night was a gaudy one and the next day the fighting was much as before, except that the kill of the last animal was a little more interesting, perhaps because many knew more of what to expect and gave the matador more encouragement to show what bullfighting meant. Some of the cattlemen from the Southwest had seen other, better fights. The man in the white linen suit, who turned out to be from the State Department with years of residence in the legation in Spain under Dan Sickles, kept silent. He was out to look after his British wife's ranch interests and wanted no trouble.

The bull that received the long Toledo blade the second day was dragged out onto the prairie and left for disposal and the crowd trailed back to town to wet their dry throats. When the owner went out for the hide, planning to tan it as a souvenir for his ranch wall, the animal was gone. Not stolen or dragged off somewhere, just gone. A few days later the bull was discovered back with his herd, apparently no worse for the experience of death in the arena.

This true story, or this windy as some who never saw the bull called it, gave Dodge intense satisfaction. The honor of the cattle country had been vindicated. But a death in town that night was a little more permanent. A cattleman from down around Goliad, Texas, was shot in a quarrel with a gambler. He and his partner had 6,000 cattle on the Dodge market and, some said, he had lost most of his share to a faro dealer. Angered, he called the dealer crooked and then was too slow on the draw. The gambler was hurried off to jail and a heavy guard set to hold off the dark knots of trail drivers gathering here and there, threatening a little lynching to end up the two-day celebration of the killing of the bulls.

Although only one of the bulls seemed to have died, the rancher from Goliad was dead, dead as Dodge, the cow town of the trails, was dead.

# DEEPENING DEDICATION

L ONG before the settlements and quarantines pushed the cattle trail beyond Dodge City some of the dedicated men felt compelled to pull up stakes once more. Not King down in south Texas. His moves were expansion of his range, improvement in the stock, and a firmer hand on what was already called King's Kingdom, not only a kingdom whose subjects and all their lives were irrevocably in the sovereign's palm but a kingdom with a railroad that would also be in his strong hand if Richard King had to build it himself. He planned to bring everything he needed, including markets, through his own ranch gates. But in the meantime his herds were going north—well-managed stock, sleek, fine, but from deep in the tick region, and wherever they walked it seemed that the grass turned to poison, so poisonous that even the emigrant's cow plodding at the tailboard of his wagon died from merely crossing the trail.

Up in Colorado the energetic Charlie Goodnight was getting mighty restless in his fine but limited canyon leading to the Arkansas. In 1869, two years after Oliver Loving died, he settled the trust he had maintained at the request of his friend, giving the family half of the $72,000, the profit from the joint herd. With Jim Loving, Goodnight took the whole sum down the Pecos in a wagon, his faithful Negro driving. So he got through the outlaw country of east New Mexico and past the Robbers' Roost that preyed on the old Santa Fe Trail and the ranchers coming into the cornering of Texas, New Mexico, and the literally lawless No Man's Land that had somehow escaped belonging to any of the adjoining divisions. Down in Texas Goodnight sold his share in the old joint herd with his half-brother. The news of these profits and that he was carrying the money spread fast and, fearing ambush if he went back up the Pecos, he slipped out horseback through Indian Territory and by railroad to Hays, and then overland to the upper Arkansas, a long way around any robber ambush but a safe one. Unfortunately he had to leave his sweetheart behind, as so many men did when they returned to their cows.

In spite of all the outlaws threatening the Goodnight Trail and the protests from his Colorado neighbors running northern, American, cattle, Charlie Goodnight kept trailing southern stock into the state, and to market. Sometimes he used the threat of buckshot and bullets to get his herd across the Arkansas. But this wasn't enough up near Denver, where settlers shot into his bedded herds at night and stampeded them, killing some. Still he kept on, and delivered the 25,000 to 30,000 head of cattle contracted to Iliff, up in the northeast corner of Colorado in the three-year period. It wasn't up to King's great herds of a few years later, but still, Goodnight was doing very well for the times, and making enemies, too. Some called him overbearing, and trimmed the term with lurid additions and suggested destinations. Others said he wasn't above filling out a herd with stolen stock, if it was handy. But the outlaws were the hottest against him. William Coe, with his Robbers' Roost gang of around forty, fifty thieves, gunmen and general cutthroats, had long threatened to kill Goodnight at sight. Although accounts of what happened varied, plainly something was done. The story that pleased the Roost's victims the most gave Penrose, commander at Fort Lyon, Colorado, the

credit. They said he marched out with a six-inch cannon
and blew the stone Roost to pieces after he captured
Coe. Anyway, a mob dragged Bill Coe out of the Pueblo
jail and strung him up. Goodnight helped capture several of
Coe's gang. Later he ran into some of the outfit hanging from
telegraph poles when he was bringing his new bride out
from Texas. Although Mary Goodnight had grown up in
the Cross Timbers, she was shocked at this wild country
and disturbed by the roughness it seemed her Charlie had
acquired during his years up among these Yankees. But
there was no easy road back to Texas and so he got her to
stay long enough to go up to his new ranch not far from
Pueblo. He worked hard to make a pleasant home for her,
had canals dug for irrigation, planted apple trees, and grew
corn until the railroad came through and broke the high
price.

Gradually Goodnight started trailing Texas Longhorns up to his ranch in the fall, when the fever danger was
past. There were storm losses, and drifting, sometimes as
far as southeast Kansas, but less difficulty with his neighbors.
He wintered the stock on a vast expanse of the public domain he called the Goodnight range. He bought some
blooded Shorthorn seed stock and worked with the Stock
Raisers Association to keep Texas, Mexican, and other inferior bulls off the Colorado range. He had also joined the
neighboring ranchers to organize a bank. Might as well put
the interest he was laying out into his own pocket, he said.
And make money off other people's needs and bad luck,
some added. But the panic of 1873 left Goodnight the in-
voluntary owner of a lot of Pueblo property barely worth the
taxes. With beef prices gone down a badger hole nobody
who could hang onto his cattle sold, overstocking the upper
Arkansas range, too. Then, as soon as beef prices climbed a
little, new ranchers moved in, and settlers. In 1875 Goodnight borrowed $30,000 at 18 per cent annually. That called
for fast increase, good calf crops, good growth and fattening, which meant new grass and spreading room, freedom

from the piggin string of regulation, government or association, and from rustlers and the pushing hoe men.

Early in the spring of 1876 Charlie Goodnight made a sort of treaty with the sheepmen and the few ranchers of the Texas Panhandle, bluntly announcing that he was moving in. He wouldn't touch the hundreds of miles watered by the Canadian River, rugged, with sheltered breaks for winter protection, and they were to keep off the headwaters of the Red River, out of all the colorful canyons of the Palo Duro cutting down from the Staked Plains. Here he would be 200 miles from a town or legal authority. He and the Mexican *pastores* would be the law, the public domain their domain, to rule absolutely.

Goodnight set a great herd on the trail, heading stock southward for the first time in his life. As the outfit neared Palo Duro, coming in across a flat tableland, Goodnight, far ahead, signaled the route from one rise after another to the heavy cook wagon rumbling over the prairie in the dust of the herd behind. Finally a bit of wind carried the man smell to the invisible canyon ahead and suddenly a far rumbling of a buffalo stampede shook the earth, and a long time afterward a mushroom of reddish dust rose from the Palo Duro. It climbed the 1,000 feet to the cap rock and the level of the plains, and the skies beyond, thinning out finally, almost like an Indian signal fire, far off.

The canyon opened before the feet of Goodnight's snorting horse, the earth falling away, a curving gash cut deep from the plain, with scattered brush and trees startlingly green against the reds and purples of the canyon walls, a narrow band of stream glistening far down, flowing through greenest slough grass, everything very clear with only a thin film of dust still in the air from the stampede down the canyon.

They took the cook wagon to pieces and packed it down the 700-foot wall on the back of mules, and the provisions the same way. The cowboys pushed the cattle in a bawling, zigzag string down the narrow buffalo trails and let them scatter along the creek to drink. Afterward they kept meeting straggling buffaloes that had to be scared off by putting bullets into the red dirt under their feet. Finally the men stirred up the main herd again, at least 10,000 head, and moved them so they would not excite the cattle, or toll some adventuresome ones away. Even after that a few young buffaloes still loafing on the steep paths that led out of the canyon, came plunging back down through the scrub cedar, and sent a couple of little black bears loping off to find better shelter while the tired cowboys roared with dust-hoarse laughter and hooted them on their way.

When the camp was well settled, Charlie Goodnight went back up the canyon until he came to the widening park he sought, where the broad bottoms were cut by a little side stream that started in a spring near the cap rock, far above. There he set his home ranch, the first within the bounds of the Staked Plains, set far up the Palo Duro canyon that drained into the Prairie Dog Town Fork. Together the streams cut a colorful stretch of canyons nearly sixty miles long and generally almost 1,000 feet deep, varying from a few hundred yards in width to extensive badlands fifteen miles across. Here was shelter from the blue northers that swept down the winter plains, with water and grass for thousands of cattle. The cedars, hackberry, cottonwood, and chinaberry trees had been fuel and shade for generations of Comanche camps. Goodnight had been told that as many as 10,000 even 12,000 Indian horses had grazed in the canyon. It was unexcelled as winter range, the high bluffs and cap rock fine storm protection and more effective fencing for animals than even the new barbed wire advertised so highly, with salesmen coming through the settlements like snake-oil peddlers showing their samples.

By the spring of 1877 times were a little better. That money Goodnight had borrowed was from John George Adair, of a New York brokerage firm. On a hunt to Kansas in 1875 the Irishman and his wife were so pleased with the open prairie that Adair moved his business to Denver. There he caught the cow fever, as infectious as any carried north by the walking herds. By the spring of 1877 he was in partnership with Goodnight and the two men were taking their wives to the canyon. Goodnight had loaded four great freight wagons with half a year's ranch supplies, got a light ambulance for the comfort of the ladies, bought 100 of the best Shorthorn bulls he could find in Colorado, and hired some cowboys to drive them along. The cowboys joked among themselves about starting a ranch with a bull herd and about the handsome Cornelia Adair starting the long trip south on a sidesaddle, yards of veil flying from her hat, whipping in the wind. But they underestimated both Goodnight as a rancher and the lady as a sidesaddler. Mrs. Adair was one kind of horsewoman these cowboys had never seen.

With Mary Goodnight driving the ambulance they reached the Canadian River and crossed its spring flood at the new little cow town of Tascosa, still mostly tents and hide shacks, but already very wild, with enough saloons, gambling dens, and prostitution for all the cattlemen, border outlaws, and *comancheros* of the Panhandle.

Once out of the broad, flat, sand-scarfed valley of the Canadian, the Goodnights were on the great unwatered plains. After two dusty, burning days without water the women were worn and drawn, the stocky, short-legged Shorthorn bulls wild with thirst. Goodnight knew he must strike ahead for a water hole he believed he could locate about ten miles out, leaving his wife to straw-boss the outfit and to follow the point on the horizon where he disappeared. But the cowboys, unaccustomed to mirages, took their first one for Indians, and circled the stock and the wagons and prepared for a siege. When evening was coming on, Goodnight backtracked as hard as his horse could go, uneasy that the others hadn't covered the ten miles long ago to the relief of the water hole. He found them barely a mile from where he left them in the morning.

Furious, he moved them out into their evening shadows, knowing he must get the blooded bulls to water or lose

the entire investment and, worse for a good cowman, watch
a critter die. But these were no rangy Longhorns to go three
days without water and make an eighty-mile march to the
Pecos. He took only one wagon, for supplies, leaving the
rest standing together, the horses unhooked and driven with
the bulls. It was a hard night push and the water hole
wasn't fresh but it was wet and apparently not dangerous,
judging from the antelope, rabbits, and buffaloes around it
at dawn, even a little herd of mustangs, almost as choosey as
stock horses about water. Goodnight rested his party here a
couple of days while the rest of the wagons were brought up.
By now the cowboys looked with admiration upon this city
wife of Adair, still cheerful, still sitting her sidesaddle in
heat and dust and wind, although the flying yards of veiling
had disappeared into her pocket.

They reached the vicinity of Palo Duro canyon just
ahead of an electric storm but the loud rumble was doubled
by the noise of a buffalo herd in rutting time, the bulls
roaring, running, and fighting. Suddenly the canyon lay before the weary party, the spotting of dark cedars along the
top, the walls red and rose and deep purple in the sun
slanting under the jutting blackness of the storm, and turning the rising dust golden off downstream where the buffaloes were. There were between 1,000 and 1,500 in the herd,
the canyon walls echoing with their noise and the rising
thunder of the storm. When they caught the smell of man
they broke into a gallop, tails up, sweeping this way and
that but not leaving the sheltered Palo Duro.

The rain moved in a curtain down the far bluffs, the
lightning glowing in a constant explosion of violet and rose,
cut by great branching bolts that reached for the earth,
the thunder crashing, shaking the ground so even the worn
wagon teams had to be held from breaking away in terror.
Occasional storm-set fires blazed for a bit in the cedars of
the canyon, for all the rain, until the pouring increased so
the water leapt down the walls in streams and the creek
boiled up over the bottoms. The storm's roar and thunder,

trapped in the canyon this first night, prepared even the Adairs for almost anything this raw and torn land could produce.

In a few days a trail four miles long was cut to get the wagons from the cap rock into the deep bottoms. A two-room log cabin was put up immediately. Here, despite the hard trip, John Adair signed a five-year agreement, he to furnish the capital, Goodnight the foundation herd, to manage the ranch at $2,500 a year and plan the expansion of the cattle under the JA brand and buy up 25,000 acres of land out of Adair's cash, all to be repaid with interest. At the end of five years the property was to be divided, one third to Goodnight, the rest to Adair.

Because the money the Irishman advanced now would buy only 12,000 acres from the Texas public lands, Goodnight hoped to get another 12,000 next year. To keep others out he bought the first allotment in a sort of crazy checkerboard, covering all the water and hay lands and the good building sites, leaving the dry range free and grazable only by his stock. The first purchase cost from twenty to thirty-five cents an acre. The largest purchase, the Tule ranch of 170,000, cost twenty cents an acre, but that was years later.

In 1878 Goodnight pointed his first beef herd north to market. He went late, with the fat of fall grass on their ribs. The Adairs returned to Denver or New York for the winters but Mary Goodnight stayed, patching the clothing, doctoring the sick and the hurt. For a long time the nearest woman neighbor was the wife of Bugbee, eighty miles to the north. The first women Mrs. Goodnight saw after the Adairs left were the Comanches of Quanah Parker's band.

Once more Charlie Goodnight had turned out a trail breaker, a ranger opener. By the fall of 1877 there were half-a-dozen other ranchers in his region of the Panhandle: Bates and Beals, Cresswell, Littlefield, Hays, the Reynolds, old-time cowmen pushed farther out by the settlements, and some others up around Tascosa. The troops at Fort Elliott represented such law as the Panhandle possessed. Near it was Sweetwater, the Hide Town of the remaining buffalo hunters. Later Mobeetie was established, and finally the much nearer colony of Clarendon, led by a Christian minister, a strange settlement for the wild Panhandle, a prohibition community named for a preacher's wife.

Goodnight bought cattle off the range and the trail to add to the herds at the Palo Duro. The serviceable cows were thrown into the main herd for calving, the inferior ones spayed, fattened, and trailed to fall market with the beef herds. He kept his blooded cattle separate in the upper reaches of the canyon, with the best bulls. Each year he culled out the inferior stock and threw it into the main, the common herd.

Other Colorado cowmen followed into the Panhandle, bringing well-bred Shorthorns. Some bought fine herd bulls. In 1881 Goodnight got 500 more registered Shorthorns, 200 bulls and 300 heifers, at Burlingame, Kansas, and trailed them down from the railroad. Near Wolf Creek they got too close to a south Texas trail herd. To avoid the fever, the blooded stock was driven up the middle of Wolf Creek until far beyond the contaminated range.

The Shorthorn's susceptibility to Texas fever was discovered early. Back in 1848 Colonel Tom Shannon was given two fine cows by Queen Victoria from her own herd, delivered at New Orleans. He hauled them all the way to north Texas in ox wagons, which, fortunately, was beyond the regular tick region and out of the path of the trailers. The ranchers on the way scoffed. A man had no business with cows that couldn't light out and walk from New Orleans to Texas and across even the noble distances of that new state.

Shannon's neighbors were particularly furious. They wouldn't have that squat blood loose on the range. Too short-legged to get over the ground that a good grazer had to cover to keep alive. The cows and their calves did well but some of the bulls Shannon brought in were apparently shot on the prairie to keep their blood from spreading. Blooded sires probably were walked to death by the Texas cattle or killed by the native bulls, although it seems that the Spanish fever might have had a part in their easy dying.

But by 1877 George Reynolds, the solid old cowman still carrying an arrow in his back from an Indian fight ten years before, was defending the Shorthorns. He predicted that they would be one of the coming breeds for Texas. He drove in some seed stock from Colorado, in addition to the over 200 carloads of blooded cattle the Katy railroad had already hauled into the state. Much of this stock went to men who once, with enterprise and millions of Longhorns, almost wiped out the beef producers in the original cattle regions of the nation—New England and the area around New York and Philadelphia. Not by the fever, although that had been a threat for many years, but because in those regions cattle had to be fed and winter sheltered, with both breeding stock and land high, so high they couldn't compete against the Longhorn from the wild, free herds, to feed on free grass, with almost the only outlay the roundups, trailing, and shipping expenses.

But as the wild cattle vanished and the range was practically all claimed if not owned, the Texan turned to better blood. Although a heavy investor in Shorthorns, Goodnight felt there must be a better stock for his range. He recalled that during the winter of 1871 he saw some Aberdeen Angus cattle out on the Laramie Plains of Wyoming—the polled blacks thick-haired and straight-backed and in good shape when many other cattle froze in the high, blizzard-swept country. But there was almost no Angus breeding stock available.

Goodnight talked the problem over with W. S. Ikard, who had seen a remarkable breed of cattle at the World's Fair in 1876—a breed of red whitefaces called Herefords, a fine, blocky beef stock said to be good foragers. Finally he had brought a few into Texas, as did several others, and found that almost no one would take the new cattle as gifts. Then in

1880 Lee and Reynolds walked seven carloads of Herefords from the railroad to the LE ranch west of Tascosa. They turned out hardy, good keepers and beefy as ever.

During the next few years Goodnight brought in substantial numbers of White Faces, too, first for the JA range, then to the ranch on the upper Tule, near the bone piles left there back in 1874 by General Mackenzie when he butchered around 1,200 captured Indian horses. Goodnight paid a flat $75 a piece for a fine herd of twenty-five bulls, over 600 cows, with around 400 calves. Old-timers who had seen plenty big four-year-old Longhorns go at $5 shook their heads when they heard these prices. Foreign capital! That Irishman was getting skinned like a fat heifer, and his hide hung out on the corral to dry.

But the Hereford blood raised the quality of the JA cattle and produced the first range yearlings in the region to bring $25 a piece. In a stretch of eight years around 10,000 purebred Hereford bulls were brought into the Panhandle. Goodnight's cross of a little of the old Longhorn for self-reliance and initiative and Shorthorn for weight and bone on top of the dominant Hereford blood made a most excellent cow for the Panhandle. She was fine to see, with her white face, perhaps with a white patch like a kerchief behind her neck, sometimes a white stripe all down the back. A good grazer, she laid on meat and fat and was still perfectly able to walk the shortening trails to market and to the slaughterhouses when they moved out upon the range.

Another of the early ranchers, one who was as dedicated as King or Goodnight and the others in his own way, started to move the year Charlie Goodnight returned to Texas. Except that I. P., Print, Olive was leaving the state. The San Gabriel region was overrun by nesters, with fool hoe men, he said. But everybody knew it was because he had become so hated that, armed and ruthless as he and his entire outfit were, he was being handed the same treatment that he had doled out to those around him, to Negroes, Mexicans, settlers—to anyone who got in his way, particularly those who couldn't fight back.

Yet some had been fighting back, as his wife apparently reminded him, striking out of the darkness upon the Olives, killing Thomas and one of their Negro hands, crippling Print and others of the help. It was no way to raise their children, their son William, already talking of killing although still a girl-faced boy. For years now there had been little except violence, with almost everybody against them except the Snyders, fine people, but there were fine Olives, too, fine God-fearing Olives.

Print must have known that although he was always acquitted of the killings by the courts, none of the outfit was acquitted in the minds of the cattlemen around them, nor of the settlers. More and more were wondering openly whether this neighbor or that one who vanished had received one of the Olive "Tickets to Hell."

By this time young Bob, twenty-two and considered the most reckless of all the brothers, was in trouble again. "Looks to me like that outfit's determined to plant a steady crop of casualties like some folks plant cotton," one of their neighbors, a good twenty miles off and plainly close enough, said slowly.

Evidently it was true that Bob had shot a Negro who, he claimed, was stealing corn from the Olive cribs. Naturally Bob was not tried for that but now there was another killing, some said his third, perhaps the fourth. It seemed that this time Bob was in a saloon drinking with a man called Cal Nutt,* whom the Olives said later they suspected as one of the gang that attacked the ranch and killed Thomas. Or perhaps he was hired to dispose of Bob because he had sworn to get his brother's murderers.

After the two men drank together awhile, Bob Olive said he had to be going. Some argument came up outside the saloon door, their voices rising, the men around them moving back as cattle would from a couple of bulls bellowing mortal .

* Sometimes Null.

challenges. Suddenly Cal Nutt fired a bullet through Bob Olive's loose-swinging vest. The report was lost in Bob's fast shots that knocked Nutt backward through the swinging saloon doors, two bullets in his vitals. This time there were plenty of dark and angry faces, and a lot of lynch talk, talk of lynching an Olive, all the Olive brothers.

But by then young Bob was gone, riding hard for the home ranch. There his brothers filled his pockets with money and hustled him off for Wyoming. GN, Gone North, as Bob Stevens. This was no time to chance a trial, Print Olive argued, with the juries going against them now. There was even some concern among the brothers, particularly Ira, about their Methodist parents and sisters. Bob would surely get a ranch job up in Wyoming, probably with Federal Judge Carey, a good friend of Dudley Snyder.

A reward of $400 was posted for Bob and now gradually the news spread, too, that the Olive brothers were moving north, not just taking a herd or even half-a-dozen herds to market but pulling out, going lock, stock, and barrel. Many went to some far hill to watch them go, holding their impatient horses long after the Olives were past. Others watched by rumor, by telling and retelling, until the going had grown to mammoth size. Some said there were 60,000 cattle and 2,000 horses, driven by seventy-five cowboys, mostly Mexican and Negro, some of them with the Olives for years. Perhaps it was allegiance; perhaps at bottom the loyalty that the Olives got from their men was some curious fear. But perhaps that, too, was allegiance.

Because the Olive herds came from down in the tick belt and were headed through settlements, the cowhands would need their guns handy, and they all had them, including young William, a blustering boy talking big, pulling his Colt at any excuse. Print had a new Winchester in the boot and his holster low over his worn chaps. Print Olive was never a Shanghai Pierce, to go unarmed, whether, as old Shang did, in south Texas or on the streets of badman Abilene. Nor was he like gun-shy Jesse Chisholm or even John

Chisum, whose hired hands were notoriously fast with gun play but Old John was always a muley, without weapon or defense.

The Olives went north with long trains of freight wagons carrying ranch tools, equipment, implements, and supplies. I. P. rode ahead, his dark face even darker at this necessity to lead this departure from his home region, the milder brother, Ira, riding beside him, his eyes and his drake-tail hair the same Indian black under the dust.

Behind them came some of the chuck wagons and the family carriage with Louise Olive looking out anxiously from among her children back along the trail to where her son William must be riding. The carriage was followed by several lighter vehicles, buggies and carts, and the wagons with the family belongings and their camp equipment. Far back, their manes and tails streaming in the wind, the loose horses followed the bell mares, and finally there were the cattle, broken into many herds with their remudas, separated by long stretches to let the dust clear off and to keep them from crowding and mixing at the watering places and the stretches of grazing. Finally, far behind the last drags came the families of the hands, mostly Negro and Mexican, and then the heavy wagon trains, moving slowly but doggedly.

Altogether the Olive outfit was strung over ten to twenty-five miles of trail, depending upon the water and the range. They traveled at a good steady rate. Any stock that couldn't keep up was dropped, the rest not hurrying but moving, moving. So a remote ancestor of the Longhorn had come westward out of Asia, except that there must have been fewer, far fewer cattle and a great many times more people —an exodus of man.

With Print Olive always up ahead, leading his herds to new grass, there was no encouragement to friendliness along the route. Once, when one of the men was asked at a trail supply store where they were going, he scratched under his dusty hat and said, "Damn if I know. I aims just to follow."

One day the Olive brothers came up on a covered wagon stranded out on the prairie, one horse dead from, snakebite, a man, his wife, and a baby in the wagon, helpless, many miles from any habitation, with no food left, no gun for hunting, not even the knowledge for a rabbit snare or the digging of an Indian turnip. The man had not eaten for two days.

Print Olive slouched over his saddle, his arms folded on the horn, listening, his sharp little eyes probing the desperation on the man's face. After a while he raised himself in the stirrups and shifted his holster. "Come along. I'll adopt you," he said.

He ordered a team hiked to the tongue, the lone horse sent back to the stock herd, and had the cook wagon stop to feed the starving little family. Then they were dropped in with the other wagons of the hired help, far behind. There were other men, brown-skinned and white, in that long, moving outfit who had come to Print Olive through some desperation.

As I. P. Olive neared the Kansas-Nebraska line he made plans for the coming winter. His family would be settled in some little town. Perhaps he knew that his wife looked hopefully toward quieter times here in the north with the Yankees, who were perhaps not so hotheaded. Certainly she could hope that there would be less here to arouse her husband to his violent angers, with pleasanter times for her children, particularly for her beloved, the young William. He was a good boy, but a little wild, his mother admitted, and as restive as a young mustang under his father's hand, as Print had been very early, Print's mother once told her daughter-in-law. "His father never understood Prentice," she had defended.

The herds were stopped at the Republican River, with fine, long grass, lush enough to feed the great herd of buffaloes once centered there, and mostly gone four, five years ago. There seemed only a scattering of cattle to fatten on these well-seeded slopes already ripening golden toward fall. Here the Olives built a great spread of corraling, the Olive Pens, to which the herds were gathered at night and turned out mornings. The methodical one for such tasks was Ira. He saw to it that all the penning was orderly. He always stationed a man in the gate as it opened, to hold the cattle back, keep them to a single file, without crowding so no horns were broken off.

"I hate and despise a critter with a horn gone," he said.

Evidently he meant it. One morning he was late coming out to the pens. The cattle were gone to the range but there were a couple of fine long horns tramped into the dirt of the gate. He cursed the Mexican gatetender, called him every vile Texas name in Spanish and English. But Leon was not the man to take this quietly as the older hands did, men like Uncle Amos and the other Olive Negroes. Caught without his gun, he whipped a knife from his boot, but before he could throw it Ira shot him down. Several men saw this coming but none dared move to stop it, or to avenge the killing. No one could be certain he might not be next, now that this quieter one of the Olives had taken to gunning his hired help down, too.

Afterward Ira Olive paid the man's widow well, and, of course, it never became a matter for the law. By this time news from Texas got around the Republican country about the cattlemen named Olive who had pushed into the region like a stray hog into a corncrib. As settlers began to move into the old Olive range down in the San Gabriel country rumors ran northward on the wind. Bodies were being found in the empty Olive reservoirs and dirt tanks—more and more bodies, apparently of some of the ranch hands and settlers who had vanished and were never heard from again.

With the Indians so recently pushed out of much of Wyoming and Dakota and most of the Yellowstone basin, and the cattlemen just beginning to move in, many wondered why Print Olive squatted in the rapidly settling Republican country. Still, he had clung to the San Gabriel and Williamson County region with settlements from before the days of the Texas Republic, when he could have started out in open country as King did, or moved, as Goodnight and a hundred others. Perhaps he needed the fighting, as the gunmen of Griffin and Abilene, of Newton and Tascosa and Dodge City needed gunplay.

Before many weeks on the Republican River Print Olive was informed he had moved in on grass saved for winter range by cattlemen who claimed the region for years. He discovered that he was hemmed in by ranchers and homesteaders, and that there was no grass for any Johnny-Come-Lately except through an army of guns, and it was plain there were too many guns here already, Texans, too, and British money, never shy about putting unruly natives down. Besides, many of the ranchers and the settlers were old buffalo hunters, men who put their trust in long-distance rifles, long-distance marksmanship. From their faces he knew they had heard his reputation and were not afraid.

"Yeh, I hear you killed nine niggers down in Texas," one of the old hunters now running cattle told Print in a bar. With his mouth tilted up he said it and then took deliberate aim on the spittoon, hit it squarely, and walked away.

But there was more to make I. P. Olive uneasy. The whole region was organized into counties, with officials and law, law that could be bought, certainly already bought, and would be mighty expensive for Rebel money or any outsider's money to unbuy. Before long Print led a wedge of his riders up to the Platte and across it into the long-grass country of the sandhills, where the fall bunchgrass ran orange in the wind of sunset. But the Texas cowman realized that this handsome sweep of grass was perhaps longer on looks than on feed value, or the other grasses around would show less grazing. Yet there must be plenty of good range farther on, in the rolling chophills, sandy as some of the region that Richard King had drawn into his cattle empire down in the gulf country. As they rode in deeper the cow chips became scarcer, and not a cow in sight, only an occasional antelope to turn and run with a toss of white rump hair, but to circle around back to look.

The region was without a rock or tree or even a shrub beyond a few little buckbrush patches or perhaps a dwarf willow shorter than the stirrup, in some low spot. The only thorns to make the Texans feel at home were those on the low clumps of red-hipped prairie roses in the grass, the spears of the soapweed clumps on the sandier knobs, and an occasional patch of bull-tongue cactus—patches like greenish hearthrugs scattered around, the sections small and dainty to the eye accustomed to prickly pear that grew taller than a man on horseback, with the gray-blue sections over a foot long, the barbed spines the size of darning needles.

Finally, riding over a low ridge, Print Olive and his men looked down on a sandy little valley, as empty as all the others except that a stream clear as spring water ran through it, filled almost level with the grassy banks that showed little variation from drouth or flood. The men bellied down to drink, the water very sweet to the alkalied tongues of the Olives and their cowboys. Wiping his bristled mouth with the red bandanna about his neck, Print took out the little map he carried and saw no humor in the name, the Dismal River.

The Olives sold a fine lot of late-fall grass-fat beeves, certainly finished out better than any they ever marketed from Texas. This was meat country and the Olives were the outfit to produce it, so Print bought around 150 two-year-old Shorthorn bulls and the next week he was stringing 15,000 Texas cattle northward in one close-trailed herd after another, across the sand-choked Platte and into the foothills beyond. Many of the Republican ranchers had been out to see him go, stopping their horses on the far ridges, as down in Texas, the men here not to be contented until the last hoof tracks of the Olive cows were blown over. Along the Platte men watched, too, the sun glinting on the rifles across their saddles. They knew it was Olive stock coming through and were prepared to see that the range-hungry Texans did not linger overlong.

Finally the last of the drags were in the protected hills of the Dismal country. Print had a few shacks thrown together for his riders. He was satisfied with the wintering, but by spring he was looking around for something nearer the railroad, nearer the comforts of town for his family, his hands, and himself, too, for I. P. Olive liked to spend the evenings in one bar after another, feeling big as he stalked through the swinging doors and saw the faces at his coming, the Yankee faces showing they knew him. True, there was no vacant range near the railroad and he would have to clear the settlers off their homesteads and push some small ranchers from the land they had been holding ten, twelve years. But they had no rights beyond the gun, not even the settlers, no matter what the law said.

Print settled some of his best men into a log house on a rented school section on the South Loup River and took a house at Plum Creek on the Union Pacific along the Platte. Almost immediately old Plum Creek, a stagecoach station not so long ago, became Olive Town, taken over by his outfit. Some Texans were surprised that Print would move his headquarters to the railroad, where there was law and courts, the latter certainly with the local cattlemen against the outsider.

"Hell, no law's ever stopped Print. Nor no courts, neither. Maybe he likes to know the men he's going to buy up got the power to deliver."

By now Print Olive, through his biggety ways, was called Nebraska's richest cattleman, the top cattle king, although some restricted the region of his supremacy to the Plum Creek and lower Loup country.

Soon after they moved in, Olive's men discovered what a fire could be in the largely long-grass region, with no large streams and no barren wastes to stop it. At the first cry of "Prairie fire!" and a pointing to the pearly, iridescent little cloud rising against the sky, teams were hooked up, breaking plows thrown into the wagons, water barrels loaded and sacks piled in to soak for pounding out the smaller flames, particularly in backfiring. The wind was gentle at first but it swelled in the heated air. The men fought as well as they could, with the help and direction of men from the surrounding ranches and some settlers, too, and fought until they fell scorched and worn out under the fierce drive of Print Olive. He was cursingly certain the fire was set by an enemy. The plowed fireguards saved the ranch buildings, but the flames swept on, the Longhorns fleeing like the occasional deer and antelope, the coyote and the rabbit. Many were caught in the deep grass of the bottoms and burned to death or had to be killed later. Settlers lost their homes, their little accumulation of corn and fodder. Finally the fire hit the South Loup and spread along the banks, making little sullen headway, edge-on into the wind, and so it died.

The transplantation of the new cattle king and his methods to Nebraska from south-central Texas, where he was almost literally driven out, caused much stir. Everything he did was big, highhanded, overbearing, bulldozing. At the ranch Print's word was law to the white men as it was to his "gun Niggers" as he called them, men who had known slavery and could bend their necks. There was soon trouble among the men now, however, all gun-armed—white, Negro, Mexican, Texas white, and the northern whites that Ira put on. Print had them fight it out—egging them against each other in his half-drunkenness, whether bare knuckled or with knives, even guns a time or two. Afterward there were the fiddlers for a little good time, regular hoedowns, generally. Often there was Sunday bronc riding, calf roping, and steer tailing around the corrals. Men from the neighboring ranches were encouraged to come, including foremen and range riders. Phil DuFran from up on the Missouri River in Dakota, foreman for the neighboring Durfee and Gasman ranch, was usually there. He was as black haired as the Olive brothers, a

Frenchy and a little Indian, too, some said, but a genial fellow who could make Fred Fisher, Olive's foreman, laugh and sometimes even the dark-mooded Print himself. When the Pawnee Indians came through the region they had called home not long ago, there was trading and horseracing and betting at the Olive ranch, until Print, with a sudden wave of his gun, shouted the alarmed Indians into hurrying their families out of his way.

When the ranch hands went to town, they emptied their guns into the store windows and shot out the large red lamp globe of the hotel, spreading a stench of coal oil over the place, and then paid for the damages with their supper bill. Olive gave them all a surprise raise in pay because the cattle increased so surprisingly, growing and fattening beyond anything he had ever seen. But then he had never seen grown cows in any region that nurtured and fattened the great buffalo herds, and very recently here.

Before long the little ranchers who ran cattle on the government land were commanded to keep their stock out of it, and homeseekers warned not to come in. This range was now Olive property. The settlers already there, and there were many, got orders to kill no cattle, brand no mavericks and no calves, and to keep their cattle off the grass, including that on their own claims. This was Olive law, issued from a ranch on a leased school section, set up over the surrounding public domain and the land legally the property of the settlers. Those who had heard rumors from Texas were certain Print Olive was preparing to shoot down everybody he wanted out of the way on the pretense that they stole Olive cattle. A man didn't have to come from Texas to know there were ways of planting a settler's brand on the calf of a rancher's cow to furnish the excuse for a shooting—or a lynching.

Several of the settlers, some with families, well-built homes, and crops planted took the hint and left their homesteads. By now the brawling, gun-jerking young Bob Olive had come down from Wyoming and even the other ranchers left the outfit alone as much as possible, put on extra line riders, ordered more guns for the hands, and waited. It was a particularly hard wait for the settlers, and hardest of all for those with wives and children. Someone would have to be the dead owl the Olives were planning to use as a scare for the others.

The expected blowup came very fast and no one could ever know the whole of it, so complex were the factors involved in this fight for grass for the cow—certainly not Print Olive or his brother Bob, with their gunmen, white, black, and brown.

Conspicuous among the settlers who would not scare out were Mitchell and Ketchum over near Clear Creek. They had filed on adjoining homesteads and built a long, double soddy across the homestead line, with Ketchum's end of the house on his claim, Mitchell's over on his. Mitchell was a slight, middle-aged man, old for homesteading in a raw country, although the Loup region was not as new as some, with a railroad in reach for ten years. He had his wife with him and two stepdaughters, the elder, Tamar Snow, a pretty sixteen-year-old who was to marry young Ami Ketchum. Like his brother Lawrence Ketchum, a government scout, Ami was a crack shot. He had brought his forge and anvil and started to set wagon tires, shoe horses for the icy ground of winter, sharpen plowshares and sicklebars, and braze an occasional gun with a broken breech tail. They were sociable people, going to the country dances and house raisings, even if two, three days away by wagon. They sat up with the sick and helped bury the dead.

Unfortunately the homesteads of Mitchell and Ketchum, although several townships away from the Olives, were a rallying center for the settlers around there, on range Print intended to take over. Soon it was said around that Ketchum was overeager to get enough money ahead to marry and that when a rancher's herd ate up his shirttail patch of corn, some of the cows left their calves in his corral. At least that was the story the Olive hands were spreading. Their friends, including Phil DuFran, foreman of the neighboring

Durfee, were glad to follow the lead of this Texan if he could clear the range they had about given up. Print Olive got his brother Bob appointed stock inspector, in spite of the $400 reward for his return to face the murder charge in Texas. He was to watch Ketchum. Maybe plant an Olive calf in the settler's corral or some fresh Olive hides around his place somewhere, old-timers from Texas and Wyoming warned. One even rode over to tell Ketchum about the "Death of the Skins" killing down in Texas, in which two men were smothered, rolled in drying hides with the Olive brands.

Ami Ketchum laughed, but others warned him, too. "You better think about hittin' it out of here," an old cowhand told him at a dance. The fiddler, who was a preacher on Sundays, agreed, and offered to loan Ami the money to go back to Iowa. Once more Ami laughed and swung pretty Tamar in a dough-see-dough.

Yet all that first fall there had been trouble in the region, stirred up, some said, by the Olives. It was inevitable, this trouble in an old range country already half taken up by settlers when an Olive outfit pushed in with their big herds, after the local ranchers were already hard pressed. Some bodies showed up on the new Olive range when the snow cleared toward spring, missing hunters, all full of bullets. Nothing was disturbed in their camp, no money or watches taken.

"That's how it went down in Texas," the southern cowhands said.

By now everybody knew that both Mitchell and Ketchum had been warned to get out of the country. Then in April word got around that the Olives had a man named Roberts arrested for stealing cattle and took him up before a justice of the peace. Roberts had dared to hire an attorney, Aaron Wall, county judge in the next county, for his defense. The Olives kept Wall out of the justice court with their guns, although he opposed the half-drunken brothers and their outfit all afternoon. Finally, by a trick, Wall got them to let the prisoner come out to consult with him a minute, and got him away, for an open trial elsewhere.

Furious, the Olives went over to Wall's court to arrest him for interfering with justice, Bob leading the cowboys. Once more, with drawn guns, they bulldozed him, but did not quite dare shoot a county judge at the bench before witnesses. Finally Wall got a deputy to grab Bob Olive and fined the outfit for contempt of court. They didn't all pay but agreed to leave town, swearing they would get even.

Things crippled along this way for a while, nobody knowing where the guns would be drawn next. Then Print Olive and Fisher, the foreman, found cattle with the Olive brand at the homestead of Christensen. There were several neighbors at the place. They agreed that Christ had bought the cattle with a brand release. He went to the house to look for the paper, with Print's boots stomping after him. Roaring and impatient, Print struck the settler across the cheek with his .45 and broke his jaw. Standing over the fallen man, Print gave him five minutes to prepare for death. But Christensen begged so through his pain and terror, promising to fetch the release to Olive as soon as he found it, that Print agreed, particularly with the armed settlers still outside. One of the men was George Brill, stepson of the Judge Wall who had defied the Olives. Besides, Brill had ridden the range with Bob Olive up in Wyoming and knew about the reward out for him. Christensen was too frightened to hunt up a doctor and the neglected jaw grew so stiff he could never open his mouth more than about an inch. In a short time he was gone, quit the country.

Afterward Print claimed that Brill and the other man at Christ's shot at him and Fisher from the brush when they left the place. "I should have killed the goddamn Swede when I had him down—"

The release on the Olive brand showed that Manley Caple sold the cattle to Christensen. Manley, son of an early rancher in the region, had been gambling heavily and was suspected of rustling to keep in chance money. The Olives had him arrested. In his confession he seemed to implicate Ami Ketchum, although apparently it was no more than an implication or the Olives would have acted at once. But in the end they got a warrant for Ketchum and had Bob Olive deputized to serve it, although everyone, including the sheriff, knew about the Olive threats to kill Ketchum, make buzzard meat of him if he didn't get out.

Then one night the Olive hands had some news to tell around the bars at Plum Creek, news about a raid planned on some rustlers over on Clear Creek. The news reached Mitchell and Ketchum, some said by the gentlemanly Texas cowboy become horse thief and traveling under the name of Doc Middleton. Others said it was Buckskin Bill, who claimed young Bill Olive shot at him twice for dancing with the kid's girl.

"Startin' early—that kid of Print's is scarcely bearding out," he said.

Although the stories of the next few days differed very much, all agreed that a stranger to Mitchell and Ketchum came to see who was home by pretending he wanted his horse shod. Probably trying to separate the two men, get Ketchum over to the blacksmith shop, perhaps away from his rifle. But the settlers were hooking up to the wagon to return a borrowed bull, and Ami asked the man to come back next day. By the time Mrs. Mitchell and the girls had climbed into the wagon the Olives and their cowboys, mostly Negro and Mexican, charged out upon them, riding low on their horses, giving a Rebel yell and shooting.

Mrs. Mitchell pushed the girls down into the wagon bed as the bullets whistled past. Bob Olive led the outfit, shouting something about "Throw up your hands, Ketchum! Throw up your hands!"

But Ketchum had already pulled his gun and fired. Mitchell grabbed the Winchester from the wagon and shot, too, while bullets splintered the wagon box around him, the younger of the girls inside crying in the hay. At first the settlers didn't shoot to kill, only brought down some horses and grazed a man or two. Ketchum had jumped out into the open to draw the fire from those in the wagon box and got a bullet in the arm. Now Mitchell took aim and at the double report of the rifle and Ami's pistol Bob Olive jerked himself straight in the saddle and started to slide from the running horse but was caught and held by cowboys on each side and carried away as the rest turned, too, spurring for cover. Ami Ketchum got in one last shot from the rifle that Tamar helped him hold.

"Goddamn 'em!" he swore in fury. "I could kill the whole damn outfit, attacking when there's women and children around—"

Off in the brush Print decided to take his brother to a neighboring settler's dugout, less than a mile off. He ordered the man to get his team and wagon ready and laid Bob on a bedding of hay. With the settler driving, Print riding alongside whipping the team along, the cowboys following, they got Bob to the eastbound train. But he died, died, it seemed, on his twenty-fourth birthday.

The body was shipped home to Williamson County, to his respectable parents and sisters, and laid beside his brother Thomas, riddled with buckshot. By rights, some said, Ketchum should have the $400 reward offered for Bob Olive's return to Texas, but perhaps that was for his return to stand trial for murder.

From the moment that Bob Olive wavered in the saddle, Mitchell and Ketchum knew they would be mobbed by the whole Olive outfit, with perhaps DuFran and others bringing their cowboys, too—clear the range by stringing up the one man nobody had dared to touch, Ami Ketchum. At least Mrs. Mitchell and the girls must be taken away before anything more happened, with Ketchum's arm swollen and useless, Mitchell a scared old man. They turned the neighbor's bull loose to go home, piled blankets into the wagon, and started across the country, whipping the team hard, the wheel tracks so pitifully plain over the late fall prairie. They didn't dare go to a doctor, for with so few in the country it would be easy to have them all watched. Instead, they hurried to Judge Wall, even though they realized that the Olives would strike there immediately, settle two grudges at one time. The judge advised them to get as far away as possible, to friends who would hide them, preferably friends the Olives knew nothing about. But all such friends were around Ami's old home in Iowa.

In the meantime a mob of cowboys gathered under the leadership of the Olive gunmen, burned the roof off the deserted sod house on Clear Creek, all that would burn. From there Print Olive sent his gunmen to scour the country, some pursuing the wagon tracks, others cutting across from settler to settler. The railroad towns he had put under guard by telegraph long ago. Within a few hours notices appeared in every saloon, post office, and crossroads fence post: Print Olive was offering a $700 reward for the apprehension of Mitchell and Ketchum, murderers of his brother Robert Olive.

Nobody dared to help the fleeing settlers now, not even give them a handout of dry biscuits, let alone shelter. To save the woman and the girls, the men let them go on ahead to some acquaintance and struck out alone afoot. But Mitchell was soon worn and limping, Ketchum burning with fever and pain, his arm swollen double in size. They made one more desperate and guilty appeal to Judge Wall, knowing they were endangering his life. Sadly, and in helpless fury, he admitted he could neither protect them nor advise them now. Wherever they were caught they would be returned to the sheriff who threw in with the Olives.

"Only the governor, with the militia, could save you and we can't get them in time. I sent a telegram. Got no reply yet."

The two settlers had known it was hopeless, and slowly they started away into the night. Olive's posse appeared at Wall's home. The judge managed to escape them but only because there was an old tunnel out of the house, big enough for a crawling man, dug back in the days of Indian scares.

In a short time the two settlers were run down on the prairie, put on horses, their feet tied under the bellies, and taken to Kearney for trial. There Print Olive refused to pay the reward until the men were delivered to him in his own region, Custer County. Over the pleading of the two settlers and men sympathetic to them they were smuggled out of jail without the knowledge of their lawyers and turned over to Sheriff Gillan of Keith County, west of there, but the only man of the captors who was willing to claim the reward. He took the two prisoners, handcuffed together, to Plum Creek by train. There, at Olive Town, Print, his foreman, and his cowboys were waiting. The settlers were thrown into a light spring wagon and with Phil DuFran driving, Sheriff Gillan in the seat beside him, they headed north, the mob following, in and out of sight. The moon came up, red on the prairie, just past full, and was lost in streaks of cloud. The cold of the December night chilled the manacled men but they were silent with only now and then a low word between them. They reached the burnt-over region, dark in the fitful moonlight.

About three miles from the Olive ranch and well within Custer County the mob rode up and Print handed the sheriff the $700 and took over the wagon. While Gillan and DuFran stayed behind watching, the Olives turned into Devil's Gap, a wild little canyon. There, in the light of the December moon, the wagon with the prisoners was stopped under a tree. Lariats were thrown over a limb and two of the cowboys put nooses around the necks of the settlers, still handcuffed together. Ketchum pleaded that they let Mitchell go. Old and sick, he was the only support of a woman and two children.

To shut him up, Ketchum was drawn up first, jerked up by a dally of the rope around a saddlehorn and a spur set to the horse. Mitchell's arm was yanked up by the chain of the handcuffs and held there, as Ami Ketchum kicked his life out. Then Olive put a bullet into Mitchell as pay for the one that killed Bob, and gave the signal to the cowboy with the dally.

Afterward a can of coal oil was brought from the spring wagon and doused up over the men. Print struck a lucifer and the two hanging men shot into flaming torches, the clothing and hair blazing, the brush under them burning, too, flaring up, the sooty smoke carrying the stench of the burning cloth and hair and flesh, too, out of the Gap and over the prairie to where sleeping cattle raised their heads a moment.

After a while Mitchell's rope parted and he fell into the burning brush and accumulated leaves amid a gushing of smoke, one arm still uplifted to Ketchum by the handcuffed wrist.

Nodding to his men, Print Olive turned his horse toward the ranch, the rest following, leaving two of the hands behind to keep the fire from spreading to the range.

It was the next day before anyone dared to follow the wheel tracks to find what everyone knew would be there. But no one was prepared for the burning. Now shock spread over the state, even to the hiding place of Mrs. Mitchell and her daughters, including the twice-bereaved Tamar Snow. It reached over much of the cattle region and over the nation. "Alleged Rustlers Burned Like Witches and Heretics!" one of the headlines cried. "Nebraska Settlers Victims of Heinous Crime Out of Inquisition!" another added. But mostly the headlines screamed out the same two words, over and over: MAN BURNERS! MAN BURNERS!"

# BOOK III

*ORGANIZATIONS,*
*CORPORATIONS,*
*AND BUGGY BOSSES*

# CHAPTER I

# DISCIPLES UNDER THE OAK
# AND THE COTTONWOOD

OF ALL the expanding cow country the only part that was ever Rebel territory, and suffered the swarms of carpetbaggers, was Texas. The anger against this exploitation not only drove out men like Goodnight but helped swell movements such as the Klan, with its hooded night riding and whipping with wet rope, but it encouraged the violent and the lawless all over the state. The attempt at regulating the early postwar cow hunts, with the general ignoring of the law, was often blamed for the custom of frying up anybody's beef but the rancher's own at his cookhouse and chuck wagon. Yet long before one Rebel shot was fired there really were people in Texas who would almost as soon eat one of their own children as one of their own beeves. To butcher his own meat for a guest was the cowman's highest honoring, a little like the Old-Testament father killing the fatted calf.

Besides, for a long time the wild cattle were there for the taking, with such county organization as existed often very far off, with counties perhaps sixty miles one way and ninety or a hundred the other. As the loose cattle grew scarcer and wilder from all the chousing, branded stock and their calf crop became more attractive to the careless, particularly as the blood was improved and the taking more profitable. Almost from the first the cattlemen saw they needed rules and some agreement on branding, the calf to go with the cow as the tail goes with the hide, and for a fair division of the mavericks, usually on a percentage of the herd ownership on the particular range.

But almost before branding dates were agreed on "Sooners" were jumping the gun, working the loose herds, taking the pick of the calf crop and the older unbranded stock, the mavericks. To separate the calf from the branded cow some slit his tongue to make his sucking painful long enough to wean him. Even easier was just to kill the cow in some thorn patch or arroyo. Some carried bows and arrows for this, leaving the arrows sticking in the dead animal.

"Damn Indians been working the range in a new way," some of the ranchers complained. But there were plenty of men who knew Indians. Some of these looked at the arrows and spit out their tobacco into the dust. "Bucks from the Short-Hair tribe—"

Up in Palo Pinto County one of the Sooners was out weeks ahead of the February 1 date, carrying his chunk of fire for the branding irons along because wood and cow chips were too wet for the flint and steel. He moved his roundup outfit out very casually and openly. Late in January he appeared at West Edwards holding pens with around 100 mavericks gathered on Edwards' range. Bold as a skunk in a hen yard he built up his fire and branded the mavericks right there under the rancher's nose. Furious, Edwards and three good hands rode out to the Sooner's own range. They traveled light, with only a blanket apiece, some grub in a *morral,* a Winchester at each saddle, and a couple of six-shooters at the hips. In two days Edwards branded 250 unmarked cattle from among the Sooner's stock.

It was said that another enterprising rancher, Haley, rounded up a branding pen full of big calves and yearlings a day ahead of the opening date, ready for the iron. That night an owner of some of the penned stock, with a few other cowmen, threw the gate to Haley's pen, drove the cattle to his own corrals, and notified the surrounding ranchers. They came, divided the young stuff figured on the probable number of cows each man had on the open range, an estimate because there was no way to be certain in the broken, brushy country.

As early as 1868 small groups of owners had organized into protective associations to keep out thieves and maverickers. Some hired stock detectives to watch as much of the vast ranges as possible and keep an eye on the pens and cattle work. As ranching spread into the open country north and westward, drovers coming through, particularly with mixed herds, got mighty careless about sweeping along any local stock handy. The idea caught on and by 1872 there were two protective associations up in Colorado, with delegations from the young Wyoming association down to observe. Up there the lead was taken by Cheyenne, with her freighting and stage lines anxious to protect their stock, horses, mules, and bulls, from rustlers. Over west the Laramie County Stock Growers Association organized in time to run the first general roundup the spring of 1873, with eleven ranchers participating. In 1879 the name was changed to the Wyoming Stock Growers Association and within a couple of years they had acquired powerful connections over in the capitol. Soon the association's stock detectives were arresting men or shooting them down if they resisted as though they were law-enforcement officials. Next the Association spread its supervised roundup and its detective system into parts of Colorado, up around the Black Hills, and into Nebraska as far as the forks of the Platte. From the first, newcomers into the free-land regions looked with uneasiness upon the growing power of the Wyoming association. Down in Nebraska settlers were openly against this outside, extra-governmental force invading their state. Somehow the settlers feared the Association and its armed range riders much more than the rustlers or the outlaws did.

By this time cattle were once more worth stealing and Texas was sprouting stockmen's associations like mesquites on new cattle range behind the buffalo hide men. Fort Griffin, on the Clear Fork of the Brazos, first only a way-station for southern trail herds, suddenly flourished under the only wealth Texas knew in the depression—buffalo hides—and drew as fine a lot of snakes, varmints, and plain trash as any gully washer ever swept down. Then, suddenly, the buffalo was gone, except in the farthest reaches, leaving only bones and lengthening grass. The men who had made fortunes either from the hunt or from the hunters around Griffin were out of jobs. Some went into cattle, but most had blown in any money they made and now found cowboy wages at $25 a month and found pretty slow pickings. Gangs of such men rode out of Griffin in the nights to the surrounding ranches, such as the Lynch outfit and others, and drove off herds of cattle. Often they waited until the rancher had rounded up his stock and then struck. Rustling became big business, flaring up everywhere, spreading like prairie fires in the wind over all the range country until solid cowmen like Jim Loving, who once stood off the Indians successfully for years, were cleaned out by the rustlers.

Not that cattle stealing wasn't old long before a cow crossed the Rio Grande—surely reaching back to the time of the first semi-domesticated bovine. The migrations bringing herds out of Asia into Europe must have had to fight off thieves much of the way. The early and very destructive raids by the infuriated Indians and the mestizo seeking food and breeding stock bedeviled the missions and then the ranchers. Later, if Indians swept stock away or it was driven across the border into Mexico, the rancher could appeal to the government for reparation but stock gone with the rustlers was stock entirely lost.

True, the practice of mavericking—the hard work of gathering unbranded stock past weaning age—had first been accepted as legitimate cow hunting, then as a sort of gentlemanly theft from great pools of cattle in the wilder brush and breaks, in strictly limited, unclaimed areas. Before 1870 horse stealing was the ultimate crime, for to set a man afoot to the mercies of the Comanches or, worse, to death from starvation and torturing thirst, was more dastardly than a bullet through the back. In those days it was an honor to help string up a horse thief, while mavericking, even driving off a few of the usually very distant neighbor's cows, didn't keep a man from being a deacon in the church or playing a spread of dominoes with the sheriff. Many ranchers had been cow-poor after the war and were actually obliged to the man who helped reduce their herds to fit their grazing ground. Rustlers usually took the tamest, the most tractable stock. Often this was the poorer and more likely to draw raiding Indians to the ranch than the brush herds. For a long time cattle stealing in Texas was at the worst a misdemeanor and the thief found guilty might pay a small fine and go on his way undisgraced, for who hadn't got his start with a rope and a running iron?

But the new rustler changed all this and cowmen shagged down to Austin demanding protection. In 1873 cattle stealing was made a felony but even then rustling by the herd was safe enough. The ranges were scattered over one third of the vast state, with almost no telegraph and no local officers. Off west and northwest were the emptying buffalo plains; just across the Red lay the ambiguous political area, the Indian Territory; north of the Panhandle stretched the forgotten strip called No Man's Land, and west was the rugged, largely unorganized, and welcoming, territory of New Mexico.

It was easy for even an eastern greenhorn to whoop a whole herd away from some watering place off to the open wilds, even easier to drive the stolen stock to market from there or to sell it, at almost pure profit and very little risk to some of the big outfits trailing to Wyoming, Dakota, or Montana.

The Comanches, too, had entered the larger rustlings.

Goodnight and Oliver Loving, in the attacks that finally took Loving's life, had discovered that the Indians were after cattle. It wasn't that they were after the meat—they found hump ribs of fat young buffalo cow much sweeter—but they were age-old traders of raided stock, with regular, well-worn trails out along the cap rock where now the *comancheros,* mostly Mexicans, brought their goods to barter for the stolen cattle and horses. There were many stories of one prominent trader, Tafoya. Backed by the commanding officer of Fort Bascom, New Mexico, and a ranch storekeeper who supplied much of the goods, Tafoya took his heavy wagon trains out to the Comanche trails. Where the Staked Plains dropped off into the canyons and badlands leading into the southeastward streams he met the Indians, usually just after the Comanche, the raiding moon. In his camp the Indians found bright calico and flannel cloth, beads, bracelets and bangles, paint, coffee, lumpy brown sugar, bags of hard bread, knives, guns and ammunition, including lead and powder. There was whisky, too, the most valuable of all, and well guarded to avoid violence.

As fast as the stock came in, sometimes with brands as far away as the Brazos and the Trinity, Tafoya's Mexicans swept the herds up the trail along the Canadian and over the state line, to be sold to the far ranches at handsome profit to Tafoya and his army friends and suppliers. One superintendent of Indian Affairs, finding New Mexico full of Texas brands, cut down the trading permits of the region to four, but by subletting the privilege or by ignoring it entirely, the *comanchero* trade went right on.

The real menace to traders like Tafoya was not the law or angry cattlemen but drunken Indians. One said he hid his whisky kegs eight, ten miles from his camp, got the Indians to turn the cattle over to him, and then, after the herds had a substantial start, he showed them where the whisky was. Then he hit it out of the country on the fastest horse he could buy.

By the time the cattlemen were talking of organizing

against the rustlers and raiders there were at least three of these *comanchero* trails or roads tapping the stock stolen from the advancing fringes of the Texas cow country. One struck the Pecos, crossed to the buttes called Yellow Houses, and down to Double Mountain Fork, another lay along the old army road down the Canadian to Las Tecovas, with a New Mexican fork turning southeast to The Door of the Plains, a large cut in the cap rock near the head of Trujillo Creek. From there the traders struck across the high, wide table to the head of Palo Duro and down it, turning to Tule Creek and the foot of the Plains, to camp at a headwater of the Pease called The Tongues because so many languages were spoken in the trade there. The third, the middle trail, hit the lakes, the lagunas, of the Staked Plains and up to the region of The Tongues, too.

This was old trading country, with an earlier meeting place just south called The Valley of the Tears. Here earlier raiders had brought their captives, white, mestizo, or Indian, to be traded and separated to complicate pursuit and bring more rapid assimilation. Mothers and daughters torn from homes in Texas and Mexico were scattered out from here, sometimes to be ransomed or rescued, but perhaps too late, as happened with Cynthia Ann Parker, who died of grief when she was taken from her Indian husband and family.

By the 1870's the *comanchero* trade carried a growing risk from organized cattlemen and from the occasional forays by the Rangers and by Indians who stole their stock back and forced the trader to pay for them a second time under threat of death. The whisky they demanded made the warriors uncontrollable by the chiefs, who considered the theft of stock from a rancher on what they thought of as Indian land much as a rancher looked on a smart deal or a merchant on beating out a competitor. A trade, however, was an honest man's agreement to the chiefs, and unbreakable.

Yet even with the growing insolence of the warriors the *comancheros* found the profits great. A loaf of bread might buy a cow, a keg of whisky, a good herd.

Cattlemen all along the Texas border and up the Pecos reported Indian attacks and losses, even entire herds. They kicked to Austin, to Washington, to the frontier posts, particularly Fort Bascom, said to be the center of the trade. Troops did pick up several thousand Texas-branded cattle at various times and Goodnight tried to get back stock he found carrying his brand in New Mexico. He finally went to the federal courts. The *comancheros* admitted that they took around 300,000 stolen cattle out of Texas, with perhaps around 100,000 horses, but all Goodnight got was the privilege of paying the court costs. The governor of New Mexico did issue a proclamation against the thieving practice but so much of his territory was still rugged as ever, and still unorganized, with the rustlers dug in.

The anger of the cowmen finally stirred up a little action. H. M. Childress, a native Texan, had trailed cattle north seven years until he was cleaned out in 1871 around Abilene. Scouting for something to do, he ran into a man authorized by the governor and some ranchers who had lost stock to make a raid into New Mexico for the stolen property. Even with the detachment of U. S. Cavalry along it was a difficult and dangerous undertaking. Childress fought seven pitched battles and killed several Mexicans but he recaptured 11,000 cattle and 300 horses without losing a man. The stock was sold up in Colorado at a good price and Childress wound up the year with a neat little fortune for his daring. True, some of the New Mexicans claimed he was no better than a highway robber himself, coming in and taking whatever pleased him, and some of the Texans complained about the big profits he made, but they didn't dare to follow him up the profit trail. Next year Childress was back in the cattle drives with a herd of his own, convivial, jolly as ever, and bighearted. And if it was true that he was a deadly pistol shot, and high-riding, there were many who explained that he wasn't really overbearing.

Childress threw a little scare into the *comancheros* and

their customers and encouraged William Hittson, the Texas cowman known as Colonel John, to try his own raid in 1873. With powers of attorney from many cattlemen of northwest Texas and three very good men with guns along to enforce his paper, Hittson rode west and up the Goodnight Trail. He let it be known that he was after any Texas cattle that the holder couldn't prove were legally acquired, and started repossessing stock right and left until he had around 10,000 head and was ready to call it a good job. In the meantime, even after he was back in Texas, he offered much free advice to the government on how to stop the traffic.

To be sure the herds recaptured were barely a drop in a desert, and discouraged the raiders and those who bought from them no more than sporadic hanging of a few rustlers discouraged that practice. The invasions did infuriate the authorities and New Mexicans in general. Texans, disliked before, were hated now, hated enough for a war if the two regions had been small treaty-backed European nations.

Next year, after the Indian attack on the buffalo hunters at Adobe Walls, General Mackenzie had gone out and whipped the Indians, Comanches, Kiowas, Southern Cheyennes, and a scattering of others, including Apaches, to their reservations and left the great pile of dead horses in Tule Canyon. Tafoya, with his vast familiarity of the Staked Plains, did a little guiding for the troops, now that the Indians who had furnished him with trading stock were gone. Other *comancheros* took up even duller work or restricted their activities more to their home territory.

The rustlers, too, were having a litle trouble, but in disposing of their stock in the hard times. Some even started to offer bills of sale. Once, while one of these papers was being drawn up, the owners of the cattle rode in over a ridge. Under the sights of their rifles they grabbed the thieves and marched them out to a tree and left them hanging in a row with a note: CATTLE THIEVES DOOM pinned to the shirt of each one, to flutter there awhile in the wind.

Over at Fort Griffin a vigilance committee had been

formed but that soon proved to be riddled by rustlers and gunmen, working from the inside for advance information on coming attacks, and to dispose of competition inside and outside of their own gangs.

By 1877 cattle prices had gone up again and rustling increased, particularly in regions like Dillingham Prairie, handy to Cross Timbers and the Red River, increased until it was ruining every stockman in that wide, unfenced range. For over a year men like C. C. Slaughter, Jim Loving, and Kit Carter had chewed over ways to fight the cattle thieves. Several of the loose organizations had had some haphazard success, mainly down along the border. John N. Simpson, rancher from Parker County, began to talk up the achievements of the Wyoming Stock Growers Association, particularly the policing of the roundups, and the range detectives. But Carter was against violence, even in defense of his property. Slaughter, son of a minister, leaned toward a firm stand against the thieves, and Simpson, hard hit by the rustlers, too, was anxious to try force where the law failed or didn't exist.

Mid-February, 1877, three windburnt, whiskered men rode over the mesquite-dotted Dillingham Prairie to Graham, not far below the Red River. One was C. C. Slaughter, forty, tall, affable, gallant, his well-groomed beard a little bushier than a goatee—still sometimes called the first native cattle king of Texas. He had started buying when he was seventeen with $520 he made hauling and trading lumber and wheat along the Trinity. He had pushed his little herd three hundred miles northwest and was now boss of the vast Long S Ranch out on the Prairie. He had a home in Dallas, where he had gone into banking—one of the first of a breed to prove very long-lived, the banker-rancher, making money on his cattle in good years and in bad stretches foreclosing on his neighbors and spreading his range farther and farther.

Beside Slaughter rode Jim Loving, son of one of the early dedicated men. He sat the saddle with more weariness and more age than his forty-one years and with much gray in his full mustache and pointed beard. He had not only lost his trail-blazing father to a Comanche arrow but, a big cattle operator and trail driver himself, he had lost so much stock to the brand-burning fires of the rustlers that he was literally broke. All he had left was a little one-horse ranch and a good name. The latter, at least, he knew he must keep.

The third man, the eldest, was C. L., Kit, Carter of Palo Pinto County, around fifty-seven, with a bushy and benevolent white beard. He was a man of integrity and friendliness, with a twinkle in his eyes. Born in Virginia, he had come to Texas young. Like Jim Loving, Carter carried an Indian-made sorrow deep in his stooped breast. Kit and his young wife had pushed out with the frontier early and it was not far from today's trail to Graham, eight years ago, that his son Shapley and eleven other cowboys were surrounded by Indians. The cowboys fought them off all day but young Shapley was one of those who died.

The three men heading for Graham this chilly February day rode like kinsmen—three bowlegged stock growers of the open country where a man had forty miles of elbow room—a region that had demanded a lot of energy, push, and guts to cut it from the wilderness and the Indians, and which now seemed even harder to hold. They were old friends, the three. They had worked roundups together, punished Indian depredators together, grieved for their bereavements together. But now they had to raise their sights.

At the little cow town of Graham other men came riding in, singly, in pairs, and in bunches, some over one hundred miles of mesquite and post-oak country. They gathered at the potbellied stove of the hotel, some looking with exaggerated envy at Burnett's big white hat, a John B. Stetson from Philadelphia—something new, called Boss of the Plains.

"You shure got to be careful with your ambeer spittin' in the wind—"

"Pounding out a couple of those prairie fires like my cook's always setting sure would black up a pretty albino belly like that J. B. you got," another offered.

But mostly the men had little time for even such mild joshing except to cover their seriousness, their uneasiness about this new undertaking, and none of the joking was about rustlers. One man there, George Reynolds, had already been in trouble over letting a thief get away. While out hunting cattle one winter his wrangler, a youth who was left in charge of the camp, skipped out with Reynolds' favorite riding horse, a rawhide lariat, and all the camp blankets. The rancher and a couple of his hands cut for sign and located the wrangler thirty, thirty-five miles off. They got the loot back, including the lariat, and started to the sheriff with him, a good stiff distance. They met a cowman who suggested it would be much quicker to string the wrangler up, as a warning.

"You know—hanging out a dead owl to scare the rest away," he said.

They looped a throw rope over a branch and told the youth to get on with his praying. He prayed so fervently and pitifully that softhearted George Reynolds decided a good thrashing would do more good than a hanging. He applied the rawhide rope solidly to the wrangler's rear, gave him an overcoat against the cold weather, and told him to hit the road.

The news of the planned lynching pleased the sheriff but when he heard about the good rawhiding instead, he sent word to Reynolds that this was a penitentiary offense and he better keep dodging. George did, for several years, but when he wanted a marriage license he got a couple of gun-packing friends to go to town with him to get it, face the friendly sheriff down if they had to. It worked out all right and the Reynolds set up housekeeping in the sod-roofed dugout on George's lonely ranch, adding another woman, like Mrs. Carter, Mrs. Loving, and Slaughter's mother, to those who never got sight of a sister soul in months and months.

Now, here at Graham, many realized they would have to give up such individualistic action as George's with the wrangler. It came hard for these old longhorns, hard as a horse pill to swallow.

Some put off thinking about this by wondering whether Charlie Dalton would show up for the meeting. He did, although seven years ago the Dalton family had sold Jim Loving a herd of cattle for $15,000 on tick, on time. After the rustlers cleaned Jim out, Charlie had to reclaim what little was left to him for the family debt. It wasn't easy to do and here would be the first time they had to meet in close quarters.

Plainly Jim Loving was edgy as a mustang before a storm and when Charlie Dalton came through the door the wind-squinted eyes of the others slipped uneasily to Jim and then away. In the silence the clump of Charlie's boot heels was loud on the rough-sawn pine floor, the clink of his spurs like trace chains clanking. There was a sort of shifting among the dark-faced men, a sort of aligning without movement, and for a minute or so all the old animosities here were laid bare, rising to life like a nest of spring rattlers.

"How'd do, Charlie," someone said.

Half-a-dozen others also spoke, pushing their hats back from pale foreheads, the group moving around a little, talking overloud, one or two laughing, for there was more than personal animosities at stake here, perhaps even lives. Only something much deeper than any personal things could have drawn others besides Dalton and Jim Loving together here at all.

There was a little further attempt at codding, joking, but it was still feeble as a heifer's newborn calf in a norther, and gradually the talk turned to the rustlers. One of the first was Medlan, converted into a granger by the rustlers who stole nearly all his cattle. He went into corn, wheat, and hay for the ranchers around him who were trying to protect their stock by corraling it more, which called for feed. Medlan had made it in cattle from around 1854 through the war and the Indian raids but the rustlers threw him. He stroked his whiskers now, admitting that he was still turning grass wrong side up. "But I ain't joined the Farmers Alliance yet," he assured the rest. "Knights of Labor are more my bunch, but both outfits tell me they're with us in our plans here, and they got power in the statehouse."

Lynch, in his thick Irish brogue, talked about his little place where the first big hauls started when that gang from Griffin swept off his whole herd in the night. He had taken his young wife to a dugout when they got back broke from the California gold rush. He moved her into a good two-story house since, but if the rustlers carried on much longer he and the lady would be back in the dugout.

Finally C. C. Slaughter spoke and everybody stopped even the moving of the jaws to listen, even those who envied him this respect. His father, Old George, was still called Sam Houston's right-hand bower, the last man to deliver a message to the Alamo, it was said, and the first one to marry in the Texas Republic, with C. C. here the first one born of such a marriage—the true Texian. The father had flourished in ranching, but his cattle were of the old wild blood, mostly hoofs and horns, with no market in Texas except for the hide and tallow at the rendering plants. By 1853 he had moved to the Indian border. To his ranching and his soul-saving as a Baptist preacher he added practical knowledge in frontier medicine. He delivered the babies of the couples he married, doctored the sick, and buried the dead. Besides preaching the double gospel of salvation and cattle, he fought off Indians and reared eleven children, two of them here among the forty men called together, the forty selected from among themselves to save their cattle business.

It was fitting that C. C. Slaughter would be the one to lead the group out of the hotel to a big winter-browned oak for the final organization where no alien ear except the sleeping squirrels might hear. The forty men stood or squatted on their worn boot heels, their hams cradled against their spurs —whiskered men, with only the youngest in stubbles. These were the first cowmen of Texas and the whole Southwest to establish a permanent organization—a formal notice that the day when a man could start in the cattle business with no more than a cow horse, a rope, branding iron and the nerve to buck the brush, was past. From now on the range here, though mostly public lands, and the cattle, even the un- branded, were no longer free for the taking.

There was long, even windy talk of range and brand control, with the story of Dan Waggoner's 144 steers stolen and a Box put around his 3-D with a bar iron. No Box 3-D was registered so he recorded the new brand in his own name and went to reclaim the steers from the brand burner, with the weight of the guns on his side, of course.

Yes, but most of the brand artists were smarter, at least smart enough to whoop the stolen stock out of the re- gion, if not to record their brands.

That was true, and in their helplessness these old cow- men, thorny as prickly pear, often sensitive as a shedding rattler, formed the Northwest Texas Stock Raisers Associa- tion to work for the interest of the stock growers of the re- gion. The territory was divided into six districts sprawled across north Texas, from near the Arkansas line westward and around almost to El Paso. The roundups would be super- vised by the Association; doubtful ownership of any stock and any question of brand or brand artistry would be the respon- sibility of the roundup boss selected by the members. When trail herds from south and central Texas came through, As- sociation members were to check them for stock belonging to any member. Kit Carter was elected the first president, with Jim Loving the secretary. The heads of the six districts in- cluded some of the shrewdest old cowmen of Texas, not only the initiators of the Association but little Seth Mabry, the Harrolds, the Ikard brothers, and old fighters like Hittson, who, it was said had brought the 10,000 head of stolen stock back out of New Mexico.

As the men scattered back across Dillingham Prairie some were content with what had been done, some hopeful. Many, however, were uneasy about a new factor brought up,

discussed, praised, and damned—the new invention called
barbed wire. Of course the menace or the boon was still a
long, long while off, but some thought that eventually it
would reach all the range. Some had seen it and these, too,
were divided about its portent.

The new Stock Raisers Association plunged into its
work and was aided by the unusually high spring flooding of
the Red River. The 300 yards of roiling, brown-red water
held up the herds there and gave the inspectors time to look
over the stock and all those detained on the trail, their campfires stretched back from the Red across Texas to the San
Antonio.

But the Association was no medicine wagon cureall.
By the second meeting at least one charter member was
accused of violating the rules against driving and molesting
cattle outside of his own district. Captain Millett offered a
resolution for additional power to stop herds or to make arrests. There were some who recalled the highhanded outfit
Millett himself ran, wild cowboys in many shooting scrapes,
a big one last January at Fort Griffin. Two of the captain's
cowboys, full of rye, had spurred for the Bee Hive, shooting
and yelling all the way. A deputy sheriff and the county attorney tried to stop them. In the gun fight two men were killed,
two wounded, one of them a Millett hand. The other got
away north, but afoot.

Yes, it would be Millett advocating arrests right and
left, but then how else could the Association be effective? The
query: "By what right do you stop me?" was answered to the
satisfaction of most of the members, at least, by the Association's power and the guns that the rustlers or trail drivers
would find against them all the way to the Red. Nothing else,
no legal right.

The fall meeting of 1878, the first session away from
the old oak at Graham, was at Griffin, where the rustling by
gangs had started. The town was pretty sleepy in its dust
these days, with the buffalo hide trade about done. Still they

managed a little excitement for the Stock Raisers, even had a little old-time talk of lynching, but quietly, because of the bloody vigilance committee, who, it was said, had disposed of eighteen men they claimed were livestock thieves. Ungallantly they strung up a lawyer apparently because he defended a woman who poisoned her husband.

People around Griffin had been missing cattle again, even the former sheriff, who had a slaughter lot in town. He said the thieves were the trickiest he had ever run across but he was working on them. Then a cowboy noticed a hide sticking out above the water in a shrinking pond near the slaughter lot, with the brand of a small ranch nearby still showing clear. He spread the word. Men gathered to plunge into the stinking water, fishing out a dozen hides with various brands. The former sheriff saw it was time to hit for the wilds but he was caught and locked in the county jail. There was a rumor that his friends and confederates would rescue him and so the vigilance committee broke into the jail, took him out for a volley of six-gun and rifle fire. To shut his mouth, some of the soured Griffinites said.

It was a sobering experience for the Stock Raisers, this session around such violence. President Carter spoke out sternly against these tactics. The Association was as anxious to round up rustlers as anybody, with so many of the members busted by the thieves, but they planned to work with range detectives and court trial rather than the slapdash of necktie parties down at the pecan trees or a volley of Winchesters.

But there were members as hot as any rustler's iron to take matters into their own hands. "Look at the private law down at King's Kingdom," one argued. "No rustlers bother him much."

"King owns the land," some of Carter's backers pointed out.

"Yeh, and the Mexies he's moved up, too, owns them."

"How about the law that Goodnight and the Mexican sheepmen agreed on out in the Panhandle?"

Well, that was mostly state land and they had no legal

basis for their action off their own property, but they probably had the guns.

The different factions pulled this way and that, not only at Griffin but later, too. As some pointed out to Carter around Christmastime, there were worse things than necktie parties. Up in Nebraska, for instance, where the Olive outfit, run out of the San Gabriel region in Texas here, was burning settlers, whether rustlers or not. Carter knew something about the situation up there, out in west Nebraska. A brother of one of his trail bosses had homesteaded west of Sidney and was run out not by a Nebraska cattlemen organization but by the Wyoming Stock Growers. Crops eaten up, his wife scared into crying fits by bullets coming through the window at night.

The problems were a little different in the North from those of the early cattle days of Texas. Up there it wasn't a matter of rounding up a lot of Longhorns by hard work from the brush, mostly wild stock about as easy to gather as deer and as hard to drive, as the brush poppers put it. The North was mostly prairie, the cattle tamer, even the Longhorns trail-quieted. Getting a stolen herd away was often much easier, with grass and water usually handy and markets, too, down almost any stream leading to the Platte, or along the canyon of the Niobrara clear to Iowa, if wished. She-stuff was profitably pushed north, perhaps down the breaks and canyons of the Powder, the Belle Fourche, or the Little Missouri.

The frontier always had many men who left home a jump ahead of the sheriff and some managed no more than that for years. Some of the buffalo hunters come north drifted into outlawry, and occasional miners, too, with the placer diggings pinching out in the Black Hills. But the most successful rustlers were former cowboys who got their time by one request or another. Experience in handling range stock was very important and such men were hardest to track, to bring in if overtaken or to string to some cottonwood. Ranchers who lost stock usually started the hunt by trying to trace down their former hands. Often the cowboy had built up a little bunch with his own brand and ran it with the ranch herd, perhaps encouraged to take cattle as part of his wages because the boss lacked cash money except market time or because he felt it helped the drifting cowboy settle down, keep him from throwing his money around in gambling dens and on whisky and women. Often a few fat cows and calves kept a hand from yelling for his time just because his bedroll got soaked or the beans happened to rattle like buckshot in his tin plate. It wasn't as easy to hit the road with a bunch of cows as with only a kack and ditty bag to throw on a horse. In the South some ranchers had used the cowboys in their dubious mavericking on other ranges by encouraging them to do a little off-time cow taking for themselves. In the North, even at roundup time, a cowpuncher might brand an occasional slick for his boss on the sly, and do the same for himself. But sometimes this led to changing even his employer's brand, or that of a neighbor, particularly if the owner happened to be an eastern financier or, more commonly, a Britisher off across the sea.

Often cowboys who got a few cows together, by honest work or the long rope, set up little spreads of their own. This, perhaps even more than the occasional theft of a critter, decided both the Wyoming and the Montana associations to bind their members not to hire men owning cattle. So they were black listed, thrown into the same pot as everybody from the known rustler to the honest ranch hand trying to get a little start. In Wyoming ranchers who hired cowboys on the black list were ordered investigated. No black-listed cattleman or cowboy was permitted in a roundup, and any foreman who broke the rule not only could be fired but forfeited the $3,000 bond he had to put up. This was a powerful weapon against any newcomer, any settler, but the bond itself kept all small operators from roundup foremanship. In Montana the black list was denounced as a way to shut out the small, the beginning stock grower, and the newspapers over the territory broke out in editorials condemning it as the act of greedy cattle kings.

Almost anyone could have a new brand recorded and some were deliberately planned to cover neighboring brand marks, as for instance, a UB could be burned over a lot of such letters and figures, single or in combination, as U, J, I, B, P, and 3, the number increased by a bar under the UB with, say, a B under that. To cover more difficult brands, those with twists, an S could become an 8, a chain, a clover leaf, or half-a-dozen other marks. With a little herd of mixed stock, old and young, legally owned and branded, a man could work up a very fast increase with a long rope and a hot saddle ring in some far canyon or in the far night. One of the most difficult brands to change was John Chisum's Fence Rail, a single bar that ran almost the entire length of a cow's side. But he ranged his stock in rustlers country and when his herd was delivered to Hunter and Evans on the Niobrara River, up in Nebraska, the trail crew included, along with some of the best cowhands of the West, some who turned out professional rustlers.

The northern associations scattered detectives over the range to watch newcomers, those with small herds particularly, even making plants to get rid of them, many claimed. In spite of them, cattle rustling without much trouble over brand blotting grew up, the stock moved down the wilder rivers, with stations at hidden box canyons and dugouts provided for both the men and the horses. Such cattle went to butchers, feed lots, into southern herds headed for Indian contracts, and as seed stock for new ranchers far from the brand registry.

Horse thieves worked the same way. The Texan who called himself Doc Middleton and was said by some to be the Jim Riley of the Newton, Kansas, massacre stole Indian ponies, ranch horses, and even the racing stock so prized in the cattle country. Apparently he worked Montana and Wyoming for horses to sell in eastern Nebraska and in Iowa and headed those he and his gang stole there up along the river to the ranch country. He invaded the settled Platte regions, stole race horses practically off the tracks, and camped every-

where, even with the Olives. Always a gentleman, he never
stole from a host unless pushed to it to get away, and then he
usually sent back as good as he took, or better.

The Wyoming Stock Growers Association hired brand
inspectors to watch at the railroad loading stations, at the
Indian agencies, and in the packing centers. All cattle bearing brands of those they called rustlers, and all brands unknown, meaning not of members, were treated as mavericks
and seized without legal procedure. This gave the Association
absolute power not only over the Wyoming cattle industry
but over anyone wanting to move into the vast regions that
the cattlemen claimed as their range, mostly government
land, public domain, legally open to any bona-fide homesteader's entry. Yet every cow or horse of the settler could be
taken up and sold as a maverick, the proceeds going into the
Association's coffers, without any effective recourse.

Such power grabbing brought opposition not only
from settlers and small ranchers but from the business people
dependent upon them. As settlement moved westward the
border law-enforcement officers often turned toward the bulk
of the voters. Suspected rustlers brought to court might very
well be turned loose in spite of overwhelming evidence because the cattle barons had grabbed such absolute power in
every other way.

Those cowmen who had approved Print Olive's burning of the settlers as a good example got a little uneasy as
more stories spread. Even after the burning of Mitchell and
Ketchum was reported to the authorities, the men were left
out in Devil's Gap several days, until Mitchell, on the
ground, was gnawed by the coyotes, so strong was the fear of
the Olives. Finally Print, sensing the feeling against him,
seems to have given a poor dim-witted man $20 to go out
and bury the bodies. He dug a shallow grave in the frozen
ground but the bodies couldn't be fitted into it, even after
chopping off an arm and a leg. So he threw them on top and
scraped leaves and dirt over them. Finally several men, led
by a Union veteran, went out from Loup City, dug up the

settlers, and after photographing the bodies, took them to Kearney for decent burial.

This was the story that sifted through the whole cattle country, and still no arrests were made. Print Olive still stalked from bar to bar in his town of Plum Creek, threw back his buffalo saddle coat, hitched his worn holster around a little, and reached for the bottle the bartender set out. To any remark he might overhear he roared that there weren't enough men in the whole goddamn state of Nebraska to take him.

"Looks like he's right," one of the men who had hung back from drinking Print's liquor finally admitted. So he had to move to the bar, too, but let the whisky slop to the sawdust. Not even the Ketchum brothers had been seen since they came for Ami's body. They had been bragged up as crack shots but somehow their aim seemed to wobble before an Olive.

There were stories that Print was making plans for expansion, for a Platte River kingdom. This was the region for him, he shouted out one night against several men who stood away from his liquor. Texas might drive him out but a man with guts could make himself king of all the yellow-belly Yankees. The Plum Creekers, the settlers, and the ranchers of all the region kept quiet and as the days and weeks passed, they began to pull to I. P. Olive's side, or quit the country.

Then a rumor got out that Mrs. Olive wanted to leave, didn't want her young son Bill brought up in such violence. "Violence, hell!" one of the settlers from the Loup snorted when he heard this. "That kid's already pulled his gun on a dozen men around here. Only the reputation of the outfit's kept him alive."

It seemed, too, that Mrs. Olive couldn't bear the newspapers with their denunciations of her husband, the demands that the governor act against the murderers, the looks she got in the stores and on the street. No matter how carefully her carriage was watched, every time she came out there were the chalk words scribbled on the side: MAN BURN-ERS.

Then there was a rumor that she and the younger children were packed to leave the next Sunday, maybe Print going, too, and taking his lawless gang along. Perhaps Phil DuFran, who had brought the settlers to Print, would join them, better join them, some said. And Sheriff Gillan from over in Keith County who had collected the $700 for delivering Mitchell and Ketchum, too.

Although neither the governor nor any county official acted, the frontier's energetic Judge Gaslin had been working quietly. He found that every possible witness had been warned that the talking tongue would be cut out at the root. Warrants issued for the arrest of the Olive gang were refused by two sheriffs who said they were not ready to die. But there were a few men ready to go through hell to see Print Olive locked up. They were deputized and with a few more willing to risk their lives, Judge Gaslin headed for Plum Creek.

The men scattered casually into town, stopping for a little business here and there. After the mail train came through, Print Olive went to the post office, the waiting crowd parting to let him through. Someone introduced two strangers to him.

"The Ketchum boys, Print. You know, brothers of Ami—"

Olive growled something, his hand hooked over his holster, and waited for the men to flee from his angry face. But they didn't. With one on each side of him they put him under arrest and before the astonished eyes of the crowd snapped handcuffs on him. In the meantime out on the street somebody picked up Fred Fisher, Olive's foreman, and a few more of the gang.

By then a crowd, a mob, was pushing up around the men. "Get a rope!" somebody yelled back toward his horse and a dozen coiled lariats were handed in over the shoulders of the pushing mob, the owners calling out, "Here! Here! String 'em up!"

But one of the arresting deputies elbowed in to face the leaders. He spoke quietly, so quietly that the mob had to silence itself to hear. He said he had taken an oath to protect the prisoners and he would do it with his dead body. He handed Print a pistol. "Shoot the first man who lays a hand on you," he ordered.

To the angry roar of the crowd, the yells of "Sell-out! Sell-out!" the deputy held up his hand for silence. "This man killed my brother, Ami Ketchum. If the law fails to punish him, then it's time enough for us and I'll do it my own way."

By dawn the two Ketchums and Sam Snow, stepson of the dead Mitchell and brother of Tamar, and their posse had twelve of the Olive gang, including Phil DuFran and Sheriff Gillan. The last man they took was the keeper of the hotel and saloon where the Olives hung out. Then they were taken away, chained in pairs, and all without a shot fired by the man who a few hours earlier had seen himself king of the whole Platte country.

"Sure caved in easy," some Nebraskans said.

There were, however, some Texans around who had seen Print Olive in the hands of the law for murder before, but none had ever seen him serve a day for any killing.

Still Olive and eight others were indicted for murder of Mitchell, taken up first as the older, the family man. It was done despite the rumors that Print had a standing offer of $1,000 out for any and all men drawn on the jury who voted against indictment. There were threats against the attorney general's life, too, and Judge Gaslin's. Nobody expected the judge to take this seriously, not the judge who had learned to lay two loaded six-shooters out before him when he opened court, to see that there would be no gun play. He was doing this back when Print Olive still shot Mexicans and Negroes down in Texas.

Olive, Fisher, and two more of the gang were taken to

the pen at Lincoln for safety. Brown, who was one of Olive's trusted hands, and the affable Phil DuFran had turned state's evidence. Sheriff Gillan certainly "criminally connected with the affair," as the newspapers put it, was unwilling to take up quarters with his fellow prisoners, suddenly mighty holy, it seemed.

The trial came up in the April term at Hastings, considered a little safer because farther from the crime and the Olive gang. But there were threats of a great mob of Print's cowboys coming to raid the court, burn the town to ashes. Many were afraid, for a man burner is a man burner. The sheriff petitioned the governor for protection. A company of troops pitched their tents opposite the courthouse and stayed.

There was suddenly a great deal of money loose in the country, particularly among those who might be witnesses, money from the Olives and from ranch acquaintances and connections. Some said that included the fine old Texas cowmen, the Snyders, somehow connected with the Olives left in the South.

Print's parents came up from Texas and at first none could believe that this I.P. of the violence, the whisky, the foul mouth, the ruthless brutal killer and defiler of men could be the son of such a gentle and religious old couple. Then they heard the mother speak of the goodness of "my boy, Prentice," always "my boy," as though he were still at her breast, as though she were still hiding his childish little naughtinesses from his father. "My boy, my poor baby," she murmured into her lace handkerchief, with no eyes for his brother Ira or even Marion, the youngest.

Two of Print's hands weakened and told of a plot to shoot Judge Gaslin and Attorney Dilworth during the trial, and added that I.P. said he had no fear of such proceedings. He had attended a dozen such weddings.

"Meaning killings?"

"Yes."

Olive and Fisher were found guilty and went to the pen, with high praise for Judge Gaslin from all but three newspapers of the whole state. Steps were taken immediately for a new trial. The case hadn't been tried in the jurisdiction of the crime—the new Custer County, which by an oversight of the legislature, was attached to no judicial district and so had no district court. A thick file of documents, including some shockingly revealing depositions, was presented to the state supreme court for a change of venue. The change was granted and one of the attorneys who got the decision was said to have received the 10,000 head of three-year-old Olive steers sold for him on the block at Hastings. "No telling what the others involved got," was the bitter comment, one way or another, over much of the state.

In the meantime the local lawyers of Olive and Fisher had been driving and riding over the entire region giving many people a choice of a roll of bills or the threat of a tongue cut out. When the rehearing came up in Custer County, in the only court that existed there, the county court, no complaint was found on the docket and no complaining witnesses came forward. The already celebrating cowboys roared and fired bullets into the ceiling of the courtroom, it was said, and Judge Boblits rose and announced, "Prisoners, get the hell out of here. It is time for another drink—on I. P. Olive and Fred Fisher."

Some said it was also time for Judge Boblits to add a good-sized herd of fine range cattle to his ranch, but then it was a good buying season. Anyway, on December 17, 1880, the court ordered "that the prisoners be discharged until further proceedings can be had." The case of Print Olive and Fred Fisher was never closed.

But I. P. Olive, said to be the wealthiest individual cattleman in Nebraska two years before, was now reported stripped of at least $250,000 in gold and property, with perhaps as much more added by others. "State supreme courts come a little high sometimes," Judge Gaslin was reported to have said. Perhaps they should have used the ropes offered them the evening they got the Olive outfit arrested.

Print, his family, and most of his ranch hands except the hated state's evidencers left for Kansas. Attorney Dilworth, marked for death by an Olive bullet, later became state attorney general but by then only Ira Olive was left in Nebraska, Ira who managed himself judiciously now, so much a good neighbor that when he needed any help it came as to any other, as though he had been orphaned, without sibling, without brother.

Down in Kansas Print Olive had joined with other cattlemen, pushed himself, some said, into a cattle pool in the region north of Dodge City and tried to recoup his herds and money any way he could. Perhaps he was right; perhaps the day of the lone hand in the cattle business was past.

# CHAPTER II

## THE BONANZA

THE cow learned to survive the Ice Age around man, who, unable to grow fur for his protection, took it from other creatures. Unable to lay up fat or flesh enough to carry him through famines or the winter as the bear did and the hedgehog, man took these, too, from the animals which could convert the grass he could not utilize. Unwilling to depend upon the uncertain chase, he tamed such animals as he could—living commissaries handy to his stone knife.

The cow, in her tolerant way, accepted all this. More, she probably hunted out man's habitation in time of deep and enduring snow, smelled out his seed caches when forage failed, and hugged up close to the caves and shelters he had appropriated or built up.

So the cow became the companion of man in his far wanderings, often the center of his existence. In all his really great treks over the earth she walked calmly beside him, perhaps bearing his burdens, drawing his wheel, sharing his triumph in fertile regions as well as his vicissitudes in famine, snow, and the devastations of war. Yet never had she been involved in such a vast man-made calamity as the depression that came sweeping out of the East in the 1870's, when drovers who had put their last cent of money and credit into great herds, trailed them perhaps a thousand miles or more to market, only to find the desperate bawling of 100,000 of hungry, unsold cattle and the angry, dark-faced trail crews demanding their pay.

In the East, in addition to the unsalable stock that reached there, great trains of cattle cars stood idle on sidings, stockyards and expanding feed lots bare and dry, the spread-ing cornfields to finish beeves heavy with drooping ears not worth the husking peg. To everyone involved it was a great loss but often to the cattleman it was a personal sorrow, for to him the cow was much more than a way of making a living.

Then in 1877 the price of beef had crept back past $2.25 a hundred on the hoof; by 1882 past $9. Part of this rise came out of the experimentation of the hard years. Some enterprising Yankee trail drivers and traders had dressed and stored the beef that they managed to get as far as the pack-inghouses and shipped it as they could, to large buyers of the East for what they would pay. In October, 1875, an initial shipment of 36,000 pounds of beef refrigerated by the new Bates Process was sent to England. Within a year the amount rose to 3,000,000 pounds a month; by the end of 1881 to 110,000,000 pounds a year—enough to break the market for British growers of beef and mutton, even without one head of the many live cattle shipped over. A cry against diseased, "sick," American meat went up, with an itch to invest in those far ranges and herds that could produce beef so cheaply.

There had been some earlier investigation of the American prairies and the reports of the British buffalo hunters but it all was too incredible, certainly more of that western exaggeration, more western tall tales. But by 1879 news of the vast Capitol Lands Reservation in Texas reached England and Parliament sent two members to look around. They returned bug-eyed from this empire of grass. Their report started the British invasion, from the Pan-handle up the Plains to Canada.

At the beginning of 1881 the Liverpool edition of the *Drovers Journal* reported on western cattle, generally Shorthorn blood on Texas cows, into Chicago from the Wyoming and Nebraska ranches by way of the corn regions, and in very good condition. As with animals partly wild, the meat often dressed out in high color, sweet and sound. Many would, however, be condemned as unfit for human consumption in England and most were not heavy enough, where cattle sold per head, not by weight.

This wasn't too encouraging, particularly for those who knew that the Chicago correspondent spoke of improved cattle, not the chute-run of Longhorns. But there was the Scottish-American Mortgage Company that had provided the sterling to rebuild fire-gutted Chicago in the panic year of 1873. The money was borrowed at low interest in Scotland and loaned at around double the per cent. The stockholders had received annual dividends up to 15 per cent. When investment in American ranches came up, this high return, with the fast money some Britishers had made as hide hunters, particularly in the fabulous Texas, whetted many a hunger. That some of the buffalo hunters had been scalped by Indians only added a bit of adventure on top of the romance of the cowboy. Money sprinkled with adventure and romance was irresistible.

Once the old trans-Missouri country had drawn the world's finest crop of travelers and adventurers, come to hunt, to view the aborigines, perhaps to live for years with the Sioux. Now once more everybody came but for a *ranche,* as the Britishers still spelled it, a ranch with cattle by the tens of thousands to bawl their fat way to market, and high-stepping horses to fork. Soon the range of all the West was claimed and fought over, even leased and occasionally bought when these were possible, as in Texas and along the railroad right of ways. Cattle by the millions were needed to stock these new ranges if there was to be money from the grass. Texans yielded their stock, even their fine young breeding heifers, for although they knew they were building up the stiffest kind of competition in the North, the price they asked and got was high. And safe in the pocket, as some of the old-timers comforted themselves, men who had seen the bottom drop out of the market as a bronc drops out from under a tenderfoot.

The Midwest, too, was skimmed of its best seed and Oregon—all blockier, heavier stock than the southern, while even much of the inferior she-stuff that usually went to market as culls was kept for breeding. Many calves usually cut for steers were now kept as herd bulls, while the dearth of their kind, usually plentiful at the slaughter pens and the feed lots, made even the canners boom.

Around Cheyenne and in Boston and Edinburgh it was said that a man could buy a calf in the forenoon and sell it in the afternoon for enough profit to pay for his dinner, with a hearty nip or two thrown in for sauce. Indeed, the only way to avoid making money in beef was not to go near the business at all or to punch cows for the other fellow at $25 a month. It was the new bonanza—not of gold but of something better, something that touched deep in man's nature, a bonanza in something he could grow and develop as his own living handiwork, a creature that stirred him twenty, twenty-five thousand years ago as the magical being that nurtured him, helped shape his destiny.

"Cattle, give us cattle!" was the cry from the San Antone to beyond the Marias of the north. By May, 1882, steers had climbed the highest since 1870, $9.35, a hundred for top quality. A steer ready for fattening on the northern ranges brought $37, perhaps even $50 in Texas, and could be sold to a Wyoming speculator for $60, beef cows at $35. There was a rumor that the British-owned Prairie Cattle Company had announced a dividend of 42 per cent for 1882, and according to livestock journals, Montana cattlemen were reaping profits from 25 to 40 per cent. Truly 1882 was the year the cow jumped over the moon, and next season she would clear the sun like an old-time, brush-popping Longhorn going over a granger's plowed furrow.

None of this could be hidden or ignored, not even
with the booming gold rush of the Black Hills. Brisbin's
*Beef Bonanza or How to Get Rich on the Plains,* put out in
1881, was being read everywhere, and the newspapers publicized what was certainly the last outpost of adventure in a
shrinking and dullard's world. Men and money poured out
upon the Great Plains. Even the most cautious old-timers, the
starters of the business, began to reach out, increase their
herds beyond what they ever felt they might swing handily,
and hunted more grass. Many of the earlier dedicated ones
spread, too, in addition to men like Goodnight who had already moved twice and I. P. Olive now crowding the others
in the cattle pool in Kansas. Ikard and Harrold, charter members of the Northwest Texas Association, added 70,000 cattle
and drove them to range lying across the west line of Indian
Territory. C. C. Slaughter bought state lands almost by the
county in west Texas until he had a pasture fifty miles wide
and eighty miles long. In addition he leased an empire of a
ranch in Montana and trailed steers up there to finish on
the hearty northern grasses.

Kit Carter, president of the Northwest Texas group,
who seldom ran more than about 8,000 head, organized a
cattle company in 1883 and bought up 40,000 acres to
guarantee range for around 15,000 cattle, come rain or
drouth. The Snyder brothers, once associated in cow herds
with Print Olive, were scattering their holdings from the
Gulf up through New Mexico, Colorado, and Wyoming to
the Pacific slope.

But the real boom capital for the cow country came
from the East and the British Isles. Although breeding stock
was at peak demand, beef prices seemed to sag a little now
and then, temporarily. Of course there were some sour
months like the *Drovers Daily Journal,* with its 1882 pre-
diction that catastrophe would result from overtrading. When
the cattlemen recovered from their first fury at this traitor
nurtured by their money, they asked what was meant by

"overtrading." Was a starving cow chasing grass overtrading? Or a calf bawling for his mother?

"We are just measuring up to the demand, sir," the Texans argue.

The East, which kept pouring money into the range country, needed no justification, nor did London and Edinburgh, throwing pounds sterling into the pot to equal if not exceed the Yankee dollar. In Edinburgh drawing rooms buzzed with stories of the bonanza. Staid old gents scarcely knowing the difference between a steer and a stone cow discussed the bonanza over port or snuff as they warmed their knees. Young aristocrats hungry for adventure, particularly if a little wild and an embarrassment at home, had no trouble tapping the family exchequer for investment. The western cattlemen were only too happy to unload their holdings at fancy prices to such investors. As always in a profit-hungry time, swindlers flourished. Paper companies put out attractive prospectuses and handsome stock certificates. Without an acre of land or a solitary Longhorn steer they raked in the money like a croupier in a boom town. And why not? A Scotsman, J. S. Tait, issued a small brochure, *The Cattle-fields of the Far West*. He estimated the possible profits as from 33½ to 66½ per cent, and added some fine success stories.

For instance, there was Searight of Wyoming who invested $150,000 in the cattle business in 1879, took nothing out, and put nothing more in, and although there was the hard winter of 1880-81, with some bad losses, before two more years had passed his business was estimated worth $1,500,000. Colonel Slaughter, president of the First National Bank at Dallas, made a similar sum from cattle before he reached middle life. Charles Goodnight, the Pioneer of the Panhandle, made, without any starting capital of his own, $600,000 in ten years. His partner, Adair of Ireland, put up around $360,000 or $370,000 the last six, seven years, and took out between $60,000 and $70,000. The remaining $300,000 of his investment was now worth $3,000,000. Tait added that Searight, Slaughter, Goodnight, and Adair could be surpassed in wealth by many cattle kings, and it was true there were a couple dozen such men—King, the Snyders, Lux, Lytle, Brush, Lawrence, Stuart, Kohrs, Carey, Kendrick, and so on, all pioneers in ranching. These were men who worked at the job, rode the range almost daily, supervised perhaps the smallest dab of tar on a wound to keep out the worms, saw the last sliver of rock salt on the far range, and caught the least sign of a buzzard circling where a critter might be dead. But now great corporations were moving in, organizations whose stockholders hired a manager, often several. Occasionally they got one who knew cattle, but most of them merely made a pleasant drive around the range in a buggy now and then while the owners talked cow over Scotch and water at their club in London or Edinburgh, played poker at Cheyenne or up at Miles City. Sometimes their hired hands rode the range and perhaps they connived with rustlers or branded part of the spring calves for themselves.

Such outfits invited the incompetency and thievery they often got. Even when they bought out honest ranchers the figures in the tally books were quite unreliable since no account was taken of the losses in calf crop or of stock that died during the winters, say 1878-79 and 1880-81. Investors seemed to think they had to buy that day, that minute, sight unseen, or lose the golden opportunity. Up in Cheyenne a blizzard story was told of a lot of cowmen at the bar in Luke Murrin's saloon gloomily trying to figure what their livestock losses would be. "Cheer up, boys," Luke said heartily. "The books don't freeze," and set 'em up for everybody.

Often, too, the pressure to show large dividends made men of judgment sell the herds down to the short hair, taking this year's profits out of next year's growth. But while many newspapers began to urge caution in the boom they feared was already slipping toward a bust, one Colorado livestock journal insisted that cattle were one investment that couldn't come too high for any man. They would multiply, replenish, and grow out of even a bad bargain. In 1883 the

*Breeders Gazette* reported that a good-sized bull calf worth $5 at birth could be a $45 to $60 steer when ready for market after four, five years' feeding on the free grass of the public domain. A thousand such animals would bring the owner $40,000 to $45,000 above their calf value. Even allowing another $5,000 for running expenses, the profit was still at least $30,000. But Bill Nye of the *Laramie Boomerang* dabbed his rope on the tallest tale of the whole beef bonanza. He told of an innocent tenderfoot who came to Wyoming with empty pockets leading a lone Texas steer and carrying a branding iron for the increase. Perhaps, as Nye said, innocence is truly its own reward, for the tenderfoot soon found himself the owner of 6,000 head of fine cattle, all but one the natural increase of his lone steer.

Yet even with Nye's paper spread out before them for a good laugh, everybody in Cheyenne speculated in steers. The *Boomerang* reported that a justice of the supreme court of Wyoming bought a $40,000 herd—good publicity to draw capital into new ranch enterprises and into some established ones, too, in need of new blood.

There were always some Massachusetts bonanza stories floating around. One told of a man from there who bought a Wyoming ranch the spring of 1883, 12,000 cattle, 700 horses, and other stock for $230,000. That fall he sold his beeves and 6,000 other cattle for a total of $180,000, which left him 6,000 head, counting calves, and 700 horses, worth at least what he had paid for the ranch. Another Massachusetts man, a manufacturer, was ordered to Nebraska for his health. He picked the cattle business for its fresh air, bought out a small spread of 4,000 cattle and drove in 5,000 from Oregon. In four years his $110,000 investment brought him an offer of $300,000 spot cash, which he refused.

The Bay State Land and Cattle Company was one of the cross-financed outfits coming in, with some Massachusetts and Maine capital in addition to the Scottish and English money. The ranch was started in western Nebraska back in the late 1870's, well ahead of the boom. They shipped out a

large frame house, knocked down, and set it up on the
Lodgepole Creek bottoms—a palace rising out of the prairie.
Cowboys came to stop their horses on the ridge and stare
awhile as they slouched over the horn. It was said they had
running water inside there, and a tub for washing all over,
like in a buffalo wallow. The carpets come boot-heel deep,
and velvet stuff was hanging over lace shutting out the windows. The grub tools looked like the silver on spurs and
there were napkins to stick in the shirt collars. Of course
that wasn't for the cowhands, but even in the cookhouse the
grub was mighty rich—canned peaches any day, and when it
was dried apples it was pie, raisin pie, too, even for breakfast,
and beans, lots of good beans baked brown and sweet with
molasses, cooked soft, too, not bouncing all around like Mexican jumping beans on a hot stove lid.

But mostly it was the bathing room and the privy
inside the house that the cowboys couldn't quite believe. Just
like a man heard tell.

Before long a second such house was dumped off the
freight and bullwhacked out to the head of Pumpkin
Creek, where the Bay State's main brand, the Half Circle
Block, was centered. By the spring of 1883 the outfit was
expanding very fast. They bought the Circle Arrow Ranch,
from Creighton, Snodgrass, and McShane for $700,000 and
that fall added the remainder of Creighton's holdings. The
next spring they bought out "Coad's Kingdom," as the
settlers called it, the Coad Ranch stretching from Chimney
Rock west to Scotts Bluff between the North Platte River
and the Wild Cat Mountains. Not large but very compact
and protected. In addition the Bay State leased Union Pacific
railroad lands and established another ranch up near Ten
Sleep, Wyoming. With these bases the managers planned to
run cattle all over the western part of Nebraska and the Big
Horn Basin of Wyoming and much of the region between.

Although they were building toward a herd of 150,000
head, their Indian contracts required outside steer purchases,
and late the spring of 1883 the new manager, John A.

McShane, went clear to Oregon and with a crew of eleven men prepared for the 1,200-mile, three-month drive back. It took many weeks to break and shoe their broncs for the rock and lava beds to be crossed, hunt up steers, not plentiful there either, throw and brand these heavier, shorter-horned cattle. Finally the herd of over 2,000 big two- to four-year-old FF steers was started east over a trail with vast stretches that made the route from Texas seem like a pleasant browsing along the grassy Platte bottoms, the crossing of the Red River only a little noontime cooling for the cattle compared to the roaring snow-fed streams they had to swim between Oregon and the hungry Sioux of Dakota.

At Old Ferry, on the treacherous Snake River, the cowboys worked the cattle out on a long bar and let them stop to drink there, belly-deep in water. In the meantime two men hurried across and brought up seven, eight head of the ferryman's herd, mostly milk cows, to the bank as decoys. Then the two waddies at the point of the herd cut off some of the leaders, including the bell steer, and prodded these into the swift boil of water, swimming desperately to keep afloat and from being swept away. The rest were whooped in after them but for all the "Yi-hoo! Yi-hoo!" that the trail drivers could yell out, the lead steer hesitated and almost went under when the main current hit him. But he could see the cows calmly drinking on the far side. His eyes lost some of their bulging fear and he struck out straight across the river, swimming strong, the rest of the herd pushed hard behind him.

They made it across the powerful snow-water stream that was not more than forty or forty-five yards wide here but so swift and deep that sometimes whole herds refused to try it at all. There were still three dangerous rivers to cross. At the Fayette the packs of barking, snapping curs set the cattle wild. This quieted a little when some of the dogs went floating downstream. The trail had many rocky stretches, including the lava beds that wore the hoofs of the herd to the quick, many long, arid sagebrush miles with no grazing, and finally the practically straight up-and-down trail at Terrace Canyon, called Tear Ass Canyon by every trailer who ever tried it. "So steep even the coyotes stop to throw on rough locks to make it down," an old puncher in the region warned the Bay State hands.

By November the 2,012 big FF steers were delivered to the Indian agent at Pine Ridge, Dakota Territory. For all the three months on the trail they were good, well-fleshed stock, better than the Longhorns the Indians usually received, stringy and trail-gaunted by the long, fast drive over burning prairie. The FF herd was just nine head short of the starting number. McShane made up a few others lost on the way, it was said, made them up in the usual manner by gathering in any strays from earlier herds, or any way he could.

The Bay State was by no means the flashiest of the foreign-owned ranches that dominated so much of the bonanza cow country. Most of Wyoming was taken up by British outfits. One of the fanciest was Moreton Frewen's up in the Powder River country before he sold it, and the Rocking Chair, coming in down in Texas, run by a British Lord for Queen Victoria, it was said, and not pretending to make money; nothing as common as that.

John G. Adair, the Scotch Irish financier who went in with Goodnight in the Palo Duro, had set a sort of pattern, more or less, but the typical Englishman entering the business in the bonanza years went in more for adventure or perhaps because he could not maintain his position at home. Perhaps he wanted a hunting preserve or came across the sea because the distance reduced the embarrassment he was to his family, who were sometimes very glad to make periodic financial payments to keep him out of sight. But the remittance man didn't stand high in the cow country except with those getting some of the remittance into their own fists.

More British ventures into the cattle country were by

company, such as the Prairie Cattle Company, Limited, the first Scottish ranch venture in America, at least of any size. In 1880-81 they brought up the so-called range rights to much of the Cimarron in New Mexico, then added the LIT on the Canadian in the Panhandle. The new company had some immediate success on the rising beef boom, and the chairman announced that a $16 calf could be fed up to a $35 value with less than three shillings outlay. This helped spread enthusiasm. Late 1881 the Texas Land and Cattle Company, Limited, of Dundee, with shareholder connections to the Prairie, had bought the 236,000-acre ranch in Nueces County from Mifflin Kenedy, former partner of Captain King, for breeding stock. In addition they got control of more land in the Panhandle and the Cherokee Strip. Both these companies had some American obligations and shareholders. The Texas also succeeded early and paid an annual dividend of 15 per cent. The next year the Scottish Matador was registered to buy $1,250,000 worth of ranch property. In six months they had 60,000 cattle, 300,000 acres of land bought on an average of $1.68 an acre, and ranging privilege on almost 2,000,000 acres.

With this demand for range Texas raised the minimum price for her unwatered state lands to $2 an acre. Still the cattle boom went on. More Scottish companies were formed, the investors anxious to grab a piece of the bonanza. One of the contact men sent out was John Clay. He came in 1880 and by 1883 he was made superintendent of the Western Ranches, Limited, up in Dakota. In 1882 the Wyoming Cattle Ranch Company, Limited, had been organized after Clay's favorable report on the 71 Quarter Circle, described as containing 4,000 square miles, 2,560,000 acres, but without stating how very much of this was government land, public domain. In 1882 the Powder River Cattle Company, Limited, took over the 76 Ranch of Moreton Frewen, who had amused the Wyomingites so much. The ranch lay along the Powder and the Crazy Woman, in Johnson County,

far from the railroad, but not too far for the great festivities
for visiting Englishmen under Frewen's management, although the land owned was nominal for the 54,629 cattle
listed in 1884.

Other, similar cattle companies were formed for the
Wyoming, Dakota, and Montana ranges and helped dominate the legislatures of these territories for years. In 1882
alone ten major British-American ranch companies were in-
corporated. Added to the earlier ones, their total subscribed
capital reached $15,500,000. The high dividends paid caused
some uneasiness in serious circles. *The Economist* thought
the public was ill-advised to suppose that these dividends
paid by the "Texas Companies" were from actual profits
but came out of the inflated valuation placed on the stock.
The rapidly increasing competition was expected to lower
the cattle prices before long. Others agreed. A correspondent
to *The Scottish Banking and Insurance Magazine* pointed
out what few had any intention of mentioning: that most
of the stockmen were merely squatters on the western land,
that they usually owned only narrow strips along the waterways and used the range on sufferance of the United States
Government. Prairie fires or a severe winter after a dry season
of short range could prove disastrous. Besides, buying cattle
by "book count" projected an estimated increase year after
year, without ever actually counting the stock, alarmed the
correspondent, as did the risk of being put off the public
range. The *Laramie Boomerang* was already reporting that
the Secretary of the Interior had begun to move against
all fences enclosing government land.

But the cattle companies kept right on sprouting in
the British Isles. In 1883 the Swan Land and Cattle Company, Limited, bought out the Swan ranch holdings of Wyoming and Nebraska. The land claimed was centered on the
Laramie River, a range 130 miles long, east and west, and
from 42 to 100 miles north and south, mostly public domain.
The price seems to have been $2,387,675, stock and all. The
next year the company bought railroad lands, which were

checkerboarded, alternate sections still the public domain and open only to regular settler entry.

So it went on, but with a little more caution among the Scots after the Swan transaction. London companies for Dakota, Wyoming, Nevada, Kansas, New Mexico, and Texas lands were still formed, including Lord Tweedmouth's Rocking Chair Ranche, Limited, in Texas, called Queenie's Cow Outfit by the neighboring ranch hands.

The general complaint against the invasion of the West by foreign capital brought a congressional investigation in 1886, which revealed something of the power of the foreign holdings in the range country. Twenty-nine foreign companies controlled 20,747,000 acres, much of it public domain, government land—a term that meant something entirely different to those from the old, old baronial and crown land holdings of Europe, particularly Britain, than it did to the democratic American, something different in mind and in law.

It also came out that several ranches promoted in England around late 1883 and early 1884 never got under way and perhaps it was as well, for range inspectors inquiring into the Prairie Company ranches reported them overstocked, which raised the charge of mismanagement. Shares dropped in value and stockholders of other companies became nervous. There was a general complaint about the packing-house combine in America, that the book counts for the ranch stock bought were always far too high and that the range on public domain was appallingly insecure now with the rising protest, public and governmental. There was some attempt to improve some of these situations. Moreton Frewen was managing the Powder River Company that bought him out, with Frank Kemp as assistant manager and Fred Hesse foreman. These men relieved him of the daily supervision to plan his own feeding and slaughtering operations down along the railroad, outlays he had trouble justifying to the shareholders at next year's meeting. Perhaps this was chiefly because beef prices were down. Compared to 1882, prices were far down, but while this was disappointing, cattle would come back. All the ranchers had to do was hold them over for next year.

In the meantime around $2,000,000 worth of blooded bulls had been turned loose on the Wyoming ranges. Old cowhands crossed their arms over the saddle horn and moved their cuds meditatively. "Them bulls shure are going to raise a fine chorus come winter, bawling around the corrals for somebody to come shovel out the feed," one said.

"Hell, they'll want to get inside. Look at them soft bellies sticking out. Ain't built to cut the wind like the Longhorns."

Still, it was plain that the cow country had confidence in the beef prices of next year, or the year after.

*CHAPTER III*

## *THE BIG DIE-UPS*

FOR some time very few men had managed to pull their eyes away from the sleek, grass-fat steers and their fine price long enough to feel the curious stillness gathering around them, see the thin, warning haze rise along the far horizon to suspect they were in a weather breeder, climatic and economic. The price collapse of the early seventies had been forgotten and the losses of the winters of 1878-79 and 1880-81, too. The profit on the stock that survived the last big winter had paid for a lot that were bleaching bones in canyon and draw. Since then the winters had been mild, the country growing warm again, old-timers like Stuart and Kohrs told each other, taking a personal pride in it. Cattle, even the unacclimated Texas herds and most of the imported eastern stock, were making it to grass without very serious losses as far north as the Marias of Montana, while native stock and second-year emigrants came through fine as frog hair.

Although the 1883 drive north from Texas was only around 260,000 head, the westward movement of American stock increased, with cattle from as far away as Ohio and New York State, even from Florida—an estimated 185,000 head, mostly young heifers, with probably 20,000 more driven in from Oregon.

The northern ranchers watched the boom in new cattle companies uneasily, but were less aware of the powerful foreigners, and feeling less able to fight them than the little outfits starting up with perhaps a log shack along some creek bottom, and a brand. Sometimes these little fellows had no intention of fighting for a piece of the free range, not even as rustlers, just hoped to sell out for the big money of the foreign investors. But most newcomers brought in cheap southern cattle and on top of the Longhorn's threat of fever was his inferior blood on the range with so much northern she-stuff good grade and the herd sires mostly pureblood.

"Ain't nothing rannier than them scrub bulls," an old rancher of the Chug country complained as he watched a dusty herd of Longhorns come in. "One of them Texas bulls'll come bellerin' clear across the table from Horse Creek and bust right in my corral if he smells a cow."

"Why don't your short-leggers, your Shorthorns, run 'im off, out of the country?" a Texan asked pleasantly, setting his hat back a little to show his humorous intentions.

"Oh, them big fellows ain't so eager," a cowboy put in, a little on the scrubby side himself.

There was a lot of laughing, not all humorous. The last few years one southern bull after another had been found dead on the Wyoming range. "Stopped a hunter's bullet," was the usual explanation.

It was true that the apparently unlimited flow of southern cattle was a real threat to the crowded North, the leggy stock able to beat the improved blood to the scarcening grass, and Montana and Wyoming had opposed all talk of a national cattle trail from the start. But when it came to a showdown, the range, the land was the main worry. Squatter holdings that exceeded a man's filing rights on government land had never been recognized and squatting had no legal status anywhere after land offices came into the region. The early cattlemen had divided the free range among themselves, as Goodnight and the Mexicans did in the Texas Panhandle, and prepared to defend their holdings in the only two places possible: in the legislative halls and on the premises, with money ready for the first, veiled or open threat of guns for the second. It was hoped that in the meantime their holdings would become classified as "accustomed range" with eventual legal standing, or that a lease bill could be forced through Congress.

While the cattlemen talked up the worthlessness of the land for settlement and homes, they took energetic steps to warn off those with ranching ambitions. In his report, 1883, to the Secretary of the Interior, the governor of Wyoming Territory outlined the difficulties a newcomer would have getting into the local ranges. In addition the Stock Growers Association pushed their law of 1884 through. This took the branding of a man's cattle, even on his own land, out of his hands entirely by making all branding illegal between February 15, before the calves were dropped in the North, and the Association's general spring roundup, the only one permitted by the law. In the roundup all stock with brands not accepted by the Association was automatically classified as mavericks and sold for the Association funds, with their hired inspectors empowered to confiscate stock and make arrests anywhere.

The Montana cattlemen welcomed the Northern Pacific Railroad's roaring approach up the Yellowstone but it would bring in settlers and make things easier for rustlers unless the ranchers could hire brand inspectors for the shipping points. It would bring in more competition, too, particularly eastern and foreign money. Without the powerful organization that stock growers could attain in the almost purely cattle territory of Wyoming, Montana ranchers had turned to their legislature with a "Cattle King" bill. It was passed in spite of the powerful mine and farm interests but the governor vetoed it, calling the bill a menace to personal liberty, a delegation of arbitrary power to unsworn subordinates, empowering the employees of a civilian organization, the stock growers, to make arrests without warrants.

So the Montana stockmen worked for control out on

the range. Through their local associations they published notices warning off any newcomers. The papers carried such a warning from the stock owners of the Musselshell, July 19, 1883:

> . . . we positively decline allowing any outside party or any party's herd upon the range, the use of our corrals, nor will they be permitted to join in any roundup on said range from and after this date.

Without the privilege of joining the general roundup on the open range a man's cattle business was soon closed out. True, without control of the legislature the cattlemen couldn't make such a boycott work legally, but few had the money or the guns to fight long. Individuals, too, staked out their range in the newspapers. The *Glendive,* (Montana) *Times,* April 12, 1884, carried this advertisement:

> I, the undersigned, do hereby notify the public that I claim the valley, branching off the Glendive Creek, four miles east of the Allard and extending to its source on the South side of the Northern Pacific Railroad as a stock range. Chas. S. Johnson.

Of course such claims had no more legal standing in court than those of the associations and so the cattlemen tried to get control of as much of the range water as possible. The rancher, if a citizen, could use his land-entry rights—homestead, pre-emption, perhaps timber claim, 160 acres each, or a Desert Act claim, first a section, 640 acres, later a half section. To these he might add such filings as he could talk his cowboys into making, trying to select those who would get no ranching notions of their own. With luck there might be the two school sections of each township open for rental, or some railroad lands for sale, unfortunately only alternate sections. That was just about the limit of his legal approaches to a wide range. If he could cover all the water, he controlled the surrounding prairie also, sometimes very wide stretches in the drier regions of Wyoming and Montana. Yet much later than 1884 some of the cattlemen didn't bother to own even the quarter of land that held the home ranch, depending entirely upon other and more immediate measures.

So long as the region wasn't crowded, all but the real range hogs had tolerated an occasional newcomer, if not too close. Some, like the Boslers, who claimed 150 miles of the North Platte water front in Nebraska, considered almost anything too close. They hanged a man from one of the government surveying outfits come to run the lines that would enable any greenhorn settler to find the numbers of the land he wanted. But the surveyor didn't scare out. He just picked up another helper, apparently from the disappointed miners deserting the Black Hills.

It was not only Goodnight and the cattlemen of New Mexico who had trouble with sheep. By the early seventies the moving gray blankets that were the herds crept in from the west upon Montana and by 1881 the assessed sheep outnumbered cattle. By 1884 three western counties of Wyoming were predominantly sheep country. Against this invasion hog wire or force was the only protection. Yet both the sheepmen and the ranchers were on government land, like tumbleweeds trying to cling to the earth that refused their roots.

To the settler neither cattle nor sheep range claims and customs existed. He saw the public domain as land held for the bona-fide homeseeker, the poor man, offering him a homestead of 160 acres for the filing fee, around $14, and five years' residence and improvements, with a second quarter obtainable by pre-emption at $1.25 an acre and often a third 160 acres, a timber claim, by planting and caring for ten acres of trees for five years.

Often the settler went boldly beyond the ranch-held waterways, sank a well or hauled his water, planted crops, to be destroyed by the range herds who might also rub down his sod house in an hour or fall through the roof of his dugout upon his bed. In return he shot at the cattle, often felt free to eat the beef that fattened on his grass and plantings. With those settlers pushing in all around the east, many cattlemen envied Print Olive his dispatch if not his tactics. There was no denying he knew how to hang out an owl that ought to help every rancher keep his range clear.

Those who looked southward with the uneasiness of a cow smelling a storm, the spring of 1884 turned out as keen-nosed as any old brockle-face. Although it was the year that Dodge City put on the big bullfight to draw the cattle trade back there, without much success, the drive, 420,000 head, was the largest since the disastrous year of 1871. More stock came in from the East, too, the heavier, blockier, barnyard cattle. The Northern Pacific alone carried 98,219 of these west-bound pilgrims to the open range and only 75,000 market stock went back. Other railroads reported the same trend.

These barnyard cattle cost around $35 a cow instead of the $24 the Longhorn brought. They were of better bone and flesh every year, quieter and gentler to handle. But long before January they would be up around the buildings and corrals bawling their heads off for hay and shelter instead of rustling the snow-swept ridges like the natives. Besides, the East was full of pleuro-pneumonia, a constant threat to the range herds. Yet the worst danger was still overcrowding, particularly after the very short summer grass of 1884 that sent the underfed cattle into winter without fat or strength. Before the boom 640 acres of good grazing land in south Texas usually fed 150 cattle, but after the grass was thinned and killed out by overstocking, with the usual invasion of mesquite, cactus, and other thorn, ten acres were required for one cow. In Wyoming and Montana sagebrush sprang up where good grass had grown, and while the cattlemen looked angrily toward the sheep as the culprits, much grass disappeared before the pungent, green-gray tangle of sage where no sharp-hoofed, root-cropping sheep had ever walked.

The success of the local cattleman organizations

brought a national stock growers' movement to work on the wider range, with the first convention set for the fall of 1884 at St. Louis. The Texans planned to fight for just one thing— a national trail to the North. But there were the deeper problems: range rights and a national lease law, the railroad monopoly, the packing trust, and the shrinking grass. Perhaps jealous that the early cattle market, St. Louis, was given this convention and aware of the criticism of Chicago's commission houses and packers, the Chicago Board of Trade put out a warning report. The western ranges were all badly overstocked; barbed wire had made many little pastures of big ones, and the mysterious Texas fever was spreading into a national plague. When the price of range cattle dipped sharply the editor of the *Daily Drovers Journal* informed his readers, "If you have any steers to shed, prepare to shed them now."

The uncertainty and unrest had brought the first Democrat to the White House since before the war, one not to be counted out as Tilden had been eight years ago. The angers of that steal seemed of another age, even to the Texans, as the men whose lives were ended that year seemed of some prehistoric time: Custer, fighter of the miserable Indians now squatting on reservations waiting for their only opportunity for violence—shooting down trail-gaunted Longhorns or Wild Bill Hickok, bad man of Hays and Abilene, the memory of him like a faded Wild West Show poster tacked to an old buffalo hide yard. Even the great herds of those buffaloes had no reality left for the men who had made as much as $5,000 or even $6,000 a season and now were perhaps punching cows for $25 a month and found. But some had a little jag of cows stashed away with a friend's herd or a relative's, and with a little luck—

There seemed so much concern for the ailing beef bonanza that only a few seemed uneasy about Cleveland. "There's a damn sight of laws on the books that could be turned up against the cowmen if he's so-minded," one of these said uneasily.

"Yeh, I hear Sparks is stirring up hell on fraudulent filings and fencing public lands over in Oregon," the newspaper readers replied.

The ranchers looked serious when this came up but were more uneasy about beef prices still sliding a little, telling each other cattle couldn't help but come back. The larger companies, particularly the foreign ones, were faced with the problem of falling dividends. To show a paper profit they sold off too much stock before the peak age, which helped the grass but cut down the number of salable stock the next year and many years following.

March, 1885, a stock journal put out a comforting report. There was really no cause for uneasiness, and with this assurance many ranchers held their beeves until late summer for a recovering price that never came. By then President Cleveland had ordered the herds expelled from the Cheyenne-Arapaho Reservation where they had grazed under old and unprofitable leases, unprofitable to the Indians. But the 200,000 cattle forced out had only one place to go, to the overstocked ranges. That or the market.

Several cowmen had hurried to Washington to talk Cleveland into stopping his order, and were told that the ranchers' cattle made trouble with the Indians—all that beef around and their families starving. In the end he turned out tough as any old mossy-horn steer that had walked to Montana. The cattle would be out on the deadline; the government had troops to see to that.

There was little time to curse the president and the railroads that the cattlemen were certain had pushed the order. The chuckwagons rumbled out and dust rose in clouds over the reservations like smoke spreading. The roundup crews worked from light to darkness and right through the moonlit nights. One rancher gathered up a mixed lot of 10,000 and headed them for the Cimarron. At nine in the morning the lead cows jumped into the river, throwing salty spray. Behind them came the great herd stretched back in a string to the horizon. At three in the afternoon the last drag was over, the banks on the far side churned to mud clear across the bottoms and into the breaks by the dripping cattle. The ranchers and the Kansas guards who had had trouble with stubborn men like Blocker and West smiled dryly. "General Miles and his troops standing around handy sure greased them cows' heels."

Finally it was fall and everybody tried to sell the last moment before the snow, with very little buying. Last spring grass-fat steers were quoted at $5 a hundred, already far below the 1882 top of $9 and over. Later this season they dropped to $3, the poorer grades down to $1.80 a hundred, the lowest since 1873.

The drouth-shorted corn in the feeding regions helped the tight system of stockyard trading, particularly in Chicago. Commission houses controlled the distribution of most of the cattle and worked together like card sharps taking a mess of greenhorn sight-seers to Dodge City.

"Yeh, it's sell at our price or take your damn beef off the doorstep," was the way one shipper told it out on the Sidney Table of western Nebraska.

"And pay our freight rate or walk them to Chicago, the railroads tell a man," another added.

It was true that beef was no lower, only cattle. Commission charges and freight rates were no lower, only cattle. The railroad monopoly had long been a bur under the saddle blanket to the cowmen. Late in 1879 Kit Carter, of the Northwest Texas Association, had appointed a committee to confer with the rail company heads at St. Louis. They got the same cold-decking that the beef trust gave out lately. The movement of slaughterhouses to the plains, the meat shipped East in the new refrigerator cars got a real push these years. The Marquis de Mores over on the Little Missouri and Moreton Frewen were two of those putting these hopes to the test, but there were dozens of others.

Last year a speaker addressing the Wyoming stockmen predicted great changes in the packing situation. "The day will come when a live bullock will only be seen in circuses in Chicago." Dressing beef would be a home industry and the commission merchant, now a necessary evil, would be wiped out.

It was true there were plans to ship more live beeves straight through to England for fattening, in spite of the quarantine against pleuro-pneumonia. Perhaps that could be side-jumped like a bronc avoiding a rattler on the trail. Frewen was sent over to see. In the meantime there was agitation for a congressional investigation into monopolistic practices and rates. There were also more threats of wage cuts for the railroad workers and other buyers of meat.

In the meantime nature seemed inclined to help a little on the overstocked ranges. Texas got a most disastrous storm over such crowded counties as Fisher. Ten days of sleet and snow sent cattle drifting with the wind, to sweep stock along clear down the edge of the Staked Plains. Thousands ended up in the Pecos River.

The old-time cowman, Ike Pryor, was caught in the storm. He had made a $500,000 deal in the fall for cattle he would deliver in the spring, on a $100,000 down payment. In the spring he had to return $30,000 of the advance, let alone deliver any stock on the rest. It was as well that he cleared this up fast, like cutting out a worm-infected wound on a steer. Later the deliveries would have been even harder to make.

After another dry summer, late December brought the first real clouds flying in from the pale haze that had lurked along the horizon for some time. The weather-wise Longhorns from Kansas down started a swinging march long before the sun was hidden, stringing southward in long lines, some halting in breaks or in timbered bottoms, perhaps to move out again, mostly in single file almost as the buffaloes had migrated, much like the ancestors of the Longhorn had marched purposefully southward before the push of the encroaching icecaps. They moved now as with some deep memory for survival stirring in them, urging them on. Cowboys and ranchers saw them go, and old-timers spoke of it in wonder. Few could recall ever seeing such a thing among cattle.

The storm came out of the north upon the Dakotas. The last morning of the closing year was a weather breeder, close, oppressive. The whistle of the new railroad heading up through northwest Nebraska could be heard clear to the Black Hills. By midmorning tatters of gray cloud streamed in from the north, boiled over all the sky, ran in a thick mist barely off the prairie. The wind came, first sneaking in little puffs here and there along the tablelands and blowing harder as the temperature fell. The mist turned to snow, thick and white, to cling to the northwest side of every weed and bush and cottonwood, until they were lost in the driving blizzard.

One of the hundreds of cowhands who had been swept into speculation by the promises of the bonanza had bought up a herd of 2,300 steers in Texas and trailed them north to the Black Hills region, planning to repeat this seasonally and after a few years to take his profit and settle down in Texas to a ranch of his own. Now as the wind hit the thin southern hides of his steers they bunched up as before an enemy, a cougar, perhaps. But this was not something to be faced down and so they turned their tails to the wind and started southward, blinded by the thick, powdery snow that choked their breath. Their backs caked white, and their heads, their blank-eyed faces as they hurried faster and faster, straight for the rim of the tableland where it fell in a steep wall straight down.

Their owner had seen them start and tried to head them, turn them into a spin, a mill, as in a stampede, but before long he couldn't even see any of them, his horse snow-caked, too, even the head lost to him in the driving snow. But he kept going, following the best he could by the dull sound of the thousands of hoofs. He heard them as they went over, plunging down the forty-foot bluff.

Slowly he turned his horse away, whipping him sidewise into the storm to keep from going over, too, in the push of the wind, seeking shelter, pulling his icy-white buffalo saddle coat about him, chilled not only by the storm but the debt that would be with him for years, for many, many years at a cowboy's pay. It was no comfort to him to discover later that the Reynolds brothers, old-timers in the cow business, had trailed 7,000 steers up to Dakota from Texas and lost them all.

The storm hit Kansas a night later. It froze cattle and people caught on the prairie, tore their little board shacks to pieces, and froze those huddled there, too. Down in the Texas Panhandle it struck a homeseeker's wagon and left the whole family dead, parents, three children, and the horses at the tongue. It drove hundreds of thousands of cattle on as it had those up in Dakota and Kansas. Some went hundreds of miles, piling up in arroyos and canyons, going through the ice of the occasional lake and the rivers. The Arkansas, Cimarron, and Canadian were full of carcasses. Farther west the ranchers of the Indian Territory had built a barbed-wire drift fence one hundred seventy miles long from their west border across the Panhandle to New Mexico, with a parellel fence south of it along the Canadian. Endless strings of cattle from southwest Kansas and No Man's Land hit the first drift fence. The leaders piled up in low places and on down slopes, going under in the blind push of those behind until the broken, the freezing, and the dead were so deep the rest clambered over them, or the posts went down, the fence flattened for miles as the cattle were driven on by the fury of the blizzard. At the second drift fence it was the same, with ten thousands of bodies lining its reaches both ways. In places the dead cattle lay in piles 400 yards wide along these fences, sometimes only the horns of the top ones showing through the drifted snow. The manager of the LX Ranch with his men skinned an average of 250 head to the mile along thirty-five miles of the Panhandle drift fence. Other ranchers did the same. Hides went east by the trainload, the only marketable product on the prairie.

Every ranch in No Man's Land showed a loss of at least

50 per cent, some 75. The Kramer brothers, after months of search, found only 2,500 head out of their herd of 20,000. In the spring the carcasses and even live cattle bearing brands from ranges as far as five hundred miles north were found in Texas. The Kansas prairie, too, was dark with carcasses, the second time in eleven, twelve years—first the buffaloes and now the cattle, almost like a retribution. Ten thousand cattle lay dead between Garden City and Punished Woman Creek. The pool that included Print Olive was hard hit, Olive too, after the fortune his burning of Mitchell and Ketchum had cost him. Now the new start that the boom had brought was cut down by the bust and the blizzard.

Up in western Nebraska the Bay State lost an estimated 100,000 head. The carcasses formed an almost solid covering between Pumpkin Creek and the roughly parallel Wild Cat Mountains, the deep creek bed choked with the dead stock for ten miles. It broke the great power of the Bay State, with all its eastern and British backing, and opened a vast new region to settlers, and to rival cattle empires.

From Dakota to mid-Texas the fragrance of spring flowers was lost in the stink of the Great White Ruin. It was estimated that 300 people died in the storm but there was no way of telling who all might have been on the plains, seeking stock, or game or land, or fleeing from some pursuer and never heard of again. Skeletons found ten, twenty years later were identified by various means as men lost in the Ruin.

Cattlemen could organize against rustlers and the tick. They could fight the packing combines and the railroads. They could even fight the grangers, the settlers, one way or another for their cows, but against such a blizzard they were helpless. They shook off the complaints of eastern stock growers that cattle, particularly cows, calves, and bulls, should not be turned out with no feed or shelter, to die like this. They laughed sourly to complaints from that new outfit of do-gooders, the Humane Society, who had objected to branding and ear bobbing from the start. Now they had turned to angry protests against letting cattle live their natural lives rustling on the range.

"Want us to stall-feed 50,000, 100,000, 300,000 cows?" the cattlemen snorted.

But only a few knew about the Humane Society and the rest. Others too low down to read or listen, rode the range where the fall had shone golden on so many cattle, yes, too many cattle, but good stock, their stock. Many turned everything over to the bank; others just quit the country, never trying to round up the few cattle left. Almost to the day that their range seemed deserted others moved in, particularly the out-of-job, land-hungry homeseekers. They rushed in everywhere.

It was the natives, the fat steers, the cows unencumbered by a growing calf that survived, or survived the calving, perhaps with the help of a cowboy who had sworn that was one thing he would never do—play midwife to a goddamn heifer. But it was the fond cursing of the beloved, and everybody knew it. Even for all their help the calf crop was almost zero. J. M. Day's big D Cross spread near Ashland, Kansas, branded 900 calves compared to 10,000 the spring before. Besides, many cattle that did survive had to be killed because their frozen feet were amputating themselves, falling off. In some regions a third of the stock had lost their tails, dropped off, too, and many horns, while some carried strips of tattered, loose hide where wolves had been at them. With so much meat around they had not needed to chase the animal, finish the job.

By summer it seemed that all the moisture of the sky had fallen in that one blizzard, to run off in one swift thaw, roaring down the gullies and arroyos and away. By June almost all of Texas was burning, only the mesquite and the cactus green. The drouth that had started the summer before spread into the midwestern corn belt, with farmers and stockmen both short of feed. It widened into Wyoming and Montana. By fall the cattlemen were spooky as a herd of steers smelling javelinas in the brush. The Chicago market was declining steadily, the papers announced, as though that could be news.

"Bottom dropped out," the cowmen told each other when they met, saying it quietly, past the relief of profanity now.

The demand for stock cattle was about gone. The southern ranchers had rushed their cattle to market to get out with what skin they might save and found prices still going down, lower than any time in range history. They had dropped ten, fifteen dollars a head below last fall, with most of the run poor stuff, drouth-thin, but better sold at any price or given away than left on the bare, baking range to die, or to steal the little remaining pasturage from better stock. Up in Montana ranchers leased large tracts in Alberta from the Canadian government. In August, 40,000 thin, dusty cattle from Dawson, Custer, and adjoining counties were plodding, slowly, with popping joints, across the border. By September over a quarter of a million Montana cattle were on Alberta grass.

While there was often incredible mismanagement on the outside-owned ranches, as was to be expected, sometimes, however, the mistakes were the foolish interference of the far owners, innocent not only of cattle but of geography as well. Moreton Frewen, the Britisher who had learned a little about ranching by the time he had lost his Powder River outfit and had to take on the job of manager, had bought up cattle right and left. By the summer of 1886 he tried to take advantage of every little inch of rope possible and gathered up the biggest herd of beeves ever seen in Wyoming—good beeves, fed on the sub-irrigated river bottoms. The foreman, Fred Hesse, got the herd to Fort Fetterman to be shipped out on the railroad due there. But Hesse received a cable from London ordering him to turn the great herd back and ship from Medora, far up the Little Missouri near the Roosevelt ranch. From there the cattle were to be routed to Duluth and shipped by the lakes to Liverpool.

Furious, Hesse turned his herd back. It was late summer and although he had kept the stock in good flesh, now he had to move fast to beat the winter. He pushed them over the long, weary, waterless stretches as fast as he could but even so he had to load the great herd in a blinding snowstorm and got them to Duluth too late for shipping through the Lakes, already freezing up. There was no range around Duluth, no feed available. Starving in the pens that cost money, the cattle were turned loose in the snow to eat dead leaves from brush and trees, to break in here and there, spreading terror with their wide horns, their wild eyes. Finally Hesse got permission to ship them to the Chicago market, gaunt and starving, to be sold at giveaway prices. Stockmen figured that the London cable cost the company at least $200,000, the cable and their innocence of geography of the West.

It was not a good fall in Chicago anyway, with the big packers having their own troubles. In October, 1,200 of Armour's beef butchers joined their pig stickers in the strike that spread to other firms. Even when an agreement was reached in November, some of the Morris and Swift men objected to some of the conditions. The situation was a heated one, with an alleged attempt to poison the family of P. A. Armour with sample packages of buckwheat full of strychnine. It sounded unreasonable and hopelessly amateurish—such a bitter poison, one that had to be hidden very carefully from the wolf and the coyote, stirred into bland buckwheat. But Chicago was in a sullen, angry mood, as was the whole cattle country.

All the summer of 1886 the ranchers of the South had looked toward Indian Territory and the reservation ranges that Cleveland had cleared of outside stock. Would the government let cattle starve while vast Indian pasturages stood in untouched grass? Plainly the government would. Up North private deals had been made with the Crow Indians along the Little Big Horn and the Yellowstone at fifty cents a head.

But it was done too late in the season, the range too near the river breaks for good grazing. Some Montanans scattered part of their cattle in small bunches of around 1,000 head through the agricultural region for winter herd. The Cheyenne paper reported large shipments of cattle to forage as far east as the Nebraska and Iowa cornstalk country. But these were all small, last-minute remedies, like scooping up a hatful of buffalo gnats from a great swarming, even with the quarter million cattle on herd in Alberta.

The real uneasiness hit the old cowmen of the North when they noticed curious and unusual movement among the wild life that fall. Animals were very scarce, even the varmints. Prairie dogs holed up early, Elk moved in determined march southward. Suddenly almost all the birds were gone, even those that usually stayed all winter, even the gay, dark-crested little waxwing. The snowbirds, after whirling like tossing leaves in the wind awhile, no longer gathered in their circles to pick up seeds, while they fluffed out their feathers in the growing cold. Instead, Arctic owls came flying on silent wings, the first seen in the Judith Basin so far as any white man could remember. Old Indians followed their ghostly flight with their narrow eyes and drew their blankets closer.

"Big cold—" they said, with blank faces, and then their camps, too, were gone.

Clouds came to the whole region of the range lands, almost the first since early spring. They brought winter, early winter. Blue northers whistled across the Texas expanses that had been hit by the Great White Ruin last January. From Montana through the Dakotas, Wyoming, western Nebraska, Colorado, and parts of New Mexico snow fell and was welcomed as a break in the killing drouth. But it kept falling, let up a little, and fell again, deepening on the ground so it buried the tallest patches of blue joint grown up where a little snowbank had lain last winter. The snow choked the streams and covered the water holes to trap the wandering thirst-driven stock. Cattle, even the rustling Longhorns, went hungry, weak and sore-footed, their knees

cut and red-iced from plowing the deep crusted snow. Then
in December the blizzards started, howling from the north
and the northwest, with the pale cold sun out a few hours between storms. None of these were as bad as the Great Ruin
of last year, but after weeks and months even the hardiest
stock began to die where there was no bark to gnaw off the
trees with the half-toothed bovine jaws. A few feeble attempts were made to feed hay from the stack or two put up
for the driving team, or the blooded bulls. But mostly these,
too, had to rustle, their short legs soon too weak to carry their
gaunted bellies dragging the snow.

Even when the sun came out little curls of snow soon
began to run again in the rising wind, the dry, loose snow
lifted to the knee of the hair-chapped cowboys, then to the
watering eyes as they turned up their buffalo coats and let
their horses find the way home. Fewer and fewer cattle remained to drift with the storms, to stumble into snow-filled
washouts, gullies, or canyons.

The blessed Chinook came early that January, 1887,
with the day bright, the sky suddenly blue, the wind wonderfully warm from the land of the Chinooks. It ate into the
darkening snow, made the river ice pop under the lifting waters. It took the kinks out of the backs of the cattle still able
to stand. They waded the slushy, watery drifts seeking out
patches of grass flattened down and soggy gray.

But almost before they had one belly full, the wind
turned, the temperature dropped so fast no lagging thermom-
eter could keep up, the slush ice hard as stone. The ground
was covered for the rest of the winter, with new blizzard snow
slipping over the ice-glazed prairies, piling deep in canyon
and draw. Spring finally came. By then a young artist,
Charles M. Russell, who, like Remington, came West to attach himself to the new bonanza, had portrayed the essence
of this bad winter on a postcard-sized water color. Working
as a cowhand he had holed up on the OH Ranch of Phelps,
Kaufman, and partners. Asked by his employers at Helena
for a report, he sent them the water color of a washboard-

sided, goat-necked starving cow humped almost knee-deep in snow, hungry wolves watching. He called it "Waiting for the Chinook" but it was later changed to "The Last of 5,000" because Kaufman had seen so many of their 5,000 dead on the range.

The spring roundup of 1887 was the darkest, grimmest ever known to all the cattle country. It was the first time that white men ever saw turkey buzzards soar the Wyoming sky in great dark flocks, circling slowly down.

The cattle up in the severe cold of Canada had been swept southward, too, some reaching their old Montana ranges as deep under crusted snow for them as for the local stock. Drifting steers that found settlements huddled against the buildings, pushing in the windows, breaking in doors, whole walls. A late rising of blizzard wind swept thousands of ice-caked, staggering cattle past Great Falls and out upon the Missouri ice, to go down on the 50-degree-below-zero smoothness, plunge through the deep air holes and into the dark open current, the sullen water drawn back deep from the cold.

Old-timers who had survived ten, twenty, or more winters were desperate. On the Canadian ranges the disaster was complete, and a little farther south, too, and much farther south. The dead were piled in the coulees, in canyons, in arroyos, and along the foot of the cap rock—along any barrier. Their carcasses dammed the canyoned creeks and smaller rivers, blocked the lowlands with the river ice when it was finally lifted by the spring thaw. A 90-per-cent loss was general over vast portions of the open range country. Even those with native or acclimated stock lost 65 to 80 per cent. Montana, with a million head of cattle, reckoned up a loss of $20,000,000. Granville Stuart, the old-timer, the patriarch of Montana cattlemen, figured his loss at 66⅔ per cent, better than most, but his friend and former partner, Conrad Kohrs, salvaged only 3,000 head out of 35,000.

Now came the great surprise for all those who had damned the whole Chicago commission and packinghouse gang. Joseph Rosenbaum, livestock commission man, came out to Helena and called in a number of Montana ranchers who owed him a total of $1,000,000. They went as ranch owners, taking one last look at their spreads as they rode away over the stinking prairie, stinking with their cows, cows trusted to their care. They went as cowmen and would return owning less than the lowest saddle bum in ragged chaps.

But instead of foreclosing on them, taking over much of Montana range country, Rosenbaum offered the cattlemen an additional million dollars to build up new herds.

The dark-faced ranchers heard him in silence, unwilling to believe their battered and frosted ears. Gradually they accepted his words, quietly, with dignity. This was not Chicago. This was the West, in the best tradition of the West, where a man pulled even his enemy's cow out of a bog, where a man's word was his bond and could not be dishonored this side of death. The ranchers were men of few words this spring but Joseph Rosenbaum was never to regret that day's work.

The poor, winter-gaunted remnants of great herds wandered in search of the sprouting grass, their ears, tails, feet, even legs and backs frostbitten, the skin ragged and dropping off. Men like Granville Stuart, who had found the cattle business engrossing, compelling, all their lives were suddenly shocked and disgusted with it. Some never wanted to own another cow as long as they lived. It was as though a whole way of life had failed them, a basic faith betrayed them, an idol fallen.

The *Cheyenne Sun,* long a powerful voice of the stockmen's capital, also became critical. "A man who turns out a lot of cattle on a barren plain without making provision for feeding them will not only suffer a financial loss but also the loss of the respect of the community in which he lives."

The larger companies had been most responsible for blowing good cattle prices into a boom, a bonanza, a sort of South Sea bubble, by buying up vast herds on borrowed money at fantastic interest, paying fantastic dividends. Now it was all gone as a tally sheet in a blizzard wind, and with them their welcomed terms "cattle baron" and "bovine king." Before the Marias and the Milk, the Yellowstone, the Little Missouri, and the Cheyenne and Platte had carried off the snow water, the Swan Land and Cattle Company, the largest of the northern outfits, the first to import White Faces, was in the hands of the receiver. They were only one of a whole generation of cowmen dead broke, busted.

Thomas Sturgis had hurried from the East to Wyoming in the lush days of the boom. He had become one of the big stockmen and helped make a power of the Wyoming Stock Growers Association, was the secretary when the chinook thaw froze to ice. He stayed until he saw the fat buzzards wheeling low, caught the stink of dead stock on every wind. Then he boarded the train east and from New York he resigned his position. The Union Cattle Company, a $3,000,000 outfit that he had headed, was gone as were a dozen eastern financial organizations that had backed the western cattle companies. The swanky Cheyenne Club, the hangout of the men who ran Wyoming and the statehouse— the headquarters of the International Cattle elite—defaulted on its bonds, and was to be sold for two winter-thin dimes on the dollar. Nearly all the big outfits in Wyoming headed into quick liquidation. Up in North Dakota Teddy Roosevelt left his blizzard-swept ranch to the hired help. The shoe company in St. Louis that had bought a great herd from Glenn Halsell for $340,000 sold out to a cowboy who had saved his year's wages.

The next fall, after the worst had been faced, the *Cheyenne Sun* congratulated its readers on the departure of the Frewen brothers, managers and promoters of the Powder River Cattle Company. Of all the English snobs of great pretentions, who flew very high and sank very low, the Frewens were probably the toppers. They had had flowers shipped out to the ranch, conducted their business on a level that was a constant surprise to even the most reckless and extravagant Americans. They had brought an important and legitimate business into discredit even in the East.

It was typical that a character like George West would face the Big Die-Ups in his own way. He had 150,000 acres of Texas land stocked with mortgaged steers when the drouth and the blizzards struck. After the last dry leaves clinging to bush and thorn were eaten the cattle were about gone, too. His men skinned until he couldn't face the bull trains of hides any more. He sent the hands out with hatchets to knock off the left horn of every dead steer found and bring it in as a record. When they had a pile of 2,200 horns in the corral, like a great rick of mesquite, he stopped them.

The summer of 1887 in northwest Texas had been a season of burned and barren range, with no rain to replenish the holes when the snow water of the second ruinous winter was gone. C. C. Slaughter sold 10,000 cattle at giveaway prices. Ikard and Harrold, gone so hopefully into Greer County with almost uncountable cows, sold wherever they could, for whatever they could get, and pulled in on their small home ranges. The Snyders, of the early dedicated men of Texas, had been in the cattle business since around 1857, were major suppliers of beef for the Confederacy, had survived the price busts of 1871 and 1873. Before the Big Die-Up struck they had been offered an even million dollars for their cattle outfits from the Gulf to Wyoming and over to the Pacific slope. In the spring of 1887 they owed nearly that much, and selling out, retrenching, they started in the saddle once more, back where they were thirty years ago. Colonel Ike Pryor, publicized as the orphan cotton picker who had been offered nearly a million for his ranch holdings, was pretty nearly back in the cotton patch.

Truly this was the end of an era. From now on cattle would have to be specially winter-pastured, and at least the cows, calves, and bulls winter-hayed and given some shelter from the fiercer storms—all pretty expensive for common southern range stock.

There were some whites and some Indians who did not think of the future, but looked back to these Plains fifteen, ten, or, in the North, even five years ago. A couple of old Cheyennes headed down toward Indian Territory as soon as the snow thawed off to visit their relatives. They saw hundreds of magpies and buzzards, too plump to do more than flap awkwardly out of the way, the coyotes and wolves so fat and lazy they barely rose to move before the snorting of the Indian horses. The men rode with their blankets drawn about them in the chill Montana morning, over prairie scattered with carcasses that were bloated round as great dark puffballs, their awkward legs sticking straight out. As they moved southward into warmer regions, they were never out of the stink of dead cattle and seldom away from the curious rushing sound of maggots working.

The Indians had seen such sights before, when the white men, in their violent way, had killed the millions of buffaloes, leaving their carcasses an offense on the clean earth and wind. Now there was another great killing, but this time it was not from the roar of the hunters' guns.

# CHAPTER IV

# THE NATIONAL TRAIL

FROM the first cow that escaped Coronado's herd, with her double burden to be dropped at ripening, Texas cattle were known for their fertility, their high percentage of sturdy calving and, particularly those from the southern regions, for the fever that struck wherever they passed. First the Arkansas and Missouri farmers lost their milk cows, then the cattle breeders as far as New York State had to see their good stock die. There was action, varying but angry: boycott, arrests, guns, rope, and bull whips. But it was the Kansas settlers with their fury and violence who pushed the Texas herds westward, using whip and rope and gun, too, and finally the courts and barbed wire to protect not only their stock but their crops and grass.

Legislation came, too, but slowly, bucking the power of the railroads and the stockyards of St. Louis and Chicago, and the booming business of the trail towns. It was even harder to get enforcement than enactment, with the long, open border to the south and the west, the trail drivers willing to use money and lead to get through, some lawless by nature but more frequently by necessity or because to them the cow could do no wrong.

Even in Texas there had been appalling losses among

the blooded stock brought in to improve Longhorn beef. While it was generally accepted in the North that the fever was somehow connected with the cow tick, some still believed that the southern herds breathed contamination upon the wind. Others claimed that traveling gave the cattle a fever, which justified their unwillingness to butcher their own beef while on the move, yet even the loudest mouth against frying his own trail meat in the chuckwagon skillets had no more fear of any fat strays in the herd than of any fat young heifer unlucky enough to be caught grazing along the trail.

The south Texans still claimed that their cattle were clean, healthy stock, as any fool could see. They denounced the quarantines as aimed against the competition of their low-cost beef. While there was much opposition in Colorado against herds straight from Texas, many ranchers disposed of their good but fever-susceptible American stock for the cheaper Longhorns. Not that there wasn't violence plenty there, too, almost from the first. Joe Curtis and John Dawson, former associates of Goodnight, trailed 1,600 head up toward Denver in 1869 and were attacked by a gang of around fifty men. They shot down many of the cattle, wounded others, and stampeded the herd. Afraid of the Texas fever, they said, but the *Pueblo Chieftain* suggested that their object was "doubtless plunder." To be sure some recalled that Goodnight and others were important in Pueblo affairs, but the trailers who heard of the attack sent back for armed reinforcements to shoot their way through, whether ranchers or plunderers.

Although the Coloradoans complained that they had asked the trailers to go around the more settled regions, beyond the range of American stock, on a perfectly feasible route, the Texans swore they would go where they goddamned pleased through any damn Yankeeland. When Goodnight was stopped near Canon City by fifteen, twenty men who refused to let the herd cross the Arkansas, he loaded his shotgun with buckshot and led the way, a hired hand with his Winchester out across the saddle pointing the herd in behind him, the rest of the trailers with their Winchesters ready, too.

"I've monkeyed as long as I want to with you sons of bitches," he said, and the Coloradoans parted, sitting their horses awhile, watching, and then went home.

Out of these conflicts a Colorado Cattle Association was organized, around 1,500 men pledged to let no Texas herds pass over the main trails between the Arkansas and the South Platte unless within the territory at least a year. The law forbidding the importation of any Texas cattle for any purpose whatsoever was unenforced and so repealed. But even the arrogant Goodnight found it expedient to swing his herds around east of the settled areas. In 1875 he blazed the New Goodnight Trail from Fort Sumner to Granada, the station on the Arkansas River just west of the Kansas line. But by the late 1870's Goodnight's Texas range lay astride the new trail routes through the Panhandle and was running expensive blooded cattle. Once more he drew his Winchester but this time against drovers stringing their coastal stock through his range. Made a difference which way the skunk was headed.

Ranchers in No Man's Land were losing their herds to the fever from trail stock out of the Gulf regions and Goodnight was in even greater dangers with his Shorthorns. After lone-wolfing it so long, he decided that the Panhandle cowmen must organize or be cleaned out. True, the use of the wide loop and the running iron had increased until the rustlers practically controlled the country, at least up around the Canadian, but now the cattle had begun to die of the fever and against this the cowmen had to stick together or go under. Cowboy couriers were sent around the more reliable ranches from north of the Canadian down to the Matador. They met at Mobeetie and elected Goodnight president of the new Panhandle Association formally launched next year, 1881.

Goodnight worked on a three-man committee to stop the coastal herds from coming through. There were powerful men down there, men like Richard King, and rambunctious ones like old Shang Pierce, but the committee made a trip to the governor anyway, to suggest a quarantine, with one well-marked trail through the Panhandle and the herds to be kept strictly within it. The Northwest Texas Stock Raisers Association had already slung together a plan for a trail with a fine of five cents a head for each day a trailer's cattle were outside of the route. This seemed pretty stinking cheap to ranchers who were finding their good herds scattered dead and dying over the prairie after the coastal stock went through.

No Man's Land, which still belonged to no state or territory, with no political organization, was a natural refuge for thieving, brand-burning outlaws. The ranchers up there had an early sort of league against them and were reviving it against the fever herds when a Texan named Moore appeared ,with his southern herd. They tried to tell him the route he must follow on to Dodge City but they couldn't agree among themselves where this was to be and so Moore went his own way. Next year when the old trailer Ab Blocker came through he told the ranchers he would drive his herd where he damned please.

"I make my own trail," he roared.

To this the leaguers had to stiffen. Go their route or be thrown out, herd, horses and men, they told him, and stuck to it. Outnumbered and outgunned, Blocker gave in. When the Texans wrote the Secretary of the Interior for an opinion about these stoppages, they were told that No Man's Land was still literally no-man's territory and open to all in a broader sense than any other region within the nation.

But now there was more trouble farther south. George Reynolds, long in the cattle business, headed a herd northward. Before it reached Goodnight's region, one of Charlie's cowboys, Smith, came riding with a letter saying that he was to guide the Reynolds herd out around the Goodnight range, adding that if Reynolds had any feeling as a friend or an acquaintance, "you will not put me to any desperate action. . . . My cattle are now dying of the fever contracted from cattle driven from Fort Worth. . . . I simply say to you that you will never pass through here in good health. Yours Truly, C. Goodnight."

Reynolds sent the letter to the *Fort Griffin Echo,* commenting that stockmen in general should know how overbearing prosperity can make a man. Not to be stopped by any Winchester quarantine, Reynolds started two herds across Goodnight's range, one under his brother. Neither was molested, but the enmity lasted. Others, too, resented the Goodnight attitude and swore to contest his self-appointed rulership of the old buffalo plains. There was, however, the plague, the fever, all the Panhandle infected, some losses up into the hundreds, thousands of dollars, yet out through the Panhandle was the last trail open to the northern markets.

Then came the news of the Kansas law against Texas cattle, this one legal in spite of the Supreme Court's decision, legal and enforceable. It provided for inspection of the herds at the border, with the power to hold infected ones until fall at the expense of the owner, and past the best sale time, even though the bonanza was still putting a very high premium on evading both the irate citizens and the law. There must be a solution, swift, clear cut, and permanent, particularly now that the British Government put a veritable embargo on American cattle against the pleuro-pneumonia and the suspicions of Texas fever. Finally the government must act, and after a bitter fight in 1884 a Bureau of Animal Industry was ordered set up, with the power to regulate the cattle traffic and suppress bovine diseases. But all this public agitation helped make the consumers mighty uneasy about the meat they were eating, and backed up those who would shut off the movement of all southern herds.

Now there must be a National Trail, the Texans decided. In November, 1884, they belligerently had their valets pack for a trip or, more often, slicked their hair down with water, threw the other shirt into a gripsack, and headed for St. Louis and the first National Stockmen's convention. They met in the hotel lobby festooned with hoofs and horns, with mounted Longhorn heads and the newer range breeds, Short-horns and the Hereford with the curly white faces, along the walls. There were wagon wheels, fancy bridles, and enough big hats in the decorations to warm the hearts of the western-ers. But even before the registration the split in the Texans was plain as the canyon of the Rio Grande. The Panhan-dlites, led by the dedicated old cowman Goodnight, were de-termined to save their stock and ready to shoot if necessary. Because large-scale shipping by rail from deep in Texas was entirely too expensive, the rest were for a national trail and the only place it could run now was through the Panhandle. Pryor, Lytle, Shanghai Pierce, and fifty other old-timers were pushing the trail, led by Richard King, of King's Kingdom. Once more he proposed that the cattlemen organize a com-pany or a federation and buy a strip of land north to Canada for their drives.

The opposition southerners thought the government should furnish the land, just as it granted great tracts to the railroads. "Something for nothing" appealed to the free-grass ranchers rather than the "Pay for it and then it's yours" policy of King, who had secured most of his grass by buying it up long ago. Outnumbered, King gave in. He was only one of the representatives of the South Texas Association and the other organizations were mostly against him, too, the young-est, Goodnight's outfit, the most Winchester-minded of all.

But there were deeper currents in the convention. Two years ago the Chicago beef interests had held a sort of national convention, cooperating mainly with the northern stockmen, particularly those who represented the big foreign investors in Wyoming—such men as John Clay, the Bay State, and a dozen others, and again last year. Now St. Louis was reach-ing out to dominate the livestock market by conspiring, Chi-cago claimed, with the southerners. Robert D. Hunter, pio-neer in early trailing, but now in the more stable livestock commission business, in St. Louis, believed that the town could become the great cattle market of the nation again. He prepared the biggest show of splendor and spending that the cowmen had ever seen. To be sure the cattle boom was already riding down a little slope but that was just getting a run at the higher rise beyond. The new-rich of the cow business gloried in their self-confidence, strutted, drank, and applauded everything, particularly the parade of beautiful women, even though some of them were their own. The old-timers enjoyed the fun, too, but they had come to see a little more than the high-stepping drum major who led the band with a pair of polished longhorns carrying a silken banner: COWBOY BAND, DODGE CITY, KANSAS, $20,000,000. The figures stood for the cash value of the ranchers represented in the new musical group. Behind him marched the band, the men in blue flannel shirts, chaps, fancy boots and spurs, braces of ivory-handled six-shooters at their hips and white Stetsons on their heads, each hatband stamped with the brand of the ranch represented.

The exposition building was lined with flowers, trees, the sage called purple, and other prairie beauties. The vases and the gavel were great steer horns, and everywhere were the banners of the states and territories represented, two from far New England and all across to Oregon, including seventy-seven livestock organizations. Captain Bedford Pim of the Royal Navy was there, admitting that the great quest of England was for food. Only a fool would try to invade her shores. The best attack would be interception of her food ships with gunboats. England and America united could knock out the world but they would never need do that. They could starve the world into submission without one blow.

The nation's bulk of livestock wealth was gathered at St. Louis—cowmen and outside investors with their wives and daughters lovely in silks and satins and jewels, the men all seeming great, broad-shouldered brawny figures, mostly bearded, few of them entirely at home in the boiled shirts, not even those recently from Boston or London or Edinburgh. There was banqueting and singing, even the old-timers joining in some of the hymns and "The Little Black Bull Came Down the Mountain." Some with too much of Hunter's whisky roared out the baudier verses in their wind-hoarsened voices, ignoring the shushings of the religious. Some easterner called for the wordless song of the brush and brought a serious quietness. That was impossible in the city, impossible indoors, meaning impossible anywhere outside of the brush.

From the first meeting it was plain that the most un-loved were the Texans, unless it was the Kansas rancher Print Olive, dark-faced and somehow alone in the crowd where everyone knew of him, many from long before he left the San Gabriel country, let alone before he left Nebraska. The Texans in general seemed to be unloved even though they were the ones who had built the beef business of the nation, of the world, out of a natural resource they found running loose on the hoof. But now that the Great Plains region was stocked to Canada, the feed lots of the spreading, the burgeoning cornlands full, they were not needed any more and were looked upon as an arrogant remnant from some pre-historic time, men who spread disease in the modern world. By their cattle, to be sure, but here a man was known by his cows.

King's idea of a national trail, bought and paid for, was thrown out early. Getting Congress to set up a fenced lane six miles wide across the country north seemed hopeless. It would have been a starvation trail, a few realized, with so little of it through well-grassed country—about all that was left unclaimed by some rancher or settler long ago.

Still the Texans from the fever regions had to fight the strangulation of their business. Their oratorical Judge Carroll demanded, even begged for a nationally financed trail from the Red River north. "There must be a trail from the breeding grounds of Texas to the maturing pastures of the North!"

At once gray-headed Granville Stuart, from up in the

Milk River country, was on his Montana-booted feet, waving his big white hat high for attention as he would from a rise out on his own range.

"What you mean 'maturing pastures of the North'?" he roared. The prairies on both sides of the Rockies were breeding ground for the finest beef cattle in the world, and he failed to see why the government should be asked to build a trail for the Texas breeders to slough their surplus stock off up there. Thousands of cattle not ready for market had been shipped east from Montana because the range was over-stocked. He, for one, didn't want the government spending his tax money to swamp the country with stock they didn't need or want. "Let them bring their cattle into Montana in the old-fashioned way—" he said.

"And don't walk them in too fast; give them time to shake the ticks off, not kill our good stock like they did last summer," one of the Wyoming Association men added.

Yes, it was true that 5,000 Longhorns had been trailed into Wyoming from the cattle trains that unloaded them at Ogallala and Sidney last summer, with from thirty to a hundred of the lot dying every day as they crossed the crowded northern ranges, threatening the life of every critter there. The cowmen had been helpless but they sure kicked to Cheyenne and Washington, with some emergency action and the promise of a quarantine of all cattle coming in by rail. In addition there should be inspection stations to keep out all infected stock. Legislation was planned for the next session at Cheyenne.

So now the fight was in the open, with the south Texans snorting as they had for thirty years at the whole idea of a Texas fever, which was plainly a sickness of northern stock. "Buy our Longhorns and have a healthy herd!" was their motto.

Finally Goodnight threw his prestige to the Texans on the condition that the National Trail would not pass near his range. The governor of Colorado didn't object to the trail if it crossed in Kansas, but before his words were really out, Russell, from Kansas, was on his feet. They had been burned by cattle trails from Texas, he said quietly. No use telling them there was no such thing as Texas fever. He knew better, to his loss and sorrow. Kansas was not against the National Trail, just against its entering her borders.

Martin Culver of Dodge City softened Russell's objections a little by coming out for the trail. But many there knew that Culver bought vast herds deep in Texas and trailed them straight through to Kansas, scattering infection all the way, and he intended to keep doing just that.

Plainly nobody really needed or wanted the trail except the coastal ranchers and everybody else was anxious to get on to his own snake killing. The 1,300 delegates memorialized Congress for a national cattle highway from the Red to Canada, to be located on unsettled, meaning unclaimed domain as far as practicable and interfering with no habitation or material interest without compensation.

With the trail fight done, most of the Texans stayed awhile longer for the speeches and complaints about the stranglehold of the packing and railroad monopolies and for the lease law, of no interest to them with their state lands both for sale and lease. But underneath there was the growing power of Chicago and for this there was no remedy, no arnica, and no iron-boiled sage tea.

A southern delegation, without the Panhandle, went to camp on the Potomac until they got a trail to pack home in their ditty bags. They made it look very good: 690 miles from the Texas line across No Man's Land north to the border, not over six miles wide, all on government land, 1,324,000 acres. The surveying and fencing; sinking artesian wells in the waterless stretches, and bridging the wilder streams would cost $1,000,000. This was only 2.78 per cent the value of the land granted the western railroads, to say nothing of the cash bonuses paid them.

With the bill in both houses of Congress, the Texans were suddenly as red faced as kids caught riding a prize bull calf. They were demanding a free trail through the rest of the nation and not throwing one foot of their own state into the kitty. Hastily a new bill was drawn up for a trail from mid-Texas to the Neutral Strip, the No-Man's Land, but only two miles wide.

The proposed raid on the treasury for the trail was fine ammunition for the northerners, but their chief complaint was the planned evasion of the quarantine laws and other state laws as well, the trail an alien strip beyond all local jurisdiction running from Texas to Canada. Mighty easy way for an outlaw to hit for the border. Kansas protested to Congress and alarmed the adjoining areas. If Kansas with her armed guards to enforce her quarantine blocked the trail there, where would the markethungry, gun-packing Texans break through? They had bulldozed their way for a long, long time, gone where they pleased, spread their disease out wide behind them. Angry livestock associations passed angry resolutions against the Texas herds, now that they did not need them any more.

The Panhandle ranches were joined by those of the Cherokee Outlet and the Cattle Growers Association of Bent County, Colorado, agreeing to block every Texas herd. The Bent County ranchers had already lost $500,000 to the Texas disease, the Panhandle $300,000, Kansas and Indian Territory $300,000 just the last season. The cattlemen agreed they were against violence but passage of cattle from the infected regions would be resisted by every legal and by every *necessary* means.

The disappointed Texans dragged back from Washington and added Winchesters to the six-guns of all their trail hands, even one for the chuckwagon, and prepared to shoot their way to market. When the governor promised them he would provide a trail out, alarm as from the pale smoke of a prairie fire swept the Panhandle. The governor must mean he was ready to use the Rangers and the sharpshooters and crack shots from the war and the Indian fighting. That he could certainly blast a trail through the Panhandle with the state arsenal even the tough-minded former Ranger, Goodnight, admitted. There were some saying that Rangers were already passing as cowboys and were ready to force the herds through any opposition.

As this news spread, any who had faltered before saw now that they must prepare for war if they intended to save their herds, their blooded stock—war, and perhaps their lives the stakes.

Many of the older ranchers had looked upon the rail-road strike against the drastic pay cuts of 1877 as the news-papers suggested, as a communistic, an anarchistic revolt, a revolution. But in 1885, with a shrinking market, the Texas cowmen took a more sympathetic view. Once more the rail-roads were cutting wages, and when desperate workers walked out, even down in Texas, the cattlemen passed reso-lutions and expressions of sympathy for the Knights of Labor and their women and children, many hungry and sick. At last the cowmen were forced to lift their eyes beyond the pasture and the water hole, even beyond the rustler and the settler, to look more closely into the national picture. What cut the purchasing power of the workingman certainly cut the market for meat.

The Texans, north and south, called a meeting to work out the trail problem, approaching Dallas like range bulls marching to battle. Some of the steadier men like Slaughter, or Simpson of the Texas Livestock Association, refused to get drawn into an open fight. Finally some southerners were asked to recommend a trail that avoided the outlawed Indian Territory. They platted it north along the state line, past Doan's store on the Red River, elbowing west to Buffalo Springs, up through No Man's Land, called the Neutral Strip now, and on to the corner of Colorado. Most of the southern ranchers roared like angry bulls all right over the extra distance in the swing around the Pan-handle ranges. The men of the Strip, still without legal sta-tus, finally decided it was better to keep the stock to one definite route than letting it infect the whole region. Of course there was still Colorado to be heard from, waiting, armed.

One man who couldn't see the cattle business without free range, great trails, and the sky the limit, was Martin Culver of the old Queen of the Cowtowns, Dodge City. Late the spring of 1885 a herd of his steers had moved through the Neutral Strip, grazing the deep grass, fattening on the seed-topped annual that brought gloss to the hair. The bristle-whiskered cowboys idled along, perhaps resting a leg swung around the saddle horn, rolling a cigarette, with the wind down and the grass green, or replenishing a cud from the plug in the worn back pocket.

Suddenly at the Kansas border a dozen mounted men spurred up, yelling, the sun flashing on their drawn rifles. "You can't come into Kansas! Head you for the jailhouse if you do!"

"Them steers're Mart Culver's, over to Dodge. You can't stop a citizen from bringing his stuff in."

But the border guards weren't interested. The dark-bearded trail boss looked around the determined men, their row of Winchesters, then back over the wide prairie and the steers piling up behind him. He motioned his men up. They came spurring, hands on guns as they jerked their horses to a stop around him.

"Bend 'em west, boys," he said. "Nothing in Kansas anyhow except the three suns; sunflowers, sunshine, and sons of bitches."

His remark was repeated around the camps and ranches for weeks, with roars of laughing, but old-timers recalled that this had been said many times since the first yellow rose of Texas came creeping up the Santa Fe Trail to flourish wonderfully in Kansas soil, in the sunshine that grew the fattening grasses and the sons of bitches fit to meet the Texans on even terms.

Culver, the adopted Kansan, didn't hear the stories. His herd had grazed up along the eastern border of Colorado while he, knowing that a million Texas cattle were spilling out of the roundups with no trail, no markets, hurried to Washington. There he got permission to drive cattle from the Neutral Strip up along east Colorado, on public domain, without touching Kansas. So finally there was a National Trail of sorts, but marked with bleaching buffalo skulls and Texas cow chips instead of the strong wire fences planned.

Always the opportunist, Martin Culver laid out Trail City where the new route crossed the railroad near the Arkansas River. It was inside Colorado but so close that a drunk stumbling out the back door of a saloon would be practically in Kansas, and safe from the local marshal or sheriff, as would any rustler or gunman fleeing out the back way, or jumping between the buildings. The National Trail, the main street of the town, would make it boom as Abilene and Dodge had boomed, but safe from the blight of the quarantine.

Culver got a couple of partners and by August, 1885, had saws and hammers going, enough to scare the herds straggling through into fine stampedes if they hadn't been trail worn. In a few days any cowboy with money could satisfy every need and desire, including a final spot in the boothill cemetery. Inevitably there was a rival town twenty-eight miles down the trail and just across the line in Kansas. It was named Borders, for a Kansas banker who established the *Border Rover* there and promised a railroad and irrigation canals to make the town a paradise of lawns and shade trees. Not only that, it was available to the thirsty cow hands long before they reached Trail City.

But the best that the *Border Rover* could find to report were the violent goings on up at Trail City. The route itself turned out just as the local stockmen had warned. Something more than bleak-eyed buffalo skulls was needed to keep the Texans from taking short cuts and even long ones to find grass for the starving herds. From the first the skull markers had to be backed up by armed guards "to assist any lost drover" to find his way back to the trail.

John R. Blocker had started 25,000 steers north in

nine herds to graze their way slowly along. The lead herd
met one of George West's up toward the Kansas line and the
two trail bosses decided they could make time by cutting
across the west end of Kansas. Together they were strong
enough to make it stick against any armed guards. But as
they drifted to the state line, a bunch of horsebackers came
charging over a row of low hills to meet them, surrounding
the foremen. They ordered the herds stopped in their
tracks. They wouldn't even be allowed to swing over to the
National Trail now, since they plainly did not intend to
stick to it.

"These are Blocker and West herds," the trail bosses
announced, as though the two men were beyond the law.

But the guards stuck to their position, and the two
leaders hurried back to notify their bosses. Many an armed
man had trembled at the wrath of Blocker and West, who
were among the toughest and most determined men ever to
look down the bony back of a Longhorn. It was said West
would fight a cyclone with a bradawl for his cattle. He was
considered to be the man who really established how far a
Texas cow could walk by the long drive he made back in
1867 when he took 14,000 cattle to an Indian reservation up
on the Missouri, little more than 100 miles south of the
Canadian border. Blocker was called stubborn as a blue-eyed
burro and was almost as great a trailer as West. The three
Blocker brothers had driven more Texas cattle to market
than any other outfit. It was said that in one year they
pushed 82,000 head up the Chisholm Trail. Both West and
Blocker believed in the frontier rancher's code: "Take a
heap of abuse before you kill a man," but now they were
really fuming.

The Kansas guards ignored them as they had Culver.
In the meantime other herds were stacking up behind them,
with the whole trail region virtually blocked by starving cat-
tle with nowhere to go. One of the drovers, a friend of
Blocker, put in his two-bits' worth. "Give the word, Johnny.
I'll take my men and kill every one of them fellers."

Blocker was so certain that the law was on his side that he held the herds while they telegraphed Washington, keeping the wires hot to their senators and to the War Department for troops to escort their herds through. When they were about ready to shoot their way to grass, a small troop of cavalry came cantering up in a whirl of dust to take the cattle up along Culver's National Trail, staying with them every inch of the way past Kansas. The guards from the Sunflower State had won.

Although the early herds were taken around Kansas, the flood of stock became too great for the border guards, and cattle from the fever region spilled over the Cherokee Outlet, into Kansas and through Bent County, Colorado. There were howls enough to foretell a month of northern lights in coyote country but even before fall dried up the movement, a kind of bitterness had fallen upon the ranchers along the route. Plainly the National Trail was a joke, a mammoth snipe hunt in which the Colorado ranchers were the tenderfeet left holding the sack. The *Pueblo Chieftain* complained that the northern cowmen were tired of losing their grass to the through herds and on top of that losing their cattle to the fever, for which not even the Bureau of Animal Industry men were finding a remedy. Possibly the matter could be settled without bloodshed but it didn't seem probable.

In the meantime winter quieted the roistering Trail City. Like its little imitations along the route the fronts of the saloons and dance halls were boarded up, leaving the main street, the trail bare to the biting winter winds. The cattle had gone through by the hundreds of thousands to the overcrowded ranges and the northern reaches of the Big White Ruin.

By the next June stock was moving again, with typhoid fever spreading, several cowboys down with it at Trail City, several to die, and more along the trail. "Boil your water in a tin cup, if necessary to drink. Better stick to coffee—"

"Or hard liquor—"

At least safer, the doctor out from Dodge for the epidemic agreed.

By mid-June there was a constant crossing of herds at the Arkansas, around 175,000 head with no buyers, now that the bonanza was done. Several rains had started the grass and the cattle could be held without too much loss. But that meant idle cowboys in town, with a lot of shooting among the gamblers and other lawless element. Then August 18, 1886, a dispatch from Trail City was picked up by newspapers all over the cow country but read most closely in San Gabriel, Texas, and up in Nebraska, where the settlers passed the papers around until they were worn and tattered, perhaps reading where a work-blunted finger pointed: MAN BURNER KILLED BY COWBOY, saying, "Well, they got 'im; finally got 'im!"

Or perhaps: "So Old Print Olive finally got what he was askin' for for years."

All who could read had to savor the print for themselves, and those who could not, or had no glasses, had to hear it over and over. I. P. Olive, cattleman from Nebraska, now located near Trail City, Colorado, had been killed by a cowboy named Joe Sparrow.

"Sparrow—it say Sparrow?" an old Texas cowpuncher asked through clamped lips, his jaw tipped up to hold his tobacco juice.

"Yes, that's what it says."

Nobody up in Nebraska seemed to know such a man although some up along the trail this summer thought they might have seen Sparrow down there, a Hard Case, so it was said. Anyway, the news of the shooting started all the talk of the Olive killings again, both in Texas and Nebraska, and brought out the story of Print's son killing a man in the Smoky Hill country not long ago. Now this fellow Joe Sparrow came out of some place away to hell 'n' gone and picked off the head of the outfit, the old bull himself, Print Olive. A man ought to know more about a cowboy like that.

Soon there were many rumors, some saying that the

fight was over a livery bill Sparrow owed Print, others that it was an old grudge from way back in Texas or that Sparrow was just traveling under that name, a man who had been living for nothing except to avenge Mitchell and Ketchum and that he had a son with the same hatred, planning to vent it on Print's son Bill. Some claimed that Bill had already been shot over a game of billiards and that the father, the Joe Sparrow, disguised as a cowboy had killed Print at a roundup of the Olive cattle.

But all these stories had to be changed later because it turned out that young Bill Olive was alive and hanging around the saloons drunk and fighting, much like his father for so many years. He had been mixed up in a killing but it was Bill who did the shooting—shot the man who killed his father. That didn't seem probable, either, not with a J. J. Sparrow standing preliminary examination for the murder of I. P. Olive, with a dozen or so eyewitnesses called in and at least a hundred more who saw the murder.

In the end it seemed that Bill Olive had killed a man up in the Smoky Hill country just to show he could do it and stood trial, one more case Print Olive had to win. He got the son acquitted but it cost a lot of money—not as much as his own release up in Nebraska but enough. Somehow putting Mitchell and Ketchum out of the way had stirred up the animals more than all the troubles in Texas, as Print complained at the time, so it was handy that the defense of his son came cheaper for he no longer had the kind of money he spent up in Nebraska.

Apparently nobody, not even around Trail City, knew much of the story behind the killing, although a Garden City, Kansas, paper reported that Sparrow had worked for Olive at one time and had some trouble, apparently over a herd of cattle. Later other stories made the rounds. Perhaps it was true that Sparrow had come in from Dodge on Sunday and happened to run into Print Olive next morning, had a few words with him, Olive pulling his gun. The cowboy grabbed it. Furious, and sour drunk, Print promised to kill Sparrow before sundown, Joe arguing all the time he wanted no trouble. The sheriff took Print away and got him to bed.

Some suggested to Sparrow that he better get out of Trail City but the man said he wasn't running. Besides, he didn't plan to have any trouble with anybody. But in the afternoon Print came through Haynes' saloon, found Sparrow, and everyone could see there was a storm coming up, that Olive had to carry out his threat but intended to make out a case for himself this time. Everybody, including the bartender, looked for shelter, preferably where they could see, most of them agreeing later that Sparrow was still trying to avoid trouble. But when Olive reached for his gun, Sparrow fired and missed—deliberately, some thought, and still talked quietly to the drunken man. Now Print fired, seeming to graze Sparrow, and this time the old rancher got a bullet through the left breast. He went down, striking his head on the doorcasing, falling on his gun hand. He seemed suddenly cold-sober but whimpering as he eased his gun out from under him. "Oh, Joe, don't shoot!" he begged, shifting himself for a swift draw.

Now Sparrow knew he had to shoot fast. This time he put a bullet through the left temple of the man who had killed so many. Then he gave himself up.

Before long some were remembering that Ami Ketchum's brother had held the mob off when they wanted to lynch Print Olive, and his words: "If the law fails to punish him . . . I'll do it my way." Perhaps Sparrow was the brother.

But that couldn't be. Surely somebody would have recognized the brother, or so it seemed. But was Tamar Snow's brother so well known? He had his stepfather to avenge, and the betrothed of his pretty young sister.

The Olive family came for Print's body and took it by train to Dodge City. The Texas relatives came up and stood sorrowfully by while the Independent Order of Odd Fellows carried out a very formal and impressive funeral for I. P. Olive, the big cattleman from Texas.

Not long after his father was killed Bill Olive showed up around Beaver City in the Neutral Strip. Since then he had been living by the moderate labor of gambling and selling the meat of an occasional fat steer he stole from the nearby ranches. On the side he seemed to be one of the younger men in one of the tough gangs of road trotters, the claim jumpers of the region—a fat practice here, where the settlers could not make legal entry, only hope to hold their land by squatters right until there was some decision where the Strip belonged, with Texas, Colorado, or the Indian lands of the Cherokee Outlet. In the meantime there was no law, no sheriff, not even a federal marshal because legally the Strip was less than a mirage in the eyes of the beholder.

At the point of their Winchesters the road trotters forced the squatter to ante up enough money to satisfy them, all he could raise, or lose his land. If the place was a good one and well improved, he probably lost it anyway no matter how much he paid. Finally the settlers got together and a couple of claim jumpers, Bennett and Thompson, were killed. This time Bill Olive managed to put his gun on the side of the settlers in time to save his hide—just one more proof to the old-timers that the gunman shot on the side with the money or the most guns.

Before long there was another Olive story to tell. It seemed that while Bill was off on a hunt, perhaps making night meat, the woman he was living with quit the country, saying Billy abused her beyond endurance when he was drunk. On his return he trailed her to the Cimarron station. Afraid to tell the truth, she made up a story. Henderson, a bartender at Beaver City, a squatter town of the Strip, said Billy was not coming back, had deserted her.

Young Olive came roaring into the saloon. Henderson denied saying it but Bill and one of his side-kicks, John

Halford, called Lengthy, went on a big spree, and after many hours in and out of the saloon, came back to shoot up the place: the lamps, glassware, and all of Henderson's personal stuff Bill could locate, with Lengthy holding his gun on anybody who might think of interfering.

There was no law to call on, no sheriff, no marshal, so Henderson just waited, backed up against the wall. Finally young Olive left, but came running back with his Winchester. He motioned Henderson outside and down the street ahead of him, the man's bar apron blowing in the wind. Everywhere people stood back from the doors and windows, out of range when the bullets began to fly, watching Henderson's boots scuff up the dust while Olive poked him along with the Winchester muzzle in his britches, cursing, striking him over the shoulder with the barrel, then prodding him along again, with Lengthy Halford buffaloing Henderson across the side of the head with his pistol a couple of times. Still no one interfered, not one of all the armed men around tried to stop this "naturally wild son of a wild father," as several remarked, keeping well out of sight.

At the edge of town, with the audience left behind, Billy Olive pushed his Winchester against the bartender's back and pulled the trigger. The cartridge failed and Henderson ran, Halford's pistol shot missing him, too. By the time Olive got the rifle working, the man was out of sight, headed into the sandhills beyond Beaver Creek.

After some time Henderson's friends picked up the nerve to ride out looking for him. They found him hugging the bottom of a washout full of old wind-drifted tumbleweeds. They talked him into coming back to town. "You got to bushwhack him," a leader of the better element argued. "We can't go on letting the Olives make everybody eat dirt. You're the man to stop it. It's you he tried to kill—with you it's self-defense."

Henderson took a long time rubbing the sand off himself and wiping his haggard face with his bar apron. Finally he agreed, provided they would keep him surrounded by their saddle horses so he wouldn't be picked off by a long-range rifle shot before he even got his hand on a gun.

The little knot of horsebackers crossed the bottoms, splashed through the shallow, sand-choked Beaver, and into town to get Henderson's Winchester, the townspeople standing behind their doors and windows, expecting Olive and his partner to start the bullets flying this time for sure.

When Bill Olive heard that Henderson had dared return he started angrily along the street, Lengthy a few steps behind, searching store and bar along one side and then crossed over to the other. Henderson, from behind a sod wall, saw Bill come. He steadied his rifle on his hand against the rough, rooty surface and fired. Bill Olive fell, the dust spurting up around him before the report echoed across the street. For a moment Lengthy looked down at his friend, as still as though dead for hours. Then he swung all around, searching out the spreading of blue smoke, fearfully, as an animal might. When he saw it he started to run from it. At a hitch rack he jerked the reins of a horse and was off in a whipping gallop.

Nobody made any move to hold the bartender. He walked back to his saloon, set the Winchester in the corner behind the bar next to the frame of the shattered mirror, and wiped his hands on his apron. Then with his fingers on the edge of the bar he said, "What will it be, gentlemen?"

So ended the Olive gang, except for Ira, settled down, quietly running the Olive property left in Nebraska, to live a long time among people who forgot that he was the brother of the man burner. Not far away, married to a brother of Judge Wall, who had stood up to the Olives, lived the twice-bereaved girl with the lovely name of Tamar Snow.

With the beef bonanza busted, the bones of two big Die-Ups bleaching on the prairie, the cattlemen were cautious and slow to buy. The *Coolidge Citizen*, across the line in Kansas, reported that while 90,000 cattle were sold at Trail City in 1887, at least 70,000 more were returned to the home regions without buyers. The *Range Journal* said that several herds taken north had found no market and, turning their tails to the home of the aurora borealis, were marching back to the Panhandle of Texas. Probably saw the bones of their brothers up there, some said, and mighty glad to get back South before the snow.

This was also the year that a land office was established at Lamar, Colorado, bringing in a stampede of settlers to the Bent County region lying directly across the skull-marked National Trail. It was about the end. Only a few tried to fight their herds through the settlements and the tightening range practices of the cattlemen after that. During the last twenty-two or three years at least 10,000,000 Texas cattle had plodded northward to óne market or another. It was estimated that 32,000 drivers, most of them hard-bottomed, hard-working cowhands, rode the trails. Chuck wagons had rutted their way clear to Canada; their campfires had blown ashes over every mile, with prairie graves and boothill burials scattered all the way.

Two of the early dedicated men did not live to see this ending, two very different men, but neither inclined to brook the slightest opposition or interference. Not only was I. P. Olive dead by violence, as he had lived, but the great exponent of the deeded pasture and the rancher-owned National Trail, Captain Richard King, was also gone. Many must have known when he spoke so vigorously in November, 1884, for his trail that he was a dying man, dying of stomach cancer, leaving his wife a half-a-million-acre ranch, plastered with half-a-million dollar debt, money gone for fencing, more land, blooded cattle, mostly Shorthorns usually so susceptible to the disease of the South. Somehow King kept them alive in the region of the fever that had broken herds and trails and men. E. J. Kleberg, an attorney once working against King, later his lawyer and engaged to marry the boss's daughter, became manager of the ranch. He was the man now faced with the problem of getting the cattle to market without giving all the profit, and more, to the railroads.

So Kleberg, the son of the German liberal who fled his

unfriendly nation for America, became boss of King's King-dom.

And so the old dedicated men were dying, and their time as well.

# CHAPTER V

OF THE GIANTS—THE XIT

AS THE prairies were cleared of Indians and buffaloes the cattle frontier crept up out of the lowlands of Texas and washed against the cap-rock barrier to the Staked Plains. It moved out along the Canadian and pushed up the deep canyons from the Quitaque, such as the Tule and the Palo Duro, so like the scorings of some giant grizzly clawing at the plains.

From the first the cattle bred in the newer regions grew larger than their ancestors in the lower bottoms, perhaps due to the iodine shortage that lengthened both man and animals over so much of the Great Plains country, and surely due to the nutritious grasses that got too little moisture to be washy, summer or winter, curing like fine standing hay as soon as the seeds ripened.

By now it seemed that all the Texas range would soon be covered, by purchase or by armed possession. The Grange, made up of farmers and small stock growers, had seen this come and aligned themselves with the Knights of Labor to work for a new capitol building at Austin, to be paid for by state lands before they were gone. Eventually 3,000,000 acres were set aside in west Texas as the Capitol

Tract, with an additional 500,000 to pay for the surveying. Many considered these lands, stretching over 200 miles along the western edge of the Panhandle, a dry waste, but planned to unload it on some unsuspecting Yankee outfit before they found that out. Then the capitol building burned and the state government was on the street. Advertisements for bids were rushed out and high time, many thought, with the cattlemen over-running the whole region since Goodnight settled there, many buying only small patches, claiming as much of the rest as they could range. These outfits would be mighty hard to shake loose if a buyer did show up. Their cowboys were already armed to protect the holdings against rustlers and any new cowmen coming to look for grass, warning them away from the watering places where only a few months ago there might have been only a little mustang herd, perhaps an antelope or two and the coyotes and their small prey, with fine flocks of geese and swan settling for a rest from the long flights spring and fall.

Soon after the news that the building contracts for the state capitol were awarded to Taylor, Babcock, and Company of Chicago, there was a rash of rumors and charges. The firm included the Farwell brothers, and State Senator Matlock of Texas had received financial backing for his outstate mining interests from Congressman Charles Farwell, for which Matlock admitted he felt "under great obligation." No telling how many others of the legislature and the building commission were under equally "great obligations" in the past, or planning to be in the future.

In addition there were protests against the transfer of such vast state-sized bodies of land to an individual or a corporation. It was against the genius of free institutions, and tended to create great and overpowerful interests. Then there was another roaring heard down at the temporary legislative halls at Austin, this time from homeseekers demanding their share of the state lands. The ranchers with their cows had been getting wealthy and powerful all these years from the free range of the state's public domain that everybody had said was grass just rotting down anyway. Now a Chicago outfit was willing to put up a massive and handsome capitol building for the farthest and the driest reaches of west Texas. If those state lands were worth such a swap, why shouldn't the ranchers be paying the state for all the grass their stock was eating, and help cut down taxes?

Some politicians saw the vote-drawing power of this issue—like a great block of rock salt set out on a sweet water range. They agitated for lease bills, loudly identifying themselves with the measures. To the cowmen this was the warning bellow of scrub bulls coming out of the brush to their choice herds. They packed their grips for Austin. But a lease bill was passed and brought the end of free grass closer here where the whole idea of free range started, and created a great industry.

Before any of this Capitol Company that was to build the Texas statehouse had seen even one foot of their 3,000,000 acres they were swamped in a gully washer of inquiries from landseekers. So Colonel Babcock, one of the owners, went out with a surveyor recently from Alabama to size up what they had cornered. Through Congressman Farwell's pull with General Sheridan, he got military trail equipment from Fort Elliott, including a tent, a Sibley stove, and an ambulance for his comfort, and a camping outfit for his cowboys who at least knew something of west Texas, and the Mexican who was to do the cooking.

In March, 1882, Babcock had headed out to the top of the tract. Before long the cowboys discovered that the big trunk in the equipment wagon had a compartment fitted for bottled goods, the remaining space filled with canned and other nonperishable foods. Babcock vowed loudly that he would never eat a mouthful of anything cooked over a fire of cow chips—cow dung—only he put it more bluntly. The tricks the ranch hands played on him over this made stories to tell all the way from Rabbit Ear to San Antone. But he was a serious man who read passages from Ingersoll's *Some-Mistakes of Moses* to the cowboys while they all waited out a spring snow in an arroyo.

Starting from Buffalo Springs, up near the Neutral Strip, Babcock found a neighboring ranch running a cow camp on his Capitol range. From there he headed down the tract, past a scattering of other new ranch shacks and great ricks of buffalo bones where the hunters had finished off the vast Texas herd, leaving nothing salable except these bleaching remains. In thirty-six days he traveled 950 miles over the Capitol lands, talking to the few people he saw and hearing that the Panhandle ranches paid 25 to 40 per cent annually, "and generally with very slack management." Apparently nobody mentioned the disastrous times for the ranchers operating back in the panic years of the early seventies, perhaps because none of these outfits were in the business then. Nobody suggested that the bonanza on now might ever sour.

Babcock did a lot of figuring in the little memo books he carried in his pocket and the papers he spread on the military field table. He came up with what he termed a conservative estimate of the prospects—a net return of over $4,500,-000 in five years from the investment of $3,000,000 in the Capitol Company's lands. With this he recommended no attempt at colonization now but that the entire stretch be turned into a cattle ranch and fenced, involving, as any rancher knew, a neat little outlay just for wire and work.

But the company had to have some immediate cash, and the land deeds were only to be delivered in designated blocks as units of the capitol were completed and approved. Down at Austin Babcock's son-in-law, Abner Taylor, was struggling with the building schedule. The rising costs forced him to borrow money, and anywhere he could, even from Charles Farwell, while Babcock was selling his Midwestern real-estate holdings to throw this ante into the pot, too, small as it was in the total need.

"All outgo, no income," was the sour complaint of the land-poor, acre-poor millionaires.

But it was plunge now or lose heavily. Babcock and Taylor got out a thirty-page prospectus glorifying Texas and particularly the wonderful Capitol tract. They had 10,000 copies printed and sent them to every promising British and European address they could scare up. A few were distributed in the eastern United States but apparently none at all in Texas.

Then John V. Farwell returned to Europe where he had made evangelistic tours with Moody, and where he and his brother, as drygoods wholesalers, had several purchasing offices, particularly in Paris and in England. Farwell talked Texas and the 3,000,000 acres—around 4,700 square miles, a region nearly four times as large as the sovereign state of Rhode Island, almost a sixth as large as all of Scotland, and larger than half a dozen of the world's smaller nations. It was truly a nation in itself, an empire.

This, on top of all the recent optimistic news of the American beef bonanza and the artificially maintained high dividends paid by many of the British-owned ranches in the West brought cables piling up in the Chicago offices. Some investors hurried across the sea, determined that no one should get to the good pickings ahead of them.

Farwell formed the Capitol Freehold Land and Investment Company, Limited, capitalized at 3,000,000 pounds, about $15,000,000, the English officials including such men as the Earl of Aberdeen and Henry Seton-Karr, M. P., with the Marquis of Tweeddale, a Scottish banker, the chairman of the board. Among the American board members were Abner Taylor, the capitol builder, and the Farwells, with John the managing director. Although the American owners formed the Capitol Syndicate and leased the property from the British company, with detailed and itemized reports due annually, the Texans always looked upon the ranch as British. Perhaps the British were of the same mind for they finally sent a man to the ranch to represent them.

The representative's incompetency didn't alter the intentions at all.

Before the ranch that Babcock advised was set up, they needed an experienced cowman as manager. B. H. Campbell was approached. He had borrowed a little of John Farwell's loose money back in 1879 for one of his curious cattle operations. Mainly Campbell was a Shorthorn man, bred them in Illinois, helped found the American Shorthorn Breeders Association, and had been through the continent and England for breeding stock.

Still here was at least one man who knew a Longhorn from a lap saddle. He was running range stock along the Kansas-Indian Territory border, branded Bar BQ, and so was known as Barbecue to every cowhand on the trails, perhaps because he was a teetotaler and demanded that his help keep dry off the job as well as on. He permitted no rough treatment of any livestock, not even a spur to touch up a lagging horse or take the morning frost out of a humping bronc. He was a short, lean man, militarily stiff and brisk, with a neat graying beard, gray eyes sharp as hail under the cloud-heavy brows, and always had several boxes of his favorite cigars handy. He could be loud mouth and overbearing as old Shang Pierce, almost, but in a pinch he settled to business quiet as a good cow horse in roiling floodwaters and quicksand.

These men made a fancy saddlebag of characters for the great new cow outfit: the Farwell brothers, together wholesale merchants, one a politician, the other an evangelist; Colonel Babcock with his volume of Ingersoll, and Barbecue Campbell, the manager, not only dry as the young woman of growing militancy named Carry Nation living not far from his Kansas ranch, but as furious as any member of the ASPCA over the bullfight of Dodge City. He understood that this was to draw the Texas trailers back and bring in eastern money, but he roared out his anger at the baiting of the bulls and loudly hoped that somehow the instigators might get a horn. Around the cow camps Barbecue was damned as being tight as hackberry bark, but as soon as he got to Buffalo Springs, selected as the home ranch of the Capitol company, he loosened up noticeably.

"Dealing with other people's money," one of his old cowhands said.

"Yeh, English money," another agreed, thinking of the galloping over the hills on the postage-stamp saddles, canned peaches at the cow camps, and the boss over at the Rocking Chair Ranch breaking out a bottle of whisky for any passing cowboy.

At Tascosa on the Canadian Barbecue Campbell found what he expected, no brass band or any welcome at all from old friends, now that he was with the Capitol, and moving in on a region where half-a-dozen ranches were running cattle, even if the Capitol owned the land. He discovered, too, that rustling was big business here, with so much of the country open and wild, the New Mexican and Neutral Strip borders just a good jump away. The big ranchers hired a special crew of gunmen, including Pat Garrett, the killer of Billy the Kid, to ride the range against the thieves, run them down. They disregarded any losses the small outfits coming in might suffer, often helped discourage the newcomers, and worse. But it was the homeseeking settlers who were considered the prime menace, potential killers of beef, rustlers of calves, and, like a Longhorn in an alfalfa patch, decoys for more of their kind. Even if the settler was an honest man he was a menace, in fact a greater menace.

The hired gunmen brought growing bitterness against the big cattle outfits far beyond their range on public lands, particularly down at Austin, already in the hands of the hoe men, the grangers, because they had the votes.

Although more and more ranchers seemed to be pushing in, Bates and Beal, millionaire shoe manufacturers from Boston, took a cautious sniff at the wind, or perhaps consulted the *Farmer's Almanac* hanging in the ranch cookhouse. Some said it was the growing violence, the rustlers and gunmen as well as the settlers. They sold the LX at the peak of the boom to the American Pastoral Company, Limited, of Britain, and went home with the money. The cow was not for them, only her hide.

Barbecue Campbell, for all his ranch experience, was certain that wire fences would keep rustlers out, and with no free land inside the Capitol holdings there would be no settlers. So he refused to join the Panhandle Association.

Campbell had one worry: water. The Capitol lands stretched down into the Staked Plains to where only a few years ago troopers and buffalo hunters had died of thirst and panic. Campbell realized that every drop falling or flowing must be saved and protected from wandering stock and trailing herds. Fences would keep outside stock away, and for water he certainly had to sink wells, many and deep wells over the vast expanse that lay beyond the walking distance of the springy-legged Longhorns.

Babcock had ordered $35,000 worth of barbed wire and hired an old buffalo hunter to run the fencing, just around a 500,000-acre range at first. Long strings of freight teams crept from the railroad toward Buffalo Springs, groaning wagons piled high with dark, bristling spools of barbed wire, others loaded with yellow new-wood kegs of staples. There were no trees and so men were sent to government land to cut millions of posts, one for every thirty feet around the great pasture, for a stout four-wire fence, strong enough to hold all but the breechiest cow or the ranniest scrub bull. The fencers had a little trouble with mustang herds attacking their horses and mules, the wild stallions squealing as they charged in to sweep off the mares, but a few well-placed rifle shots usually sent them off, their fine, long manes and tails flying in the wind.

Then the big blizzard of the winter swept cattle from the Neutral Strip and from Kansas into and through the Capitol lands, icicles on their muzzles, eyes and ears lost in the snow caking. They piled up along the stout new fence or went over or through it, pushed on by the blinding blizzard wind, not stopping except for death before they reached the canyons and the timbered strips of the Canadian. At night herds of pronghorns, frightened by the big hungry wolves, hit the frost-tautened wires on the higher tables, set them singing, the terrified antelope cut and torn in their panic.

Though prices had slid from the bonanza peak, Campbell recommended contracting for only 20,000 cattle, steers and she-stuff, for the summer of 1885. Buy only the best, Farwell ordered, which was easy with the Texas market glutted, not only held for a rise but for a trail to get through to the North, so the very best was available for a little down payment in advance.

Ab Blocker, the man with hell in his neck, as the West called it, worked hard to get his herd, 2,500 head, in first. He knew of the Goodnight Winchester quarantine of the Palo Duro region so he cut around east, past Fort Elliott, and then swung back northwest to Buffalo Springs, the Capitol headquarters. It was farther, but he pushed his men and stock on by starlight—old Hell-in-His-Neck for sure. When he got there the branding corrals and a long, tight chute were ready to handle up to twenty-four head at a shot. But Campbell had no brand.

"Biggest ranch in the world and no brand?" Ab said scornfully, pushing his dusty old hat back from his forehead as he let himself down to his boot heels. A brand needed three things. Got to look good and sound good, be easy to run, and planned so it wouldn't fit under any other brand around or any possible for the brand blotter to make. An X was always good, so was a bar or a diamond, with any good-sounding letter. Stretching out a bowed leg, Ab Blocker scratched three enormous letters in the dirt with his worn boot heel: X I T.

Campbell marked it off in the dust for himself with a weed stalk, tried to blot it, change it as a rustler would. He couldn't make anything else of the XIT and so it was adopted. Because there was no iron ready they used a single bar about five inches long forged across the end of a wagon rod. Then Ab Blocker burned it on one steer to see how it would look and hurried off to help his brother John, in trouble with the Kansas border guards.

Campbell had tried to hire him to manage all the branding but he did get a start at a ranch crew by picking up forty men from the trail outfits delivering cattle to him, many ranchers glad enough to let them go, with money much too tight for big crews now. Barbecue had sent a sixteen-mule team to haul cottonwood and piñon from the draws on Neutral Strip, a good forty miles away, for the branding fires, the wheels cutting deep ruts back and forth.

As the stock arrived it was herded through the crowding pens into the long chute where one man with a pole pushed through across the back could hold a critter tight and motionless for the hot iron. The hands kept twenty of the new branding irons going, twenty red-hot irons from the fires that trailed pungent smoke toward the low ridge of hills beyond the spring. It was a big enough job of branding finished in sufficient speed to have impressed even old Hell-in-His-Neck if he had stayed, 22,000 head carrying his brand, his XIT. It wasn't much for 3,000,000 acres but enough for the range that was ready. They were around 43,000 head short of the 65,000 the delivery contracts finally covered but the Capitol was lucky they didn't come. By 1886 prices had dropped so far that they saved money on new contracts.

Before fall some of the new cattle found their way down to the old trail by which Coronado must have brought the first cows into Texas. The stretches, so hard and dry that the Spaniards had to pile rocks and clods and whitened bones to mark their passing for the herd coming behind, were still the same.

From the first the XIT proved hard on the chute run of practices so fixed in the cow country: hard liquor, pistols at the hip, the rancher's precious water holes free to any outfit coming along, partly, of course, because the rancher usually didn't own them either. Campbell was against stocking good range with Longhorn blood, killing another man's cattle for beef, and Sunday work. Worse, the XIT fence was closing the range although at least technically they owned what they fenced. And old Barbecue Campbell seemed to be everywhere. With his sturdy buggy and high-stepping horses he traveled fifty, sixty miles a day, the most energetic buggy boss of them all.

Then one night some hands riding in to headquarters saw a glow rising into the sky off toward the Neutral Strip— almost like northern lights before a blizzard, but not quite.

"Prairie fire!" one of the men yelled out suddenly.

It was mid-December, the range bare, the wind sharp from the north bearing down on Buffalo Springs. The cowboys spurred their tired horses for the ranch. Supper forgotten, Campbell sent one outfit to meet the fire, slow it, taper it, split it in any bare spot, any arroyo or canyon or dry wash. Others hurried out to round up the horses and mules, get them to some bare stretches, hold them there against their blind, panicking fear of fire. The rest of the hands worked to backfire around the ranch buildings and corrals, starting little fires north of any bare strips and patches to burn slowly into the wind.

Old-timers who had seen the Panhandle burn before realized they could only try to fight such a fire now. Some knew of the one that the army set against the Indians back in 1865, along a hundred-mile stretch of the South Platte, to come roaring down through Colorado and west Kansas and the present Neutral Strip into Texas. Men and animals were burned in that, whole herds of antelope and buffaloes killed, the fire not stopped until it died on the barren stretches of the Staked Plains. Even jumped the broad, sandy bed of the Canadian, some said, carried by smoldering tumbleweeds sliding across the ice of the frozen stream.

Nobody was too hopeful now and by the time Campbell had the XIT organized, the fire seemed less than fifteen miles off and coming like the express train of the Santa Fe, all the night sky a burning red, the shadows of the boiling smoke rolling black over the prairie. Up north the firefighters had spurred their lathering horses through panic-blinded antelope and deer, wolves, too, even rabbits and smaller creatures frightened from the safety of their burrows. Here and there the flames leapt up twenty, thirty feet in the dead grass and reeds of a low place, sending smoke to billow black and flame-shot into the burning sky as the fire raced on up the slopes before the growing wind.

The men sought out any barrier that might hold a backfire, any possible place to split the head flames, narrow them. Once a bunch of cattle passed, running, tails up, bellies low to the ground, horns clattering as they went head first into washouts and over banks, others upon them, and over them, when safety lay only a few hundred yards to the side. Finally, when the fire seemed almost upon the men, the sparks, the heat scorching their faces, they shot a lone cow, ripped her open, and with lariats dragged the body across the edge of the fire, working inward, and on the barer knolls, the horses faunching under the spur and quirt, wild in the searing flames and smoke, the embers burning in the manes, the men beating them out and from their scorching clothes. But it was useless. All they had hoped was to narrow the fire a little, hold it back some on the barer strips, but even there the heat exploded the dry grass beyond, and the flames raced on again to overtake the head fire, many miles wide now, and as much beyond the power of man as a hailstorm or the black blizzards of dust.

Whipped, their beards, brows, and lashes burnt to their blistered skin, the men gave up and started back to the ranch, riding their worn horses hard to outrun the fire, small bobbing figures against the red sheet of flame around the north. They found Campbell sweating, too. While his men burned off the worn grass around the ranch he carried buckets of water, dogtrotting with them, to help hold the backfires, and wetting down his few young trees as the smoke and soot on the wind lashed his face and stung his eyes.

When the first tongue of flames hit the black strip of backfiring at the ranch, the fire spread to both directions, leaping high in weed patches, the flame-shot smoke rolling over the low roofs where the men beat out smoldering sparks, drenched down curling boards beginning to smoke in the heat. Several times the wind carried the fire over the burnt strips and was beaten out by wet sacks and saddle blankets, while the main head swept around on both sides of the ranch and, rejoining, roared on, leaving the squatting of buildings and corrals behind in the smoky darkness. The men, using lanterns now, searched out smolderings and twists of smoke in the corral dust and the cow chips, in weed corners of the garden and the trees, even in the old swallow nests under the eaves that Campbell had protected all summer.

The fire ran on unchallenged now, whipped southward by the growing gale, burning every fence, every windmill and tank across the XIT to the Canadian. There, in the broad, sandy bed of the river not even this hungry fire could make the jump across and so spread in feeble tongues sidewise into the wind along the worn banks, smoldering a while in the cow chips along the bottoms. Cattle, those still able to run, and the smaller creatures fled out beyond the Canadian valley, running as long as they could, for the stink of the smoke pursued them on the wind far, far from their accustomed range.

At sunup every XIT man was in the saddle, his horse kicking up spurts of soot already running in dark curls over the blackened plain, the knolls bared to the yellowish earth where the wind would bite all winter. They found burnt animals here and there, antelope with their delicate hoofs charred, to be shot; singed cattle wading the gray ashes around the fallen windmills and the cracked and drying watering places, bawling for the water they knew should be there. A million acres were burned and although most of the stock escaped, winter was upon them.

Campbell ordered his men to throw the cattle out on the unburnt range beyond the fallen fences of the XIT.

About 5,000 head were trailed into east New Mexico, the rest south of the Canadian. Driving XIT stock to range claimed by others stirred up a lot of anger. Newspapers complained that a short time ago Campbell had declared himself independent of the stock growers association and other ranchers. He had even refused to let the Prairie Company look for stray cattle within his vast enclosure, saying they would be informed of any carrying their brand.

"An apology would now be a clever thing," one paper suggested, but without any chance of Barbecue Campbell coming across.

The fire had killed thirty head of cattle on the LE range and Reynolds, one of the owners, sent a letter as scorching as the fire to Taylor down on the capitol job. Reynolds was positive the XIT fence crew had let a camp fire get away in the wind and were responsible for the damage. He claimed pay for the cattle and burned fences, threatening suit. Taylor replied there was no proof and besides the fencers were independent contractors. Riders reported the blackened strip started up at the Arkansas River. The LE claim looked like one more try at bleeding a big foreign outfit.

Long before this the snow had started, marbled in ashes at first then pure white. The XIT cattle, for whom fenced pasture had been so carefully prepared, were now wandering on overstocked, summer-grazed range. The snow turned into the roaring blizzard called the Big White Ruin, which swept so many cattlemen out of business. It struck the unprotected, gaunted XIT stock, with no familiar range to hold them.

By the end of winter the losses of the great ranch were the talk of the country. Not that others hadn't lost, perhaps everything, but bad news about a big outfit is bigger news. It was said that the spring roundup scared up a scant 10,000 head, the spring calf crop below 900.

"Yeh, them thousands they lost last winter must have set the Britishers back no less than $200,000."

"More than that, if you figure the fencing, the wells, and everything. A hell of a lot more."

But Barbecue Campbell wasn't the man to side-jump at the sight of a little bad luck. Immediately after the fire he had the fencers out rebuilding the lines, in midwinter. Slowly the posts and wire crept over the burnt prairie and beyond, to grass. A second fire came, this one blazing up suddenly out of New Mexico on a strong west wind. The fence crew whipped the horses and mules with the equipment into a wide dry wash and saved themselves. But ten miles of new fence went up in smoke, the posts charred butts in the ground, the wire crisped and worthless. Patiently the men rebuilt the stretch. Campbell contracted the large southern section, eighty-five miles at $100 a mile, with a loss, the contractor complained later, of around $30 for every mile he built.

Although gates had been set every three miles as required by law and enforced by the Rangers to stop the earlier fence-cutting wars, organizations all the way from Texas to Montana were fighting to outlaw all barbed wire. Unconcerned, the XIT kept stringing their fences on their own land, owned by deed or by contract that promised deeds as the statehouse at Austin progressed. By the fall of 1886 the ranch had become a showplace of Texas for at least one thing—the fences, one stretch of 150 miles without a jog, and altogether over 750 miles enclosing all the XIT except 35,000 acres of outlying sections that the owners hoped to trade for land that would square up the ranch. The fence riders had 575 miles of outside line to watch against wire cutters, gate throwers, rustlers, fighting bulls, blizzard-drifted stock, perhaps lightning or prairie fires, particularly maliciously set. That second one, from New Mexico, looked like a good try at burning the XIT out completely.

Up to 1886 most of the XIT was treeless as the palm of a roper's hand. Then in January three big freight wagons had arrived at Buffalo Springs and unloaded sacked bundles of what looked like rough brush brooms upside down. The cowboys ankled out to see, and gawked in silent disbelief. Trees: 5,000 one-year-olds tagged as catalpa, box elder, white ash, maple, black cherry, and other stuff. The big burlap bags that looked like goober sacks were tree seeds. Almost nobody remembered seeing the seeds of any tree except the scrub acorns the javelinas hogged down, the chinaberries that made the wild turkeys taste like soap in season, and the mesquite beans the cattle carried all over hell and gone. In addition to the trees there was machinery; breaking plows, planters, and cultivators.

"Goddamn nester layout!" a gnarl-toothed old cowhand snorted and spit his cud far out, to roll itself in the sand.

But the XIT would have shade and the cowhands would plant it. They planted big gardens, too, and alfalfa and corn. Campbell's assistant estimated that the corn would run forty-five bushels to the acre. There would be 100,000 cattle, with the best bulls to be bought.

By July the XIT had a thin scattering of cattle spread the length of their holdings, at least so long as the water holes lasted. Farwell reported to the London office that they received 51,116 head of cattle, nearly all of high breeding, which must have meant something besides Longhorns, or even Texas crossbreeds, in that far land of blooded stock. Still Campbell was buying the very best possible, and he had contracted for purebred Shorthorn and Hereford bulls. The range was in fine condition, Farwell wrote, the cattle doing well.

If the stock was doing well it was because Campbell had hired some of the best cowhands ever to sit a saddle and then put them to ankling, as they called it, to such foot jobs as digging ditches to lead water miles out over the thirsty range to dirt reservoirs, perhaps to old buffalo ponds or wallows. Deep furrows were plowed, scooped out and plowed again until the canals were low enough to draw the water along, some as far as eight, nine miles from the source. The mowers and hayrakes came, and the Texas cowboys who had never pitched a forkful cursed Barbecue Campbell for running a goddamn granger outfit. But when they went to call for their time they remembered that jobs were scarce as a prairie hen in a hailstorm. Besides, the grub put out here was mighty good and a man got Sundays off if no cow fell in a well or a fool horse got into the bob wire.

Soon weather-beaten, bowlegged old cowboys were mowing creek bottoms while others were well-digging in gangs, sinking holes perhaps eighty-five feet deep. If the vein turned out a strong one, it was walled up and a windmill set over it to pump day and night in the eternal winds of the Panhandle.

All this was very fine but apparently there would be no profits or dividends for a long, long time and the British investors wanted to withdraw. They were encouraged to send representatives over to look around the vast holdings, see the alfalfa patches green as good Irish sod, listen to Farwell preach a Sunday sermon to the congregated hands in front of the bunkhouse.

On the way back to Chicago Farwell bought 100 Aberdeen-Angus bull calves, blocky and as shiny black as a prairie raven's wing. Fortunately Campbell put off the delivery to spring, as he did most of the undelivered portion of the 110,721 head bought and under contract.

The Big Die-Up followed last winter's Big White Ruin, with even the tallest weeds buried under snow and the cow chips lost to the cookstove and the heaters for a month at the least. In the depths of the snow some of the cowboys recalled an old coal mine over near Rabbit Ear Mountain in New Mexico. Campbell sent a man to see, and bought eighty acres there. He wished Babcock to know that the XIT had burned its last cow chip. The ranch hands not only plowed and planted, mowed and dug. They mined coal.

There were several burs under the saddle for Barbecue Campbell and the XIT. Beyond the general antagonism against such sprawling vastness there was a growing hatred of foreign outfits competing on the cattle market. With costs at the statehouse at Austin still going up and beef falling, there was no return for the protesting British investors, and neither Campbell nor the Farwells could see any way to make the situation look good.

Campbell managed to contract for twenty-five wells bored in the south half of the ranch, in the driest portion, where ten years ago, those men of the Lost Expedition died with thirst-blackened tongues. At least twelve of these wells were to be near the bluffs called Yellow Houses, and working in time for the new herds about due. The receiving camp was ready in time but there was no water, not a single well put down, and with the drouth the cattle from down in the Colorado City region would come in from a fifty- sixty-mile barren stretch from three water-crazed days. There was only the small and shrinking laguna at Yellow Houses and a little spring in the canyon. Thirty thousand cattle—cows, heifers, steers, and bulls, the best stock that Campbell could scare up —were headed here, and while he raged and bounced over the dry prairie in his buggy, seeking some way out of this box canyon in which he found himself, the long-brewing range trouble up at Tascosa on the Canadian blazed into a gun fight, lurid even for that wild cow town. Three LS ranch cowboys and a bystander ended up in Boothill—died of the bitterness growing between the large cattle outfits on one side and the small ranchers and settlers on the other. Outside for the present, a sort of bystander, was the XIT, the largest of all, the most hated by both sides.

But Campbell was occupied with the desperate search for water, improvising plans and equipment. The drillers had hauled up big machines, big enough to aim for artesian water, but they struck dry formations and a whole string of trouble. As the time for the herds came very, very close, Campbell roared his complaints and the contract driller moved his rig into a valley. This time water came flowing. Everybody was excited. A mile south another well was sunk, with more flowing water, but then somebody noticed that the first had dropped far down. There just wasn't enough water for two wells on the Yarner there, as the old-timers had long assumed.

Any other cowman would have headed off the incoming herds, sent them on to the Canadian River, but not stubborn Barbecue Campbell. He would need water in the Yellow Houses region for the cows eventually and he would show all the wrinkle-horned old cowmen that he could get it.

Finally the drillers struck a seepage, but a good one, at only six feet near Yellow House Spring and another at eighteen feet. The fencing boss called his men in and set them to work. With plows and shovels they dug out big supply tanks or reservoirs to catch the seepage and set up treadmills run by old cow ponies, to lift the water by endless chains of sheet-iron buckets. It was primitive, as primitive as the equipment of prehistoric man along the Nile, where bullocks perhaps plodded the treadmills, or of Asia, where the cow roamed very early, sniffing the lifted water and drinking deep of it.

Campbell had stout wire fences built to regulate the cattle approach to the water. It was the best he and his help could devise. After all, men experienced in the region had died for water on the trail to Yellow Houses.

When the tanks shimmered in the heat dance of early June and the dust began to rise from the horizon and grow like puffballs, Campbell stood bareheaded to watch for the thin, wavering line that would approach like an enormous snake, a rattler—no, more like some giant coachwhip humping over the low ridges, raising the great trailing of dust. The bawl of the cattle came hoarsely on the wind, from swollen tongues, Campbell knew. At the first sniff of water their tails went up, and the stock broke into a hurried and shambling trot. The cowpunchers spurred in, yelling but hoarse, too, swinging their ropes like whips to break the herd into small bunches, let them in to water a few at a time, hold the rest back from the desperate crowding at the cottonwood troughs. As fast as they had drunk a little they were punched away to the branding corrals, to make room for more of the crazed stock, the weary men cursing, their eyes red-rimmed holes in the dust-caked faces. At last the first herd was done, Campbell still watching, his bare head forgotten in the broiling sun.

Finally night settled over the bare prairie, dotted with trail camps and their fires, the pumps groaning on as the old horses still walked the treadmills. Thirsty cattle still bawled, crowding, pushing in the darkness, the men silent now, their ropes popping.

Checking his remaining water holes, Campbell found a big Matador outfit watering at the XIT Spring Lake. He demanded where they were going. Arizona, the brawny, bearded trail boss said, hand on his gun, but easily, as though just resting it. There was a stretch of 111 miles to the next water and he wasn't pulling out until it rained.

"I can't allow that," Campbell said. "I have cattle coming in every day with their tongues hanging out. This is XIT land and water."

Now there was no doubt why the Matador foreman's hand was on the holster, his cowboys drawing in at a motion, letting the cattle spread. They were all armed, Campbell and his few men as always without guns. Finally the trail boss said he wasn't unfriendly but if the XIT tried to move his herd away it would mean lead.

Campbell ordered a man to ride out to round up the hands. "Tell them to bring all the guns they can."

At dawn the men started coming in, wondering, but ready. With a good force about him, Campbell rode over to Spring Lake. But the Matador herd was gone. Luckily they hit rain farther west. Campbell felt relieved. A gun fight would have blown the Farwells sky-high, and with the Matador, too—the big Scottish-owned ranch. Sky-high wouldn't have expressed what would have happened over in England.

Thirty thousand cattle were delivered during the next month at Yellow Houses, with growing talk of fraud in the tallies and in the age count, yearlings turned in as two-year-olds, or even three or older, perhaps one head tallied as two and three, or the cowboys hairbranding some of the stock, burning only the hair, the critters to be rustled later, when the brand was grown out and gone, the cowboy's own mark put on. There was much talk of one of Campbell's relatives, some said a cousin, deep in the thieving schemes. And this was the man who came with such stern rules—and drier than Carry Nation.

Still, the herds were delivered and somehow watered, at least their swollen tongues wetted. The cattle showed thirty different brands, representing some lifelong cowmen like C. C. Slaughter, who sold 10,000 head at the giveaway prices. The Snyders, who had seen a million dollars wiped out by the bust in the beef bonanza and the Die-Ups, were happy to turn their cows into a little XIT cash. But there were stories of the new stock dying of thirst on the prairie, some along Campbell's wire fences, trying to return to their home range, as cattle will, and nobody bothering to drive them back to such water as there was a few times until their feet knew the contrary route.

When Campbell was swamped by the herds crowding in, he had called on A. G. Boyce, up with the Snyder deliveries, for help with the count and the watering. A. G. tackled the job and got the aid of the trail outfits, not because they were friends of the XIT but of Boyce. There was still fraud among Campbell's hands, and many cattle died of thirst before Boyce or Campbell could get to them—seventy-six in one of the large open wells, the smell of water tolling the desperate animals as it tolled rabbits and even the wily kangaroo rat.

For a while Campbell had tried to be everywhere, watching with some satisfaction as the XIT herds grew and improved in quality. Most of the later cattle were from above the fever line, the larger, better grade stock of west Texas. By the fall of 1887 the herds totaled nearly 120,000 head, with around half of the bulls quality Shorthorns and

Herefords, in addition to the Polled Angus, with their long, glossy black coats in the chill of fall, but dusty and burning in the heat of summer. The crosses of these bloods with the range stock was producing a heavier, more manageable cattle but less hardy and far less picturesque for the English visitors. Still it was good; the XIT was out to produce beef, not hoofs and horn.

Eventually there was water, too. Many little dams were built to hold the runoff, and around 125 wells, varying in depth from ten to 400 feet, were put down, the windmills set upon them spinning their wide and shining wheels, like flower faces turned not to the sun but into the wind. The pump rods ran silently, spouting water through the lead pipes into cypress tanks, the overflow running into ponds and reservoirs.

The drouth after the Big Die-Up brought starvation to the settlers of Texas, their teams too weak to haul bones to market or even to carry them and their families back to the in-laws somewhere. The Quaker colony that had established Estacado the fall of 1879, the first settlement above the cap rock of the Staked Plains and with such high and noble hope, gave up and left. The *Dallas News* demanded relief for the suffering homesteaders and in a special session the Texas legislature appropriated $100,000 to rescue the drouth victims. To the cattlemen this was like throwing money to the infidels, giving tax money to keep the grangers alive. With beef prices gone to hell, the stock growers could do with a little saving themselves, but not on $100,000, not with the second summer of drouth driving even southern stock off the range. The XIT had profited from this buying but it took money, as the fences and the wells had taken money. At Austin the statehouse was still about two years and $2,000,000 short of completion. The Capitol Syndicate was that much short of the final deeds to the XIT.

Several plans were considered to quiet the impatience Taylor found in England and to raise a little needed capital. Taylor suggested that Campbell drive 1,000 or 1,500 steers to

Kansas and sell them at a good stiff price in time to appear on the year's balance sheets. He could have his cousin at Wichita take them and guarantee him against the loss. It was very desirable to fix a good price on the cattle this year, Taylor suggested, for their friends on the other side of the water.

But Barbecue Campbell replied that an arranged sale at a fictitious price to make an impression could only be an act of desperation. Even so the stiff price would be against them next year if beef didn't come back up. Although he knew that Farwell was in a practically hopeless struggle to keep the company together, Campbell advised against it, and Farwell fought on somehow without the sale.

The English, hearing many rumors from the neighboring ranchers and perhaps settlers and politicians, too, tried to keep their eyes on the XIT. They had sent a man out early to act as general manager while Campbell was off organizing the ranch. His name, Walter de S. Maud, was too much for some of the cowboys and their common contempt for foreign outfits. They called the new general manager Lady Maud. Not that he wasn't roostering it around the ranch with girls brought in by the wagonload and whisky by the keg. Much of the time he was off gambling at Tascosa, taking up this American game called crap shooting with the enthusiasm of a convert.

On top of the appalling mismanagement of the new herds received the summer of 1887, evidence of other gross negligence and of graft was piling up. Apparently Campbell, in spite of his stern entry into the Panhandle, had no more control over his employees than over a shirttail full of lizards. The ranch had become a hangout for rustlers, outlaws, and plain Hard Cases.

Suddenly John Farwell acted. He sent a trusted young man from the Chicago office ostensibly to look after the bookkeeping of the ranch but to lift an eye above the shimmering horizon now and then to see what was going on at the other ranch division headquarters. In addition Farwell hired Matlock, the former state senator, who had borrowed the money from Charles Farwell, and in return, it was said, helped get the Capitol contract for them. He and the book-keeper were to investigate the general situation for Farwell and for Goodnight and the LS ranch, too, all anxious to get rid of the rustlers they claimed were dug in at the XIT and operating on the surrounding ranges from there. How much self-interest was in the protest of these neighbors one could guess and yet plainly something drew all those buzzards soaring.

At Yellow Houses, Matlock reported, he found the range boss a man he saved from being hanged by a mob some years ago. The man had his brother-in-law there, too, a horse thief—a good example of much of Campbell's pay roll there. Farwell fired Barbecue Campbell, away from the ranch at the time—skipped out, some said, with XIT money. Actually he had gone to Chicago to sell his interests in the ranch, and then home to his family, still in Wichita.

Farwell hired Matlock to run the ranch with Boyce to help. The new manager started clearing out at Yellow Houses, firing most of the cowboys and the foreman. He had no trouble replacing them with able men but there were loud and frequent threats against Matlock's life. The dis-missed range boss and eight, ten of his gun packers returned to take over but the new manager faced them down and was still around the next day, the gunmen gone, later to appear in New Mexico. What Chicagoans and the British didn't un-derstand was that western gunmen did not shoot important people, whose killing would bring certain action. Print Olive shot only small men, until a small man killed him. Hickok, the most publicized of gun fighters, would shoot a southerner, a Reb in northern territory in 1861 but never a man of any consequence. "Only halfwits and greenhorns pull down on a man of any substance," was the common con-tention of men like John Chisum, who never carried a gun, even with vast sums of money on him. There were others like him.

But there was plenty of dirty work still going on

around the XIT. Fences were cut between every post for miles along the New Mexican side of the Yellow Houses range, a mile of fence and a windmill went up in smoke, and half-a-dozen small prairie fires were set. Farwell suggested big rewards for conviction but spite work proved hard to nail down.

Nor were things good at the other headquarters of the ranch, with gambling, thievery, and harboring of outlaws very common, particularly at the Escarbaba, only a good jump from the New Mexican line. Some of the little outfits were building up their herds mighty fast—almost everybody working foreign-owned stock. Often a man too considerate to touch a grouse or wild turkey on another man's range went to great trouble to steal from a British-owned outfit, the bigger the better.

Although the XIT herd was not much under 120,000 head with some fine big steers, nothing had been sold, no beef income had reached the books, and the British investors were very hard to hold together. Henry Seton-Karr, M. P., and a major shareholder in the ranch, was picked to go investigate. Taylor returned from London furious to find, as many in the Panhandle believed, that Campbell was apparently fired on "trumped-up charges," and an incompetent political friend of Charles Farwell put in. With the capitol building still unfinished and the deeds of the land incomplete, quarreling among the American shareholders would wreck the British company, as the Farwells knew. They agreed to the angry Taylor's insistence that he be appointed manager of the ranch with the power to prepare for Seton-Karr's coming. Nothing of the charges against Campbell must be mentioned, no hint of negligence or dishonesty. Taylor, with a fine nose, delicately flanged, and the appearance of a very learned man, and with a handsome statehouse going up under his hand, impressed the British visitor. By then the railroad, aimed at Tascosa, had reached the Canadian River. With a substantial right of way on their land, the XIT got the railroad to lay the track diagonally across their holdings to the northwest corner of Texas, giving the land value a fine jump, if only on paper.

So far there had been only one attempt to get an XIT beef sale on the books. A thousand of the biggest and best steers had been rounded up and trailed the 120 miles to the Santa Fe railroad. But prices were so low then that the first loading didn't pay the freight, and the Chicago managers wired orders to trail the rest back to the water-short range. It was a sad and dusty job. For the Farwells, too. Once more John had to talk the British into standing by for another season.

In 1888 the New Order, under Abner Taylor as non-resident manager, took entire charge, with A. G. Boyce managing the ranch. Boyce was a short, stout, chin-whiskered cowman with sun-narrowed brown eyes in a leathery and lined face. The general headquarters were moved from Buffalo Springs, at the very northern edge, to Alamocitas Creek, nearer the middle. With the move came a jolt like a man's cutting horse going down in a badger hole for the cowpunchers—250 copies of a little book of ranch rules, one for each employee, were handed out and 90 copies of the twenty-three new laws written by Taylor were to be posted at every camp. These rules and laws broke entirely with the range country customs and furnished many jokes and jibes. But Boyce had to tack them up. Not only did they regulate the relationship of ranch worker to employer but undertook to run what the West always had considered a man's own business—his private life. No employee was to carry a pistol, dirk, Bowie knife, knuckles, or slingshot "on or about his person." There was to be no gambling on the ranch, or even card playing, and no liquor was permitted any employees "during their time of service with the Company." No grub-line riders were to be fed, no hunters permitted anywhere.

Unfortunately the weather was beyond even Taylor's twenty-three steel-jacketed rules. In January, 1888, Boyce and the Chicago bookkeeper stood at the ranch window and saw what had been summer temperature turn to a white and howling norther, shutting out everything before their eyes, the wind so powerful the city man was struck silent. Boyce was silent, too. He was making plans for the skinning crews. They stripped 3,500 carcasses bare and estimated that 1,000 more were never found. The loss in expensive bulls and heifers was appalling in number and in cost. The two-day storm that killed so many people farther up the Plains cost the XIT nearly $100,000 above the value of the hides.

Now at last they were where the hair was short. Wages were cut, the great ranch divided into seven very distinct divisions, under separate foremen. Families were brought to the ranches, the first women permitted there, officially, and telephones, that new invention to the Panhandle, were installed, to tie the vast cow empire into a whole.

The next few years the XIT went on its unwestern way. Trees and gardens were put in at each of the seven ranches, in a larger way a little like Faver's gardens and peach trees in the Big Bend country. Great reservoirs were dug, cemented, tarred, and still found to leak. Finally the bottoms were plowed and the rock-salt blocks put there for a while, the earth packed stone hard by the milling cattle. Big dams were thrown up, one 115 feet wide at the base, twenty-one feet high, holding twenty-five feet of water at the deepest and spreading to 300 yards in width, nearly a mile long. Double fireguards were plowed around the 3,000,000 acres, thirty-five feet apart, the grass between burned off— grass that alone would have made a good-sized ranch even in Texas.

Although Charles Farwell seemed busy in the Senate now, his brother John was firm about lawlessness around the XIT. Foremen with reputations for short rope with rustlers were hired and Winchester-packing fence riders made it dangerous to be caught anywhere near ranch-owned wire and post. There was no hesitation about following rustlers or anyone suspected of tampering with stock, range, or

fence anywhere, even across into New Mexico. Angrily this
was called armed invasion but it had been going on from
back in the early *comanchero* days and before.

But all these things took years and cost money, as the
cattle had cost money. No well-run ranch, understocked as
the XIT was all this time, sold off more than the steers and
the culls and dry cows. The investors, however, were tired of
anteing up and wanted a smell of the kitty, the profits, that
the prospectus had promised. The great profits. Now they
would have them, or there would be hell in Texas.

Yet there was still the combination of railroad and
packer monopolies. Kit Carter, president of the Northwest
Texas Association, said people told him that cowmen must
be getting mighty rich at the prices they had to pay for beef.
Yet his steers barely paid the shipping costs. It was the big
packers and the railroads working in cahoots who were sitting in the easy chairs, reaping the cream of the cowman's
saddle-pounding work. Under Governor Sul Ross, Carter's
old Indian-fighting brother-in-law, Texas chalked up her
first anti-trust law. C. C. Slaughter was appointed a delegate
from the 1888 Association to the Farmers Alliance and
Knights of Labor, organizations that were proposing a cooperative system of refrigeration and distribution of beef.
The fight between St. Louis and Chicago as top cattle market
was up again, with Senator Vest of Missouri getting a Select
Committee appointed to ride herd on range problems. Vest
was the chairman, Coke of Texas and Farwell of Illinois, and
the XIT of Texas, on it.

But Kit Carter died before anything was done, or
times got better. A. P. Bush, new president of the Northwest
Texas Association, appointed Goodnight, Cape Willingham,
sheriff of Tascosa, A. G. Boyce of the XIT, and Murdo
Mackenzie, who had made the Dundee-owned Matador a
cattle empire, to hammer at the Select Senate Committee for
results. Slaughter, a born Texan, in the cattle business almost
since he could climb an old horse like a boar coon goes up a
tree, blamed the beef trust for the poverty of the western

ranges. Hard work and judgment weren't enough, and everybody knew that he had reason for his opinion. He had found that when he wouldn't sell his cattle at Kansas City for giveaway prices, Chicago could tell him exactly what he had been offered down there, and St. Louis the same.

Beaty's little packing plant at El Paso managed to get the contracts to supply refrigerated beef to Los Angeles and San Diego, but soon the railroad refused the cars to haul the meat. "Along about the first of February Mr. Armour concluded that our business could not continue; that it was detrimental to his interests," Beaty said. "The moment Mr. Armour put his refrigerator beef into California the customers of Beaty had to ship their steers to Kansas City and sell at a loss."

Senator Vest insisted that St. Louis should be in as advantageous a position as Chicago in purchasing and shipping cattle. Five firms in Chicago controlled the price of beef. Every butcher felt it and shippers had to accept what the packers would pay.

The investigators blamed Armour for encouraging vast overproduction by financing the ranges for the slump. Philip Armour denied any attempt at price fixing or control of cattle or dressed-beef market and although the fight on the packers didn't get any results at the time, harder battles were planned for later. In the meantime attempts at packing on the range, such as the Marquis de Mores' up in Dakota, were squeezed out, as Beaty was at El Paso, by the railroads. To avoid any such nuisances in the future, the Big Five of the packers spread into the country, to Omaha, Fort Worth, and so on, underselling the little operators everywhere, until they were frozen out.

In 1888 the magnificent capitol building of red Texas granite was finished and dedicated. Now the XIT owned all the 3,000,000 acres and because cattle from the northern ranges brought more than southern stock, they leased range from the VVV up near the Black Hills of Dakota. Boyce rounded up 15,000 steers and by the end of May had the last hoof set on the trail north, with men ready to see that the herd got through Colorado, where the quarantine had tightened up. In the fall he sent some XIT steers to market. They brought $13.40 each, at a $16 a head loss. Finally he sold 30,304 head for an average of $24.77 each, $750,000, but they had cost more than that to produce.

Still deeper in the red, Farwell gave Boyce the job of general manager, now that Taylor was done at Austin anyway, and warned him that economy must be the watchword. Early in 1890 Boyce leased 2,000,000 acres between the Yellowstone and the Missouri rivers in Montana—bringing the XIT range to 5,000,000, the giant of them all. With such distinction and prestige from their American ranches, could the Britishers cry for profit, too?

# BOOK IV

*PRIVATE EMPIRE*

# CHAPTER I

## THE THREAT

U P NORTH, particularly in Wyoming, the ranchers were in what they realized was a fight to the finish if they would preserve the free range as the private empire of their cows. True, they knew that the Cheyenne Club might never offer the extravagant glories of 1884 again, or even of that final autumn of 1886. Paulus Potter's huge painting of the bull of some effete and sheltered Dutch breed would not draw another angry and critical bullet of a beholder in the club. Nor would the cattlemen gather there with the old exuberance in their Herefords, as some called their white-fronted evening attire appropriate to those formal and elaborate days. But those occasions, with food and drink fitting the exalted and lovely guests, equal even to Harry Oelrich's friend, the Jersey Lily, were gone. Never again would such a display of wealthy young men turn up in the Territory of Wyoming from perhaps halfway around the world, to spread themselves around Cheyenne, to ride out like the lords that some of them were, observing their minions conduct the rituals and the dispensations of the roundup spread over the new spring grass.

The Wyoming Stock Growers Association looked back to those golden times much as a Longhorn steer would to a season in some settler's lush green stretch of corn. When the

first little rise of beef prices had come, most of the new territory of Wyoming was without county organization or sheriff,
and the Association had established itself as The Law. Since
then any man who tried to run cattle without their full approval was automatically operating outside of that law—a
rustler. It had been easy at first because Wyoming was so
essentially cattle. Texas had the vast agricultural regions,
with wide stretches of snowy cotton fields and other crop-
pings, too. Kansas and Nebraska had their corn and wheat;
the Dakotas, particularly the eastern and northern sections,
their bonanza wheatlands. Colorado and Montana were mining camps before one Longhorn came stringing his hoof dust
northward, and later South Dakota, too. Only Wyoming was
cattle from the day the Indians were driven off the old buffalo
plains, cattle and practically nothing else.

The first officials of the new territory of 1869 included
men to go high in the ranching business, such men as Carey,
appointed U. S. Attorney for Wyoming, from Philadelphia;
Wolcott, Receiver of the Land Office, from Kentucky, later
the manager of the Scottish Tolland Company's VR Ranch.
Other officials to turn to stock growing included Surveyor
General David, to become general manager of Carey's ranches,
and Warren, the territorial treasurer.

From the first the territorial officials and the Stock
Growers Association overlapped, but as much of the range
law and enforcement as possible was kept in private hands,
away from the meddling voters. As cattlemen they assessed
themselves a cent a head on their herds and hired gun-armed
stock detectives and inspectors to protect the interests of the
Association members while a few of them ran the government and enjoyed their private preserve beyond anything
they could have dreamed of a few years ago, even better than
carpetbagging.

In 1883 there were only two ranch holdings not to be
termed large between the upper North Platte River and the
Missouri, deep in Montana. The stock growers, particularly

the Wyoming men, planned to keep it that way. Of the more than 400 Association members in the Territory, all but eighty already owned over 1,000 head of cattle each. Then in 1884 they managed some pretense of legality for their practices through the Maverick Bill that made branding a maverick a felony, all mavericks to be sold to pay the Association inspectors. "All rustler brands and all stray brands for which there are no owners to be treated as maverick cattle."

"That means anybody they decide to call a rustler is out of the cattle business. I can't even brand me the mavericks that's hanging around my herd without going to the pen," a member of the Henry's Fork Stock Growers Association roared.

"No. Guess not. Them big outfits's got their start and now they're shutting the gate on the rest," another member agreed.

By the spring of 1885 the Henry's Fork group was rejecting the roundup foreman the state association sent out. They put in their own and branded their mavericks in the old, old way—for the man on whose range the unmarked critter was found.

This open defiance was only one instance of a growing rebellion against the big outfits, especially against the domination by the foreign money behind so many of them, including the financial interests of John Clay. Clay was the American representative of W. J. Menzies and his Scottish-American Investment Company and other Edinburgh capitalists. Although a newcomer, he agreed with many others of the Wyoming Association, particularly members from the Sweetwater and the Powder River that there should be swift and drastic punishment to stop the ranchers at Henry's Fork, crush this bunch-quitting before it spread. But down at Cheyenne those with their own money at stake were more concerned with the falling beef prices.

Not that the extra-legal hand of the Association was to be unfelt by the little fellows, as everybody realized when Frank Canton was put in as range inspector to take over the

criminal work of the range and then was made sheriff for the
newly created county of Johnson in the Powder River
country. One of the stock detectives and roundup foremen
up there turned out to be Phil DuFran, gone to Wyoming to
tend a little bar soon after he had delivered the handcuffed
Mitchell and Ketchum to the Man-Burner, Print Olive,
down in Nebraska, and then turned state's evidence against
him. Some thought Olive would not have had to buy himself
out of the pen if it hadn't been for DuFran's testimony.

The Association found Canton and DuFran valuable
for years. Canton, who had left his past and his name behind
in Texas, as many others before him, was arrogant and ready
for gun play or ambush, yet always agreeable to those who
paid him. DuFran, the affable and Indian-nosed Frenchman,
was liked by almost everybody, rancher and settler, although
there were some on both sides who were easier in mind when
he tended bar.

It was time to discourage all the newcomers settling
over the open range, make a sort of example for them, hang
out a dead owl to scare the others away. For this somebody
selected the Young brothers over in the Sweetwater country where Clay's firm had bought the Quarter Circle 71, and
a half-a-dozen others of British roots or money were running
ranches. The three Youngs were building up their herds
very fast. Next thing the settlers heard was that Porter Young
had been arrested by a Pinkerton detective from Chicago
with a sheriff's posse. Young was ironed, it seemed, and taken
by train down as far as Omaha and around by Denver, Santa
Fe, and south Texas. At every stop he was exhibited as an
example of the way Wyoming managed cattle thieves. People
came to look at the helpless man as they had stared at captured Indian chiefs a few years earlier. Nobody told them
that Young was arrested for an alleged murder back East,
and not for rustling or anything else done in Wyoming.

The bust in cattle prices and the Big Die-Ups had
cleaned out some of the largest ranches of the West, with

little outfits popping up like cottonwood seedlings the moment the wind brought down the great old tree that had shut out the sun. Often before the remaining ranchers could agree on a peaceful division of the vacated public domain, settlers and former cowboys swooped in and covered the waterways and hay flats with homesteads, those poor man's kingdoms, inviolable to all except death, even free from taxes for seven years. Some, as those who slid in around the lordly old Frewen holdings on the upper Powder River sensed this kingship particularly, and they would not be driven out even by that age-old threat—the dried ear stuck to the claim shack door with a nail or knife blade, or a rope knotted into a noose thrown at the step.

The antagonisms were perhaps stronger because many of the remaining ranchers got their start in earlier and less-regulated days, with cows that had twins, and older stock picked up in the night. That was before Sir Horace Plunkett, manager of the EK, got most of the cattlemen to boycott any cowboy who owned a place he used or even had a little bunch of cows.

"They claim they're afraid that a man with stock'll be sneaking some of theirs," one of the Swan cowboys complained. "Some of them ought to know—"

Besides, many ranchers used to hire cowboys for special expertness with the long rope and the running iron and paid them an extra $2.50 to $5.00 or even a competitive $7.50 a head for all the mavericks branded for the boss. Now, with the collapse of beef, many of those cowboys were out of jobs and might use the tricks they learned to build up herds for themselves. The Britisher, Fred Hesse, started as a cowboy. While foreman for Moreton Frewen, back in 1882, he started a herd and his 28 Ranch. When the gay and spendthrift Frewen saw the end of his British company after the bad winter, he sold the bulk of what remained of his herd, once estimated at 80,000, to Pierre Wibaux, Montana's French cowman. The remnants he gave to Hesse, as did several others of his countrymen. Hesse claimed 50,000 acres

of the public domain up near Buffalo, with additional interest in range and cattle down in the Sweetwater country.

It was not surprising that to many Wyoming of the
1880's meant not merely cattle but British-financed cattle.
The region was never directly on the  trails from Texas to
the larger Indian reservations nor did the Reconstruction-
minded territorial government attract southerners. Further,
most of Wyoming wasn't open to cattle until the early promise of bonanza profits had drawn the British, who turned
there naturally, out of old attachments. Back in the days of
the big-game hunting and the Noble Red Man, the region
had drawn such sportsmen as the Irish Sir Gore and his
forty servants. Even earlier the Scottish Sir William Drum-
mond Stewart came to live among the Sioux for years, back
when the only cow of Wyoming was the Indian's mother-
creature, the brooding buffalo.

The decoy to toll the young Britishers was the Cheyenne Club, organized by a group of gay young blades from
the East: the Daters; two of the Sturgis family; young Edgar
Beecher Bronson, nephew of Henry Ward Beecher and of
the Harriet Beecher Stowe who wrote *Uncle Tom's Cabin,*
and the Oelrichs, C. M. and Harry with his English Drag
said to be worth $4,000, the only one west of the Mississippi,
one of the few in the nation. Soon the club was swamped by
the actual foreigners.

There seemed little thought about the power of the
outsider and outside capital in Wyoming, perhaps because
except for those like the breed family of Elias Whitcomb,
almost everybody else was an outsider, and even Whitcomb
owed John Clay money. There was a little uneasiness around
the club, however, after the dinner the British members
gave for the Americans back in August, 1883. It was elaborate, formal, and impressive, but in the midst of it some of
the earlier ranchers noticed two old-timers were missing, and
suddenly saw the Britishers as their permanent hosts, solidly
in the saddle.

"They made us look like grub-line riders in our own

Wyoming," Jack Hunton was reported to have said. But then he was a southerner, and a little thin-nosed anyway.

There was no denying that the British cattle interests and their employees were determined to have the Wyoming range regulated and orderly. Perhaps they looked upon the American public domain as something like their own early backlands, to be gifted by the king to his favorites or appropriated by any aggressive chieftain with the long bows to hold it. Anyone setting foot upon it thereafter was a trespasser or a poacher, not too different from the predatory animals with a bounty on their ears, or, taken connected, their scalps. The early British colonists had put a bounty on the scalps of the Indians, introducing the aborigine to the scalp knife. In the West the bounties were on predators of cattle—wolves, mainly, and Indians, occasionally *comancheros*. The settler or small rancher moving into the free-range country, whether rustler or not, was considered most predatory of all.

There was no legal way to get empires of grass from the public domain anywhere except in Texas, through the state lands, as Goodnight and the XIT did it. While the organizers of foreign-cattle companies often hid this from their investors, their American representatives and ranch managers tried to hold their government grass by armed men, by herds on grand and overawing scales, and often by great ranch houses with handsome imported furniture, chefs, valets, Irish hunters, and monkey saddles, while perhaps even the grand houses were on free land that any bona-fide homesteader could file on, improvements and all, for the $14 fee, if he liked hot lead. Gradually, however, many ranchers asked their guests, citizens or foreigners with their first papers, to file on the waterways and the bottomlands, making what the guest might never understand was a fraudulent entry by swearing he intended to live on the land, and later perjuring himself by his oath that he had lived there for the final proof. Many old ranchers as well as the foreign interests scorned this procedure, as many frowned on fencing the public lands. They had the free range, possessed it, and any such concessions as filings or fencings seemed to admit doubt of their eternal right to keep it.

Because the Maverick Law had not been enforced and produced too little money to pay the inspectors, the cattlemen pushed the legislature to set up a Board of Live Stock Commissioners to take over the detectives and inspectors, and to supervise the roundups and the sale of the mavericks. The Board was composed of the leaders of the Association, and only the source of the money was shifted, the range control given a little more legality.

Some of the big outfits still hired their own inspectors. Besides, with the Herd Law of Nebraska making the owner liable for damages by his loose stock, even for a homesteader's unfenced corn patch, eastern Wyoming ranchers had to set up a Line Riding Association to turn their cattle back at the Nebraska border. Mike Shonsey, stock inspector and long foreman for the Guthrie and Oskamp Cattle Company, was made foreman of the Line Riders.

The Wyoming Live Stock Commissioners gathered no more mavericks to be sold for the inspectors' salaries than the Association had, and the cattlemen, particularly the large absentee outfits, complained that no man's stock was safe from rustlers. To this many replied that the cry of "Rustlers, rustlers!" was raised to fool faraway shareholders, to cover losses from bad winters, mismanagement, and from substantial thievery by employees.

Still, no one could deny that the situation was serious. A Cheyenne paper not overly sympathetic to the large interests agreed that cattle stealing had become almost respectable. Men of good reputation frankly raided the stock on the open ranges and bragged about it. Sometimes overwhelming evidence against a cow thief stealing from the large companies, particularly foreign-owned, brought no indictment. Those caught in the middle feared for their stock and their lives from one side or the other, and so managed to see nothing done by the hired gunmen of the big outfits or by the actual rustlers.

To be sure the ranchers understood that the great loss was the land but the settler's filing was legal and so the only charge they could bring against him was that of stealing their stock. It wasn't working. Whole townships, whole counties were being cut out of the range country, chopped up into small holdings, with a few cows, a little breaking, a garden, perhaps only a dozen barefoot children, and a couple of milk cows. Buffalo, up in Johnson County, jumped to over 1,000 population and helped throw Frank Canton, the Stock Growers Association's range inspector, out of the sheriff's office. In spite of Canton's capture of Teton Jackson, a genuine horse thief, and Packer, the man eater, the voters put in the bristle-mustached, stubborn Scotsman, Angus, Sheriff Red Angus.

There were 5,000 brands of one kind or another in Wyoming and the overlapping ranches from outside the Territory and scarcely over forty Association members, all but eight of these from big companies, mostly foreign-financed. But the president, John Clay, now of the Clay, Robinson commission house of Chicago, still had his hand on an empire of Scottish-financed ranches, including the old Swan spreads, taken over since Alex Swan went broke owing money to the John Nelson Trust of Edinburgh, through Clay. Under Clay's strong leadership the Association armed for one last mighty effort, "a sort of crusade," one man called it at Clay's induction into the presidency and laughed a little. But Clay did not laugh.

Now the inspectors at the markets and shipping points were ordered to enforce the Maverick Law to the letter, to attach every head of stock bearing a brand not approved by the Association. Any man who questioned this could face the Stock Commissioners and try to prove to their satisfaction that the stock attached was rightfully his, had never been stolen, and that he was a man of good repute, not what they called a rustler.

During the first ten months, with limited staff, 16,306 head of stock bearing unacceptable brands were confiscated at various shipping points. Of these 5,238 were sold and the $13,949.83 held back by the Commission—money from stock not proved stolen, carrying the brands of men never convicted of rustling, most of them never accused of it.

At this news the corral-fence and brass-rail lawyers let out bellows like old herd bulls under the knife. Was this America, where the burden of proof was supposedly on the accuser, this stock confiscated without proof of a crime committed, of any such cattle stolen anywhere? These buckshot scatter-gun methods could only drive the settlers and small ranchers into the same corral, up the same box canyon, with the actual thieves. Towns like Douglas, Glenrock, and Casper as well as Buffalo, began siding with the little fellows. The press, really dependent on the advertisements of the large cattle companies and those who lived off them, dared join judges, juries, and the general public against the Stock Growers Association. The officials of the organization complained that they were making the members look like thieves. The editor of the Cheyenne *Sun* in what was still called "The Holy City of the Cow" was ordered "to appear before the executive committee at once" because the Association didn't like his editorial.

The newspapers stood their ground, with great blank pages where ads were withdrawn by order of the Association. The Cheyenne *Leader* backed up the *Sun,* deploring the un-American spirit of dominance that would force "the weaker elements to immigrate or crawl, cowed and subdued, to the feet of the fierce and implacable oligarchy."

Long before this violence had come once more to the settlers of the Sweetwater country. The Bothwells, with the Sweetwater Land and Improvement Company, started Bothwell as a coming metropolis of the cattle barons and a place for the cowboy to spend his money, offering everything he might want, even a newspaper. But a settler, James Averill, took up a homestead not far away and opened a small store and saloon, in the heart of the country claimed by the Bothwells, Clay, Hesse, Sun, and their associates. Although Averill was personally a quiet, peaceful man with many friends among the cowboys as well as the settlers, he wrote fiery letters to the papers denouncing the big cattlemen as range tyrants and grabbers of the public domain. "Is it not enough to excite one's prejudice to see the Sweetwater owned, or claimed, for a distance of seventy-five miles from its mouth by three or four men?"

Because he shouted words that many in the Sweetwater country would not have dared whisper, he became a threat. Although many agreed that Jim Averill had not one head of cattle and was apparently never accused of rustling, Ella Watson, a woman who lived nearby, was called Cattle Kate because she entertained cowboys and, it was said, took cattle in trade. Perhaps she was Averill's wife, as some said, and was using her maiden name to take up a homestead. There was a rumor, too, that the Averills had a small son off east somewhere. Anyway, Kate was a strong, husky woman in her late twenties, and in addition to the supposed entertainment, she washed the cowboys' shirts and had a mighty smooth hand with the sadiron if a man was going back East and wanted to look good. Gradually her homestead was stocked with cattle, around forty head, some guessed; at least eighty, others claimed, with many more marketed at the railroad.

"That ain't likely, not with them brand inspectors grabbing 'em," a settler said as he looked over a hot letter from Averill in the Casper paper. "I ain't seen no marks for Kate in the Association's *Brand Book*—"

Although Averill and Kate received some warnings and threats, everybody got them. Neither carried guns, and there was still the notion that if Chisum could go through the wild Texas days and the Lincoln County war unarmed, a mild, pacific Jim Averill out on his homestead should be safe. Apparently the cattlemen were just talking about the rustling; they made no attempt to take the two to court, although they controlled the county officials.

But it seems that Averill contested some land that Connor had covered by a filing. His protests to Washington made trouble for Durbin in his final proof, too. Besides, Averill kept Bothwell from fencing all the Sweetwater country against all comers.

Then one day in July, 1889, the crippled boy living around Averill and Kate's places slipped out to the hired hands, Buchanan and DeCory. Some men were making trouble back at the store, he said, picking a fight—

The two hurried over. Later it was reported they found ten in the outfit, including Fred Hesse, still looking like a genteelly-bearded solicitor and his range manager George Henderson; Bob Connor, also high in the Association; John Durbin of Durbin Brothers, already buying cattle from the Snyders in 1871 and delivering beeves to Iliff's slaughterhouse corral near Cheyenne in early 1872 and now of the Durbin Land and Cattle Company here in the Sweetwater country; Tom Sun, the Canadian Frenchman early in the region, and Bothwell of the town.

It seemed they had gone to Ella Watson's place. Durbin kicked the staples from the wire and drove the cattle out of her pasture while a couple of armed men kept her from coming out of the house. The cattle were freshly branded, because, she explained, she had just managed to get her brand recorded at Cheyenne and hoped it would be accepted for the fall roundup. The men laughed, and Bothwell forced her into the wagon by threatening that he would drag her there at the end of a lariat if she didn't go. At Averill's store they made him get into the wagon, too. Jim, who often spoke of the man-burning Print Olive, said quietly that he was reminded of Mitchell and Ketchum in their drive to a lynching, but of course Wyoming would not hang a woman.

They took over Averill's place and when the hired men came up, jumped them. DeCory was knocked out and when he revived, everybody was gone, Buchanan and the crippled, sickly boy, too. Ralph Cole, who happened to come to the store, helped DeCory. Getting guns, they followed the mob by wagon track and pistol shot to Spring Creek Gulch. There Buchanan had crept up close enough to drop a few long-range rifle bullets among the mob who were putting the nooses on Averill and Cattle Kate, the woman fighting them, fierce as any Longhorn cow on the prod.

While several of the men drove Buchanan back to some rocks with their gunfire, the rest threw the rope ends over a long limb of a twisted tree hanging out over the gulch. Then Bothwell shoved the slight Averill off. While he jerked and swung in the air, the contemptuous and defiant Kate was pushed out, too, mainly by Henderson. The arms and legs of both jigged what seemed a long, long time, the young woman's Indian moccasins flying off, her skirts blowing and ballooning in the updraft and the slow dying.

Sickened, the men in the rocks tried to crawl closer, DeCory vomiting as he moved forward, yet was compelled to see, to know for certain just who such men were. Finally the two bodies hung still in the cooling shade of the old tree, with the sad and desolate forward-tipped heads of the hanged. Then the mob gathered up the sick boy and rode off, bunched as for protection, taking some parting shots at the men in the rocks.

DeCory and the others knew their lives were not worth a busted smokehouse check now, and they scattered to hide out, but at last Buchanan had to report the hanging to Casper. He got lost in the night, it seems, but sent word to the sheriff's office and named the men except the three that Hesse said were officers from the fort although dressed like the rest and acting as lynch-hungry.

Most of Wyoming knew about the two settlers hanging in the July heat of the Sweetwater country but no sympathizer or anyone else went to cut them down. Finally a deputy sheriff was directed to the place by Buchanan. It was dark in the gulch when the bodies were lowered, in horrifying condition from the July heat, but by rolling them in waterproof tarps they got them to Averill's store for the coroner's inquest and then buried them right there in the yard. News of the findings swept to the farthest claim shack. Apparently the stories of Buchanan, Cole, DeCory, and the Crowder boy had been told and the coroner's jury called it death by hanging at the hands of A. J. Bothwell, Tom Sun, John Durbin, R. M. Galbraith, Bud Connor, E. McLain, and one unknown man, said to have been George B. Henderson.

"Where was Hesse? I hear Canton was there, too?" settlers asked each other.

"Well, Hesse anyway. Everybody says he led the mob. He and Henderson."

The men named were put under $5,000 bond and held over for the grand jury, the witnesses heard, and now they knew their danger, particularly Buchanan, who had ridden for the sheriff. He slipped away to hide from those hunting him down. But the cattlemen smelled him out and headed him east, to hold him several months, or so it was told around Casper and out among the settlers as far as Buffalo and Newcastle and down the Platte below the Olive country.

While waiting for the grand jury some of the eastern papers protested the reign of lynch law in Wild Wyoming, and made it romantic, too. Some called it Border Justice meted out to the couple who had rustled twenty, twenty-five calves from Bothwell early in July and killed the cows. Westerners knew that in early July calves, in the late breeding region of the North, would still be too young to live on grass alone and nobody claimed they saw Kate trying to bucket-feed any wild young range stock. Another story was that the two had branded Bothwell cattle and took them to the rail-head, where they certainly would have been grabbed up for the Live Stock Commissioners' fund.

Still, a lynching in Wyoming looked bad just after attaining statehood—Wyoming which had given women the vote twenty years before and now added one of the few woman lynchings in the nation's history to that record.

Averill's brother came from the west coast and quietly, as Jim would have done it, he went around raising money for the prosecution. Ella Watson's father came up from Kansas to stay until the grand jury sat for her lynching as Cattle Kate.

But the anger and protest couldn't be covered by sod and a prayer, and when Wyoming seemed to be getting a little warm for the lynchers, Buchanan was shipped out of reach of a subpoena, off to Hesse's contacts in England, and set up in a little business there, so it was said. He had been under $500 bond as material witness but Frank Canton, the Association man up in Johnson County, got some friends to put up the cash so that the forfeit was all within the circle. Cole and DeCory were never seen again, and the sickly boy, taken away by the mob from the hanging, died after some weeks, so there was not one witness left. The grand jury failed to find a true bill, and there was celebrating at Bothwell.

But there were plenty of rumors. One was that Ralph Cole left the Averill place after the hanging and got as far as a surveyor's camp for the night. Next day he headed down toward the Union Pacific railroad and was overtaken by Henderson, shot, and the body burned to ashes.

"Another man burner!" a cowboy named Cole down in Nebraska was reported as saying. He was supposed to be a brother of Ralph Cole. Nobody heard him say more or saw anything of him for a long time after that, although there were rumors that in the ashes he identified the remains of a blocky little hand-forged bullet mold his brother sometimes carried.

Some said that Henderson got rid of DeCory, too, but if anything as identifying as the bullet mold was ever found for DeCory, no word of this got out. Although nobody was jailed even one day, the hanging at Spring Greek Gulch was not forgotten. Henderson, who used to travel under the name of John Powers, had been a strong-arm policeman around the iron and coal mines back in Pennsylvania in the Molly Maguire troubles before he became range manager for Hesse and Clay's Quarter Circle 71 in Wyoming. He was openly accused of killing the vanished Cole and DeCory as well as the lynchings, but his job as range manager of the 71 gave him powerful friends in Casper and Cheyenne. Besides, where were the witnesses to swear to anybody's connection with the lynchings or the killing of the two missing men?

Henderson had a lot of trouble with his cowhands and around the saloons after that, and finally ended in an encounter in which no smart lawyer or important connections could save him. He quarreled with a nighthawk of his own outfit, over wages, it was said, and got killed, although John Clay insisted that the killer was a "rustler at a small ranch." Clay admitted that George Henderson unfortunately gave way to drink at times and became garrulous and unreliable. Perhaps the dutch courage that had carried him through the lynching of a woman had slowed his hand on the draw. Not much more was known about the man who sometimes called himself Jack Tregoning, sometimes Smith, than about Joe Sparrow down at Trail City, the one who finally picked off the man-burning Olive.

Maybe wages were as good an excuse as any, the cowboys at Bothwell and Casper and Buffalo told each other, pretending to be busy with their drinks and to know no more. Some did hear that a couple of Cole's brothers from down in Nebraska someplace had been up, men who knew their way around Wyoming. Perhaps DeCory had relatives, too.

But others thought that Henderson had died because, by now, he knew too much, particularly for a man often "garrulous and unreliable" from drink. Anyway, it seems he found the cow business in Wyoming a little tougher than the black mines of Pennsylvania.

Over in the Sweetwater country Henry H. Wilson contested the homesteads of Ella Watson and James Averill on the grounds of desertion. He filed on the land and after final proof sold it to Bothwell. It was said that Cattle Kate's log shack was moved to Bothwell's ranch and used as an ice-house there for thirty years.

The settlers, instead of scaring like a flock of band-tailed pigeons at the crack of a gun, seemed more united, more determined to get to the ballot box. They talked Populism and squeezed out a little more from the coffee and shoe money for an old shotgun or maybe a pistol, and shot a few tin cans off the fence posts to get the feel of the sights. None of the small ranchers had been scared out, either, and not one rustler, so far as anybody could tell.

But the campaign to clear the range had only begun. The big outfits, particularly the foreign-backed, were gathering more gunmen than cowpunchers to their pay rolls. Next there was news out of the northeast, from near Newcastle. A thrifty German homesteader named Thomas Waggoner had started a little horse ranch there some years ago, trapping mustangs, breeding his stock up carefully, trading here and there. Around dark in early June of 1891 Tom Smith, former deputy U.S. marshal, Hall, a foreman of the 21 Horse Ranch, and two other men rode up and called Waggoner outside. Claiming they were officers with a warrant, they took him away. His wife and the three small children first supposed he had gone with friends, but he didn't return, and eight days later his body was found hanging over a gulch, decomposing, flyblown, the face blackened and the mustache that his wife had admired so much dropping away.

There was great excitement around the settler towns. Tom Smith bulled it through, frankly admitting that he led the hanging. Tom Waggoner had looked guilty, he said, and a man who stole a thousand horses didn't have a trial coming. The officials took the horses away but not a head of them was ever established as stolen. Later the big cattlemen changed their story. Waggoner was really an honest and hard-working man, they said, and the rustlers lynched him because he knew too much. The settlers, bolder now, too, threw Tom Smith's brags about the hanging into the teeth of his employers. But that didn't make Mrs. Waggoner less the widow, give her children a father, or get the thousand horses back.

Evidently somebody was spotting the attacks carefully over the map of Wyoming. The next one was another mustanger, but up in the Sheridan region. The man refused to leave his homestead. The Big Horns made a fine blue wall against the sky and glowed a rosy red in the fire of sunrise, the veiled head of Cloud Peak standing far off and aloof much of the day. One night a masked gang came, stripped the mustanger to the raw, and set him running naked across the dark prairie with bullets to hurry his bare feet. His horses were scattered by rifle shots; some bearing his brand were found fifty and more miles away.

Although many in the ranch country were as loose-rooted as the fall tumbleweed, no one could vanish now without the suspicion of a dry gulching. A few of the more timid, or those with small children, left their places. But not enough, and not from the more settled regions, where it seemed a man was surely safe, or a woman.

But there was a great deal of stirring from one big ranch to another during 1891. Up in Johnson County Frank Canton still refused to accept defeat as sheriff. Down east of Casper another man remembered more satisfactory times. The Scottish Tolland Company established the VR in 1877 along both sides of the North Platte River and as far back as the cattle would graze. The manager, and acting like the owner, was Frank Wolcott. He had come to Wyoming as receiver of the U. S. Land Office twenty years ago and now was fighting the settlers and small ranchers pushing in and challenging his hold on the vast area of the public domain that he was once paid to protect from just such exploitation as his ranch.

That Major Wolcott had his enemies was proved by his neck, wry as a bronc whose head had been pulled down by a careless rope. Wolcott's, it was said, came from a beating that a hired bruiser gave him, hired for a forty-dollar suit. The squat major was cocky, with that curious and often tragic cockiness that comes to some young officers upon victory in a civil war. It was a little like that of a small boy after he had overcome an older brother—so different from the eternal grief of the older officers, whether defeated or victorious in the spilling of fraternal blood.

There were those who knew that Wolcott had borrowed $80,000 back in 1885-86 from John Clay's British connections, the John Nelson Trust, and that after the Big Die-Up he was practically to the wall, compelled to realize that sooner or later he would be closed out, and with no profession, no earning power. The time of such foreclosure lay in John Clay's calculating hands.

The Fourth of July, 1891, Clay was up at the VR for a talk with the major. The two men went out to the alfalfa field where the hay crew was raking and stacking. The commanding Clay and the stocky Wolcott strode along the uncut edge, the purple bloom striking their knees as they walked, heads down, speaking low although there was no one except a drowsy bumblebee close enough to hear. Out of this stroll in the alfalfa came a plan, one said to have been Wolcott's and partly Frank Canton's—a plan to solve the problems of the big ranchers everywhere. By Wolcott's scheme the real trouble spot, Johnson County and the surrounding regions, would be cleared of the rustlers and the homesteaders, and of their sympathizers in Buffalo, beginning with the sheriff. Much of Wyoming would be freed and the Association, under Clay as president, would be re-established as the power in the state.

Years later Clay said that he told Wolcott the plan was impossible but there were doubters who asked if Wolcott wasn't really helpless, his entire future in the palms of his creditors and their representative. Anyway, Clay was still the canny Scotsman, preparing to be in Britain and on the Continent when the time came to put Wolcott's plan into action. But there would be certain expenses and $100,000 was raised for these—to hire men, buy horses no one would recognize, the latest model Winchesters, three Studebaker wagons to haul the supplies which included some items only mentioned in whispers. A few of the big ranchers and ranch managers were dubious but they anteed up their share of the money. Some were neither consulted or told.

A long time afterward many spoke of seeing the two men stalking the alfalfa and told of what went before, and after, each telling it in his own way, depending upon where his eyes were at the time, his feet, his pocketbook, and perhaps his heart.

When everything was in order Wolcott and former Governor Baxter, the West Pointer who was now general manager of the Western Union Beef Company up in Johnson County, headed for Colorado together. They went to raise a force that would clear out the rustlers, the rabble, and trespassers, all those poaching upon the sacred premises of the cow.

In the meantime others were beating the farther brush. Tom Horn, the outlaw who had worked for the Pinkertons until he was charged with a gambling-house holdup, was sent off through the Dakotas to hire gunmen at $150 a month and expenses, with a bonus of $500 for each man killed, Horn to lead the force he gathered. Hiram Ijams, secretary of the Board of Livestock Commissioners, went up to Idaho, talking openly about a cattleman "Invasion" of Johnson County to kill the rustlers, including Sheriff Angus and some other officials. That would scare out around 300, maybe 400, more and clear the range, be a lesson to settlers all through the cow country. He talked up the safety of the job—many of the homesteaders were without even a bird gun. The Invasion force would be hundreds strong, with bounties for all. Tom Smith, who had led the very successful Waggoner lynching, was back home in Texas recruiting twenty-five of the bravest gun fighters of "impeccable" character, at $1,000 each and expenses. It was said that Smith was getting $2,500 for the organization and leadership.

Things had not been quiet in Wyoming. One November dawn four men kicked in the door of a Powder River shack, come to hang Nate Champion and Ross Gilbertson sleeping there. In the dusky room they shot at Champion, still in bed. He jerked his gun from under the pillow and fired six times, almost in a solid roar, one bullet striking a man in the ribs and another going up his sleeve before the gang could crowd out the door and get to cover in the gray morning light, their boots loud as running hoofs on stone. They all got away but there was a lot of blood where they rested awhile. They left without their horses, overcoats, bedding, grub, ropes laid out handy, and Frank Canton's new Winchester saddle gun that Tom Smith had given him as a present.

The men had been so confident there would be no witnesses they hadn't masked as those who ran out the mustanger up near Sheridan did. Champion and Gilbertson recognized three of them as Association men: Canton, Tom Smith, and Joe Elliott, a stock inspector, the fourth a drifting trigger man called Coates. Plainly they had come for another lynching but Champion turned out a little fast with the gun.

Even before this both men might have known they were marked. Gilbertson had used the last days of the old law to brand up a handful of fine mavericks right under the eyes of the roundup foremen, although any stock he might try to sell would go to the Live Stock Commissioners anyway. Champion, a good-looking man with a brown mustache,

around five foot eight, had been a steady top-pay cowhand
in north Wyoming, and very good at getting the proper share
of mavericks for his bosses. But after the Big Die-Ups he was
dropped, with many other good cowboys, for cheaper help.
Since then he worked with his few cattle and jobbed around
as extra hand, sometimes with his brother Bud, and Ross Gilbertson, working for such outfits as Plunkett's EK, the Hoe,
and the 21, and maybe helping Matthews gather up odd
marketing stock of those brands that was missed on the
roundup and shipped for the owners. Even Champion's enemies admitted he was not only top help but likable, soft-
spoken, and gentlemanly, of good Texian stock. His mother
was a Standifer of Williamson County, with fighters for
Texas independence on both sides of the family, and long-
time enemies of the man-burning Olives while still down
there.

The cattlemen now claimed that Nate Champion
was a member of the Red Sash gang who terrorized the country although he was never around the rest of them and was
known as a peaceful man. They said he had been run out of
Colorado for rustling, not saying whether for homesteading
—rustling land—or for swinging the long rope. Anyway, they
never mentioned this while his rope worked for them here.
Away from the cow country they told of Champion and his
men, heavily armed, coming in on Bob Tisdale's roundup
outfit. Tisdale's men were holding 1,500 wild range stock
ready to brand. Seems Champion's outfit roped and tied all
the calves and scattered all the stock. It sounded like a good
trick to scatter a lot of cows while their calves were tied
down—a good trick and a likely story. Later some did admit
that the calves roped and branded belonged to the settlers
and small outfits barred from the roundup run by the Association. Nobody except Champion had the guts to brace the
outfit and save the stock from being turned into the maverick
fund.

Champion and Gilbertson reported the attack on
them on the Powder, but only Elliott was arrested and put.

under $5,000 peace bond. Gilbertson, Champion's only wit-ness, vanished, scared off or picked off, nobody seemed to know which.

But now Nate Champion was doubly marked, for Canton was not the man to overlook this second humiliation on top of his defeat for sheriff. Worse, the little fellows, hearing that Nate had run off four of the Association's hired gunmen while still in his underpants, made him their double symbol of resistance, particularly with the wholesale attack coming, as many feared. Even some who had been ready to hitch up and quit the country decided to try it a little longer.

There was strong talk among the settlers and little ranchers for action, with the actual rustlers pushing their two bits' worth in now, and not many honest men standing against them. The cow thieves had the good guns and the will to use them when the attack came. All the little fellows had to unite, arm, stop these killings, known and suspected.

"Let's ride against them big outfits in the night, fire the buildings, and shoot the rats when they come running out in their shirttails, like they would do us," one gaunt, bearded man kept shouting over and over at every crossroads, at the country post offices, and out on the streets of Buffalo.

Seeing where such talk could lead, a few with cooler heads tried to point out that this was getting down on the level of gunmen. Besides, most of the larger outfits would surely be against any mass killing of settlers. Some of them did try to ride herd on their stock, keep them away from the homesteader's crops, if only to protect the blood from the scrub bulls loose in the country. Some worked for irrigation on the state and national level, for railroads and post offices, even while they resisted settlement. But when the settler was actually there they paid lease for his land, maybe gave him a little meat for his kids, even flour and sugar and shoes on tick, on time, at the ranch store. But these were not the outside forces behind men like Canton and Smith, or the lynchers on the Sweetwater.

Because the loudest voice against all violence came from Buffalo's Sheriff Angus, there was complaint against him, even from his closest friends. "By God, Red, you better be deciding which side you're on before the bullets start," Black Jack Flagg warned him at a political meeting.

But Red Angus didn't like talk about shooting.

Buffalo, under the blue granite of the Big Horns, was the only town in Johnson County and had grown to around 1,200 population. But if anyone thought that size was any protection, they soon changed their minds. A month after the attack on Champion and Gilbertson two men were dry gulched right in the Buffalo region. The first was Orley Jones. The Jones brothers, well liked, had come up from Nebraska with a buggy and a span of mules that they traded for Indian mares. They went to punching cows, saved their money, and bought a few heifers. Orley, known as Ranger, was a jolly young man, temperate, and particularly popular. After five years of riding for the big outfits and saving his money, he took up a homestead in the range of one of the big cattlemen and got himself engaged to be married. He drove up to Buffalo, ordered lumber to finish the house for his bride, and on his way home was shot from under a bridge. The wagon was drawn off into a gully, the horses unhooked and turned loose.

But before his body was discovered, Charlie Basch came spurring in to Buffalo to report that Johnny Tisdale had been killed. Basch had heard shots off the road a piece and saw Frank Canton tear away from a gulch. Riding over to see, Basch found a wagon drawn in there, the horses dead in the harness, and Tisdale with a bullet in the back. Johnny, apparently no relation to the ranch Tisdales, was headed for his homestead sixty miles out with the winter supplies and the family Christmas presents. He had been warned in Buffalo that his life was in danger from the rancher down there; he even overheard Canton tell Fred Hesse that he would "take care of Tisdale." But Johnny's wife was alone on the homestead with the small children and expecting another. He had to get home, and by following the open road, for a man with a loaded wagon couldn't cut across in that rough country. He did buy a shotgun in addition to his pistol but he had known they would get him sooner or later if they were after him. They made it sooner.

Sheriff Angus sent a posse out for the body. They found Tisdale slumped down in the seat, his blood frozen over the Christmas presents for his children.

The men sat silent and dark on their horses, holding their impatience in the cold wind. "Any man that won't fight them sons of bitches after this ought to be run out of the country," a young puncher named Baker said angrily, and set the unnecessary spur to his faunching horse.

Before long men like Baker had more reason for anger. About the time Tisdale's body was brought back to Buffalo, Orley Jones' brother came riding in, uneasy that Orley hadn't reached home.

"Oh, hell! He left here three days ago!" the lumberman said in alarm.

A search party spread into the gullies and draws along the road, expecting the pattern set in the shooting of Tisdale to hold. It did. They found the body slumped down over the grain sacks and boxes of groceries in the wagon, frozen stiff, the eyes open and staring.

"By God, this one was Hesse's, as Johnny heard them plan," one of the men from Buffalo said.

Now men came streaming into Buffalo from all up and down the great range lands that lay up against the Big Horns, some from as far off as 100 miles and more. Their women were afraid, crying to leave the country or grimly taking gun in hand, shooting at tin cans about the distance that a man who came to kill would start firing. Rustlers, the Association had called these settlers, yet Waggoner, Jones, and Tisdale were known as quiet, hard-working men, making no trouble, fencing their places to avoid range-cattle damage. But they were plainly men who would stay. True,

Allison Tisdale, Johnny's brother, was called a rustler as
were all the others out with the nester roundup wagon, by
law not allowed to operate until the big outfits had combed
the range and were done, and not encouraged then. Even so
it wasn't Allison they shot but John, who had been range
boss for Roosevelt over on the Little Missouri for several
years—Johnny the solid family man.

Canton was arrested for murder but he managed to
get a preliminary hearing before Justice of the Peace Parmalee, also commander of the local National Guard and one
of the few cattlemen friends left in office in Buffalo. Although Canton had the attack on Champion against him, and
a mighty shaky alibi for the day that Tisdale was killed, with
Basch an eyewitness to his presence in the gulch at the time,
Parmalee released him. Some said on orders from DeForest
Richards, state commander of the Guards, and a big cowman, too, and banker.

Now there was a real bull-roaring up and down the
winter streets of Buffalo against both Canton and Hesse. Only
the solid, law-abiding Scotsman, Sheriff Angus, could hope to
hold angry mobs from riding out to burn down one ranch
after another, clean out the big cattle companies, and get rid
of all the hirelings of the foreign interests. At the least they
must string up Canton, Canton and that Britisher Hesse.

Angus managed to hold them off long enough to give
Canton and Hesse a chance to skip town in the night, with,
it was said, Sutherland, Hesse's brother-in-law, riding with
them. Even so they had a couple of real scares from little
gangs that tried to cut them off on the dark ride to Gillette
and the train that Red Angus recommended they take to get
out of the state fast. Later, when a lot of new evidence was
turned up, Acting Governor Barber refused to issue ex-
tradition papers to have Canton brought back from Chicago.* When he returned in March to join the coming invasion he was given a fast hearing and put under $30,000 bond

---

* In his posthumous autobiography, *Frontier Trails*, Canton says he was called
to his wife and daughters, visiting in Chicago and ill with diphtheria.

for murder, signed April 4 by the leaders of the Regulators,
as they called themselves, by all except Major Frank Wolcott,
who, it was said, couldn't bail out a two-bit whore.

During the holiday season a long article in the Washington, D.C., *Star* had characterized the people out in Johnson County, Wyoming, as rustlers and bad men generally. No
one cared to recall that the state's two U.S. senators, Carey
and Warren, were ranchers who claimed vast stretches of
government land illegally, both still members of the Stock
Growers Association, with its record red from the blood its
members and employees were shedding. Papers from Omaha
to New York made a great story of the wrongs suffered by
the cattlemen, perhaps not understanding the meaning of
the term "public domain" or willing to side-jump it if they
did. Very few understood that even the actual rustler was
no more than an excuse for what was really a cattle war—a
war of the ranch interests against the government and its
avowed public-land policy: free land for everybody, a 160-
acre place for every bona-fide homeseeker. This was the essence of what America meant to peoples of the earth and
against this the cattlemen were warring, the crusade being
joined.

Late in 1891 the newspapers of north Wyoming
warned in huge headlines that the next step in the campaign of terror, of the bullet and the noose and the torch
started with Averill and Cattle Kate and carried through
Jones and Tisdale, was a great invasion of the Powder River
country. Every man, woman, and child on the range was to
be slaughtered so the settler holdings would revert to the
public domain, the domain the cattlemen considered their
preserve by a sort of divine right.

In the meantime the small ranchers of the Powder
River region looked ahead to spring-branding time, hoping
to protect their stock from the Association's general roundup
that would put the wholesale label of "maverick" on all their
stock and throw it into the coffers of the Live Stock Commis-

sioners and the pay envelope of men like Canton, Smith, Elliott, and their kind. In the past the settlers had put out a partnership roundup wagon under Jack Flagg, individuals coming to it for a few days each and taking away their stock that had been collected. But they could only move to the range after the big outfits were done. This year the Northern Wyoming Farmers and Stockgrowers Association was organized and notices sent out of their roundup, to start May 1. This was well before the Wyoming Association's official date, although everybody knew that some of the big outfits did a lot of "soonering" even before May. Bill Walker, a young cowpuncher riding for Fred Hesse down around the Sweetwater, once ran into a bunch of Hesse cowboys putting the iron to a calf out of season. He rode toward them, and got a chunk of lead set into the grass ahead of him. He knew they recognized him and thought they were joking, but the next bullet got him in the shoulder and so he quit and went to trapping furs.

In reply to the notice of the independent northern roundup, the Wyoming Association publicly enlarged their black list to include all but the top of the Johnson County ranches and ordered their inspectors to hold back everything carrying the newly outlawed brands, with or without a bill of sale.

# CHAPTER II

# STETSONED CRUSADERS

THE day the $30,000 bond was signed for Frank Canton, former Governor Baxter presided over the regular spring meeting of the Wyoming Stock Growers Association in the absence of President Clay, off in Europe. Forty-three members were present, still only eight from ranches owned by individuals. Nothing of the meeting was to be remembered and no minutes were kept.

All the next day the gun counters did a rushing business in Winchesters charged to the Association, in addition to the full case that the governor had donated from the state's arsenal. Two days later a special train of six cars drew in from Denver. Three were full of horses, bought and branded in Colorado by R. S. Van Tassell, one of the main backers of the Invasion. For a while he had been a partner of Tom Swan, and the son-in-law of Alex Swan, whose empire was lost to Clay and his financiers. Another car held the equipment and the flatcar was piled with the three new wagons and the camping stuff.

The blinds of the one passenger car were kept drawn close, but rumors flew like gray snow on the April wind. Some realized that this was the start of the long-planned invasion of Johnson County. Inside were Tom Smith's twenty-five Texas gunmen, with their saddles and ammunition, and two adventurers who had attached themselves to the group, a young English rancher from Colorado and Dr. Charles Penrose, younger brother of the Pennsylvania senator and the Colorado mining engineer, perhaps induced to come because he had been a medical classmate of acting governor of Wyoming, Dr. Barber. Two newspapermen came to join, and the one recruit that Ijam's trip to Montana and Idaho produced, nobody from Tom Horn's search of the Dakotas. Twenty-four Wyoming Regulators got on at Cheyenne, most of them in great contrast to the rough-and-ready Texas gunmen—many of the northerners well educated and cultured and cosmopolitan. Two were the owners of the Duck Bar Ranch in which Theodore Roosevelt was said to have an interest—the elegant Teschie, H. E. Teschemacher, Harvard bred, a world traveler, his parents living in Paris, and his polished and handsome partner, Fred DeBillier, owner of a villa in France. There was W. J. Clarke, state water commissioner and rancher on the Crazy Woman Fork; J. N. Tisdale, state senator and his son Bob, both with ranches up north; A. B. Clark, owner of the DE; the Englishman R. M. Allen, general manager of the British-owned Standard Cattle Company over on the Belle Fourche not far from the Waggoner hanging and tied in with Baxter; J. C. Johnson, the eccentric partner of Tom Sun who had been in the lynching of Averill and Kate; C. A. Campbell, a Scotch-Canadian who lost his cattle in the 1886-87 winter and went in with the Clay-Robinson Company; Billy Booker under Clay in the Swan Ranches; A. D. Adams, the burly Scotsman who managed the Ferguson Land Company and today was delegated to ride close to Pap, E. W. Whitcomb, the gray-haired old cowman, in the country from back in the beaver-and-buffalo-robe days and much too old and wise to be riding the stormy trail to Johnson County today. But he was under repeated financial obligation to John Clay, too.

There were many other ranch managers and foremen along, and several Association detectives and inspectors and occasional deputy U.S. marshals, including Canton, Elliott, Smith, and Morrison with Tom Horn hiding out but to join them somewhere when ambush was possible, the only way Horn liked to operate. Phil DuFran was coming in later with a report on the situation at Buffalo, and Mike Shonsey, Baxter's foreman up at the Western Union Beef, was out spying on Champion.

The train started from the Cheyenne yards under the command of the short, strutting Major Wolcott, as was planned with Clay, eight, nine months ago in the alfalfa patch and now put into action, even against the wishes of some of the Association members. Second in command was Billy Irvine, of the Board of Live Stock Commissioners and manager of the Ogallala Cattle Company, tied in with Clay's Swan empire. With Billy was his bodyguard, "Quick-Shot" Davis, never far from his side. The lieutenants selected for Wolcott were Canton and Fred Hesse, back in Wyoming, too, and now doubly anxious to help clear his range up north of settlers and to punish those who drove him out after the killing of Jones and Tisdale last November.

Afterward it was said there were fifteen members of the Association on the trail, representing most of the big outfits in Johnson County and around its fringes. Their total property was said to be 4,657 horses, $500,000 worth of improvements, and only 86,000 acres of range for their 116,905 head of cattle—little more than enough for holding pastures at roundup and shipping time. In addition, however, they claimed an empire larger than the state of Connecticut from the public domain, and it was this free grass they wanted to retain for their cows. To accomplish this they had the three wagons on the flat car behind them, with bedding and other supplies that Wolcott borrowed at Fort D. A. Russell and ammunition and dynamite enough for a fine little war. And in Frank Canton's valise was the long list of names made up during the last year, the list of Johnson County men called rustlers, ranging from Sheriff Red Angus, the new mayor, the commissioners, and other officials and businessmen down

to Nate Champion and some that perhaps really were rustlers
—a Dead List of seventy men.

Gunbelts slung over shoulders, their boot heels loud
on the frozen cinders, the Invaders left the special train out at
the Casper yards and looked around for the force of cowboys
that some still hoped would meet them there. The Texans
had been promised a large local force, with around 100 men
to join at Casper from the Sheridan region, 75 from over at
Newcastle, 50 from Douglas, and perhaps up to 100 from the
Big Horns and beyond. But as down at Cheyenne, not a
cowboy appeared. So far not one from all of Wyoming had
joined up, and the Texans grumbled, some cursed, but all
stayed for the pay.

The men to drive the wagons and cook for the expedition were waiting and the guides, three stock detectives,
showed up, and H. W. Davis, called Hard Winter, some said
to distinguish him from Quick Shot and a dozen other Davises
on the range. Hard Winter's nature was belied by his neat
Delawarian speech and neat little mustache and eyeglasses,
fitting his Spectacle Ranch up north. He was president of the
Association back in better days and now itched to get
moving.

Mounted, the Invaders started north, Hard Winter
and Wolcott leading the column, with scouts out at 200
yards all around to warn travelers away before they could
identify anyone, as though there could be much secrecy now.
Few except Pap Whitcomb, long with the Indians, married to
one, knew that here twenty-seven years ago painted and
feathered Sioux had come charging down from the Powder
River country to destroy the Platte Bridge, convinced that
their cause was holy, certain they could drive the white
men out forever. Now the Stetsoned riders were heading
northward with impatience and fervor, too, each to his own
kind and measure. Their plan was to strike at Buffalo first,
where their men waited at strategic points over the town,
ready to bring down the city marshal and the sheriff with

the first two bullets. With these men and other town officials, and the county commissioners out of the way, and with Parmalee, and his National Guard on their side, they could ferret out the thirty or so on the Dead List in Buffalo. Dynamite squads would blow up the courthouse and the store of Foote, the white-bearded fanatic who might rally a foolish resistance. After that the only hurry was to tromp down the scattering rats as they took to the breaks. The Invaders would spread out through the country, picking off the rest of the seventy before they found out what was happening. Then the trails would be dark with settlers hitting it out of the country.

The Invaders rode at a good clip. The sky grayed and the scattering of shaggy, winter-haired cattle they passed were seeking the sheltered slopes, feeding busily, with the urgency of a coming storm upon them. Once a cow hooked a couple of the others away, but only so far as the swift thrust of her horns reached. Then they all fell to cropping the winter-bleached prairie again.

There weren't many carcasses around, the winter easy, promising a good cattle year. Add the work of the major and his followers here to that and it would be a year from which to count time.

But there was real uneasiness among the men that nobody was joining from up here. Even the range boss from Senator Carey's outfit, supposed to cut the one telegraph line north, apparently got cold feet, or the senator objected, glad, as always, to let others do his dirty work for him. The hired man who was sent instead had protested but he needed his job mighty bad.

The grumbling of the older Texans grew with the storm. "Looks like the country sure ain't with us. We was told we was just to spread the responsibility a little, bring in some strange faces, cut down the chances of you all up here being ambushed later."

The wagons were a trouble, too, and finally one had to be dragged out of a spring bog with the lariats. Carelessly a couple of lone horsebackers were allowed very close, staring at the long string of riders with no sign of a herd anywhere, new Winchesters in the scabbards, the horses new branded, scarcely peeling. One of the strangers was put in front of the column with a Texas gunman on each side. "Keep looking straight ahead!" they ordered. After four, five hours he was turned loose, and the other man, too, with the warning to hit for some sheep camp and stay there with their snoots buttoned down.

By now Dr. Penrose had found his horse too rough and wild and so he climbed in on the bedroll wagon. "Our fancy Tender Bottoms didn't last long," the Texans drawled, as they eased the set of their guns a little. Towse, representing the Cheyenne *Sun,* developed fainting spells and also took to the wagons. As the noontime passed and a gray filtering of snow rode the north wind, the men seemed to become more alike, the flashy Texan with a yellow neckerchief knotted at the nape, boots fancy enough for Bill Cody, rode as hunched over in his slicker as Mynett, in flopping old chaps bent to the bow of his legs, his clothing tattered from brush popping down home.

Gradually the April flurries whitened the sage of the dry divide toward Salt Creek. Even the whirls of snowbirds were gone, and only the column of men moved in the early darkness. The Texans shivered and cursed, bit off more tobacco, and goddamned this Yankee country, good enough for Yankee cowpokes but not for a good soft-handed man. Jack Tisdale, the state senator, offered the sullen, freezing men his professional cheer. His ranch was just up ahead, with hot grub and a good rest waiting.

They reached there around dawn, and although Canton argued hotly for pushing on, even Wolcott had to admit his men needed rehabilitation. This wasn't a hardened, disciplined military outfit, he had to admit. Not even Custer could have pushed on with this collection of saddle wolf in his Seventh.

During the day Mike Shonsey came in. He had been trying to raise a force from the ranches up ahead. He had 100 horses at Baxter's ranch grained up for weeks, ready and rearing, and talked big about this to cover up that not one cowboy was coming to join them, not even from Baxter's, where he was the foreman.

But Shonsey did have news. Last night he had stopped to spy on Nate Champion at the old Frewen line camp called the KC Ranch. Champion was wintering there. Rented the place with Nick Ray, who had a homestead up a mile or so. They fed Shonsey and gave him room for his bedroll, as was proper in the cow country, even though they knew he was connected with the man behind the lynchings and the threats and even the attacks on Champion.

"Many of the rustlers you are looking for are hanging around there, have been all winter," he told Wolcott and Irvine. "Billy Hill, Starr, Long Henry, and a lot of others with the rustler roundup wagon. They all swear by Champion, even Red Angus, since Nate ran Canton's outfit off."

Nick Ray was camping there steady, Ray the man Billy Irvine claimed was wanted for murder down in Texas and who had followed Billy when he drove the 40,000 steers from Nebraska to his ranch north of Douglas—had been following him for years, picking off stock. Perhaps Shonsey knew that only Irvine's eagerness to get Nick Ray drew him to join the invasion at all. He was against the whole idea, preferring the old range detective system that had worked pretty well in the days before the settlers were allowed to get such a toehold.

Seventeen, eighteen men were hanging around the KC, Shonsey said, and all of them would hit for the Hole in the Wall country the first wind they got of the invasion. "Swing around by the KC and clean out that rustlers' nest," he insisted, banking on the power of former Governor Baxter and the Western Union Beef outfit behind him.

Frank Canton was set against it. They couldn't go

clear around by the KC and get to Buffalo in time to back up their men he had staked out to stop Angus and his deputies and the rest.

"Hell, my men got orders to drop Angus and everybody who can swear in deputies if they don't hear from us by tomorrow night," Wolcott bragged.

Canton openly doubted Shonsey's story of so many men at KC, with the old line camp only big enough for six, seven to spread their bedrolls without double-decking. But Elliott and Tom Smith were anxious to get the wily Champion while they could, remembering that he drove them off in the attack last fall, if Frank had forgotten.

" 'Fraid he'll turn your own Winchester on yeh?" the big-mouth Texas Kid, with his first man to kill, put in.

For a moment there was dead silence in the room, with an old anger blazing in Canton against Smith and all these Texas gunmen of his, some knowing that Frank had left Texas ahead of the sheriff. Slowly, without moving, the men seemed to divide into enemy camps, with too many hands casually near the guns.

Wolcott, with his saddle wolf stiffening his movements, stepped between the men, his wry neck twisted. "Hell, Frank, you got it in for Champion more'n the rest of us. We better be moving."

The two pack horses of extra ammunition came in from Irvine's ranch. With this on the wagons, the Invaders pushed out into the clouded night toward the KC, Canton still working to head them straight for Buffalo. But if he couldn't, KC would take no more than an hour or so and they could still make town by tomorrow night, if the Tender Bottoms held out.

By now the whole state was alive with news and rumor. Suddenly every gun, every cartridge, was bought up, the loose powder and bullet molds, too, with men here and there stooping over the smell of molten lead, some wishing they had Ralph Cole and his homemade mold, claimed found in his ashes after the Averill hanging. There was particular stirring around Douglas, Glenrock, and Casper, the towns that profited from the spreading settlements to the north, and from rustlers, too, when they managed to get a little money for their cattle. The one telegraph line north from Douglas to Fort McKinney at Buffalo was kept cut by the Invaders. Nobody dared risk a ride up into the Powder country for information, and so rumors sprouted like horse-weed around an old corral.

Somehow the roundabout mail route had been over-looked and the evening of the eighth Sheriff Angus received a letter about a suspicious-looking train routed through Cheyenne three days ago. Red mustache bristling, Angus was hurrying around to the likely victims among the officials, the businessmen, and to the preachers. About the same time the Invaders, on fresh horses, left the night-shadowed Tis-dale ranch. They traveled light but Elliott carried ten pounds of giant powder behind the saddle and a hank of fuse.

Instead of lengthening the column at Tisdale, they lost men. Hard Winter Davis let his extra horses get out and followed them to his place, twenty miles away, promising to meet the Invaders at Buffalo. Towse of the Cheyenne *Sun* and Dr. Penrose stayed behind as the dark string of riders hunched into the north wind spitting a little wet snow. The Wyoming men had their Stetsons tied down with necker-chiefs to meet the collars of their buffalo saddle coats, the Texans in their hen-skin slickers cursed the climate. To-ward dawn the thin snow stopped and four miles from the KC they gathered around a few wet sagebrush fires in a deep gulch. While they thawed they waited for the spies out under Shonsey to size up the place, particularly for the blasting powder or the dynamite after the wagons came.

The spies returned, wet and chilled. Shonsey drew the lay of the place at the firelight for the outsiders. The little log shack and the stable with some pole corrals squatted out on the snowy bottoms along south of the cottonwoods that lined the Middle Fork of the Powder. The bluff that stood across the southwest was cut by the road that angled down past the buildings and corrals to the bridge and off north to Buffalo. They had found a lot of noise until late last night, people passing by, a dog barking and running over toward Shonsey and the others, and a man coming out to look around. Fiddling and singing lasted until toward morning, cowboy stuff, and Johnny Reb, and somebody starting Jesus songs.

No, there was no telling who the visitors were. Even Mike Shonsey was against using the blasting powder, even if they could. Night before last he would have been blown up with the rustlers. Besides, the dynamite back in the wagons would work out better.

With Canton and Smith as lieutenants to compete from opposite sides, Wolcott distributed his men around the little line camp before daylight. Those sent to crawl up to the stable wished they had a chunk of fresh meat. Baited up with a good dose of the well poison they had along the dog would soon be a goner. But instead they took a piece of whang leather with them and garroted him when he came around the stable and dragged his carcass off into the weeds down behind the building. Then they waited for the cold morning, watching the log shack, ready to shoot down every man who stuck his head out.

The Invaders had received their orders quietly, almost without interest. Only the stripling of the southerners, the Texas Kid, was still spoiling for his first fight, and so Canton and his partner took him along to watch at the stable, less than a good pistol shot from the doorway.

In a little while the door opened and Jones, an old trapper that Canton knew, stepped out with a bucket and started for the river. The moment he came around the stable he found two Winchesters on him and the barrel of a pistol motioning him to the river. He stumbled down to the cottonwoods where Jack Tisdale took him over, questioned him.

Next the old man's partner, Bill Walker, came out in his flannel shirt sleeves. He flipped a rock at a couple of cackling sage hens and was grabbed, too, when he turned the corner of the stable. Down at the stream he stared in amazement at the men he had known for years, and heard of others along—Hesse, his former boss, and Billy Irvine whom he knew as far back as Nebraska.

Hesse and Wolcott and Canton, too, talked strong for sending the two men back to the house and sneaking up behind them, to rush Champion and Ray, but Jones and Walker refused.

"I ain't no stalking-horse for a murderer," old Jones said, and it was plain that he would not be moved.

For a long time there was no stirring up at the house from the men, two men, if the captives were to be believed, surrounded by over fifty ready Winchesters. Impatiently the Texans and Canton looked up at the gray sky running in low-rolling windrows of cloud that carried more snow. Finally the door opened and a tall, lanky man came out. It was Nick Ray, and the overeager Texas Kid couldn't hold himself, but shot. The man went down and before the report had rolled over the frosty valley he was on his knees trying to crawl back as replying shots came from the shack. Slowly blue smoke spread upward from the old loopholes between the logs, enough to keep the attackers back while the wounded man made his desperate, faltering crawl, blood streaming down his face from the bullet through the head. When he neared the door, Nate Champion jerked it open, and with bullets spurting all around him, striking the ground, splintering the casing of the door, hitting him, too, he fired with his left hand, drawing blood from the reckless Texas Kid as he dragged the wounded man inside with his right. The door slammed, Champion sent bullets and blue smoke from the windows and loopholes of the house, both front and back.

The Texas Kid was excited by his hit, but most of the others, even Irvine, who wanted to get Ray, had watched the two men in amazement. Yet now was the time for a rush on the house Irvine argued, hurrying in his buffalo coat from one man to another. Now, before Champion had time to collect himself, barricade the place. But some of the Texans, even those who had never heard of Nate Champion, knew of the family. Others had heard that he was the best pistol shot in the country and saw his nerve here. So Champion managed to hold them off, shooting from one side and then the other, making even their blasting powder worthless because no one could get up close. That first hour one of the Texans was hit in the arm, another in the thigh, and so they kept down, although five, six were as close as the stable now, and watched the impatient Canton throw a rope out the door and drag it back several times, wondering.

Toward nine o'clock a neighboring settler, Terrence Smith, rode over to investigate all the shooting. Cautiously he crawled up to look into the smoke-blued valley, saw men clustered here and there behind cut banks and brush. New bursts of fire showed him others—forty, fifty men held off by a little scattered firing from the log shack.

Back in the saddle the man spurred out to rouse the country. At Crazy Woman Creek he met half-a-dozen men heading for Gillette and the Democratic convention down at Cheyenne. Instead, they scattered to warn the settlers. Then he headed his lathering horse on to Buffalo.

At KC the Invaders knew nothing of Smith's ride but they were wasting ammunition and no telling when the wagons would get through. In the shack Champion was keeping the men back and trying to ease his dying friend and write snatches in the little memo book from his pocket, a little story of an army shooting against two lone men. Between runs around the loopholes he managed to write a few words, or several lines:

> It is now about two hours since the first shot. Nick is still alive; they are still shooting and are all around the house. Boys, there is bullets coming in like hail. Them fellows is in such shape I can't get at them. They are shooting from the stable and river and back of the house.

The delay infuriated Canton and the Texans. The joint attack was planned for tonight at Buffalo, with all those men to be killed for bounty, and the loot and booty to take. "What's to keep the whole stinkin' outfit up there from getting away and hitting it for the wild breaks, to pick us off if we follow?" Canton demanded of Wolcott for the tenth time, one way or another.

It was true that the men were worn and hungry, and as is usual with creatures of prey, the urge to kill, and the fear of it, lay very close to the surface here. Old animosities and new ones flared up. Half a dozen of the men were watching each other like coiled rattlers, poised, it seemed, to strike with lead. The saddle-sore DeBillier tried to joke a little, and Wolcott made a puffing circle among the men, stooping to keep his twisted head down as he ran. "I'll get the son of a bitch out of there," he promised, and sent men riding to a ranch a few miles off for hay to burn Champion's place. Two, three hours later they came back without it. This was April; no winter hay within twenty miles.

In the quiet Champion wrote a little more:

Nick is dead, he died about 9 o'clock. I see smoke down at the stable. I think they have fired it. I don't think they intend to let me get away this time.

But the men were just warming their trigger fingers and the toes of the Texas Kid in his tight boots. They made no move to face the gun of Nate Champion. Instead, they settled to waiting, watching, some of them dozing a little, wondering what had become of their wagons. In the shack the man looked all around the valley and then took out the little red book again:

Boys, I don't know what they have done with them two fellows that staid here last night. Boys, I feel pretty lonesome just now. I wish there was someone here with me so we could watch all sides at once. They may fool around until I get a good shot before they leave. It's about 3 o'clock now.

Outside somebody saw a wagon, stripped to the running gears, come over the hill from the south, the boy riding the bolster having trouble with the bronc on his team, faunching and shying, trying to run, to drag his gentle old teammate along. Horseback behind the boy came his stepfather, Black Jack Flagg, high up on the Dead List of the Invaders because he ran the settler roundup wagon and had had Johnny Tisdale and his wife and children around the ranch before they moved to the homestead.

There had been no firing around KC for a while and nobody was in sight as the wagon rattled down the hill, past the KC, and out upon the rumbling bridge. By then Flagg had turned his horse back toward the house door for a greeting, and suddenly found himself faced by two men hidden at the corral, one throwing his Winchester down on Flagg. The settler laughed, thinking it was a joke, but then he saw it was a stranger, and, pivoting his horse, he stooped flat over the saddle and spurred for the bridge, bullets flying all around him.

"Shoot the bastard! That's Flagg!" Canton and Elliott both yelled, as though nobody had troubled to fire.

At the first shot the boy had lashed the old mare into a gallop beside the bronc, off the bridge and up the road, until a bullet struck the wild horse and sent him up on his hind legs. By then Flagg was alongside. He helped cut the team loose and with the boy on the gentle mare, they whipped over the ridge. Half a dozen of the Invaders, horseback and hard after them three, four miles, got a couple of bullets from Flagg, in broken country now, and they let him go.

After the sound of rifle fire stopped Champion wrote:

There was a man on a buckboard and one on horseback just passed. They fired on them as they went by. I don't know if they killed them or not. I seen lots of men come out on horses on the other side of the river and take after them. I shot at the men in the stable just now; don't know if I got any or not. I must go and look out again. It don't look as if there is much show of my getting away. I see twelve, fifteen men. One looks like Frank Canton.

With Flagg, so high on the Dead List, gone to rouse the country Wolcott knew a thousand men would probably be riding against them by morning. Somehow they had to cover the sixty miles to Buffalo before he got there. Nick Ray was checked off but there was still Champion, one of the kingpins of the resistance up here.

There was fuming and uneasiness that the wagons hadn't come in with the dynamite, with grub, too, but mainly the dynamite. Finally a couple of horsebackers dragged Flagg's wagon up by their saddle ropes. Planks torn from the stable were laid lengthwise over the bolsters, four, five high, with split pine knots from the wall piled on top, and the little rough brush and weeds from the mangers added. Wolcott, Jack Tisdale, Big Dudley from Texas, and some others pushed this breastwork before them, moving with the north wind. Awkward as a great dung beetle, it crept toward the shack, the men with matches ready, their pistols drawn if Champion made a break for the open.

Through a loophole he saw the go-devil come and planted bullets around the feet of the men, but almost at once they were out of sight and Canton's Winchester, even in Champion's hands, wouldn't carry through the breastwork. Besides, he had been hit again, not bad, but hit, and his ammunition was very low. He glanced over what he had last written:

I think I will make a break when night comes, if alive. Shooting again. I think they will fire the house this time. It's not night yet.

Outside the go-devil wobbled slowly to the barricaded window, flared to the matches, and under the flames and smoke that whipped over the log building the men escaped. As the logs caught, the wind drove the fire running up the wall and over the roof. Smoke blew thick along the ground southward across the bottoms, the grass along its path smoldering from the sparks as the pitch of the dry logs exploded. The Invaders scattered down along its trail, watching for the man to make a run for it, come out shooting.

The flames spread until all the building was a blazing, roaring pile. Yet no one came out. Could Champion have shot himself? It would be a great disappointment.

But he was still alive, still fighting smoke and heat and the falling chunks from the roof. The room was a blazing box, searing Champion's face, his eyes. Now he had to go. He threw a blanket over Nick Ray's body and ended his little account:

The house is all fired. Good-by, boys, if I never see you again.                    Nathan D. Champion.

With the memo book in his pocket, his clothes smoldering but his hat set tight, the Winchester carbine in his hand, Nate Champion leapt from the blazing window into the rolling smoke that the wind carried southward thick and low.

"There he goes!" somebody yelled as a shifting gust exposed the bent and running man.

But it was only for a moment and the bullets missed him. He made it to the gulch crossed by the thick smoke, running hard, coughing, blinded. But as he dodged down the cut, he ran straight into Canton and Tom Smith's sharpshooters. Champion fired one shot, just as a bullet from Dudley's pistol got his gun arm. Another struck him in the breast and then a whole volley flung him back, lifted him a little, like a dark overcoat thrown back by the wind, and dropped him flat upon the carbine. The Invaders swarmed in, running, yelling, coughing through the black smoke. Major Wolcott came, too, puffing, and stood looking down upon the shattered and bleeding body a long time. Finally he spoke. "By God, if I had fifty men like you I could whip the whole state of Wyoming."

With their rifles across their arms, most of Wolcott's

men were drawn to see this lone man who had stood them off all day. They did not come too close, as though still afraid, and for a long time none of them spoke or moved. Then, as Dudley edged a little closer, perhaps to reach for the Winchester under Champion's arm, his by right of the first hit, Frank Canton pushed in.

"That's my gun," he snarled, and as big Dudley looked angrily around the dark faces, the Wyoming men nodded. It was Frank's gun, all right, lost in the attack the four men had made on Champion on the Powder last fall, but now that seemed less a cowardly running—four men driven out of the house by a barely awakened Nate Champion—certainly less cowardly than these fifty men here who let themselves be held back a whole day.

Somehow no one seemed to think that the score had really been evened, although after a while a card, CATTLE THIEVES BEWARE, was pinned to the blood-soaked, bullet-ripped shirt of the man. By then most of the invaders had scattered to their own needs. Wolcott pulled out his copy of the Dead List and checked off the second name for the day. In the meantime somebody ran through Champion's pockets and drew out the blood-soaked little memo book torn by a bullet. It was passed to Wolcott, who glanced it over quickly and handed it to Canton. He rubbed his name out and handed the book on. There was a shouting from the dying fire, where Billy Irvine and some of the Texans were dragging out the charred body of Nick Ray. A long time the rancher from Nebraska looked at the man he had hated for some deep and private reason. But Nick Ray was only a flattish roll now, black and unrecognizable, smelling more of charcoal than scorched human flesh.

"Phil DuFran ought to see this. Better job than they did burning Mitchell and Ketchum down there in Nebraska."

By now the three supply wagons were coming into the valley and the Invaders got their first hot meal, their horses a little grain. The three men hit got their wounds dressed as well as could be done, now that the expedition had lost Dr. Penrose. Two of them were sent back to Douglas, to go on to Cheyenne if Douglas proved too unfriendly. The captured Jones and Walker demanded pay for their stuff burned: their guns, bedrolls, even their overcoats and Walker's $50 fiddle. The economical Billy Irvine wanted Walker to accept Champion's Stetson in place of the one he lost in the fire. Finally Bob Tisdale, son of Jack, the senator, gave them a note to his ranch for blankets, wearing gear, and a little grub. From there the two men were to be taken south, out of the country. "And keep your mouths shut if you want to go on living," they were warned.

Canton could hardly hold himself together while the others ate and swallowed burning coffee from the tin cups. "Night's coming on, and no telling what's happening to our men up to Buffalo," he kept reminding Wolcott. Finally the expedition started on the night ride of thirty miles to the ranch managed by Baxter and the fresh horses Shonsey promised. They rode hard, still hoping to make Buffalo by dawn. At Baxter's they switched saddles to new horses and set off wearily once more. They were out of the thin snow by now, with only thirty miles to Buffalo, the grained horses rearing and bucking in the frosted, cloudy night air, hot to go.

Toward the Carr ranch on the Crazy Woman old Pap Whitcomb got off to put an ear to the ground. There were riders up ahead somewhere, many horsebackers and stopping out in the sagebrush, he said. In a little while one rifle shot cut a red streak through the darkness, apparently a signal to the Invaders, because they swerved, snipped the Carr fences, and, following the dark blur of Shonsey's horse, swung around through broken country and back to the Buffalo road. They changed horses again at the Hesse ranch and once more at Harris TA, empty but with the horses ready. They were only fourteen miles from Buffalo now and Wolcott ordered a short rest. In the meantime Charley Ford, the foreman, wanted to ride over home to see about his wife, Wolcott grumbling at this delay almost as much as Canton. Would one of Custer's sergeants have asked to go see his wife when the Sioux camp was just ahead?

Big Jim Dudley, who wished he could get back to his wife in Texas that easy, had had saddle trouble all the way and now insisted on going with Ford to get another horse, an easier rider. They didn't come back and finally a cowboy loped in through the April dark. Dudley had tried a big tender-mouthed gray with his hard Spanish bit and was thrown. In the bucking the Winchester was jerked from the scabbard. It went off, shot Dudley in the thigh.

The story sounded pretty tall but plainly Dudley was no bronc peeler. He was, however, one of the first to hit the escaping Champion, so Wolcott borrowed Ford's spring wagon and sent the wounded men to the hospital at Fort McKinney up near Buffalo. "Remember to say he's a cowpuncher looking for work, and got shot when his horse threw him and the gun," he ordered.

The Invaders straggled away, Canton far ahead, determined to make the last hitch without a stop. But with the graying dawn two men came spurring in—Phil DuFran and Sutherland, the relative of Hesse's wife. Phil had been planted in a saloon at Buffalo as lookout. Always pleasant and agreeable, he managed to talk to everybody in spite of his known connection with Man-burner Olive and the Association.

"Turn back! Turn back!" he warned from far off. A mob of at least 100 men was on the road here, the whole country around Buffalo up and riding. To this Sutherland agreed, with some uneasy side talk to Hesse.

Wolcott roared his fury at the blunderers everywhere. Now he needed the ammunition in the wagons but he couldn't weaken his force to send back for them, or even protect them from the rustlers. They had to dig in some place themselves.

"Back to the TA!" he commanded, and spurred his horse into a run that showered pebbles into the dawn-gray sagebrush.

Now Canton, Smith, and the other range protectors had the ranchers on their side. They rode to overtake the major. "We'll never fight our way out of the TA alive!" he protested. "We'll be starved out."

"Burnt out!" another added, with horror in his voice.

"Perhaps we should make an orderly retreat to the railroad," Teschemacher suggested, his Harvard accent still clear although he had been separated from his sleeping bag in the wagons far too long. But Hesse and the others with ranches up here insisted on a hard ride for Buffalo, agreeing with Canton's "Hell! We can't quit the country now. That means giving up everything we got!"

Wolcott whacked his loaded quirt hard against the swell of his saddle. "Goddammnit, who's in command here? It's all arranged with the senators in Washington to get us troops any time we need them, and I got plans for a little bushwhacking somewheres along the road if they have to come—empty a few of the McClellans, make it look like the damned rustlers done it. That ought to get Van Horn shooting in the right direction."

Reluctantly the men fell in behind the major and now Smith found himself blocked by the Texans. "Give me my pay. I'm heading home," one demanded, for all.

"You try it and you'll carry something besides money in that belly belt of yourn," Smith roared out loud enough for all those gathered around him to hear. And because his hand was on his gun, and most of the Texans here were only kids and odd-job men, they fell in behind him. But Smith reined back behind the drags so at least his back was safe, with Shonsey and Elliott riding flank for him.

Up ahead Wolcott spurred on as to an overwhelming attack, but there was uneasiness among his men. A couple of them slipped away into the canyons. One of them was Tom

Horn. He was more determined than ever to work alone, from ambush, clean, with nobody shooting back.

At Buffalo, Sheriff Red Angus had listened to Terrence Smith's story of the attack on KC and then headed right out there, hoping to stop the killing, even though he knew the invasion was aimed at him first of all. Two forces were raised, one to follow him toward KC and intercept the Invaders, the rest to defend Buffalo.

In fourteen hours Angus was back from the 120 mile ride, a dour and an angry man. He slid heavily from the settler's horse they had borrowed on the way back, and told the gathering crowd what he had found. The Invaders were gone, the KC a smoking pile of ashes in the new light snow that lay over the bottoms. A man, probably Nick Ray, had been dragged out of the fire, burnt to a cinder, another scorched offering to the cow. Champion lay where he had fallen, the snow caught upon him unthawed, reddened on his torn breast and all around him, but pure white on his hair and mustache, the eye sockets drifted full.

Now nobody could remain neutral. Angrily men from everywhere streamed to the main street to be deputized to capture the Invaders, hold them for the brutal murders, hold them or something better. In the meantime a messenger rode in from Dunning, the man that Ijams of the Association had hired up in Idaho. The messenger told the story of the recruiting, the bounty, so much a head for every man they wanted killed—including the sheriff, county officials, businessmen. This news spread over town like a prairie fire in a high wind. Foote, the storekeeper, rode through town on his black pacing stallion, his long white hair and beard blowing to both sides, raising men for the fight. "My doors are open to you!" he shouted into the raw wind. "Take anything you need: guns, ammunition, saddles, grub. Take everything you need to fight the White Cap Invaders!"

In the meantime Sheriff Angus had gone to the Buf-

falo National Guard for protection of the town, for help to
capture the Invaders, and was told Parmalee had special notice from the governor not to move to any request except on
special orders from him no matter about the law of Wyoming,
compelling response to the sheriff's call. The telegraph was
still down for Angus, at least, and so he swore in 100 of the
waiting men as his deputies.

"Take the Invaders prisoners if you can but they are
murderers, man burners!" the terse-mouthed Scotsman told
them, his voice hoarse from weariness, the long, cold ride,
and the fury and shock of what he had seen. Then he sent the
men out under Snider, the former sheriff, Arapaho Brown,
and Jack Flagg. Two hundred more men joined the Defenders, with more and more hurrying up as they rode out to
meet the Invasion.

Sheriff Angus watched them go, the wind lifting the
thin wisp of reddish hair left at the top of his head. Then he
put his hat on for one more errand before he dared let himself sleep. Wearily he rode the three miles to Fort McKinney.

"The posse going out is in a dangerous mood, Colonel.
There will be bloodshed, bloody slaughter," he said.

But Colonel Van Horn reminded him that he could
make no move without orders from his superiors.

The TA was set on the pleasant bottoms among rolling hogbacks. The ranch buildings, large, sprawling, and
weathered beside a pile of new lumber, were enclosed in a
seven-foot fence of logs set too close for much more than a
limber-boned weasel to crawl through, with a stout barbed-
wire fence around the outside. The ranch house had been a
place of gay entertainment once, of hunt dinners and balls,
but it stood empty now, the blank windows staring upon the
Invaders as they settled themselves. They dug out a little fort
on a knoll, the dirt thrown up in breastworks for the sharpshooters under Senator Tisdale, with water, food, and some
of the few blankets inside. The new lumber—planking and
square-sawn logs ten inches thick hauled in for new build-

ings—Wolcott used for barricading the house, the rambling stables, even the icehouse and the hen coop. Realizing that the supply wagons were surely captured by now, a couple of steers were driven in from the range and one of them butch-ered—thin but meat. Because they must get word out to Chey-enne and Washington, as well as reach supplies and ammuni-tion, if possible, Wolcott had sent Allen, manager of the Standard Cattle Company in east Wyoming and in Nebraska, and tied in with Baxter, to Buffalo. Unknown up there, he might get Billy Irvine's order to friends. It didn't work. Al-most before the Invaders were unsaddled at the TA, Allen was in the Buffalo jail.

Fortunately the Invaders had all day to prepare but the scouts knew that the Johnson County Defenders, now to become besiegers, were gathering, coming all night, too, with a camp set up prepared for a long stay. At dawn of the eleventh, while the first smoke rose from the chimney of the TA ranch house, the besiegers appeared on the rises to the north and the .45-70's began to throw an experimental thunder over the valley, answered in a scattering fire from the TA. Then the horses were sent back and Flagg's men began creeping up closer, slowly, worming along like Sioux Indians, the firing increasing as more men came in. Now those who had Champion surrounded in his little KC alone a couple of days ago had trapped themselves.

It was impossible to keep rumors from reaching the railroad and the telegraph service—wild stories of a wild un-dertaking, with great numbers of men killed on this side or on that. Eastern newspapers tried to send men in, but every-body was afraid of being caught by the Invaders or the so-called rustlers. Wolcott's men had kept the little telegraph office on the Powder in their hands yet somehow Angus got a message through to Sheriff Campbell at Douglas about the KC fight and requested him to hold all suspects, even though he was one of the Britishers, Angus, the Scotsman, admitted dourly. Two of Campbell's county commissioners were Wol-

cott with the Invaders, and E. T. David, Carey's ranch manager, who was to keep the telegraph cut. What a mare's nest
of connected interests were after the men of Johnson County.

But the fact that one message got through that far
scared the ranchers and the line repairmen got threats and
bullets whistling over their heads. There were also big bills
or gold coins in bottles beside new gaps cut in the wire.

Now suddenly it was the Invaders locked up, at the
TA, and the besiegers cutting the line. Already the governor
had been asked for the National Guard to avoid bloodshed,
meaning Invader blood, but his orders to Parmalee of the
Guards at Buffalo apparently never got through.

Gradually the outside was getting a little more understanding of what was happening in Johnson County. Down
in Denver the *Rocky Mountain News* protested the action of
Wyoming state officials as without comparison in the history
of a civilized country. "If the ringleader's object is to kill off
all his personal enemies on this trip, about half of the population must be on the list."

Then the findings of the coroner at KC got out: eight
bullets in Champion's body, Nick Ray charred, the legs below
the knees and the arms practically burned off. When the
bodies reached Buffalo, the excitement and fury ran like a
lighted fuse toward dynamite, and once more Angus hurried
to the fort. The men surrounded out at the TA would be
blown up, massacred when the coroner's findings got out to
the besiegers there. The Invaders must be rescued, held for
murder, yes, but rescued while there was time.

The spring wagon with the gunshot Dudley came in
right after the bodies arrived from the KC. It was stopped by
outraged citizens who thought the man's story a bald-faced
lie, a ruse to get a message from the Invaders to the fort. Coroner Watkins was called from his sorrowful task of writing up
his report on the dead before he slept. He came, pulled the
blanket back. Seeing the swollen and bullet-shattered leg, he
ordered Dudley to the post hospital immediately and then,

overcome by all the violence and horror, fell in a stroke right there on the street and died.

Now even the churchmen were aroused. Six months ago the Reverend Rader had thrashed a cattleman on the street for calling his militant Methodist congregation a nest of damned cattle rustlers, it was said. Now the preacher gathered up forty churchmen of the town and started out to slay a few cattle kings, not with the jawbone of an ass but with the latest model Winchesters they could scare up at this late hour.

All over Wyoming and adjoining cattle country settlers were sleeping out in the sagebrush or the willows or bunch grass, away from their usual beds because ranchers were riding the country in posses. One from Billings and Big Timber was in a gun fight with rustlers at the Wyoming line. There were rumors of large cattlemen movements against settlers in Dakota, too, but less because there were more Texans up there, with little sympathy for the Yankee carpetbaggers and for the Britishers who controlled most of the big outfits in Wyoming. But it was rumored that ranchers even in Wyoming were loading up their families and streaming in to Douglas and Gillette, even Newcastle and Cheyenne, too, for safety. "Clay knew why he was getting out," one of the men leaving said ruefully. It was true that the president of the Stock Growers Association was safe off in Europe while his associates, connections, and debtors were dodging bullets at the TA and Sheriff Angus was working so hard to keep the Crazy Woman Fork from running red with their blood.

At the besieged ranch Canton was still arguing that they must break out, but Wolcott knew they were safer right there. If Angus and the other officials had been killed as arranged, there would be only unorganized mobs like the one around them here, and as soon as word got to the governor and Senators Carey and Warren, troops would come at a full gallop. Van Horn at McKinney knew something was up; he had been told to take in three new Studebaker wagons if they had to hit for the post.

In addition Wolcott worked out his plan to sneak a few good men in among the rustler line when the troops were about due. They would drop a couple of bluecoats from the saddles and make it look like the rustlers' doings. That ought to bring on a good fight, particularly if the troops came in the dark. Meanwhile he and his force would be making a run for Cheyenne, where reinforcements would be ready for a return. Next time they would count tally on every man who dared pack a gun against them.

"Bull! That's just plain Yankee brag and bull," old Mynett drawled. "I plan to make a run for it if the clouds hold out, but for Texas, and tonight."

"You won't be going out of here alive, not before the rest," Tom Smith warned him, with Canton and Elliott to back him up now, and the boy-faced Texas Kid moving in close beside them, feeling an important killer now that he had bloodied his gun with Nick Ray.

"There's no call for talk like that," Wolcott interrupted. Troops would be coming and anyway he was sending another messenger out to get double word to Buffalo and Cheyenne, if Allen didn't make it. Somebody suggested Phil DuFran. He knew the country for years, and probably nobody outside would suspect he had been anywhere near the TA. He could just let on he'd been off on private business.

But DuFran shook his dark, shaggy head with his usual good humor. "The fellers out there, they catch almost anybody they shoot him. Me"—pointing his thumb at himself,—"me they burn."

Some of the Texans looked on this as bad Frenchy humor but others didn't need it explained. Anyway, there was work to do, laid out for everybody except Calhoun. He was in such pain from Champion's bullet at KC that he was bedded down on blankets although with 200 men plainly not troopers sweeping in over the ridge at a gallop his gun could come in handy. Through Wolcott's field glasses he saw that Angus was the leader, with the powerful Arapaho Brown on one side and the fighting Methodist parson Rader on the other. He could have guessed that. The rest were the lot of new deputies and a general posse of small ranchers, settlers, clerks, gamblers, a few genuine rustlers who hadn't hit for Idaho or Montana, half-a-dozen plain adventurers, and some of the churchmen. But they didn't charge. Instead, they dug in, taking advantage of cut banks and gullies, making a wide, broken circle around the Invaders and apparently settling down to a wait, firing now and then, but without much urgency. For an hour at a time the only smoke might be from some pungent old cob pipe or a little hand-warming fire.

More besiegers came in through the stormy night, reporting to Angus headquarters set up at the little Covington ranch a mile and a half away. They watched but Wolcott got Dowling out past them all in a thick flurry of snow while Shonsey made a diversion on the far side. Afterward they saw where the horse had slipped on a snowy bank and knew they would have to work fast, particularly those who intended vengeance.

By morning the watchers were chilled as wet dogs, so they left a few guards and went to breakfast. The headquarters were so crowded there was barely standing room, with provisions and bedrolls and ammunition boxes in piles all over the yard—enough for a month of siege.

Inside the TA, Calhoun's wound was so inflamed and festering that it was plain he must get to a doctor. They helped him into the saddle and, swaying to the run of the horse, he got through, with only a few desultory shots to hurry him. Because this had been so easy, the Invaders all started to saddle up in the corrals, and got a hot fire that drove them back into the barricades as Dead Center Dave steadied his heavy old Sharps 50 buffalo gun on a forked stick and picked off the horses, firing out his six, seven cartridges, reloading them from the caps, powder, and bullets in his pockets and firing again, the horses plunging each time, perhaps one to fall, or stand, head hanging, and then go down to kick awhile in the corral dirt. Dave and the others got twenty-six before the Invaders made a run out to drive what was left into the barn.

The temperature dropped, the snow thickened a little until the valley was pure white over roofs and breastworks. It hurried the besiegers. They scattered bales of hay brought down from Buffalo and began to slide them along the snowy grass, pushing in as they shot from behind them, the ring of smoke closing in on one side, then another. But with the TA and the little fort sprawled out and the angle of return fire so wide, it became dangerous.

Midmorning the three Studebaker wagons were brought in to the Angus headquarters. The drivers talked freely enough, and for the first time the sheriff and the others discovered just who the invaders were. When Colonel Parker's cowboys realized that they had been shooting at their boss they slipped away, the rest letting them go, for Parker was a reasonably decent man. There was no accounting for some of those caught over there in the TA.

The three drivers claimed they knew nothing of the loads they hauled, particularly nothing of the two cases of dynamite, the bottles marked POISON with the red skull and crossbones, and in Canton's valise the copy of the Dead List with the seventy names marked for extermination.

As this was read off there was a heated run for the ammunition piles.

"Kill every son of a bitch like you would stomp out a nest of rattlers!" one of the homesteaders shouted, his words dark as the angry, the infuriated faces around him.

Half-a-dozen men stepped forward, each naming one or more as his private target. "Canton's mine," a quiet, stooped little clerk said, to start.

"Not yours alone! We'll take Canton, Hesse, and the others who tried to lynch Champion together," several others interrupted. "But we'll let you in." Others demanded this and that name: Wolcott, Shonsey, Irvine, even Phil DuFran, and so on, and Smith, Elliott, and a dozen others taken early.

But Arapaho Brown stood in their path, a hand up. "Stomping them is too costly," he said. "Somebody'll get hurt. I have been planning a go-devil for the dynamite, an Ark of Vengeance, the Reverend calls it."

Rader nodded, and some of the men hesitated, then all turned back to listen. There was no denying Arapaho was a handy man with a saw and a hammer, with machinery, and the Reverend was a scrapper; had a mighty true eye on him for men and for a target.

While Arapaho scratched thoughtfully under the tangle of his long, curly beard, one of the Covington ranch shacks was torn down and, under Snider's direction, built into a fort on the running gears of two of the new wagons set side by side. If the horses failed under fire, twenty, thirty men could push the Ark up close by the tongues while others fired through the loopholes, trying to get close enough to throw the dynamite with short fuses into the little earth fort and over to the house. It was dangerous but even the tenderest among them was ready to destroy the last man in the TA, many others as determined as Allison Tisdale, brother of the ambushed Johnny.

Uneasily Sheriff Angus watched this fury grow and rode for Fort McKinney once more, spurring hard. Colonel Van Horn was in a bad mood. Perhaps Foote really had come offering $5,000 for a cannon, as rumored. But Angus argued that his men were beyond taking captives now, planning to wipe out the entire force of the Invaders. They got their hands on the Dead List with the seventy names on it, he told the stern-faced officer. Names of their mayor, part of their county commissioners, their sheriff, even ministers. Found enough dynamite in the wagons to blow up the courthouse, half the town, and some of the churches, too, it seemed. Vials of poison for water holes and wells, so one of the wagon drivers thought. If the Invaders—madmen—had succeeded it would have meant civil war, turned Wyoming into a slaughterhouse. Not a cattle king or a company official would have been left alive. The besiegers were bound to pay the Invaders for this but the men at the TA, with state officials among them, had to be saved, no matter how guilty of murder and man burning. If they died, the consequences for the people would be almost as bad as civil war.

It was a long, long speech for the close-mouthed Red Angus, but Van Horn still couldn't move without orders. Wouldn't.

At the hills and ridges around the TA hundreds of men were waiting, coming, going, but mostly waiting. Inside the ranch below there was waiting, too, waiting that turned into anger and then despair as the men saw the great awkward go-devil, much heavier than theirs at KC, for this one had to withstand fifty rifles instead of one, and from a very wide angle. The ponderous little fort tipped and staggered forward as the drivers whipped their teams that pushed the fort from behind. The Texans squinted at it through the barricades and swore grimly, the cattlemen, gaunt and paling under their windburn, searched the rim of the valley, now dark as in standing pines, so thick were the besiegers. Plainly Wolcott's messengers were being captured or their cause here had been deserted everywhere from Buffalo to the White House. Senator Tisdale talked earnestly for a break made in force. "If we skulk in our hole here they'll get us all," he argued. In a break at least some would get away.

But Billy Irvine protested that not half could make it. "Tonight, yes—"

"Tonight will be too late."

"—tonight if the moon is hidden, but not in broad daylight," Irvine finished. Even with the provisions about gone and the ammunition low, they had to hope for rescue before that go-devil out there reached them. Someone must come. If not troops through Carey and Warren, then cattlemen perhaps from Montana and other Wyoming regions

It was grim waiting as the much too unwieldy Ark of Vengeance moved each painful inch with forty men pushing from behind after the horses reared and faunched when bullets struck around their hoofs. There was fire from the dirt fort and the ranch, grazing the legs of the men pushing, too, and clipping boot toes while far off. A dozen times the go-devil stuck against a bank or soft ground, sinking deep into gopher holes. But its fire grew more dangerous as, by dark, it was only around 400 yards off and still moving doggedly, very slowly, but moving in the clear April night.

As the moon brightened, the bullets began to penetrate the thinner barricading so the icehouse and the hen coop were abandoned with much uneasiness about the sharpshooters out in the earth fort, with the dirty rustlers certain to fling their dynamite into it. At the house Tisdale still wanted to make the break for freedom. Tomorrow the food would be gone. At least they would go down fighting, not be blown up in their holes, or burned like rats.

All around him men nodded soberly, too worn and discouraged, too scared, perhaps, to speak or to remember the KC.

Up at Buffalo the town was swarming so that Dowling had to hide out for hours and when he finally got to Parmalee of the National Guard, the telegraph was out again. Finally that night of the twelfth they got through to the desperately anxious Senators Carey and Warren. The two men rooted President Harrison out of bed. He stirred up the War Department and at last orders were dispatched out to Douglas and along the one thin wire to Fort McKinney.

Although the moon had gone under clouds early, with little running showers and sleet, at daybreak the go-devil was plainly closer, and as the light grew the lurching fort began to move again, with a black neckerchief of "No Quarter" flying at one corner, Arapaho Brown's red bandana at the other. Out in the dirt fort the sharpshooters fired in desperation, if only to slow the heavy movement a little, help the

impeding rain-softened earth and the rise toward the ranch.
But the Ark kept coming on, foot by foot, in spite of the
futile and suddenly scarcening bullets. There was a growing stir at the TA, loud shouts and cursings. At the earthen
fort a man climbed out on the wall, standing there in one
challenging, perhaps surrendering, moment, and was knocked
back by a bullet.

The men behind the go-devil pushed a little faster
now, puffing hard, afraid they would be cheated by a suicide
break. On the bottoms horsebackers rode fast from one wet
bale of hay to the next, and to the little breastworks thrown
up in spots around the ranch, some not much over thirty,
forty yards from the house fence now and drawing almost no
fire any more. "Be ready!" the riders shouted to the waiting
men. "Be ready!" Shouting it particularly on the far side
from the Ark, where men lay with their rifles aimed on the
doors and windows beyond the fence, ready now that most
of the barricading was gone there. Once one of the doors was
thrown open, a man in it a moment and then jerked back as
the bullets helped slam the closing door, hitting it like hail.
Up on the ridge Dead Center Dave and his men waited, too,
Dave's handful of long cartridges reloaded, the men looking
anxiously up to the sky, afraid the rain would thicken, cover
an escape.

The ponderous, lurching Ark was still moving, painfully but steadily. It started up the little slope to the ranch,
blue powder smoke clinging around it in the wet air, the
dynamite men ready, with their fused bundles, their matches
safe and dry.

Then suddenly the go-devil stopped, everything
stopped. Far off, thin and faint, but clear, a brassy call
sounded on the rainy wind. A shout went up from the Invaders and was choked off by loud cursing and arguing
voices. Again the clear trumpet call broke the stillness
as a blue column topped the low ridge and started down
the slope at a gallop, guidons flapping heavily, Colonel Van
Horn, his aide, Captain Parmalee, Sheriff Red Angus, and a

newspaperman riding abreast, the blue double column lined out smartly behind them.

Down at the dirt fort a head appeared and a dirty rag was raised high, and another one at the TA ranch house.

So Wolcott and his lieutenants surrendered, making it pointedly to the colonel, not the bristle-whiskered Sheriff Angus, in whose custody they rightly belonged—all the forty-six still there, twenty-four of them the hired Texans and many of the rest prominent in ranching and ranch finance, and in the government of the state, all whiskered, soiled, and rumpled, gaunted out.

Van Horn accepted the surrender but with plain distaste. An hour later, in a hard shower with sleet to bounce from the saddles, everybody mounted, all except the wounded men, including the one whose falling pistol put a bullet into his stomach at the little fort this morning. Dunning, the Idaho man, was missing, too. He was hidden in the attic and none sought him out. Others were planning to get away along the trail, Bill Booker under Clay at the Swan ranches and eight, ten others. It was bad enough that Wolcott, Whitcomb, Hesse, and a dozen such men were too well identified to escape. Their embarrassment wouldn't be theirs alone but state-wide, international.

The trumpet sounded Forward, and as the weary, gaunted Regulators, as they still liked to call themselves, rode out, rain dripping from their soiled and sooted Stetsons, the troops closed in around them, making a protective square, a wall to hold the bullets out. Even so some of the besiegers charged down toward them in their anger and frustration. They stopped a good distance off, held back by the determined bluecoats, but they gave a loud and derisive yell that echoed up and down the Crazy Woman Fork and far out over all the cow country.

# CHAPTER III

# SCATTERED TO THE WINDS

B Y THE evening of April 13, 1892, the Invasion of
Johnson County was over, the Invaders safe at Fort
McKinney, to be delivered only to such civilian authorities as
Van Horn's superiors directed. But who could say when the
effect of such action, such a crusade in the land of the cow,
could ever be done. The Regulators, the Invaders, had attempted to return to the wilderness days of twenty-five years
ago, when those marked for extermination were only Indians
—thieving, murdering, bloodthirsty savages, now that the
white man wanted their lands, although only a short time
ago they were the Noble Red men that the world came to
see. There had been an arrogant charge in where the men
had no right be be then, too, only a few miles north, up along
the Big Horns. Unfortunately Captain Fetterman had no
political pipeline to Washington to bring help galloping in
time. He and his men had to die in their entrapment.

Now Buffalo still had the dead from KC to bury and
two days after the surrender people came in over the gray
spring prairie from early morning. They came by wagon,
horseback, afoot, many from far off and never to the town
before. They came in time for the morning funeral of Coroner Watkins, who had dropped dead on the street after he

returned with the bodies from KC. It was a large and digni-
fied service, conducted by the Masons, the K. of P., and the
G. A. R., each group including men who bore arms in the
cattle war, men on the Dead List, and men among the Invaders locked up at the post.

People kept coming into town until the Main Street
hitch racks were crowded. Soon after one o'clock the townspeople gathered into the crowd, women clutching their
hoods and their shawls, or perhaps clinging to feathered hats
and sweeping skirts in the sunny April wind, the men grim
and silent, their boot heels loud on the boards as all began to
move toward a vacant store. There the women went in, the
men filling the street outside, spilling away to both directions, waiting.

Inside, on the mourners' side, were two men, the
brothers of Nate Champion, and in the back, under shaded
lanterns, two handsome coffins rested in a great mound of
flowers that had come by carriage, by stage, and mule train.
There were many simple little bunches, too, perhaps brought
carefully in newspaper pokes and twists from some remote
settler log shack or soddy. It seemed that every geranium,
every fuchsia and begonia for a hundred miles had been
shorn of its precious bloom. In this surrounding of color and
fragrance Nate Champion's face had the quiet and the re-
moteness of the courageous dead, but only the black burial
coat of Nick Ray was exposed. All the rest of the charred
body was covered by the flowers, even the burnt features
shaded to spare the horrified eyes.

The Baptist minister began with the Scriptures and
the prayer, then Reverend Rader spoke a little, his voice so
quiet it could scarcely be heard. "These men have been sent
to eternity. We know not why. They were not criminals.
They were of Christian parents. Ray leaves five brothers and
three sisters. His parents could not be notified, as the wires
were cut. But the same honors have been paid as if they were
here."

Many were in tears, many sobbed softly as they moved

past the coffins and away through the back so all those waiting out in front might eventually enter, too. Afterward the
procession moved up the main street, the ministers leading,
then the hearse, followed by carriages, buggies, carts, wagons,
a long string of people afoot, and finally a rear guard of 150
horsebackers, with three women and two boys among them,
some from those who had lost their men to the rope and the
ambush. Last of all Jack Flagg led the saddle horses of
Champion and Ray, the stirrups hooked up over the horn.
And far out from town people stood beside the road in the
pleasant April sun as the funeral passed, their faces naked.

Later that night some gathered in the saloon where
the easy-talking Phil DuFran from down around the Olives
of Nebraska had tended bar and spied on them all. Here,
too, the Britishers led by Fred Hesse and the young Cana-
dians, Hesse's brother-in-law Sutherland, and George Wellman, from Blair's ranch, had gathered for a warming drink.
Here, with the Association's inspectors and detectives, such as
Canton, Smith, and Shonsey, and a dozen others, they found
companionship in an unfriendly town, unfriendly even before Hesse and Canton had to skip out after the attack on
Champion and the ambush of Jones and Tisdale. Not that no
one ever challenged them here. Once a slightly tipsy Irish
cowpuncher strolled in to shout that he was willing to fight
every damned Englishman in the house, "In this damned bar
of Victoria, Empress of Wyoming." But Phil DuFran had
coaxed him away with a bottle, even told him he was a little
late, that the bar had been known as Clay's Inn by the rustlers for years.

Tonight there didn't seem to be anybody there except
those so-called rustlers. There were rumors of new management coming, the bartender already a settler. It was here that
Foote's words of the afternoon were repeated. "The burning
of Ray, and Champion's stalwart fight awoke us, gave us
time to save the rest of the Dead List and many, many more.
A great red flood would have swept all over the ranch country if the Invaders had succeeded, yes, perhaps reaching even

into the statehouse and the legislative halls for men like Senator Tisdale."

There was much complaining that around eleven of the Invaders had got clear away, including those who slipped out before the surrender in addition to some who evidently cut down a canyon or a ravine on the way to the fort—men like William Booker, range foreman of the Swan ranches under John Clay and potentially most embarrassing to him and the foreign owners, as most of the others were, too.

By now three of the Invaders had died of gangrene, caused, as Wolcott announced, from "accidentally shooting themselves," perhaps so the cattlemen wouldn't have to pay the promised damages to their families. Jim Dudley, the young Texas giant, who, of all the eager gunmen, had stopped the escaping Champion, was buried without a mourner, some wondering about the wife he had missed so much. Perhaps the telegraph was cut for her, too, and she might never know the end of the venture she resisted from the start, or receive the promised bounty.

By now the newspapers were carrying stories of the kidnaping of Jones and Walker, the two men who happened to be at the KC the morning of the attack, the only outside witnesses to the murders and burning. Although charged with no crime they were held in jail and then moved down to the Nebraska Panhandle, with threats and possible attempts at ambush. Bill McCann, George Wellman, and Jim Craig of Johnson County were apparently in the mob that took them over down in Nebraska, when they had managed to escape. After A. E. Sheldon, a former homesteader running a newspaper at Chadron, managed to get an interview with them, gave them a write-up, the two men vanished, killed, many believed, while others whispered of a man named Dixon back in Rhode Island who had been hired to "look after" witnesses against the Wyoming Association in the past.

Men still kept pouring into Buffalo, demanding the

Invaders be turned over to Johnson County for trial. Hastily
Governor Barber got a change of venue to Cheyenne and the
Invaders were escorted south by troops, and properly so,
Sheriff Angus agreed, and brought abuse upon himself, even
a gun stuck in his ribs for it. Down in Cheyenne the Invaders
were nominally in charge of troops but they were loose on
the town, even the Texans, all local heroes and bragging they
would soon return up north there in force and "clean the
rascals out."

Up north there the Johnson Countyites turned their
anger on everything of the Invaders. The rustlers from the
Hole in the Wall and along the Montana border had picked
up stock from both the cattlemen and the settlers during the
week of the Invasion and the excitement afterward. Now the
ranches involved were raided in earnest, not only by outsiders and known rustlers but by settlers and little ranchers
on the Dead List. The foreman of the Ijam outfit sneaked
out of the country and Pap Whitcomb's man over near Newcastle was threatened with lead in his guts if he returned
there. Charlie Carter, foreman of the TA now that Ford was
detained with the Invaders, was ordered out of the country.
Chambers, foreman of the Ogallala Company, tied in with
Clay's Swan, managed by Billy Irvine, was warned out, too.
Alarmed, he hurried the Irvine children to their father at
Cheyenne. At the Hesse ranch an unidentified mob shot the
piano to pieces, destroyed the furniture, and divided the
packable loot among themselves, including much fancy stuff
from the Frewens. All those known to have aided or perhaps
even seemed to favor the Invaders around Buffalo left, too,
or walked a line narrow as the old hand-wide buffalo trails.
Even DeForest Richards, banker and mayor of Douglas, and
commander of the Wyoming National Guard, had to defend
himself by protesting that two weeks before the invasion he
was instructed by the governor and the adjutant general to
obey only orders "from these headquarters." There were
rumors that he and some other officers resigned, declaring
the orders cheapening. Others said the orders were illegal.

But always there were some who questioned whether this was more than enlightened hindsight.

Cattle were worth very little above the freight and commission charges, now that the panic was deepening in the East, yet the stock of the big outfits was disappearing as fast as gold nuggets almost, and the Johnson County commissioners asked the ranch managers to send in trustworthy and discreet hands to look after their property. Instead, the Wyoming Stock Growers Association, chiefly Blair, Baxter's Western Union Beef with Shonsey the foreman, and Billy Irvine of the Clay-dominated Ogallala Cattle Company, got an injunction against the "outlaw" roundup of the new Northern Wyoming group, but it was dated May 10, five days after the northern wagons moved out. It named many men on the Dead List and stirred even Red Angus to heated words again. So far he had kept the guns cool partly because the Invaders found that state and national, even some British, opinion considered them arrogant lawbreakers and cold-blooded murderers. Instead of more overt action they turned to the advocates of indirection, some, like Billy Irvine, saying "We tried to tell you—"

Then in May George Wellman was shot. He had come as a youth from Canada and rode the local ranges for eleven years, lately for Blair's Hoe Ranch. After the KC attack he helped kidnap Jones and Walker, the men who were captured there. Wellman married since then, on the money he got for ridding the Invaders of these two eyewitnesses to the killing and the burning at KC, it was said. Although he was warned to keep out of the country, he took over the foremanship of the Hoe while Laberteaux was "detained" with the rest of the Invaders down at Cheyenne. In addition Wellman was appointed deputy U. S. marshal, apparently to serve the Association's injunction papers against the independent roundup, the riders already far out and moving. Others thought he was going to Buffalo to post the declaration of martial law.

Anyway, Hathaway, a former cowhand at the Hoe,

brought the news to Sheriff Angus. He said he was riding beside Wellman to Buffalo. Down south of the George Harris ranch bullets came from a ridge, or a draw, and Wellman fell in the road. Afraid to hang around, Hathaway left him there and hurried to Buffalo. No, he didn't see anybody, just heard the shots and then caught Wellman's horse.

Angus went out to investigate, alone as usual, but afterward some of his friends decided this might be a decoy report, to get the sheriff out to a dry gulching. They followed, but Wellman was dead, a .44 carbine bullet in his back.

Although some suspected Hathaway, chiefly because he told so many conflicting stories, the ranchers blamed the Red Sash Gang. Hank Smith, Clayton Crews, and Charley Taylor were arrested. Taylor and some of his cronies did wear strips of red flannel under their cartridge belts to keep the grease of the shells off their clothing. But nobody believed they killed Wellman because they weren't anywhere around there at the time. Some said it was Ed Starr, a friend of Champion, picked by lot to kill Wellman, as a man had been chosen to dispose of Hard Winter Davis, only Davis hurriedly took his eastern caution and his bodyguards down to Nebraska and showed no immediate nostalgia for north Wyoming. Of the nooses left on the Spectacle Ranch porch back in April, one had Wellman's name on it, another Hard Winter's. By the time the blame for the Wellman shooting was laid on Starr, he was gone. In the meantime most of Johnson County decided that the shooting was a typical Canton and Hesse job, that Wellman was killed by one of their own men to help them bring martial law to the Powder River country. The large outfits did sign a request for troops. The soldiers came with Hotchkiss guns and scattered over Johnson, Converse, and Natrona counties, which included the Sweetwater region and the ranches of the men involved in the Averill hangings and Wolcott's VR—most of the ranches respresented by the Invaders, most of those in which the Clay's interests were involved. Among the troops were some Negro cavalrymen who had been rioting at other stations. One night forty-four of them shot up a saloon at the little tent town of Suggs, in the oil-seeped valley of the Powder, up near the crossing of the new railroad headed for Billings. The saloon was an early settler's log shack and here several members of the Invaders' Dead List hung out. Apparently they were still worth the Stock Growers Association's bounty. Anyway, the Negro troops, with a civilian among them, fired a volley into the lamplit saloon from across the road, and when the men got to the Winchesters stacked behind the bar and fired into the darkness, the troopers ran, falling over tent poles, yelling and cursing. They made it to the railroad embankment and riddled the whole tent settlement, everybody, women and children, too, hugging the earth as the bullets whistled by. Finally they were driven to the river and to camp, leaving one trooper dead on the ground.

Certain that the soldiers would return in force to clean up Suggs, the handful of women and children were put into the old settler's cellar and the armed men distributed for such defense as they could hope to make. Cavalry came at a trot, with the rumble of a Hotchkiss gun. This looked like the cleanout the Invaders had failed to make, and the men who had been held back by Red Angus and old Arapaho Brown from clearing out the TA with the Invaders' own dynamite cursed them to hell. What if the man creeping up with the dynamite had been detected and died? He would have died a hero, wiping out the worst den of rattlers the country ever saw.

But even the most violent men fell silent when the troops were so close that their saddles creaked. Everybody held his fire and there was no fighting. The officer had heard the rifle shots and called a fast roll to find out just who was missing. He brought the Hotchkiss along for an emergency, mostly to manage his own unruly troops. He gathered up the dead man and went to hunt out the culprits.

Messages had been sent out at the first firing into the

saloon and this time nobody of the region held back. By morning men came riding in, around 150 of them, and stayed until they were mighty certain that the soldiers really weren't planning to finish what the Invaders had started. They were doubly suspicious when it was discovered that the civilian with the attacking troops last night was Phil DuFran, just released with Sutherland by the authorities at Cheyenne because he could prove he wasn't at KC for the killings any more than he was actually at the lynching and burning of Mitchell and Ketchum down in Nebraska.

"Looks like that bastard DuFran's around every time there's trouble," a cowpuncher from down at Plum Creek complained. "He'd turn state's evidence again if there was any state action."

Slowly the dust of the great crusade of 1892 settled. John Clay was back, working hard with former Governor Baxter and others to get the Invaders released. Clay seemed anxious, with so many of his connections hogtied—respected men like Campbell of the commission house and Irvine and the others from the ranches—men who could make the country mighty hot for him. Wolcott, too, should be out and working, with beef prices falling like stones. The Swan company had been reorganized when Clay was in Scotland in March. Over 280,000 acres of their railroad lands not paid for had been sold. This wasn't culling, but selling down.

Besides, Johnson County was bankrupt and unwilling to pay for the lengthy keep of the Invaders down at Fort D. A. Russell at around $100 a day for the nearly fifty men, although everybody knew they were loose and scattered all over Cheyenne, free as the high country winds blowing along the dusty streets. What Johnson County wanted was to get the Invaders tried up at Buffalo, but obviously that would never happen. There was a pretense of a trial at Cheyenne, with around 1,000 men drawn, it was said, to get a jury before the judge accepted a motion for dismissal. The story

sounded fishy as a dead bullhead in the sun, but Johnson
County was helpless.

So the Invaders were free to scatter. The delicately
nurtured DeBillier had a breakdown, "snapped over," as the
cowboys called it. He thought the Texas gunmen, rowdy, impatient, and very surly, were out to get him. Anxious to
escape, he and Teschemacher had turned their ranch over to
their cowboys and jumped bail, DeBillier to the doctors,
Teschie to Europe where his brother had killed himself over
a Russian princess, some said. Others suggested the world-
wide notoriety of the "most ill-advised Invasion," and a dozen
other causes, but some recalled that Teschie's mother had
written to several matrons in Wyoming when he first came
out: "Please look after my dear, dear boy," and knew something of the lifelong favoritism shown this elder son, the
Wyoming rancher.

For a while after the release at Cheyenne men stalked
each other in the Powder River country like hungry mountain lions come down from the hills. Young Dudley Champion was shot by Mike Shonsey. Some claimed Dud got loud-
mouth, threatening to avenge his brother Nate by a little
killing, preferably that scoundrel Shonsey, who had used the
hospitality of the men at the KC to destroy them. Others
said Shonsey killed young Dud out of bad conscience; dry
gulched him in the best cattleman fashion, then claimed that
this Champion was pretty slow on the draw. But soon Shonsey and Baxter were both gone. Seemed they were caught
doctoring the books of the Western Union Beef Company to
get 2,000 cattle for their own brands by blaming the loss
on the rustlers of Johnson County.

Many others from the Powder ranches found the climate healthier outside of the region, even outside the state.
Hesse went to North Platte, Nebraska, down around his
wife's folks, some said, and worked for the Bay State Beef
outfit. He wrote Ijams and Clay and others repeatedly, complaining about his cattle losses up in Johnson County and

built plans to market what remained without there being a "kick" about it from Buffalo. He admitted that the situation had changed considerably the last year.

Billy Irvine kept his professional bodyguard with him at all times, and Allen of the Western Union Beef and the English-owned Standard Cattle Company went to the 101 in the sandhills of Nebraska with two bodyguards along, a couple of Hard Cases that even the half-a-dozen others who fled there, too, found unacceptable. Wolcott also was in trouble, apparently caught running his iron on a calf whose mother carried a neighbor's brand.

"Seems to be catching, this rustling business," Johnson Countyites told each other with tight faces.

Some of the Texans came to sudden ends. Tom Smith, the Association inspector who had rounded up the gunmen, was shot on a train down around the Red River. The Texas Kid, who put a bullet into Nick Ray, was getting himself hanged for killing his girl. He blamed it all on the Wyoming Stock Growers Association for enticing him into his first murder.

On the Johnson County side, Flagg started *The Voice* at Buffalo after the independent roundup was done. Several of the less-rooted men on the Dead List ended violently up in Montana. An obscure one was killed robbing a drugstore up there. Allison Tisdale, brother of Johnny ambushed the fall of 1891, was reported shot in a gun fight up there, too, and Ed Starr, supposed to have killed Wellman, also ended in Montana. To please his wife he had quit carrying a gun and when he was cornered into a fight and had to go dig it out, the cartridges in it had been changed for blanks. Many were certain that Arapaho Brown wouldn't be allowed to live very long—not the big, fearless man who had thought up the go-devil at the TA, a man with a library, a reader, a talker. There were stories that he had done a little killing himself. Anyway, he was attacked, apparently by Canton and the Bill McCann who helped kidnap Jones and Walker. They shot

Brown on his homestead sitting at his supper, threw him on the woodpile, and burned him.

"Is there to be no end to these burnt offerings on the altar of the cow?" Reverend Rader demanded from the pulpit the next Sunday.

If Frank Canton was guilty, he escaped paying for this murder and this burning, too, and lived into old age. But he had to leave Wyoming again, first for Nebraska, where J. Sterling Morton and Weare, rancher of Wyoming and Chicago, hired him as superintendent of the Nebraska City Packing Company. But Frank found the Missouri River town pretty tame, with little gun play, and so he turned to chasing outlaws as far as Alaska and later was appointed adjutant general of Oklahoma, where he had important relatives. But he never went back to the name he jumped when he left Texas so long ago.

E. W. Whitcomb was killed, too, apparently by lightning on the Belle Fourche. In some ways old Pap was the saddest of the Invaders. After thirty years of sturdy life on the wild upper Platte and a record in such civic interests as relief for the blind and the dumb, he was sucked into the unhappy venture by his obligations to an outsider like John Clay. A foreign money slicker, Mrs. Whitcomb's Indian relatives called the outsider thirty years later.

Not that names broke any bones for John Clay. He had been called murderer by Mercer in the *Stock Growers Journal*—the murderer of Ray and Champion and, by inference, of all the others killed by men connected with Clay through employment and obligation. Mercer had included C. A. Campbell of Clay-Robinson in the Invasion as Clay's hired hand in the murders. Up in Buffalo they heard that as soon as Campbell got released he went after editor Mercer with his fists. Perhaps the rumor that the newspaperman had gathered up a book about the Invasion sharpened the Scotch-Canadian's need to defend his boys and his Scottish backers.

Campbell's death in 1896 was hastened, Clay believed.

by the rigors of the Invasion and the humiliation. By that time Clay had been fired from the management of the vast Swan holdings and his range boss, the William Booker of the Invasion, with him. There were rumors that this grew out of the deep involvement of his Scottish backers in the Johnson County War, which was denounced so energetically in much of the British press. Or perhaps it was because the venture failed.

Not that Clay left the ranch country. He had a genius for organization and management and even without the Swan Company there were the commission-house interests and other Scottish companies happy to keep him in the cattle business. Many years later, in his *My Life on the Range,* he spoke of the good he believed came out of the Invasion:

> Great reforms are brought about by revolutionary methods. The Boston Tea parties, the victories of Washington, were protests flung world-wide against a Teutonic dictator.

Even some of the Invaders still alive thought this a curious statement from one of his origins and his backing.

That other Scotsman, Red Angus, lived out a long and reasonably quiet life up in Buffalo, Johnson County, a town and county official almost all those years. Later the place of sheriff went to the son of Johnny Tisdale, only four years old when his father was shot in a gulch by the Canton who had said he would "take care of Tisdale."

But the hard times of 1893 brought even more settlers—

*CHAPTER IV*


# COW HORSE AND
# BETTING BLOOD


THE darkness upon Wyoming and the shadowing over
the entire range country the last few years had shut out
almost all fun, all sport, all gaiety. Yet there would be natural gaiety in a region that grew such long bones in its animals
as Wyoming did and brought such exuberance to the Sioux,
the mountain men, and the early traders and settlers along
the trails. Back eight, ten years ago there had been a kind of
transplanted foreign high spirits at the Cheyenne Club and
the larger of the British outfits like Frewens. The smaller
ranchers and the settlers had their native doings and dances
even with very few women in the country. The last five years
there were more girls, particularly the sisters and daughters
of the homesteaders, welcomed by the cowboys if not by
their employers. Yet the sound of laughter and the fiddle had
been mighty scarce, so scarce that the spies of the Invaders
around the KC spoke long of the fiddle they heard until
almost morning the day the shooting started—the fiddle that
was burned, too, before the day was gone.

All these years there had been more gaity over eastward, particularly in the Dakotas, with the Frenchies and the
breeds, and then all the Texans who came to the region that
lay like a curved hand from northwest Nebraska around east

of the Black Hills, with its roistering Deadwood, and up to the Little Missouri and the edge of Montana.

Most of the gatherings for fun were centered on the fiddle or the horse. Between roundups, fencing, and hay time there was an occasional Sunday off at one ranch or another, with perhaps a little get-together for some calf roping and bronc-riding—particularly outlaws and wild stuff that had never felt the rope and spur. Even at first there was usually a girl or two, maybe the foreman's daughter or perhaps outside friends come to sit on the pole corral watching the fight to the finish between man and a wild and infuriated horse.

"There ain't no horse what can't be rode; there ain't no man what can't be throwed," somebody would tell them, perhaps trying to hide the mouthful of ambeer, the girls perhaps exchanging looks, laughing a little, not understanding.

The Arbuckle Brothers, who later supplied the cow country with its coffee, had a private railroad car to haul out guests for their ranch down on Pole Creek, Wyoming. One summer the sister of William Force, the foreman, brought out a New York friend, who fell in love with the bronc riding of William and married him. Their daughter Madeleine became Mrs. John Jacob Astor, saved in the *Titanic* disaster in which her husband was lost.

Occasionally a man was crippled by a bronc, even killed, for with the rare opportunity to show off a little, chances were taken, the younger riders trying to outshine each other, perhaps climbing aboard an outlaw with only a hackamore, nothing to keep the horse from bogging his head between his knees and bucking until the tough mustang blood in him was done, nothing to hold him from crashing through the little pole corral and taking out across the prairie, perhaps over some cut bank or into a badland canyon. Maybe the bronc was ridden slick-headed or without saddle, too, only a rope tied around the middle, bucking and squealing to rid himself of this flapping, spur-heeled creature clinging like a cougar to his back.

Sometimes these ridings were made a part of the Fourth-of-July celebration, a soldiers' reunion, or the wedding of some French or breed rancher, which usually turned into a prolonged blowout for all the region. Back in 1887 Fred Dupree put on a real shindig for his daughter Marcella when she married D. F. Carlin. Fred was a French-Canadian trapper into the Dakota region in 1838. By 1887 he had an Indian wife and ten grown children and was running his Circle D with something like forty relatives living around him, Fred the only one who spoke understandable English, of a kind. For the ten days of the wedding he brought in four freight wagons of outside food—grub—two ten-gallon kegs of whisky, a cask of imported wine for the women, particularly the more delicate city guests, in addition to the barrels of wild-grape wine Fred made and liked. He had thirty fat beeves ready in the butchering lot and four young buffaloes out of the herd he raised from calves caught in the last great buffalo hunt on the Grand River. The barbecue pits were readied for the match, washboilers and tubs polished up for the coffee, stacks of roundup tin plates brought out, the tin cups hanging in rings strung on twine. Everybody within prairie notice—news on the wind—was welcome.

Fred's son Pete played the fiddle and Xavier the bull fiddle. They were spelled by relatives and friends and by other instruments, perhaps a cowboy's guitar, the sky pilot's folding organ, and a hammer harp from one of the Tennessee families over along the river. A couple of enthusiastic cowboys "borrowed" a piano to be hauled over in a hayrack before they were told how well provided with musical instruments the Dupree household was.

There was dancing every night and some afternoons, perhaps an old French dance or two by the visitors from St. Louis, somebody's aunt playing sad and stately little melodies on the mandolin. There were a few reels and a polka and so on, but mostly they danced square dances. The girls, particularly the breed and Indians, laughed and flirted, their feet flying. Many were very well dressed, willowy, svelte-waisted and pretty, the cowboys stomping their boot heels as they swung the girls and set their skirts to whirling. Over 100 whites and 500 Indians came to eat, dance, play poker, and race their horses for the ten days, while Fred, with other ranchers, looked on and made cattle plans and deals over their quiet pipes and cigars, their hands leisurely on the whiskies. Yes, Doug Carlin would make a man a fine son-in-law.

As the settlers pushed their farming westward they brought the trotting circuits, but in the cow country it was still the running race as it had been with the Indians ever since they got their hands on this great creature of the white man's. They were very partial to the hot race, the short run, whipping their fastest animals into a second wind before the start as they did for the war charge. When the army officers came to the frontier posts they brought the larger horse, often the thoroughbred, for the longer stretch.

To the cowboy his horse was the most important piece of his outfit. The lariat man needed a good roping horse, one fast enough to carry him up on a critter, strong enough to set against perhaps a four-year-old steer, a fat eight-year-old cow, or sometimes a grown horse, and bust any of them end over end as they went against the rope. He had to have a horse that held while he went down the manilla, one that kept facing the critter, taking up the slack, holding it while the man worked, steady, alert. Then at the slightest jerk of the hand on the rope the horse gave slack to release the noose. And finally the good roping horse stood for the man, even with an enraged Longhorn cow charging, to pick up the rider and carry him away.

Then there was the most valuable range animal, the cutting horse, short-coupled, fast, able to turn on a dime and give two bits' change. Such a horse, once shown a critter among a hundred or ten thousand, pursued him through all the herd if necessary, turning, cutting in here, heading off there, dashing, dodging, always on the tail of the animal, so swift in the changes of direction that he came out on the other side with the right critter, whether the rider was still with him or not.

Then, for roping or cutting, and no matter how full of buck on a frosty morning, the horse the cowboy had to have was one that never left him in a piece of bad luck on the range alone, when perhaps thrown by a running foot into a prairie-dog hole in a night stampede, or a bullet from ambush, or even when thrown during a surprise fright and bucking. The good horse stayed close by, came to the whistle, let the man pull himself up the stirrup even with a broken leg or stood over him as a signal for searchers if he was gut shot or broken clear to pieces.

The memory of such a horse has brought the swift stab of homesickness to many a wanderer half a world from the range country, perhaps brought even a little mistiness to time-hardened eyes.

But there was another horse deep in the affection of the cowboys, of the whole cattle region—the runner, the race horse. There were little race tracks scattered all over the cow country, to be stirred to dust by fast hoofs when the spring roundup was done. In the Dakota country this came when the sweetness of the sand lilies and the golden banner along the slopes had blown away, the swarms of white butterflies and the statelier orange and black ones, drawn by the metallic fragrance of the wild plum thickets, were gone. By then the spring calves, their brands peeling, romped on the hillsides, and the Shorthorn bulls and clean-faced Herefords walked ponderously among their cows or fought in the flats, their bellowing a fury in the air where so recently the buffaloes clashed with ground-shaking impact, and, farther south the great battles of the wild Longhorns sometimes ended in death. Now was the time, if ever, to bring on the fast horses.

One of the real gamblers in this competition of the horses was Jim Dahlman, who had traveled with some speed out of Texas under the name of Jim Murray, much as his father had left Germany back in the 1840's, except that Jim went North because he shot a man. His father, like the grandfather of Bob Kleberg who married Alice King of King's Kingdom, had left Germany for his liberal political views.

Although Dahlman worked as inspector and detective for the Wyoming Stock Growers Association in the Nebraska-South Dakota border region, he had a much greater fondness for a fast horse and a heavy bet than for running down rustlers of either cattle or land, or for pulling a gun on anybody.

In Dakota on this one point—fast horseflesh—the Texans, Frenchmen, breeds, and Sioux Indians were alike in their wild partisanship and their betting. Some of the hottest rivalries grew up around the Pine Ridge Reservation of South Dakota, in Dahlman's stomping grounds. He usually had at least one fast horse to run against the reservation stock which was mostly from Big Bat Pourier's tough old racing line or an occasional cross of thoroughbred blood that drifted in. Then Joe Larvie took a gray thoroughbred as his share in the town site of Hot Springs in the Black Hills and cleaned up on the best that the army posts around could put up, or Pine Ridge Reservation, and the ranchers, even those with imports from the British Isles.

In the meantime Jim Dahlman, down in Texas buying cattle, got his hands on a blood bay called Fiddler. He matched the horse all the way north from the Pecos and never lost. Fiddler became the pride of the dying cattle trail, and Dahlman picked up some good money from such outfits as the XIT and got part of the little that was left of I. P. Olive's fortune. At Ogallala and a dozen other places he took on every local pride. The blood bay's sudden bursts of speed were the talk of all the trail and of all the Texas cowboys around the tricorners of Wyoming, South Dakota, and Nebraska. They were both loyal, and gamblers, and put everything they had on Fiddler in a challenge to the Larvie Gray.

The Sioux hurried to back the Gray with money, blankets, beadwork, horses—everything. The Frenchmen of the region and the wealthy breeds were horse lovers, too, and laid their money down.

Cowboys from far beyond the region began to place bets, hoping to see a big run, particularly those from the Dakota ends of the Texas outfits like the Driskills, the Hashknife, Turkey Track, Flying V, and the old Chisum ranch hands who had followed the Jinglebob herd when it was sold north to Hunter and Evans—men like Johnny Riggs, sheriff of Sheridan County which butted up against the Pine Ridge Reservation, and Charley Nebo and others who had their natural bent indulged by the gay and wagering ways around the old French trader families and their Indian relatives. Some said even Doc Middleton, the outlaw, had money down, although it was more than likely, some thought, that his gang would try to sweep off both Fiddler and the Gray. Perhaps that would be a little daring even for Doc, with all the guns sure to be handy. Besides, to protect the cattle of the Sheridan County region from his outfit, Doc had been made deputy sheriff.

As the day of the race neared stories of Fiddler's great speed got around and the backers of the Larvie horse began to falter a little, think of ways to back out. Then Big Bat laid $1,000 in cash on the line for the Gray. Interest grew immediately, for Big Bat was a most knowing man when it came to the hind leg of a horse. Tension mounted between the Texans and the local boys, particularly the breeds, and the stakes grew, too, until it was plain that one side or the other would be cleaned out, stripped like a gully in a cloudburst.

Very confident until now, the Texans began to get a little uneasy over all the show of money and promised a bullet to the man who rode the Gray, first slyly, then in open threat, which only raised the betting ante. Buckskin Jack Russell, the Gray's trainer, was a cold-nerved Indian scout but with so many genuine sheriff dodgers in the region packing guns, he had to remember that he was a family man, and so he backed out. Now there were days of despair among the Indians and the breeds until Brady, a little cowboy with a good hand for a horse and an eye for one of Joe Larvie's handsome breed daughters, offered to ride the Gray. Threats scared him, but not enough.

The race was to be run at White Clay, Nebraska, just south of the Pine Ridge Reservation. The low flat had begun to fill up with campers a week ahead. Indians dropped the harness off their ponies down along the creek and while the women set up the smoky tents the men gathered in little knots and circles to talk horse. Ranch outfits came in with roundup wagons and camped, too, and small groups of soldiers from Robinson and Meade and farther away. Sporting women showed up and a couple of wagon saloons opened for business in addition to the regular ones at White Clay. Later comers poured in over the dusty summer prairie from Pine Ridge, the Black Hills, across the Badlands, and from the Niobrara, the Belle Fourche, and the Little Missouri.

The day of the race thousands of Indians moved in to the track before daylight, sitting up very close within touching distance of the stripped dirt route, with cowboys and ranchers coming later to line the track all the way. A good place up near the finish line had been staked out for the old carriage of Joe Larvie and his family, particularly his handsome daughters, including Nellie, who was married to Crazy Horse the short summer before he was killed, and the youngest one, showing her French blood in the pretty dark eyes that were made bolder by it. Yes, one could see why Tom Brady risked a bullet by riding the Larvie Gray.

The betting ground, covering two acres, was cluttered with horses of all kinds, saddles, rifles in circular stands, and a great deal of other cowboy stuff. There were Indian ponies, wagons, beadwork, and regalia at the base of the Sioux betting post. There was a pile of currency and promises of money and cattle weighted down by gold coins, about a dozen pistols, and a tangle of cartridge belts with holstered guns. Here the reservation people had thrown their wagers down in Indian fashion and were covered. There would be a fine haul for a Fly Speck Billy or a Dunc Blackburn, but only against the thousands of guns here on everybody, even the outlawed ones under the blankets of the Indians. A couple of sturdy, unmoving Indian police in thick, woolly uniforms stood by the betting post, and a handful of new deputy sheriffs wandered around, looking and talking important.

As race time neared, the shouting, the excitement, and the dust rose. Many of the horsebackers coming in were ranchers, a few with their women and girls, looking very ladylike in their sidesaddles, with so many Indian women astride and some settler wives, too, perhaps even riding bareback on a folded apron. The cowboys, too, pushed their horses in closer, a few with dark Indian faces. Here and there a horse started to kick, raising a flurry of return strikes and nippings, quieted by sharp cuts of the rein ends and muttered curses.

Then Dahlman rode out to a great cheering and a rousing Rebel yell as the shiny blood bay plowed quietly, daintily, through the great crowd of Indians pushing close to look him over. But almost at once they drew back, making swift little gestures of concern to each other, their immobile faces somehow darkening. There was a quiet sort of signaling relayed back through the people and then someone pushing, elbowing up slowly through the jam to the 600-yard straightaway course. It was Young Horse, whose family had been mustangers. He crowded through and out upon the track. There he dropped his blanket, looked all around along the narrow lane between the spectators. Then he squatted down and touched the racecourse with his hands, palms pressed into the soft dust, doing something that the watchers could not see. If he said any words, they were lost in the roar of ridicule and joking from the cowboys.

Slowly Young Horse rose and drew his dusty blanket

up about him. "Let the red horse run past here," he said to the Indians standing close as a wall. Then he edged sideways off between them and was gone.

When Brady came out on the Larvie horse a great whoop and the shrill Sioux woman's cry of approval went up from the Indians. The little cowboy touched his heavy quirt to his hat when he passed the Larvie girls. It was a fine sight, with the excitable gray rearing high against the bit, to come down faunching at the close rein that held him prancing, springy as a deer, the foam flying.

At the starting end Fiddler was quiet at his side of the track, well trained, an old-timer of many, many races. Jim Dahlman sat him confidently, his white hat down close over his nose as he always wore it, waiting. The gray broke several times, was called back, until finally they stood for one moment side by side. The gun cracked and Fiddler shot out, a full length ahead, to the thin, alarmed cries of the Indian women. But Brady whipped from the first jump, and the gray crept up through the heel dust to the flying tail, the flank, then to Dahlman's stirrup, the Indians whooping to see it. And when he reached the bay's neck, Fiddler just laid his ears back, lengthened his stride, and turned on that famous wild burst of speed for home.

But little Tom Brady had bet everything on the Gray, his cow horse, his whole outfit, even his gun, and by all this the girl he hoped to win. The quirt cut the gray hide as the rider whipped to both sides, Indian fashion, and the horse ran but was losing, so Brady leaned far over and gave the high, penetrating Sioux war cry into the horse's ear. He shot ahead now, coming up even, and so they ran, neck and neck in the whitish dust that was like fog, like fine winter snow flying, running so close together that one good buffalo robe would almost have covered both. They came like the wind, like that blizzard wind out of Dakota, and yet for all the spur and whip Brady could pour on, Fiddler was pulling away, only the width of a finger at first, then farther, a full length, both the Indians and the cowboys yelling.

Then Fiddler reached the place where Young Horse had touched the track. Suddenly he faltered, broke his rushing stride, shifted his gait, ran wide for a few jumps, the Indians falling back like grass before the wind, Dahlman cursing, setting his spurs, whipping the bay with the reins in his fury. In the meantime Brady cut the Gray with the butt of the quirt and the horse went ahead by a length, by two, running low, belly to the ground like a coyote fleeing scared. Dahlman, a matchless horseman, settled his darling of the Texas trail. Under the leather Fiddler exploded in a burst of speed such as the northerners had never seen before. It brought a great cheering from every horse lover there, but it was too late. The Larvie Gray was already past the finish, still stretched low, running far out into the valley of the White Clay before he could be stopped.

Jim Dahlman was back first, face grayish under the deep sunburn, hands shaking. He dismounted, loosened the cinches. To the angry, profane cowboys and ranchers who moved up around him he had only one foolish, feeble answer, one he said over and over: "Something happened, I don't know what. Fiddler quit for the first time—"

"Probably stepped in a gopher hole," one of the cowboys who never bet anyway suggested reasonably.

"That little buck probably sprinkled some Indian stuff other horses hate—"

By night the Indians had packed up everything in sight and retreated across the reservation line with it, before anybody could decide to reprieve his losses.

"Young Horse has made good medicine this day, very good horse medicine," they told each other, some smiling a little, as they clucked their ponies homeward.

Unfortunately Brady didn't get the girl after all. Seems she preferred the agency blacksmith who had never won such wealth for her mother's people or ridden such a race. But then she was a beauty in a land of few women, the people up around there said, their voices moderate.

The cattlemen had been accused of agitating for troops against the ghost-dancing Sioux in 1890, helping to bring on the killing of Sitting Bull and the massacre of Big Foot and his fleeing band at Wounded Knee. Certainly the alarming letters of some ranchers to their senators about the impending slaughter of settlers, some, in fact, already killed, helped bring those troops. Local correspondents for some New York papers sent in reports about blood flowing on the Indian frontier although their pieces were usually written in bars at Chadron or Rapid City, drinking cowman whisky. Some didn't know that not one Indian had left the reservation or that the whole essence of the ghost dance was one of non-violence. In the meantime, some of the timid settlers did pull out and the ranchers got more reservation range for less lease money out of the confusion and despair among the Sioux.

With the troops and the contractors that an Indian war always brought, there was even more interest in horse racing. This time Jim Dahlman helped work up a real man-and-animal killer: a 100-mile race around a five-mile route at Chadron. Once more the Texans, the French, and the Indians were excited, particularly the latter, when they heard of the first prize, $1,000 "for the best horse of the northwest" with $500 and $250 for the runners-up. Everybody knew the Indian horse was the toughest and certainly could come out the winner.

Good long-range horses were brought in from everywhere, to be grained and hardened on the long, dusty route. Cowboys shagging by stopped here and there along the track to lean over the saddle horn a while and watch. Soon, however, even the Texas cattle scarcely lifted their horned heads as riders whipped past without reining out after them.

Dahlman, turning an ear toward the young orator, William Jennings Bryan, had shifted from stock inspector for the Wyoming Association to a little ranching for himself, but mainly to the offices of sheriff and mayor at Chadron. Even so he was asked to put a horse into the long race, for the publicity. Why not run his bronco cow horse Baldy, just for the hell of it?

"I know Baldy's been out on pasture and grass-soft," one of Jim's cowboys said, "but nobody's ever wore him down."

Baldy was brought in. Dahlman ordered the rider to put the horse through the first fifteen miles in the short lope his mustang blood could hold so long. After an hour's rest he was to be put in again, rested, and run again, so through the 100 miles.

The race started at the little cow town, a whole long line of horsebackers, Indians, and breeds riding in it, too, and one Mexican. Some of the Texans shifted their bets to the Mexican. "White man rides a horse down, Indian gets on for another five, ten miles, Mexican sets fire to his tail and runs him ten, twenty more," they argued with each other.

The horses were a shaggy lot, some real broomtails but good enough to ride down. Dahlman's bald-faced red looked no better. The other horses started off in a hard run, and were whooped on when they came around and around, Dahlman's Baldy far behind, but dog-loping along, easy as though carrying a fence-line rider, with a fine, sunny day ahead of him. Before the twenty-mile round was done, three horses were out, two dead back on the track, it was claimed. After that they thinned out fast, Baldy the only one to finish the 100 miles and still going, grass belly and all, but pretty gaunted down. And when the Humane Society came in with warrants for everybody, twenty of the Sioux braves in regalia were hired to run a foot race down the Main Street. In the excitement and the crowding, pushing, everybody connected with the race got away.

Other towns saw that the race had brought business to Chadron, even in these hard-time years. Early in the spring a horse named Doc Middleton was taken up to Wyoming from Chadron, brought in casually as a "fancy buggy horse" and hid away at Charley Richards' ranch down at Bates Park, to harden and work out for the Fourth of July. Of course the news of Doc got out and some sports at Casper sent word to Jim Dahlman, at Chicago just then, for a better horse. He bought one called Sorrel John to be sent out a week ahead, with a professional jockey. Doc's backers went to take a look and came back with their chin whiskers dragging, scared. Charley only raised his bets on his horse but a lot of Sorrel John money went uncovered.

The Fourth came with a $500 purse and all the bets placed before the fast workouts of Sorrel John scared off any new money. Somebody hunted up a third horse who drew the outside of the roughly diamond-shaped track, with the Sorrel at the pole.

There were the usual false starts of the professional jockey until he got Sorrel John off to a ten-foot jump on Doc. At around 200 yards this was closing up, and it was neck and neck until the homestretch, where Doc drew away to win over the professional rider and the imported horse to a great whooping and roar.

Immediately Sorrel John's backers demanded a return race. This time Charley Richards put up all he had and could borrow, as did a lot of other ranchers and hands. Doc won again. Dahlman, with his usual sporting spirit, decided he would make up the $1,000 personal losses at the gaming tables that evening. He started at faro along about sunset and although the dealers worked in relays around the clock, Jim gave up at midnight, down almost $1,600. He took the train back to Chadron.

"That's what you get, betting against your own town," Charley Richards told him. "But we're always glad to take your money."

But now the biggest race of all came up: 1,000 miles, Chadron, Nebraska, to the Chicago World's Fair. The man behind it was John J. Maher, the hoaxer who, with his sensationalized accounts of the nonexistent Sioux uprising, helped bring on the Wounded Knee massacre. He made up the story of the great race, but it caught on so well over the country that Chadron businessmen felt trapped. Then Buffalo Bill Cody, at the fair with his Wild West Show, took it up. A combined purse of $1,500 was gathered. Photographers and newspapermen came out, and with a big crowd watching the ten riders started the relay run that was to be "The Greatest Horse Race of All Time," and surely "The Supreme Test of Man and Horseflesh!" Doc Middleton, the notorious but gentlemanly horse thief, was going along for the publicity and the fun. This time the Humane Society had men there from the start, mounted and ready to work the route in relays with the riders. Daily news dispatches were carried by the papers from points along the way. Two weeks after the start the first of the six riders checked in at Cody's Wild West Show, but he was disqualified, because, Chadron heard, he had studied the route too well ahead of time. The next man was accused of riding the cushions or at least the hard seat of a caboose after he reached the more civilized regions along in Iowa, his horse in the flatcar or something better. For a long time all anybody at Chadron knew was that Rattlesnake Pete, one of the two genuine cowboys in the race, was very late because his last horse gave out on him. Doc Middleton was also late. He turned out a real soft-bottom, openly riding the cushions, but then he only went for the trip.

The newspapers finally announced the prizes: the $500 from Cody's show divided among eight men, the top, $175, going to John Berry, $25 to Middleton, the $1,000 raised in Chadron went to seven men, Berry not in the money here at all, although Middleton got $75. There was general disgust, and if Chadron or the region had been inclined to much personal encounter, as say, in old No Man's Land or New Mexico, there would have been shooting and bloodshed. But Chadron took things a little easier, particularly on such a good conversational topic. The town got the publicity, but the real honor went to the western cow horse—standing up so well that even the Humane Society seemed pleased.

Yet when the dust of the big race settled it was clear that cattle prices had not halted their downward slide, the grass of the western ranges was still burning to brittleness and blowing away in the wind that tore at the bare snowless earth all the next winter, too. Soon there was very little laughter, not even around the Frenchmen of Dakota or towns like Chadron; scarcely anywhere from the Rio Grande to Calgary.

# CHAPTER V

# KINGS OF THE FENCED RANGE

THE prospect of eternal free grass had tolled investors as surely as the settler's corn patch drew the tamer range cattle, with less horn, and much less fear of a woman's high-pitched voice or her flapping skirts as she ran out to drive them off. Most of the larger ranch outfits of the north were very certain that they could keep homesteaders from their sacred domain, so certain that many never troubled to own an acre of their range, not even the ground on which their headquarters stood. Theodore Roosevelt, according to the assessment records at Medora, owned personal property there to the time of his Rough Riders, yet he never acquired title to the land under either the Maltese Cross or the Elkhorn's home buildings, bought in 1883-84.

In Texas the nesters, the grangers, had come early to all but the farthest, driest reaches, yet long before any cattle except work oxen on the trails stole one mouthful of grass from the buffalo herds, a few ranchers had seen wisdom in owning the grass for their cows. Not only Richard King, who began by buying up Spanish grants, and the XIT, but many others owned their range. True, this was easier in Texas, where the state-owned public domain was generally open to both lease and purchase in vast lots. Elsewhere government land was, in theory at least, intended for the home-less of the earth and parceled out to bona-fide settlers. But they came by the hundreds of thousands and cut so deep into the range that the cattlemen managed to obtain the Act of 1891 from what the settlers called a Robber Baron Washing-ton, repealing the pre-emption and the timber-claim filing. By limiting them to the homestead, to 160 acres, it seemed certain that on the higher, drier reaches of the cow country the landseeker must certainly sing with Frank Baker of west Kansas:

There's nothing will make a man hard and profane
Like starving to death on a government claim.

But many cattlemen soon regretted the Act of 1891, particularly with the collapse of the Johnson County Inva-sion that was to put the fear of God into settlers all over the Great Plains and restore the old open range. If the ranchers had to cover all their grass with filings, or even the land un-der their fence lines, it would have been much easier at 480 acres a throw than at 160.

Even in Texas, in the newer regions, there were often unsold school lands scattered through the private holdings, and these became a point of conflict when homeseekers be-gan to settle on them, as in the Spur ranch, the British-financed Esquela Land and Cattle Company of around half a million acres. It wasn't as big as Rhode Island and only a shirttail patch compared to the XIT's 5,000,000 acres in Texas and Montana but it had been described as a "handy," a convenient size to the foreign investors. Well fenced and organized, the managers kept extensive records for their company, including a diary giving much of the daily occur-rences, with such frank entries as, January 25, 1887: "Lo-max and Davis went down to see about firing out the set-tlers on the Catfish." It was customary procedure. The LX had been a rustler hangout while the shoe men, Bates and Beals ran it, managed by Bill Moore, who stole from every-body, apparently chiefly from his employers. Then in the mid-eighties the LX was sold to the Scottish Arkansas Valley Land and Cattle Company, a freehold of 204,000 acres, and controlling 700,000 fenced acres, which took armed protection to hold. They hired it, as did the neighboring LS, which had the notorious Ed King on the pay roll.

By 1896 the drouth and the panic prices put the managers of many cattle companies into a hole with the investors, particularly if foreign. It was easier to blame at least part of the ranch losses to thieves and the manager of the Spur was reporting that cattle rustling was a constant worry. Six school sections within the ranch pasture had apparently been filed on by settlers who were "living the land out." Because they had a legal right there it made a good layout for thieves, right in the midst of the Spur range, if the settlers were inclined to shield them, or take part. That there might be honest settlers among these trying to make a living was not mentioned at all, perhaps because the Spur manager had them all watched by known gunmen. Along in August one of the suspected men left, uneasy perhaps, or, as was admitted, perhaps for personal reasons. The ranch spies never managed to find anything against him.

A couple of years later there was good news to send to the home office. A suspected cow thief on the Catfish had been killed in a gun fight. "His sudden taking off has, I think, rather disconcerted some of our neighbors," Horsbrugh, the manager, reported tersely. Next year he hired a detective to add to "the famous Standifer" he already had on the pay roll and who was lately acquitted in the case in which he killed the worst thief "we had down at Clairemont last year." Besides, Standifer drove out the man that the Spur had tried to send to the penitentiary. Apparently encouraged by this, Horsbrugh hired additional range-riding help and a detective and then wrote the home office:

I am operating in the books an account to be called "Protection A-c" to which we will put the expenses thus caused by the employment of these extra men. The detective will have to be treated differently. Nobody knows about him. Will pay him through his Denver firm.

His connections with the Spur unknown, the man was to work himself into the confidences of the thieves and settlers while the known protection men, Standifer and Tynam, caused uneasiness among them. The stealing declined, and by 1899 two families of "well known thieves" moved out and others were looking to go. The Denver detective was not re-hired, but with more settlers pushing in on the strip of public domain down near the Catfish, the two protection men were kept on. Standifer, at least, also worked for the neighboring Matador, owned by a Scotch syndicate of which John Clay was a member, and working for them since the Swan Company fired him in 1896. These protection men did nothing but hide out at night, to watch, "and are prepared to act as occasion requires." Most of the settlers had dugouts in the scrub waste, the shinnery, and "can't make a living without stealing, so the moral effect of the two men known to be fearless and on the lookout is valuable."

But guarding against the rustlers and the equally unwelcome settlers became more difficult because the ranches couldn't depend on the ordinary cowhands for range protection any more. They were faithful, Horsbrugh said, but they wanted to keep on friendly terms with the settlers, and often rode far around to keep from seeing anything.

For all the alertness of the professionals, one man bedeviled the Spur from the early nineties until they finally bought his land in 1901. He had come in with thirty-five head of cattle and sold, the ranch management claimed, around 100 head a year. He must have cost the ranch $15,000, in addition to the time chargeable to the Protection A-c.

In 1903 Tynam quit, and the job went to Pinckney Higgins, one of the leaders of the Horrell-Higgins feud that scattered dead men all over the Lampasas region back in 1877. The Spur and the Matador hired the "two ostentatious gunmen to ride the range to strike terror into the hearts of the cow thieves." Pink Higgins soon proved that his reputation really shorted him. It seems he came upon a man who was preparing to skin one of the cows Pink was hired to protect. He shot the man, ripped the dead critter open from chin to tail and stuffed the man's body inside. Then he rode into town to tell the officers where they could find a real freak of nature—a cow giving birth to a man.

After that cattle thieving did seem to ease off a little on the Spur and the Matador range protected by Pink Higgins and the worn Winchester in his saddle boot. But this had been Standifer's stomping grounds for a long time, Standifer the boss, the top gun. Now this Pink came moving in on him with the old tricks of the days when the Olives and the Higginses were running things down around the Lampasas and San Gabriel rivers.

Eventually it came to a showdown between Standifer and the new man, with Standifer dead in the dust. For this the Spur dropped Higgins and hired a range inspector from the Northwest Texas Stock Raisers Association instead. But they were glad to have Higgins stay around as deputy sheriff, operating and planning with the new inspector. Early one fall morning the two men and a Spur cowboy along as witness appeared at a nester's little weaning pasture. They found a couple span of calves necked together and some others wearing heavy weaning yokes to keep them from reaching a teat. The settler was away, probably hiding off in the brush, Higgins said afterward, but a woman came running out, wiping her arms on her apron. In spite of her angry protests, the men stripped off the weaners, turned the calves out and drove them to the Spur cows they had previously located. One of the calves sucked.

Still the settler's wife claimed they were all her husband's property and that they must not drive off his stock. "At least wait till he's home," she insisted. Horsbrugh wrote about this case to the owners. The woman protested that she had been mistreated, but such people often make this charge. There was trouble getting convictions for a foreign company in the local courts here.

Some of the other settlers raised their voices against Pink Higgins, too. They claimed he was an old hand at planting sucking calves in a man's corral at night and then finding them, particularly when the settler's wife and family were alone. He was also good at sticking a settler's brand on a calf and then turning it up beside the Spur mother, either with witnesses around, or while ready for a fast draw, whichever came handiest if the outfit paying him for protection wasn't particular.

Anyway, Standifer was dead, and only a few recalled that the Nate Champion killed up in Wyoming by hired gunmen was a Standifer of Williamson County, too, on his mother's side.

As the range grew scarcer people outside of Wyoming began to stretch their necks like hungry cows looking toward the vast empires of grass owned or claimed by the foreign, the outside, companies—perhaps eastern but very many actually foreign, with the evils of absentee control.

"Where you gonna get at the man what's behind the one who pulls the trigger?" a settler asked bitterly after his neighbor down on the Catfish was killed.

It was the question asked a thousand times, particularly during the hanging of Averill and the Johnson County troubles. Was it the Cantons, the Hendersons, and Elliotts and the rising killer Tom Horn who were guilty, and the Britishers like Hesse, grown large as foremen for the strutting Frewens or similar outfits? Or was it the Scottish John Clay, American representative of a great Edinburgh financial group besides Wyoming rancher, Chicago commission man and president of the Wyoming Stock Growers Association and who had so many of his connections in the Johnson County invasion while he was safely and pleasantly touring Europe? Or were the Scottish owners behind him the guilty ones, the Lord of This and the Earl of That, with their great ancestral seats and the tradition and the actuality of defending them against the landless and the hungry for 1,000 years, holding them off with the justification of divine right.

Many asked such questions although very few in Texas knew of Clay's connections with the Matador, and most of those would not have believed that he could be aware of the professional killers on the pay roll. Clay was an honorable man, but so were all of them—those he represented, too —honorable and upright men who had learned long ago how to deal with the poachers upon their lands and their shooting. Men like the Farwells of the XIT had trouble understanding such attitudes and had stopped the hiring of two blatant range killers, even after the disastrous man-set fires a few years back. But the Farwells were from Chicago, and had power enough in their English company to have influence, too, with no nonsense about the divine right of anyone, man or beast.

"Time them goddamn foreign outfits quit shootin' down Americans," was heard in one wording or another around the bars and over sweaty plow handles and where roving range cattle were driven from a settler's corn by shouts and clods and perhaps cracked rock salt in a shotgun shell, later or by the more impatient buckshot.

"That's dangerous, shooting stock. The ranchers got a good excuse to come shooting back, even if it is your own land. You liefer kill a man's kids than his cows in this here country."

"They come shooting even faster if you take up a foot of their free range. What's a few cows compared to a quarter section of land?"

But that was still the cows, wasn't it?

It was also the range manager's business to make a good showing on his reports to investors sitting around their clubs in London, Edinburgh, or Dundee, men unable to grasp much of the principle behind the public domain and quicker to understand losses charged to rustlers than to hard times, drouth, or the cold and drifting of winter blizzards or the seldom-mentioned rank mismanagement.

"Yes, they couldn't know about the drifting off onto other ranges, and to other brands, maybe," settlers along the Catfish told each other. "You notice how many of the ranch managers turns up with good herds soon's they're shut of their jobs. Sometimes looks like the nesters and the rustlers're getting to be like the devil in the old hell-fire religions—mighty handy to lay the blame on."

Not that there weren't American ranchers who kept their own versions of the Protection Account, at least in their heads. Usually they did it less openly, their gunmen less conspicuous, often selected to shade off into the regular ranch hands. General John A. Logan, who had made such a remarkable career for himself with very little schooling or opportunity, had a valuable ranch in the American Valley of New Mexico. But by the early eighties the range was filling up with settlers that Logan claimed were depredating his stock, but really mainly his grass, taking it up right under the noses of his cows. Logan was a U. S. senator with higher ambitions, including the nomination for president, but he had to accept second place to Blaine. Even so he found time to move against the settlers and hired a long-hair named Courtright who had soldiered under him, served as police chief at Fort Worth, and then as marshal in the mining regions of New Mexico. Logan put him on as foreman but actually he was to rid the range of settlers. Although the law was on their side, Courtright sent word around, ordering them to get out. Two Frenchmen on a nice piece of watered bottoms seemed a little slow in moving and so Courtright and another gunman rode down that way. The Frenchies refused to leave their land and they stayed, two bullet-torn bodies on the ground.

The shooting stirred up an unreasonable amount of anger and noise, considering that the settlers were a couple of foreigners and the rancher a U. S. senator, more, a general very popular with the most powerful voting block—the G.A.R. But warrants were sworn out and talk passed around for the quicker rope, thrown over a tree someplace, the end fast to the horn, a spur set to the horse.

"Ain't no occasion to bother with a tree," a wind-burnt settler said loudly. "There's that good old Mexican drag I seen a time or two when I was punching cows down along the Brava—"

The killers quit the country, one heading straight for South America, Courtright following later. But he came back and ended up stopping a bullet when he tried the border shift.

One of the last regions tapped by the range-hungry cattlemen was one of the best—the sandhills of Nebraska, a great egg-shaped region blown in on an old lake bed. The sandhills were almost 250 miles long and from thirty to 100 miles across, with barely a rock and scarcely a tree—a fine, unbroken, long-grass country. Except for the narrow border of low chophills all around, the region was a series of high, generally grassed parallel ridges running southeastward, the tops of the highest wind-torn, sand flying from an occasional blowout, altogether like a great sea running, with here and there a crest to break. Many slopes were dotted with soapweeds, yuccas, and rippled in orange-tinged grasses to the protected valleys often hard land or down to the black dirt of the old lake bottom in broad hay flats, with around 1,000 lakes, all but the most westerly sweet water. These drew great clouds of ducks and geese, and the thin, twisting lines of migrating sand-hill cranes, and flocks of swan, snow-white on the dark blue water.

Altogether the sandhills were one great sponge. With no runoff water, every drop of moisture soaked in, to follow the shallow water table that formed the lakes, and, as the land fell away, seeped out in little veinings of clear, steady streams that grew and headed southeastward for the Platte.

Ranches had crept up the lower reaches of these streams even before the moccasin of the Indian was gone, followed by the Olives, determined to drive out the settlers already there, the Brighton Ranch, listed in 1885 as having 125,000 acres of government land fenced illegally, and a dozen others, crowded hard by the settlers.

Around the north of the sandhills, like a gently curving arm, lay the deep canyon of the Running Water, the Niobrara, swift, cutting its way along the hardland table across north Nebraska. Back in 1878 the protected river canyon drew two Texas outfits, the Newman Ranch, where Dahlman worked when he first came up from Texas, and Hunter and Evans, who had bought up Chisum's New Mexican herd and took on the trail hands who brought the cattle up, some of the men from the Lincoln County war, tough cowboys, tough in the saddle and with the rope and gun.

Everybody knew about the fine grass of the hills, belly deep and more, full of deer and antelope and drawing the regular fall migration of thousands of elk, but with the ridges and chophills so broken, it was difficult roundup country. Both Newman and Hunter put in line riders to turn stock back, but some always slipped past; some winter drifters never returned. Finally a cowboy, hunting strayed horses, returned with loud praise for the fine, fat mavericks he saw around some of the lakes. A wagon was sent out and several thousand head of stock rounded up, some branded, many of them slick, a few of the moss-horns with far Texas burnings, perhaps lost five, six years ago from some herds trailed through the hills to fill beef contracts at the Rosebud Indian Reservation. When the stock was brought up to the river, there was astonishment at the size and sleekness of the cattle. A few choice cars were made up and topped the Chicago market.

"That's cattle country, by God," Newman said, showing the returns of the shipment all around.

But with the railroad creeping up the survey not much farther from the Niobrara ranches than a good man could spit his ambeer into the wind, things looked bad for the future ranching here. The country would be crawling with grangers come spring. Then a great prairie fire driven by a powerful wind swept over most of Newman's range, leaving it blackened and smoldering a long time in the cow chips of the bedding grounds. The grass would come back next spring, yes, and in a few years even cover the knolls laid bare to the winds of winter, but the N— cows had to have range tomorrow, today. Newman threw the whole outfit on the trail and hit for his territory up in Montana.

Bartlett Richards was a dedicated man of this later period as surely as any of those who first felt the pull of the great herds of Longhorns running wild and free in the bottoms and breaks of Texas—men varying from Richard King to Print Olive, from Kit Carter to Chisum and Goodnight. Bartlett Richards of an old New England family came West as a youth of eighteen to the Wyoming of 1877, with the boom of gold in the nearby Black Hills and the final defeat of Crazy Horse and his Powder River Sioux. Within six years young Richards managed and controlled a dozen brands of various ownerships and financings, and over a range from the headwaters of the Little Powder, Donkey Creek, the Belle Fourche, to the upper reaches of the Niobrara and White rivers. The next year as president, with an older brother, DeForest, as vice-president, Bartlett Richards started a bank at Chadron, up in northwest Nebraska. He was apparently little disturbed that he was ordered to take down his illegal fences around almost 61,000 acres of government land within the Lakota Cattle Company holdings at the edge of Wyoming.

Two years later DeForest Richards, with carpetbag political experience in Alabama, was appointed treasurer of the new county at Chadron, and Jim Dahlman, of the race horses, the sheriff. By then Bartlett had ridden his range and looked down upon the piled carcasses of his cattle caught in the Big Die-Up. While many of his eastern and British

friends and ranch financiers, many members of the Wyoming
Stock Growers Association and the Cheyenne Club, were
leaving the country for good, Bartlett Richards decided he
would stick, but not without winter feed—hay. Unfortunately there was no hay worth a real crew on all his holdings, not even in wet years, and the few ranchers around him
with meadowland on their government range were prepared
to protect it against even Bartlett Richards with guns and all
the remaining power of the Wyoming Stock Growers Association, against all such expansion.

He noticed another thing along the fringes of his
Three Crow range, cattle dead all along, but some not from
the storm—from bullets, rifle and pistol, one place thirty
within a mile-and-a-half stretch. It was true that the ranch
herds drifted down upon the settlers, eating up a man's winter range saved for his own stock, even the ricks of hay put
up for the milk cow. They crowded into his little stable,
rubbed down his soddy, or fell into the dugout and endan-
gered his family. Yet Bartlett Richards was particularly
furious about this killing of his cattle because he had tried to
help some of these poorer families, even loaned them harness and horses for a bit of breaking to grow a little crop,
maybe beans, potatoes, or turnips for the children, in patches
of sod corn.

"Planning to get your place, by getting you in debt to
him," an earlier homesteader told a neighbor who was working with a Richards team. But there was little way of collecting from a poor man if the borrower decided not to pay up.
The homestead couldn't be mortgaged until proved up,
patented, and that took five years and could be put off to
seven.

Now, after the Die-Up, Bartlett Richards knew he
must have two things: range with hay flats, and freedom
from settlers. He went down to the Niobrara to look at the
region Newman left after the great fire, but there were settler soddies all over the hard-land table that was cut by the

black track of the railroad across the prairie. North was the Pine Ridge Reservation where Richards hoped to contract cattle, and Rosebud, too, over east. South, beyond the river, a scalloped gray-blue wall stood low against the sky. There he found long, empty stretches of rolling hills and beyond was the wet-valley region, with the hayflats he sought, lying between the parallel sandhills, valleys half to a mile wide, stretching no telling now how far eastward in the curious blue haze always over the sandhills. There was a scattering of cattle, some wild as the old brush poppers of the Trinity country, with several brands, but nothing that looked like fixed holdings of any size, and such as there were Richards felt could be taken over. With Cairnes, his young Irish partner, he started the Spade Ranch, the brand the ace of spades, hard to burn into anything else. If he thought of the superstition surrounding this card, the death card, he dismissed it. He looked over the fine sweep of grass, growing on thick mattings of old stuff, most of the range barely touched except by strips of prairie fire since the buffaloes vanished. Here he would restore his finances and those of his associates, British and American. For himself—well, a man could become a king here, the most powerful cattle king of all.

Bartlett Richards was the man for such a dream, with his smooth, womanish, even cherubic curve of cheek and the Mephistophelean turn of eye. In addition to his softheartedness for an individual in distress there was an arrogance and ruthlessness toward anyone in his way, whether a slow-footed cripple before his fiery driving team, settlers in number, or outside pressure from gossips of Cheyenne or Chadron, or governmental edicts.

"Highhanded as his foreign backers any day," a newspaperman from Chadron said. But he said it to his wife. No telling when he might need a loan at the Richards bank, and certain he would get it if he did.

With not enough timber in the sandhills for a fairsized cookhouse, Bartlett Richards moved some of the old Newman buildings from the river and sentimentally hauled a small log shack down from one of his western ranches pole by pole. His trading station was up the old trail, at Gordon, toward the Sioux reservations, but soon the Burlington cut through the south hills and he built a store, a hotel, and shipping pens at Ellsworth—the entire little cow town, except the depot and the water tower, the property of Richards and Cairnes. By then he had taken over several smaller ranches, just bought up their few shacky buildings and the cows running loose—no land. Even the Spade home ranch was on government land. He shipped in great herds of southern cattle to stock his spreading range and to fill his Indian beef contracts, with permission to hold up to 10,000 head on the reservation pastures until issued. By then the Spade, with several other brands, reached over and around the few holdings and settlers in the region from the Burlington railroad to the Niobrara and the White River, with very fluid herds, perhaps around 40,000 head or even toward 50,000. He had a big fencing crew, a hay foreman, a cow boss, and a stout bull pasture to hold his fine Hereford sires. His brother Jarvis, named for the distinguished family of their mother, was general manager, purchasing agent, and all-around utility man in charge of everything from windmills and mowers to hiring wolfers to clear out the gray wolves that pulled down yearling heifers in winter snow.

Bartlett Richards organized the ranch so he could spend much of his time at Chadron and around Cheyenne, to look after his other interests, including many sheep. Then suddenly, it seems, he did something that didn't surprise his neighbors at Chadron or up in Wyoming—he decided to marry his niece, the pretty and dashing daughter of his banker partner and brother, DeForest Richards. He left the quiet, religious Jarvis to run the sandhill holdings and went to Germany where they could marry. It heightened the gossip such romantic figures as Bartlett Richards always carry with them as a bright winter sun carries his sundogs. The Texans had hated DeForest as a carpetbagger and looked with scorn on the equality given the handsome young mu-

latto servant girl the Richards brought up from Alabama.
"Damn Yankee Nigger lovers," they complained of the
DeForest Richardses. Now the daughter was marrying her
uncle Bartlett.

"Well, if they are planning to set up a cattle dynasty,
Bartlett Richards's the man. He came here with down on
those pink cheeks twelve, fifteen years ago and now he's
running a good piece of Wyoming and Nebraska, probably
three times as big as his entire home state of New Hampshire
—banks and all—" the Chadron newspaperman said. "The
Ptolemies married their sisters, you know, and kept the
power in the family."

When Bartlett Richards returned from Europe, he
discovered that a lot of stock had vanished under Jarvis' easy-
going management. He flew into a cowman's fury and started
some real investigation, but when the trail got too close to the
Spade hired help, they pushed the blame off on some likely
settlers. With the county officials tools of the ranchers, prosecution would be easy.

But kings, even cattle kings, are impatient with
courts, and with the laws of others. Bartlett Richards knew of
the procedures worked out down at the Spur and the Matador and elsewhere, all individual action, with no unfor-
tunate public noise, nothing disturbing like the noxious
hangings and burnings. Perhaps it was a choice encouraged,
too, by the fact that, as Richards put it, Cleveland's gang was
back in Washington and that father of a bastard would surely
be calling the army out against the cattlemen if J. P. Morgan
and the hard times weren't keeping him so busy propping up
the U. S. Treasury. Probably be barking at the heels of the
ranchers as he was back in eighty-five, making all that stink
about the fences on the public domain, with even Bartlett's
own Lakota ranch plat spread out in the New York *Herald*
labeled "Illegal Fencing," for all his eastern relatives to see.
Not that it made any difference with the Richards backing or
credit rating. The cow business was above such gnat bitings.

Although Bartlett Richards was an honest man if an arrogant and ambitious one, he could see that a few swift killings over the remaining free land region could get the same results as dropping a few bullets into a herd of elk—scatter them in all directions, running in blind panic, but running. Although he was disturbed by the cattle losses while he was gone to Europe, the number of new settler shacks and soddies disturbed him even more. Many had strips of breaking that would certainly have grown corn if there had been any rain at all, and many were edging in upon his range, both in Wyoming and in Nebraska, some boldly homesteading on the best of his sandhill meadows.

Up in Wyoming the Swan company under Clay had brought in Tom Horn, the professional killer. Horn had been a good cowhand once, and a prize contest rider and roper, it seemed, but as Pinkerton range detective he learned the methods that Siringo* protested so emphatically as overbearing and illegal, even plain evidence fabricating. Horn found the Pinkerton methods restricting. Like being hobbled. "Killing men is my specialty," he always said when applying for jobs to be done. He proved so effective for the Swan outfit that John Clay made a personal friend of him and the Wyoming Stock Growers Association put him on the pay roll, some said unofficially.

For a while after Bartlett Richards brought his young bride back to Chadron the sandhills seemed very quiet, like the stillness before a storm, strange with so many refugees from the Johnson County war hidden out there, not only ranchers like Allen and his bodyguards but hired hands like Shonsey who showed up there a while and half-a-dozen others, but mostly these had seemed only the usual drifting of jobless cowhands in and out of the Spade region. Now, however, the regular cowboys began to stand away from some of the new men in the country, one of them Dave Tate, the Texas gunman who was making Richards' Spade Ranch his

* Chas. A. Siringo, *A Texas Cowboy or Fifteen Years on the Hurricane Deck of a Spanish Pony,* 1885, First edition.

headquarters. He wasn't as ladylike as some, nor soft-fingered, but he did no more cow work than his kind. He liked to hang around Gordon and other settler supply towns and shoot every cat that crossed his path, even some in store windows, his gun hand darting down and out, swift as a rattler.

Although the drouth and hard times of the early nineties were shaking all but the deepest-rooted settlers loose, to drift like tumbleweeds on the wind, many were tough enough to stick. These got warnings to quit the country. Here, too, they were called rustlers, some without as much as a milk cow to their names. But they believed the rains would come and a man could hope to make a living for the family. They would stay.

Then suddenly, in 1894, three of these stubborn ones were found dead, only a few weeks apart. The first one was Johnny Musfeldt, over west of the Spade. Warned to get out, he remained and was found dead at the plow on his wife's homestead. Tate, the cat killer from the Spade Ranch, was arrested, but turned loose for lack of evidence. Musfeldt's in-laws, the Greens, got warnings, too. Get out or be carried out. With Johnny dead they knew this was no bluff and they took the letters to Old Jules,* a lame-footed locator and surveyor who had been helping homeseekers get land. He had hunted the sandhills with the Indians, who called him Straight Eye, knew the hills like the breech of his gun before the cattlemen moved in. A few days after the Greens got their warning letters Old Jules rode in at the Spade Ranch on a horse conspicuously carrying the Green brand. He talked about hunting gray wolves and did a little long-distance target shooting when the ranch hands were around to watch. He was treated well at the Spade cookhouse, and the Greens stayed on, unmolested.

But by midsummer two more men were found dead, these over east in Cherry County, in the meadow region connected with the Richards holdings. One, Jason Cole, had

* Jules Sandoz. See *Old Jules.*

five years' residence on his three quarters of land—all patentable now. But he was a family man and started in Polled Angus cattle, including a registered sire, to build up a little herd of the handsome blacks. Plainly Cole had ambitions and would stay. So he was found shot off his mower, with no sign except the tracks of a saddle horse stopped beside the machine. Apparently it was someone Cole knew because there was a little pile of whittled weed stalks, as Jason Cole often made while visiting with an acquaintance. He was found dead beside the whittlings, a bullet in his head.

Cole's brother received threats, too, and, afraid of making more trouble for his brother's family, left his homestead and headed up to Wyoming. But Mrs. Cole and her two small sons stayed. Because the local officials seemed to make no effort to find the killer, she hired the Pinkertons but ran out of money. In the meantime, she may have discovered that they were supplying detectives all over the range country to spy on men the ranchers wanted driven out, and also what men like Siringo had to say about them. Anyway, she stuck with her land, although by that time Will Dunbar was found shot dead on his homestead, not far from the Cole place. Nothing was done about this either, and no telling how many more settlers or landseekers were left face down in the tall meadow grass or packed off into some blowout for the circling buzzards, although public discovery and shock were very important for their scare value.

Mrs. Cole stayed, knowing that a woman had been dragged away and hanged up at Bothwell, Wyoming, as recently as five years ago, and that some of the cattlemen behind that were also interested in the sandhill ranches. Besides, she had her two sons, four* and two, who must be protected as much as possible. But she stayed in spite of everything and apparently nobody was hanging women in the sandhills of Nebraska.

By this time curious rumors were sifting down from

* This son is State Senator D. J. Cole. The Jason Cole homestead is still in the family.

Wyoming, saying that Cole and Musfeldt had both worked for Bartlett Richards on one of his ranches up there before they homesteaded in the hills. Then somebody recalled that there were Coles in the Bothwell region back in 1889, and that one of them, Ralph Cole, saw the hanging of Averill and Cattle Kate, but disappeared, as all the witnesses had, to be followed by the killing of Henderson, after, some said, Ralph turned up so burnt that only his little bullet mold was left to identify the ashes.

Maybe it was just the commonness of the Cole name, with no relationship between Jason and the Thad Cole on the Johnson County dead list, either. Maybe the Coles referred to were the two settlers down in an isolated little flat of lower Cherry County, an unfriendly couple of men, who, it was said, had a tunnel out of their shack off into a washout full of brush. There were rumors plenty about them and the several names they used besides the Cole that slipped out on some legal papers, it seemed. One story called them the brothers of a man killed because he knew too much about the Wyoming cattle fights. One of the Nebraska brothers, it seemed, went up and cleaned out three of the killers but he fell with six, seven bullets in him and was left for dead. His brother slipped up and smuggled the apparently dead man out of Wyoming under a tarp, with cedar posts he cut in some canyon on government land ricked carefully around the wounded man. That was when the two first appeared in Cherry County, but nobody saw them much for a long, long time. Then, because lead is poisonous only when it is hot from powder, the brother recovered and got around, but he was always careful, always with the Winchester standing between his knees in the wagon, or across the saddle after he managed to pull himself up that high.

Some said that the uninjured brother was the man called Popsey or sometimes Copsey who worked as range boss for the Parmalee Company up across the South Dakota line. He was considered one of the best bronc busters in the country and sometimes he admitted he was an Englishman who had worked for an English syndicate in Wyoming back in the cattle wars and was hiding out around the sandhills since then. But that put him and his brother on the cattleman side, maybe avengers not of Cole or DeCory or the others ambushed by the cattlemen but of Wellman or maybe Henderson or someone like those men. Often the earlier story, that these men were really named Cole, cropped up again. Plainly nobody who knew the truth of all this was telling, and that left many to wonder where such hatreds and hunger for revenge might break out, or when, and on which side the guns would be barking. At least nobody among the settlers seemed to know.

By this time the pattern was coming out plainer elsewhere. A settler was a settler. Lewis, an Englishman, was found dead on his claim over in the Iron Mountain region, within forty, fifty miles of Cheyenne. He had been accused of rustling and warned to get out. He stayed and died, Tom Horn got the credit publicly and claimed it privately in letters as reference for further jobs. Even some Association members protested, embarrassed that a man like Horn was headquartering at the home of Clay, their president. Others complained that even if the rancher contention that no jury would convict a settler held true in some regions, Cheyenne, stronghold of the cattle interests, wasn't one of them, and if there was no evidence, Horn knew how to produce it, give the case a good natural look. But he preferred the clean ambush, with nobody shooting back. After a while most of the out-of-job cowboys hit for healthier country, and many settlers deserted their homesteads. In the meantime, as in the sandhills, it wasn't long until another man was shot not far from Lewis, near the Wyoming range of Allen's Standard Cattle Company, with Bartlett Richards connections. For that matter, they were also near the Boslers, who had a long reputation for hiring killers down along the North Platte in Nebraska.

Anyway, the one-armed settler, Fred Powell, had been too tough to scare out so he was picked off from ambush in plain sight of his hired man while cutting willows to make a hayrack. Afterward this man talked about his boss "taking in" company cattle, and while some suspected the hired man might be the killer, Tom Horn got, and welcomed, the credit. There was another story, too—that Powell, warned to get out, was hurrying to leave but was caught before he could escape. After all, he was worth Horn's regular $600 fee dead.

A brother of Powell's wife started to run the little place and was given three days to leave the country. He left, and once more Horn received congratulations, and no interference from the sheriff. By now his name was the terror of the Wyoming range and his appearance in a community scared out many, who, guilty or not, were fond of living.

But thievery didn't stop, not in Wyoming or in the other free-range regions, and so a few tried the law and got some convictions down in Nebraska. Dave Tate was still around the Spade Ranch, getting more arrogant every day, until finally he shot a man in the leg to get his saddle and then skipped out with it and a couple of horses, a six-shooter, spurs, and even five dollars from the bunkhouse. Now, at last, Bartlett Richards was angry enough to offer a reward for his gunman. He would not harbor a thief.

As cattle prices came back, rustling grew up again, particularly with war clouds rising over Cuba. Richards had a talk with the other ranchers who called themselves the vigilantes, but secretly, among themselves. The Nebraska Land and Feeding Company, Richards' new concern with William Comstock, an Englishman, instead of the Irishman Cairnes, grew out of the boom from the sinking of the *Maine* and what was called Hearst's war. Around the West many had known old George Hearst when he bought in on the Homestake Mine in the Black Hills and boosted the fortune that gave his son the newspaper power to promote the war. He also bought beef for the army, and if it was spoiled, that meant more "embalmed cow" had to be bought.

Then the dry gulching of McKinley from amongst a

forest of people brought Theodore Roosevelt, Rough Rider
and cowman from the Little Missouri into the presidency.
The cattlemen, from the Rio Grande across the Marias country, lifted their glasses to this piece of plain barefoot luck.
With a former rancher in the White House there would be a
new Golden Age of the Cow, and an end to the persecutions
by such cheap men as Sparks and his successors. The old feeling of power would be running strong as hell in the cattleman's arms once more.

By the end of 1901 they weren't so certain. Still it
seemed Teddy must be on their side and there were other
problems to take up their minds. Range in North Dakota
and southward was mighty scarce after another season of
drouth and prairie fires. Some cattlemen from north of the
White River had been down to the Rosebud Indian Reservation and found grass there, untouched grass, fine to winter on.
When the river froze over, they eased their stock over into
the Indian lands without sending so much as a horse wrangler to tell the agent or the Sioux. The government had a
fixed price for the range but with Teddy in it was only reasonable to assume very little money would actually have to
be paid. In addition to the deliberately moved cattle, the
winter storms drifted in more, some of them deep into Nebraska. By spring the earth was eaten bare and May 25,
when the Indians were beginning to butcher some cattle and
the grass of 1902 was well started up on their own ranges,
the largest spring roundup of the Dakotas was started in the
Rosebud country. Stock of sixteen large outfits was in there,
the 73 Ranch claiming around 30,000 head alone.

The roundup varied from twelve to sixteen wagons,
each with up to sixty men. Part of them started on the fifty-
mile front from along the Pine Ridge Reservation border,
going east, with a similar push of wagons heading westward
from the Missouri River breaks, to meet on a line with the
forks of the White. It was wide, rough country, but the cuts
and canyons were scoured for stock, the calves branded, the

cattle separated into day herds until too cumbersome. Then they were thrown north across the White River, the herds, held there until finished or too unwieldy, were trailed to their usual pasturage ahead of time. By the Fourth of July everybody was done and all his stock on his home range.

There were a few attempts to get some pay for the Indians for all the grass, the overgrazing, but nothing came of it. "Old Teddy knows grass is worthless until a cow sticks her nose down in it," a rancher said at the Association meeting that fall. "He's one of us."

But Washington rumors warned them that there were investigations of fences on government land, and the large cattle outfits hurried agents out to scratch like badgers to get the land under the fences covered by filings, if not deeded. Because old soldiers' and sailors' widows could apply the period of military service involved to the required five-year residence for a homestead patent, the ranch agents combed the pension rolls and scoured the country over, eager as quail dogs around a brush patch. For a small fee, usually most welcome to the poor pensioners, they filed on the land under the range fences, entries not "reasonably compact" as the law required but strung out into long strips of forties. The entries were from lists of names wherever possible, half-a-dozen hired fronts, elderly women, and men like old soldiers swearing to the filings where this extreme was necessary, some making dozens of entries.

Even if the homesteaders actually made the filings their oath that they had seen the land and intended to make their homes on it was false. "A mere formality," the personable agents assured the war widows who could understand the oath. "A formality like the 'obey' in the marriage ceremony."

These filings, mostly by people no nearer the land than perhaps Chicago, Philadelphia, or Boston, gave the ranchers a sort of legal rim or rind to their government range, at 160 acres a throw. And they were certain of one thing: none of these would come bobbing up wanting to live on their land for themselves, as happened with their cowboys so often.

In addition the cattlemen worked for a lease bill, giving them practically permanent hold on the public domain. It was announced that the Alliance, Nebraska, land district with the one adjoining, encompassing much of the sandhill region, contained 6,146,200 acres of government land under cattleman fences, pasturing 344,326 cattle valued at $8,575,350—without fetching one cent for the grass into the public till. Why not lease these grazing lands and help raise the revenue to run the government?

It was a good point, but it pleased none of the land hungry. "Legalizing their steals, shutting the homeseeker out forever," they said bitterly, and without hope, certain the bill would pass.

In the meantime Roosevelt's Secretary of the Interior was ordering the fences down. Really uneasy, cattlemen from everywhere hurried to Washington to flatter old Big Teeth a little, herd him into the bunch, back into it, they would assure the damn bunchquitter. Bartlett Richards headed the Nebraska delegation and worked for Wyoming, too. He was well fitted for the job, with his distinguished ancestral background that was certain to appeal to Roosevelt, and with real charm and grace of approach when it suited him. But as one rancher reported after their untriumphant return, all they got from Roosevelt was, "Gentlemen, the fences will come down."

When the land lease bill passed Congress, there was celebrating from Chicago to the Oregon coast, and in London and Edinburgh. For that one night the fine blowout at Cheyenne reminded some of the gay days when the pretty young bachelors ran the Cheyenne Club. But only a little. Most of the cowmen celebrating in Cheyenne now were tough as old range bulls.

It was as well that they were, for Roosevelt vetoed the lease bill and already had Colonel Mosby, the famous Rebel cavalry leader turned Republican out smelling around for illegal land practices in Nebraska. Mosby's appointment infuriated both the Texans up North and the northerners. "I sure want to see DeForest Richards' face when that turncoat Mosby starts working on that carpetbagger," a Texan who left the south in sixty-seven wrote to a friend. Many of the cattlemen still tried to believe that this was all just Roosevelt's shrewd New York-style politics, to fool the little voter and get a strong Republican Congress re-elected, but the belief came harder.

In the meantime, there was a reminder from Washington that it was illegal to enclose government land. Every foot of the public domain must be fenced *out* of a rancher's pasture. Over in Colorado Jarvis Richards was in trouble for including the alternate government sections in his stretch of railroad lands within his fence line. There were rumors that down in New Mexico the Interstate Land and Cattle Company, with Charlie Goodnight an owner, was seeking an extension of time, due to the vast improvements, to get their fences down from the 3,000,000 acres that they controlled, some said 30,000,000—a bit of tall tale.

Bartlett Richards, the Nebraska cattle king, had been ordered to remove his fences from around sixty townships of government land in the sandhills, over 1,000,000 acres. But the same order had hit the older outfits back in the mid-eighties, the homeseekers counseled by the Secretary of the Interior to cut any wire barring them from free land they wished to homestead. Proceedings were started then against such barbed-wire kingdoms as the Swan, with 130 miles of illegal fencing and Bartlett Richards, with forty-two miles of such fence around the government land inside his little Three Crow Branch, up the Niobrara. Back then some of the cattlemen had rolled up their wire and got their blooded stock mixed with scrub bulls. But working together they forced Sparks' removal and eventually got rid of Cleveland, too, even though he made a return but with his tushes considerably dulled and his land crusade forgotten.

Somehow it didn't work out that way with Four-Eyes Roosevelt. While he was damned as a renegade by both his class and his fellow ranchers—a bunch quitter, Mosby's wire cutters were out. From the Omaha Commercial Club west and New Mexico north protests and resolutions hit Washington like a blizzard sweeping in from the Dakotas. Suddenly all the cattleman organizations and the newspapers they controlled, the cow companies and the individual ranchers, rose in benevolent concern for the settler and the public. The cattlemen were making their government land produce all that could be expected, and to interfere with them would be harmful to the whole country, cutting down on the feeders to eat up the vastly increased corn crop of the Middle West, raising meat prices for the poor man, losing the rancher's tax money. Further, it was criminal to encourage a poor man to take his family out to the government lands, where every foot available for farming in ordinary seasons was under cultivation. Even the most elaborate systems of reclamation would be useless in such places as the sandhills of Nebraska, for it was patently impossible to irrigate a wilderness of sand heaps. Let the government call in its men with the wire nippers. Help keep the poor settler from starving to death on a government claim.

In December of 1902 there was a rising optimism in the range press. Mosby had blown a loud blast and it had died away in the wide-open spaces. The fraudulent filings by war widows existed largely in the colonel's imagination. In the meantime, the land lease bill was to be resubmitted to Congress and in the bust of Roosevelt's pet persecutor of the cattlemen it could be passed over his veto, if he dared another veto.

But where the fences had been removed the cattle were mixing hopelessly and drifting, the settlers and small outfits helping themselves to the beef gathered around their places, and to calves, with no Dave Tate and no Tom Horn to shoot them down.

In fact, Horn was in trouble with the law at last, perhaps due to the Roosevelt cloud over the whole range country. He was arrested for shooting a sheepman's son, a boy, although a neighboring cattleman was arrested, too, and then turned loose.

Tom Horn had been over in the Browns Park country, which rode the Colorado-Wyoming line like a jay bird on a fence. Operating there as Tom Hicks, he killed Rash, the president of the Browns Park Cattle Association, a Texan in the region since the middle eighties and generally respected. Rash owned around 700 cattle and no one claimed that he stole one head of the lot, but the cattle baron of the region wanted the Park cleared of the small ranchers, so the top man, the leader, was shot. Perhaps because Horn liked to work by twos, he also killed Rash's Negro cowboy, one of the best cowhands in the country.

An angry Colorado posse intercepted Horn before he got away. He wounded one of them mortally but was knifed himself. As soon as he was up and riding again he was back at work without opposition until the Nickell boy was killed, apparently by mistake because he was riding his father's horse. This got Horn to jail, but money poured in for his defense, perhaps to keep his mouth shut during this Roosevelt Inquisition, when evidence of any intimidation of settlers, let alone murder, might make things mighty hot for the cattlemen already in trouble over the fences and the fraudulent land filings.

Horn was loyal and for this and perhaps as a special precaution he was helped to escape. Recaptured, it was said he confessed to all the known killings, including the Nickell boy's. Some said Joe LeFors, a stock detective, got the confession; others pointed to Phil DuFran, somehow always involved, whether it was a man burning by the Olives, the Johnson County Invasion, or now this hired murderer. Apparently Tom Horn implicated no one directly except the Bosler outfit in any of the killings, and the Boslers only in the deaths of Powell and Lewis over near Iron Mountain. It was estimated that more than $100,000 was spent for Horn's defense. Many ranchers testified as character witnesses for him, including John Clay, who said Tom had headquartered with him for years, as everyone had noticed.

In 1903 Tom Horn was hanged, an ironic end for a man who, a few months earlier, needed only to be seen riding through a region to drive almost any settler out, whether accused of rustling or not. Three had left their homesteads up in the north Laramie River country in one week because Tom Horn had been up that way.

By now changes were coming upon the Richards cattle and banking empire, with sheep, too, up in Wyoming. De-Forest Richards, governor of Wyoming, died in the spring of 1903 leaving sheep and banking interests to his children and so to Bartlett, with plans to move some of the sheep down to the Niobrara River north of the Spade, under Paul Richards, a relative.

Bartlett's efforts to build up his herds in the long grass of the sandhills were beginning to show. The Spade won the silver cup for the finest carload of Hereford range yearlings at the Kansas City Stock Show in 1903. It brought newspaper praise and editorials regretting the persecution of men working so hard to improve the American beef stock. But the Spade, characterized now as a fine, quiet place, the range hospitable to any settler who wanted to come looking for a homestead, had a nice murder on its hands. Nothing as clean as a gunman's bullet. Wofford crept up behind a man called by such names as Cummins and Reinhart, hit him on the head with a club, and rode off. Cummins died, a sheriff beat a mob to Wofford, and Bartlett Richards spent good money to put the murderer into the pen, although the two men were now characterized as mere tramps hanging around his ranch.

Then, June 28, 1904, the Kinkaid Act went into effect in certain regions, particularly in the sandhills of Nebraska. It permitted every bona-fide homesteader to take up 640 acres of land. If the settler had received a 160-acre homestead in the past, he could enter 480 now, the new homestead requiring five-year residence and $800 in improvements

Ostensibly intended for the great flood of landseekers pouring in from all the world, actually the cattlemen took advantage of the Kinkaid Act to cover their range, at least any land that a settler might want. Strung out in forties, a section could automatically cut the heart out of four miles of meadowland or put a legal floor under four miles of wire fence, at least until further investigations, and surely Roosevelt wouldn't be in the White House forever. So the agents of the cattlemen wrote out bushel baskets of Kinkaid filing papers and had them ready behind the land office windows for prior entry on opening day. With the fences down, locators and surveyors plodded over the prairie with landseekers, hunting out the government corners obliterated long ago, intentionally, or trampled down by the cattle, the wooden stakes buried in the holes or burnt by prairie fires. Each region had its locators and surveyors, perhaps combinations of the two. In the western reaches of the Spade Ranch Old Jules Sandoz, who had come shooting target practice there after the Musfeldt murder, was one of these. He had hunted deer with the Indians all over the sandhills and remembered where many corners, even the carefully destroyed ones, were and knew about some of the cattleman tricks, such as burying old mower wheels or other massive iron nearby to throw the compass needle off. He had the ability and the patience to line up the probable site of a corner and then to skin off vast areas of the sod to find the rings that showed where the section holes had been.

Weeks before the Kinkaid opening, landseekers went to camp around the land office towns and began to line up before the windows days ahead. War veterans came in their old uniforms and received priority to the land, the old bonus practice established almost before the guns of the Revolution had cooled.

There was great settler disappointment because even the first one to the window on opening day found all the good land already covered. "Fraudulent cattleman filings," Old Jules told his homeseekers. "We'll protest the entries, contest those we have to. We'll kick until we get a good investigation going."

But there were some who still considered bucking the cattlemen dangerous and tried to warn him, and members of his family, as other fighting locaters were warned.

Dozens of cattlemen were haled into court in the "Roosevelt Roundup" over the range country, from New Mexico up across the last reaches of North Dakota. The Wyoming contingent included several men in the Johnson County Invasion and A. J. Bothwell of the Averill-Cattle Kate hanging. They spent twenty-four hours in the custody of the sheriff and were fined $500 each.

All the cow country was aroused at the thought of this renegade Roosevelt. The settlers were furious, too. Five hundred dollars for stealing whole empires of the public domain and holding them by the mercenaries of empires? They met in groups to protest the land lease bill, always up in another form for passage, signed petitions, fired hot letters to the papers and to Washington. Jim Averill had died for writing such letters but perhaps those days were past.

November, 1905, Bartlett Richards and his partner, Will G. Comstock, were brought to trial for illegal fencing of public lands. At the trial last June they had said they would show in the fall court that they had never seen the land, knew nothing about it, and leave it up to the government to prove by surveys in the vast region of obliterated land corners that they had broken the law. But the surveyors worked all summer under the protection of Secret Service men and the ranchers dared not interfere. By fall Richards and Comstock pleaded guilty of fencing 212,000 acres of government land and because they had taken down most of their wire, and were saved the charge of intimidating settlers that others like the Krauses faced, they were fined $300 apiece and given six hours in the custody of their attorneys in Omaha. It was a not-unpleasant interlude, with a great champagne dinner and toasts, and promises of a great future for the cow in the sandhills.

"A farce!" the newspapers cried, including many who had backed the lease bill and, until now, most of the cattleman actions. Such ranchers as Richards and Comstock, they reminded their readers, could pay such a fine every day of the year. The small fellow who had a quarter section of free land inside his fence would have been hit for the limit and given perhaps months in jail. "Don't steal a quarter of sand hills, but gobble up the entire country," the *Rushville Standard* told its readers.

Roosevelt blew up like a North Dakota thunderhead when he discovered what had been done in Omaha, on top of the light punishments drawn elsewhere. The settlers heard that he got U.S. Marshal Mathews fired for letting the men spend their custody time at their club, decapitated U.S. District Attorney Baxter for insufficient vigor in the prosecution, and was furious that he couldn't touch the federal judge, appointed for life. He rounded up a whole herd of ranchers and their agents and got indictments against them for conspiring to defraud the government out of vast tracts of public domain and for subornation of perjury. Bartlett Richards and his family were in Europe and newspapers carried rumors that he had sworn allegiance to the Kaiser to save his skin. Apparently the rancher hadn't considered indictment possible, but the fact that their confidential land agents were included looked bad. Special agents of the land office, under the constant protection of the Secret Service, sought out the extent of the Spade range.

Hundreds of witnesses were scared up all over the country. The trial lasted a month, the jury took less than three hours, including time for lunch, to return a verdict of guilty. In March the sentence was pronounced: Richards and Comstock fined $1,500 each and one year in jail. Lesser officers and employees of the Nebraska Land and Feeding Company received smaller fines and sentences. Now the appeals began. In May, 1908, the U.S. Circuit Court of Appeals acted, sustaining the lower court on most counts, charging the nine men involved with securing sixty-three men and women to make fictitious homestead filings and conspiring to induce these sixty-three to perjure themselves in swearing falsely to the papers filed at the land offices.

"Sixty-three!" some of those who passed the newspapers around at the Spade post office exclaimed. "Hundreds and hundreds!" the settlers said openly, bold as breachy cows in a corn patch now.

But the time of the hired killer was not past. Midsummer one rode into the yard where Emile Sandoz, brother of Old Jules, the locator, was milking his cow and in the presence of his wife and seven children shot the settler down. There was no rumor of cattle rustling, only a flimsy story that Emile had talked about the character of one of the girls at the local road ranch. As soon as the news of the shooting spread, neighbors warned that this was only an attempt to get Old Jules into a gun fight and kill him.

The locator was away in the Spade range with some homeseekers and had no news of the murder for a week. By then the sheriff had been forced to make some move and the killer had to leave the country to avoid arrest. But another one came riding up through Old Jules' orchard and around the corner of the house, hand on holster, to find the locator in the doorway, his rifle up. The gunman didn't draw, and after a long moment he set spur to his horse and was gone.

The Woodmen got a conviction for the killing of their lodge member, Emile Sandoz, but only manslaughter. It was, however, the first conviction of such a killer in all the region.

The winter of 1909-10 was a long, snowbound one. The cold bit the lungs, made thawing ears stand out stiff and purple, and froze fingers and toes. Most of the big cattlemen were in Florida or the more fashionable California, Bartlett Richards among these, waiting out another appeal. But back on the northern ranges no one had hay enough to last, and the Spade, with a lot of southern cattle, was hit very hard. Much of the imported stock was too winter green even to smell out the deep drifts but walked or staggered straight into them on the level flats, and died there in the bright, revealing sun. The feed hands, with no hay left to shovel, had time to skin the carcasses as the snow thawed off. It wasn't a winter like the Big Die-Up but neither were the times like the 1880's. Richards and Comstock felt the loss deeply.

All spring the Kinkaiders realized it, too, and complained to the state Board of Health about the stench and the flies from the range cattle that had drifted up around their soddies of board shacks and died there. By June the Spade had contracted summer range at thirty-five cents each for 10,000 head in the new government reserve for forestry experimentation down along the railroad. This was to take the place of the land the settlers occupied now, most of the ranch's summer pasture. As soon as the cattle were moved the Spade laid off all the regular hands except the cowpunchers. "The beginning of the end," the newspapers predicted.

By the fall of 1910 almost every section in the sandhills had a settler on it, and little except the correction-line strips and the roughest chophills remained public domain. Now, finally, the Spade was paying for all its grass and hay, mostly leased from the settlers—those who lacked the cattle to eat it up—and buying out as many of them as possible as fast as the patents came through. Many got in debt at the store, through Richards' liberal policy of groceries on tick, on time, but many Kinkaiders were staying, too many, and going into stock farming despite all the discouraging talk around the ranches. They planted corn and rye and alfalfa, put up wild hay, raised cattle and hogs and chickens and turkeys. They stayed, far too many of them.

The land-fraud cases were refused review by the Supreme Court and Bartlett Richards and Will Comstock had to come to their sentence as others had all over the cow country, and even some horse ranchers, too, such as the Huidekopers of the Little Missouri River, one of the few ranch outfits of any kind up in that region with much public domain enclosed. They fought hard, depending upon their old ranching assocation in the Badlands Country with Roosevelt, and on Senator Boies Penrose from their home state of Pennsylvania. But they got no further than men like Senators Carey and Warren did. Although their enclosure of public lands was only about 21,000 acres, the Huidekopers were fined $1,000 each and their manager, who tried to bribe the special agent of the land office, was hit for $300. Not that others didn't offer bribes, too. Perhaps that was why the manager got off cheap. In addition to the fines all three men were given twenty-four hours in the county jail "or its equivalent," as the settlers around there called it. By then the ranch was sold to Pabst of Milwaukee for around $300,000. Later a cousin, Wallis Huidekoper, made a fine record as breeder of Herefords over in Montana and sponsored the development of improved stock growing past the middle 1950's.

Wibaux, the Frenchman who had made money up near the Badland region from the Frewen stock that was hardy enough to survive the Die-Up, had disposed of his stock cattle back in 1902 when he saw the settlers swarm in thick. He had been an adventurous figure in the cattle business, a fine-looking man, boxer and fencer, driving handsome trotters, with a house that contained ten rooms on the ground floor alone. His wife was from an artistic English family, regal and charming, but very democratic and idealistic. A handsome figure on her spirited horse, she reminded many of that other handsome woman of the north, the auburn-haired wife of the Marquis de Mores and also of Cornelia Adair down in the Palo Duro country thirty years ago, sturdy, elegant, and handsome after many days side-saddling through the Texas Panhandle to a ranch in the wild new country. Later women ran ranches of fine blooded stock, kept the pedigrees straight, built up the blood lines, managed the hired help as well as the publicity becoming as necessary in ranching as mere meat production.

But there was no old cowman who wouldn't doff his Stetson to the memory of the early beauties of the cattle country, and then to those other women, too, the hardy resolute fighters against the wilderness and Indians and loneliness, perhaps thirty, forty miles from a neighbor. Sometimes they bore their children alone, nursed them in sickness alone, even buried them with none to stand by their sides, for the men were so often far away, on the trail, chasing Indians or fighting rustlers. But perhaps none endured a travail equal to that of the wives left behind by the Johnson County Invaders, some coming to the gradual realization of the deeper power that drew so many of their men to the futile crusade, a realization that came very slowly, for the women had no need of such identification.

Nor was the long battle with the government over the range upon which the cow walked easy for the women. The wives of Richards and Comstock must have been weary long before the men had to admit defeat. They had fought Roosevelt, the former cattleman turned avenger, and went to jail under Taft, the former lawyer turned golf player. They and their associates were permitted one concession Old Four Eyes might not have tolerated. They were given a choice of institutions and picked the county jail at Hastings, Nebraska, instead of the state penitentiary. There, according to the newspapers, they lived in luxury that they brought with them: expensive rugs and lace curtains; a well-rounded library; the daily papers and all the magazines they wanted; a pantry well stocked with choice foods and beverages; and a Japanese cook. Cartoons showed them living on the fat of the land—like the millionaires they had been for years. The *New York Times* said: "palatial quarters were allotted to them" where they had frequent banquets.

Whatever the truth in all these stories, Mrs. Comstock did move to Hastings to be near her husband and his jailmates, but Bartlett Richards would not permit his mother, his wife, or his children to see him a prisoner. Even his enemies were saddened by this, and a little proud of him, too. It was true that many settlers, particularly those who had suffered from the Spade of the early days, took these changes gleefully. The ranch postmaster, the storekeeper, and the cowhands kept their mouths shut, unless they were hired settlers, as many were. Even Marquard Petersen, the foreman, had little to say although, having discovered that the home ranch of the Spade was on government land, he had homesteaded it, buildings and all. When the owners tried to fire him, he threw this in their faces. They couldn't fire him or even put him off the ranch. He was on his homestead, in legal residence, and they could get the hell off any time they didn't like what he did, but they were leaving everything that stood on his land there.

Even some of the earlier settlers looked around the shrinking ranch, the shabby, rundown place it had become, with the loafing cowboys, the haphazard way of the fence, and windmill riders, the hay crews, and were saddened by the fall of the cattle empire. Many of the Kinkaiders had been living on Spade groceries, against their land lease and final sale when the patents came. Some skipped out, selling their land elsewhere, or stayed and dared the ranch, with the owners in the pen, to sue a settler. Suddenly it was the cattle kings who had no rights.

Toward spring Bartlett Richards discovered that the managers of their Wyoming holdings were going bad with whisky. His health was reported as poor; the jail, without a prison yard, was too confining. His first application for a pardon never got to the President and on advice from the Department of Justice he refused to discuss the matter at all, it was said. His mother saw this in the papers and against his orders went to spend some time with him. In June, Bartlett Richards got permission to go to Mayos' for an operation although many pointed out that lesser prisoners had to be content with what Nebraska offered. Up at Rochester a deputy U.S. marshal was stationed outside of his hospital door as with a dangerous, an ordinary criminal. The operation evidently didn't help much. At least he still complained of phlebitis. Six weeks after his return to the Hastings jail, it was reported that Bartlett Richards was rushed to the hospital with a gallstone attack and died, some said on the way, others soon after he arrived.

But there was no doubt that Bartlett Richards was dead, died September 5, 1911, one month short of his release —at fifty-two, with thirty-four of those years spent in the cattle business.

It was the end of a latter-day dedicated man—and the end of the cow held above the law.

# BOOK V

*BEEF FACTORIES*
*AND FESTIVALS*

# CHAPTER I

## *NEW  BREED —*

NOW the free-range days were surely done, and the dedicated men gone. A few old-timers hung on as buggy bosses, perhaps in the new gas buggy to make their rounds, with a couple of young mechanics to help push the city automobile out of the sand or off rocks and high centers. Even Charlie Goodnight had moved to town and up in Montana Granville Stuart, the grand old man of the cow business in the North, was puttering his time away as librarian of the city of Butte.

The old brush poppers were mostly gone, too, although an occasional stove-up old-timer still limped around the livery stables of the cow towns and was surly with the dudes awkward in their cheap slant-heeled boots and fancy shirts asking for "a cowboy horse to ride out," but looking uneasy even after they got a grip on the horn, the reins sagging.

It was a sad passing of the cattlemen who considered paying for the grass an indignity, an affront to their cows. Most of them knew they were dealt out when the settlers began to overrun the country, even many who hired range protection, or went broke defending themselves against the federal government, the invading government as they saw it, come claiming land that their stock, their cows had walked on for years.

But if the range had to be bought, taxed as deeded land, then ranching became a hard business profession, worse—no better than rooting a living out of the sod, or working on the railroad or mining coal. Every acre would have to produce the most meat possible, for the highest price. The northerners always claimed, and the southerners agreed at least tacitly by taking their stock north to finish out, that their range grew more beef, of finer quality, brighter in color and with the fat finely laced through the meat, making it more flavorsome, juicier, tenderer, and from better grade of stock in the first place. To be sure, the pastures of the South, if not actually lush and green all winter, were at least grazable. There was no call for hay and feeding crews, and no real winter loss of growth and weight, almost no loss of actual stock even among the new calves.

But the South did need a better strain of cattle, one free of tick fever and other insect invasions.

Frequent dipping was found to be one preventive of ticks as well as the spreading scabies, itch, but not if the neighbors were neglectful. The solution, if there was one, would probably come through an immune stock, perhaps by crossing with the coastal Longhorn, who managed to live with the tick. Unfortunately, when enough beefy blood for good meat was added, the immunity vanished. The first effective crosses came from the Brahmans of India. These cattle had been brought into South Carolina back in 1849 and only later were found fever-immune and fitted to heat, humid or desert dry—a tough stock but tough-meated. Long and imaginative experimentation was carried out on the King Ranch. The captain's great trail herds once spread ticks and hatred all the way North and even brought him and Goodnight, that other towering figure of the early Texas cattle period, into open conflict. Out of the opposition to King's bulldozing of settlers and stock growers along the trails came the need and the determination that eventually made a great experimental laboratory as well as a great beef factory of the modern King Ranch under the Klebergs, who worked in a fine racing stud, too, and an oil kingdom.

This first purely American breed, the Santa Gertrudis, named for the original location of the King headquarters, originated in the cross of the Brahman and the heavy, tender-meated, but tick-susceptible Shorthorn, fixed by patient and calculated breeding to carry much of the heat and disease resistance of the Brahman with a little of the distinguishing hump. Added to this was much breadth and bulk of good eating meat from the Shorthorn.

Kleberg put the first Santa Gertrudis bulls up for sale in 1950. Since then herds of the blood had spread around the world. A steer will grow big and grass-fat on an acre of good hot-climate forage, such as, say, the pasture lands of Florida, instead of the fifteen to twenty-five acres required on the King or in regions of Arizona, the Middle East, or the dry land of Australia. The Santa Gertrudis are good rustlers. The breed matures fast and at market age averages around 200 pounds more than other breeds of the same age and pasture. Often they feed on experimental plots of imported and hybrid grasses, also a King Ranch venture.

But other Brahman crosses are already being developed: with Angus, the Brangus; with Hereford, the Braford; with French Charolaise, the Charbray, and more coming. Men like Buttram and Slick are becoming known for their meaty, hardy, jet black Brangus. Farther north, at the Lasater Ranch in Colorado there is a fine herd of Beefmasters, half Brahman and a quarter each of Shorthorn and Hereford— beefy but proud and aloof red animals, fine for drouth regions. In fact, the crosses are spreading so fast all over the beef world that perhaps fifty years from now some of the standard breeds of 1900 will have to be preserved as the Longhorn is now.

Long before the free land was gone small outfits of cattlemen hard pressed by drops in beef prices or die-ups from storms or even tick fever tended to drift into sheep. Usually they received stern warning from any ranchers around, as the Richards did when they brought sheep into the Niobrara country north of the Spade. Often the protestors went into the woollies, too, perhaps even within the year. But most of the cattlemen, while still fighting settlers, had drawn imaginary lines across the free range against sheep because they ate the grass roots out of the ground, cut up the sod with their small cloven hoofs, and turned much of Wyoming into sage plains, helping to finish the overgrazing begun by cattle. The cowboys usually whooped any herds that crossed the lines into writhing gray piles at the foot of some deep cut bank or in some canyon. The dogs and the herders, too, might be killed if they were foolishly slow in moving, or refused the warning to take the herds off the range and the water holes, which the sheep roiled so that only a sheep horse would drink. But the rifles the herders carried against eagles and wolves penetrated the flesh of ranch hands as well.

Yet even after violence and shootings, some of the sternest resisters of sheep had to give up and go into the business to pull themselves out of the hard times of the Roosevelt Inquisition and the new depression looming up before the war, particularly the years when the tariff on wool was high. Long before 1900 there had been conspicuous examples of cattlemen running sheep—even in the special regions of Wyoming and Montana, men like Senator Carey of Wyoming and the Richards, both DeForest, governor of Wyoming, and Bartlett, and in 1905 the Swan Company.

The big weakness in ranching treated strictly as a business or as a manufacturing process is in its curious long-range nature. A ranch can't be shut down like a pants factory or a mine or even a steel smelter. Expenses for feed and care of the stock go on, and increase, while the prime stuff ages into canners. If the ranch is closed down, three, four years are lost putting it back into running—that long from cow to salable steers unless a ready-made, mixed herd can be bought, very scarce and expensive in times of rising prices and probably much higher than the selling price of the herd turned off.

After the Spanish-American War beef prices fell like drifting cattle hitting the Chugwater bluffs or the cap rock of Texas, driven down, it was claimed, by the manipulations of the Beef Trust. The ranchers, through the American National Cattleman's Association, accused the big packers of violating the antitrust laws and insisted that the railroads were in cahoots with them. President Taft promised an investigation but it was left for the Wilson administration to show that the Big Five—Swift, Armour, Morris, Wilson, and Cudahy—together controlled 514 companies and had interests in 762 more, dealing in 775 commodities including nearly everything from the loans that paid the cowpunchers to the fertilizer and tankage left from the cow as well as dozens of other products that no one would expect to find in the packing business, including, of course, the newspapers of the packing towns.

"Yeh, it's not only take what they offer us or go to hell," a usually unprofane old rancher admitted, "but pay what they ask for any of the 775 commodities we got to have. And tell us what we got to pay to get our steers to Omaha or Chicago to boot."

It took a long, long time from the promise of Taft, but in 1920 the packers agreed to get out of everything except meat packing and closely allied lines, and to operate under the shadow of the U. S. courts.

By then there were only the ranchers who survived the Roosevelt recession of 1907, when banks closed all over the country, even if not for long. Beef prices didn't pick up until toward 1910, moving moderately until the boom of 1914, with the war demand for meat.

By then many, many who had survived the Big Die-Ups and the hard times of the 1890's, even the fencing and land-fraud trials, were gone. The Spur had closed its "Protection A-c" and sold its holdings in 1908, paid the debts, and had a little left over to apply to the twenty years of outstanding dividends. The Western Ranches, managed by John Clay since the Swan outfit fired him, had passed dividends, too, and finally liquidated, to reorganize as an investment company. "Loan the cowman money and let him take the risks with blizzards and hard times," was the sour comment of a man who had to give them mortgages on every foot of land and every cow he owned to pull himself through the bad years, although no one could promise much future, with the growing ranges of the Argentine and Australia and fleets of ships rolling off into the water, cargo hungry. All this time the rancher operated on the open market while everything he bought and that his customers bought, except meat, was protected by the high tariff of the McKinley days, almost unchanged on anything except wool and hides.

There were more sour comments on Clay for other reasons besides the loan business. One was a speech he made before a feeders' convention in 1914 attacking the cowboy of his Wyoming cattle company days:

> The chief obstacle of the range at that time was the cowboys, who were mostly illiterate, uncivilized; who drank and thieved and misbranded cattle, and with a kind of rough loyalty, never told on one another in their crimes.

"Hell, he's still mad because none of them would join the Regulators, the Invaders, gone to clean up Johnson County," one of the feeders told his neighbor at the table.

Out on the Laramie and the Cheyenne, the Belle Fourche and the Powder there was a certain amount of laughing, now that most of the Clay interests were off the range. "The cowboys were good enough to make a lot of money for a foreign hired hand like old tight-fisted Claybowels, with his sly way of getting everybody in debt to him and then gouging them hard," one of the Whitcomb relatives said, speaking not only for old Pap but a dozen others around him.

One ranch owned by the Scottish groups that included Clay as a member was still running, due largely, many thought, to the years of Murdo Mackenzie's excellent management. The Matador was the only British ranch to make a decent profit for its investors, although its dividends had almost vanished from 1903 to 1908. But with the upswing from the declaration of war they rose as high as 20 per cent, much of it from British meat sales. Mackenzie was the finest cowman the foreign ranches brought in, many thought one of the finest cowmen anywhere, foreign or American. A booklover, he was considered one of the West's most influential supporters of the government in the fight for conservation of national resources and for shaping the government's policies in the interest of the small settler and homeseeker, although not all agreed on them. There were those, too, who recalled the range protection that the Matador hired with the Spur, to keep settlers from running tick-infested cattle into the Matador herd, Mackenzie claimed, although that wasn't the story the settlers told, nor the Spur. When one of the hired killers proved a real troublemaker for his employer, threatening to kill Mackenzie, the rugged Scotsman went right on, unarmed.

But many of the old free rangers spit into the dust at any talk of Murdo Mackenzie's good will toward settlers. Yet they had to admit that he was a powerful man in the fight against the railroads, with his admiration for, and friendship with, Theodore Roosevelt, even through Old Four-Eyes Inquisition, which didn't affect the Matador much. Most of the southern land was deeded and the northern ranges usually leased from the Indians, through Roosevelt's intercession in the Indian Bureau, the other ranchers said. Mackenzie, with Turney, the Big Bend rancher who followed the Scotsman as head of the cattle association, called on the whole cow country to stand solid against the high freight rates. When the Interstate Commerce Commission decided for the ranchers, the railroads went to court against price fixing and won. In 1904, Mackenzie visited with the President and got a plank for railroad control into the Republican platform. That brought legislation for rate fixing by the ICC, and changed the entire conception of the government's right and authority to regulate.

Needing northern range to finish their excellent-quality steers for top market prices, Mackenzie had leased half a million acres of Dakota Indian Reservation lands. But he struck trouble up there, including hard winter storms for his soft southern stock, also the problem of getting cattle across the Missouri to the Milwaukee railhead at Evarts, the old river town on the east bank. Ferries ran in floodtime, really paddle-wheeled flatboats like floating pieces of stockyards, with enough small pens to hold forty to sixty head and keep them from sliding to one side and dumping the lot into the brown, muddy depths of Big Mizzou. To help the stockmen get their cattle to the crossing, the Milwaukee railroad provided a sort of trail, a leased strip of land six miles wide between the Cheyenne River and Standing Rock Indian Reservations. It started up near the slope of the Black Hills, was lane fenced all the way, with watering places about every twelve miles, natural or from big dams and reservoirs built by the railroad, all large enough for several herds of 1,200 each a day. Gates opened from the ranges of the Matador, the L7, the HO, such Indian outlets as LaPlante's and Narcelle's NSS brand, and the Turkey Track, and many others with range neighboring on the Strip. When heavy shipping was on, waiting herds might reach as much as twelve miles back from the river.

Another problem was fires. One August day, with the sun almost hot enough to ignite the dry, curling grass as from an empty bottle concentrating the rays, the Matador was gathering beef. They had about 1,000 head of steers on the divide between the two Moreau rivers, cutting out the shipping stuff, when somebody happened to look up from the dust and sweat to see a great boiling of whitish smoke on the horizon.

"Prairie fire!" he yelled against the wind. "Big fire coming out of the west!"

Every horse was set back on his haunches at the uplifted arm, the pointing gauntlet of the warning cowboy. The wagon boss ordered the herds whooped away out of the fire's probable path, started the chuckwagon off for water, and sent a hard-riding puncher to the line camps for the fire drags. The Turkey Track, gathering beef some twenty-five miles south, turned their herds loose, too, and spurred in to help. The big drags, twelve-foot squares, looked like great bedsprings of netted steel chains woven through layered sheets of asbestos, a heavy bar across the end for the lariats. Snubbed to the saddle horns they were pulled by six strong horses, the work so heavy and so hot that the horses had to be changed every two hours. But in a wild gale-driven fire like this one little could be done except to guess where the head tongues of flame might come and backfire there. The streams and even the larger canyons all ran eastward, and the fire was coming down between them like stampeding Longhorns down a country lane. There was no barrier against which extensive backfires could be set, to burn safely into the wind. If they got away, they would be as damaging as the one roaring in from the west.

Mainly the cow crew worked the drags along the sides to narrow the spread of the fire. But the asbestos soon wore out and steers were killed, split and piled, entrails and all, on the nets of chains while Indians and white men followed to beat out the remaining pockets and smolderings. But they couldn't help much. The fire had started nearly 100 miles west of the Missouri and spread to a twenty-mile front as it came like a Milwaukee express train before the shifting west wind, burning in zigzags for two days and nights on its way to the river. One prong turned southeast, jumped the Big Moreau, and ran to the banks of the Cheyenne fifty miles away, while the main fire swept this way and that, as though to clean up what might have been missed. Finally the last flames died along the worn banks of the Missouri—over a million blackened acres behind them, much of the Matador range gone, with the stock to hold fat for market, and strengthened for the hard Dakota winter.

The men of the Drag V, the Matador of the north, had trouble around the wild Missouri River towns during the winters. Lebeau, particularly, drew the reservation and river riffraff, the gamblers, con men, and gun slingers loafing the dull season away around the saloon run by the dark-shadowed Phil DuFran. After the Johnson County war he had hit out for Arizona as a healthier climate for a while. But he didn't do so well as foreman of the Aztec Land and Cattle Company and came back North to work as brand inspector for the Black Hills Stock Association and represented Rosenbaum Brothers of Chicago on the side, a well-liked firm because Joseph Rosenbaum had saved the Montana cowmen after the Big Die-Up. Now Phil DuFran was back running a saloon again, and some recalled his stretch at bartending up in Buffalo while he spied for the Invaders.

"Wonder whose fire he's heating his iron on now?" one of the punchers asked. He had been working for the Hoe outfit over in Johnson County at invasion time and got fired for not joining up. "Somebody'll feel the burn of his mark, I'll bet."

The winter months dragged for the Matador hands, many of them laid off to spring or at least not busy now that the ground was frozen and little feeding to do, nothing much except keeping ice chopped out of the water holes so the cattle could drink. Murdo Mackenzie's powerful son Dode, managing the ranch, seemed to feel the inactivity the most and took to spending his time, and money, at Lebeau, particularly at Phil DuFran's saloon, perhaps because Bud Stevens, a former Matador hand, tended bar and listened to his dreary complaint and sent him home to bed if he could.

Then after a night spent in hell-raising, Dode made a final round of DuFran's saloon. By then his drunk was souring on him. Cursing everything around him, he staggered

up to the bar and demanded a drink. Stevens, perhaps saddened by the condition of this son of the firm and upright
Murdo Mackenzie and his sturdy breed, tried to talk young
Dode out of it. But this time it didn't work. Infuriated, Dode
pulled his gun, leveled it on the bartender. "Damn your
bossing heart! This time I'll kill you!"

Bud Stevens drew and beat him to the shot.

Astonishment slid over Dode Mackenzie's face. He
staggered back from the stinking blue smoke and burst out
the side door, into a man's surprised arms, and slumped
through them to the frozen walk. When they picked up
Dode's gun it was empty. Looked like it had been empty a
long, long time, somebody said.

Once more, for the fourth important time, Phil DuFran
had a lot to tell the officials, this time about violence against
a son of a cattleman. There were rumors and whisperings
about many things all that winter. One claimed that DuFran
had used talebearing to work on Dode Mackenzie, telling
him Bud Stevens was always trying to run him, telling
him what to do. "Damn kid ain't got the gumption to go
around the corner without being reminded," DuFran was
supposed to have reported that Stevens said. And much
more.

The Matador outfit never went to Lebeau again, let
alone to Phil DuFran's Hell Hole, as many called it. But the
killing of Dode brought up talk of DuFran's Wyoming days,
and the loose rope ends left raveling from the Invasion.
There had finally been news of the two men captured at the
KC and kidnaped as the only two witnesses against the Invaders. The younger man, Bill Walker, who rode for Hesse
on the Sweetwater some years before, reappeared and told of
being held in Rhode Island by Dixon, at times in charge of
other men the ranchers wanted kept out of the way. With the
Invaders freed, Jones and Walker had been told they could
cash their checks, reported to be $2,500, as payment for
their property lost in the KC fire. But the checks bounced
and Jones, newly married, headed back to Wyoming to in-

vestigate. He was never heard from again, it seemed. Walker
said he went to law about his money, to collect it, but his
trunk was rifled and the bouncing check stolen. Still, he got
away alive, and that was something to be thankful for. Seems
he didn't play the fiddle much after that night at KC.

There was a lot of general talk those days about the
hard feelings among the Frenchmen and the breeds against
the big outfits like the Matador coming in on the reservation
leases, crowding out everybody, even such old-timers as La-
Plante, around the region back when Indians and buffaloes
had it all. But he was forced to round up his stock and get
moving, just like the rest. In addition to the outside herds
pushing in, there were the settlers, demanding reservation
lands for homesteading, and brand inspectors like Phil Du-
Fran snooping around everywhere. Some of the men with
soft, uncalloused hands appeared around up here, too, as
they had down in Texas and the sandhills and Wyoming for
years. Many recalled Kid Rich of several years before. Some
said he had a penitentiary record and a growing tendency to
drink and raise hell, although he had been brought in by one
of the big outfits some time before to do a couple of killings.
Because he hung around afterward, shooting off his mouth,
he was picked off on the road. There were other stories, too,
as with Henderson and Wellman and a dozen others.

The Indians still liked to tell of finding the Kid one
February morning in 1903 down in the Cheyenne River
country below the mouth of Bull Creek. He was dead on the
frozen snow; his horse, a little roan, was standing patiently
nearby, frosted skin shivering in the cold but held by the
fallen reins as though staked where the man had slid off,
carrying the far stirrup over the saddle as he went. There
was nothing except the dead man on the snow, with little
blood but a cud of tobacco coughed out as he died. He had
been shot from the back, so close that a three-inch spot was
burned on his sheepskin coat, otherwise clean, the bleeding
internal. There were tracks of another horse ridden beside

him to the killing and then one track heading on up Bull Creek and so lost on a bare spot of frozen ground.

It turned out that about ten o'clock a man had come to the Cavanaugh place where the Kid worked and from the dark beside the door asked for him. The Kid got up, slipped his six-shooter into his belt, and went out and then returned for his sheepskin coat. He gave his wife no reply to the anxious question "Who is it?" saying only that the chief of the Indian police had sent for him.

Perhaps she thought about Waggoner leaving his family over on the other side of the Black Hills with some unidentified men in the night back in 1889. Still, that was long ago, and so Mrs. Rich went back to bed. Later Jim Cavanaugh said it had been too dark to tell whether the man who came for the Kid was white or Indian and when he was reminded that he knew every man in the country, he agreed. "But the less I say the better—"

During the rumors and concern it was recalled that the Kid had come down-river about ten, eleven years ago and worked for the French-breed, Narcisse Narcelle, married to a Sioux and running a big spread, much of it on reservation lands. After a few years Rich had married Narcelle's sister. They broke up and although both married again there was still some trouble between the Kid and Narcelle. Now the Kid was dead, perhaps out of personal hatred or because he had to be shut up, with the government agents out everywhere scratching up any evidence that settlers or little ranchers had been intimidated by the big outfits. Or perhaps the shooting was revenge for some man killed, one of the two found or for some other one, perhaps face down in the grass somewhere, picked clean by buzzard and coyote.

Anyway, now that Dode Mackenzie had been killed, Lebeau was given the goby and even Phil DuFran left, moved to Evarts for a while. One fire after another struck through the board shacks of the deserted town, until there was little except the cellar holes.

But Murdo Mackenzie's concentrated efforts to improve his herds had begun to pay off. In 1908 the Matador steers won prizes at the International Livestock Show at Chicago and got a lot of attention at Kansas City. In 1911 they captured the Grand Champion Award at Chicago. Such reputation, hooked up with the general rise in beef, pushed their steers to the top of the market. In 1914 the government canceled the Cheyenne River Indian Reservation lease and most of the Matador stock was withdrawn to Texas, where adjoining range was bought from the Prairie Cattle Company. The war boom justified the outlay. In 1918 Matador steers pulled down an average of $120.03 a head against the $34.75 average in 1903, and lucky to get that. Many took much less.

The old outfits that couldn't make the economic jump from free grass were gone and with them most of the old ways, although some, like the Matador, clung to the horse-drawn chuckwagon, the open corral, and the throw rope instead of the squeeze chute and the cross fences, the smaller pastures. But new problems arose with the new times. The list of cattle diseases doubled, tripled, and more, particularly as the blood improved and the old hardiness of the Longhorn was lost. Some recalled that the coastal steers could keep going when they were gray with bloodsucking ticks.

The Plains were once as free of cattle diseases as any region new to a species usually is. Some kind of *rinderpest*, perhaps foot-and-mouth disease, had swept up along the larger streams a couple of times in the first half of the nineteenth century, destroying millions of cloven-hoofed animals. Some regions, like the Laramie Plains, were left stinking and empty. The salt licks of the present Lancaster County, Nebraska, were once the center of buffaloes, deer, and other salt eaters and they suddenly were left dark with carcasses and avoided as poison by the Indians for years. There was a scare of foot-and-mouth disease as late as World War I.

Epizootics came and went but the tick fever apparently was there from the first cattle, perhaps from the first cow. The South had the screwworm, too, infecting any break of the skin, particularly castration before the bloodless emasculator was put on the market. Then came blackleg, spread all through the cow country, fatal to great numbers of the finest young stock, the animal lame for a little while, the leg swollen, the victim down a few hours and dead. The disease was easily identified by even a range child. A thrust with a quirt handle or a boot toe on the swollen leg made a rushing sound. The disease was thought to be spread by coyotes, wolves, and dogs that had gnawed at a blackleg carcass. So in addition to dipping for ticks and itch there was the seasonal vaccination for blackleg and then for such diseases as pinkeye, *hemorrhagic septicemia,* and a dozen more. The antibiotics came into general use and saved many cattle, particularly calves. Increased weight in feed lots is produced by the addition of aureomycin and stilbestrol to the feed mix but there is some public concern about the overuse of the latter, a fear of effeminization of the traditionally very masculine beef eater. It is true that the Plains Indian lived almost entirely on buffalo cow, and the cattleman, even the trail drivers, preferred a fat heifer for meat, but perhaps the natural hormone is in less concentration. Besides, the Indian wanted his meat well cooked if there was time and fuel, and the cowman would eat his beef no other way.

There is still a constant struggle to clear out the infectious abortions, particularly Brucellosis, Bang's disease, which destroys many cows for calving and causes undulant fever in man through milk from the infected cows. Many fine herds have had to be replaced from the ground up because of Bang's. Now, however, a calf vaccine is coming into general use. But leptospirosis is rising.

Where, fifty, sixty years ago, "immune Shorthorn" meant immune to tick fever, now strains are watched for inherited susceptibility to eye cancer, say, with the recommendation that the eye be removed, the calf fattened, and both mother and calf sent to the slaughterhouse. The last eight,

nine years a new problem, the "sinister gene," the carrier
of dwarfism, has cropped up increasingly among fine beef
cattle, the result, some think, of the overclose breeding for
the blocky, squat, spraddle-legged look, the one that prize
judges favor and that feeders pay premium prices for. If a
bull carrying a gene of dwarfism is mated to a carrier cow,
one fourth of the progeny will be dwarfs, one half carriers,
and only one quarter clean of the taint, and who's to say
which is which until proved out? A carrier bull mated to a
dwarf-free cow produces a normal-appearing first generation
but half of these will be carriers.

There have always been bovine dwarfs as there have
always been dwarfs among humans, but with the recent
alarming increase in the three main beef breeds—Shorthorn,
Hereford, and Aberdeen Angus, this has become of great
concern. Often the dwarf calves are born dead or short-lived,
the year's work of the cow lost. If they survive, they are
often killed to hide the blight on the herd, which has already, in some cases, reached as high as 12 per cent—far
above the losses required to bankrupt a breeder if the loss
continues.

The only solution now seems to be the radical one of
clearing the bloodlines. To make certain that a bull, whether
of $500 or $50,000 blood, is free of the taint he must be
mated to at least fifteen carrier cows, which takes time and
can involve the loss of the cow's year if he is a carrier. Other
methods are being developed, the profilometer, to detect the
slight bump on the bull's forehead which indicates that he
may be a carrier, or examination by x-ray for the so-called
crumpled vertebrae that some carriers have. But it is a slow
process, and as the stock is bred lower and lower to the
ground the sinister gene becomes more common—one more
problem unknown in the days of the leggy Longhorn that
could outrun a good saddle horse for a nice stretch.

Before the firecrackers and cannon boom of the false
armistice had died away over the fall range, war veterans

discharged early were seeking land much as the soldiers had hurried to Philadelphia with their Revolutionary muskets barely cold, demanding homes, farms. There wasn't much left now, mainly isolated plots in Wyoming and Montana too far from water for the improved cow to reach on her shortening legs, the grass too sparse for slow feeding. But to a man who had spent months, perhaps years in the close confines of mud and blood in the front-line trenches, with the roar and crash of war over him, dry landing looked mighty good, out where only the wind, the coyote, and the prairie dog owl broke the night stillness and a flaring red sky was northern lights. Anyway, with his war service deducted it wouldn't take long to prove up on the place, to get his patent. Instead of singing "Starving to death on a government claim," while the blizzard shook and rattled the tar-paper shacks of the settlers, they usually kept to "I'm always chasing rainbows." They got them, too, summers, after the high, dry-country thunderheads had spent their swift crashes of thunder and lightning, spattered a few rain drops into the dust, and were finally swept away in white mare's-tails against the far sky. But no lily-fingered range protection came riding through to warn these settlers to clear out. No latter-day Tom Horn brought death with him as he dogloped his horse along a rise.

The boom of war prices was swept away like a tenderfoot's camp in a gully washer. Beef fell, everything fell, and around 6,000,000 workers were unemployed, with strikes everywhere against wage cuts that went to 20 per cent and higher in cotton mills, coal mines, meat packing. The railroads ordered a $26,500,000 annual wage cut for 325,000 workers. The newspapers managed to keep the seriousness of the postwar depression from the public, but there was no way to keep it from showing on the cattle market at Chicago and Omaha and wherever beef cattle were put up for sale. It cleaned out many cattlemen who had gone in deep on the encouragement of the public and the government.

Old John Clay made speeches for holding on. Basically the cattle business was sound. He got some sour lip from those who had memories beyond yesterday, particularly those who recalled his denunciation of the cowboy, and those who had deeper reasons for packing a grudge against the Scotsman. If Alex Swan nursed one, it was ended. He had been the big rancher of Wyoming and western Nebraska for a long time, one of the principal men in the formation of the Union Stock Yards of Omaha. But then the Big Die-Up came and eventually Clay took over for his financial backers until, after the Johnson County Invasion, Clay found himself out, too. Eventually the old Swan place became one of the finest Hereford ranches in the world. Long before that Swan had gone to Ogden but apparently couldn't get started again and died in an asylum almost forgotten except perhaps by a few like R. S. Van Tassell, who had helped get the horses for the Invaders. The second Mrs. Van Tassell was Alex Swan's daughter, his eldest, his favorite.

By now old C. C. Slaughter, the Texian, was dead, the last of the three men who were so important in the start of the Northwest Texas Stock Raisers Association out under the oak at Graham back in 1877. Conrad Kohrs, up in Montana, was gone, too, another of the solid, old-time cattlemen. He had come out of the Big Die-Up with 300 head left from his herd of 35,000, and was saved, along with some others, by Rosenbaum, the Chicago Livestock Commission man. Kohrs returned the favor twenty years later, when, during the hard times of 1907, Rosenbaum faced ruin in the Grain Exchange. Kohrs and the others went in together and loaned Rosenbaum $1,000,000, saved him, and got their money back very soon.

In 1924 John Clay published his book *My Life on the Range,* including a little about the Clay-Robinson commission house. Every rancher grabbed a look into the account, and settlers did, too, if they could get to a copy. Neither side was pleased, particularly, perhaps because no one except Clay could have seen his past in such an un-Scottish glow of self-approval. Perhaps that came out of his long years in America, where he died.

When the prices had first gone to pieces the old cowman, Ike Pryor, pleaded with the big cattlemen to pay off their notes at the banks so that the smaller ranchers, many sure to go under if called on now, could be carried. Here and there a few of the younger cattlemen got together on cooperative schemes but many were squeezed out, their land taken over by the bankers or the banker-ranchers, the big fellows, always the big fellows.

"Yes, that's what they want," some said bitterly. "Hard times of the nineties they done the same. Like the song says, 'The rich get richer and the poor get children.' "

But some of the big outfits or once-big outfits went down, too. Will Comstock of the old Richards and Comstock outfit outlived his partner by only a few years. The foreclosure on the old Spade Ranch failed court confirmation but finally it went for the mortgage, 22,000 acres—all that was left of the spread over sixty townships of government land twenty years ago. What there was left of it went into the hands of a settler's son, one of those that was supposed to starve to death.

Up in Wyoming the Swan company transferred the entire management to an American board in a sort of admission that the foreign management had been a failure and that the land assets would probably never cover the capital investment.* In the meantime the Matador dropped the Canadian leases, partly because of the heavy protective duties put on by both sides of the border. They substituted a short-term lease on 350,000 acres on Pine Ridge Indian Reservation in southern South Dakota.

In the midst of the beef slump news came that somebody had managed to get away with a steal worth billions of dollars out in the cow country. Cattlemen were recalling that twenty, even fifteen years ago the government had hounded some of them into bankruptcy and the penitentiary

* In 1956 some real estate was still held for a rising price.

for fencing government land illegally, or obtaining parts of
the public domain in mean little 160-acre chunks fraudu-
lently. The steal was north of Casper, on the trail to Johnson
County, over the high, dry hump with the shallow depression of Salt Creek through it. A standing rock shaped like a
teapot had pleased the saddle-weary Britishers of the Invasion that day in 1892. Now all that dome was gone, but
not stolen by cattlemen. President Taft had set the region
aside as an oil reserve for the U. S. Navy. Under Harding
it was shifted over to the Department of the Interior, and
Secretary Albert B. Fall turned the valuable oil pool over
to his cronies. Fall was a rancher from New Mexico, that
state so favored by cattlemen who were first of all national
politicians as Wyoming had drawn cattlemen who were Britishers. Secretary Fall had to resign and finally, after a long
delay, was convicted of accepting bribes, and sentenced to a
year in the penitentiary and fined $100,000. Bribery and
conniving in the theft of billions of oil essential to the defense of the nation and the culprit got one year in jail—
the same one year that was doled out to a Bartlett Richards.
It was not only that there was a difference between a Theodore Roosevelt and a Harding; the Bartlett Richards had
acted out of an age-old allegiance and affection.

The financial boom of the later twenties brought little
prosperity for the ranchers. Only the cowmen with money in
Wall Street got ahead, now that prices on almost everything
except ranch and farm products were soaring high as the eagles over the Spanish Peaks. The farm bloc in Congress was
a constant threat but never more than a threat to the un-
balanced economy under unreceptive presidents. Beef was
just beginning to pick up a little before the collapse of October, 1929. The ranchers, clinging to Hoover's optimistic
confidence, held up their usual fall shipments, hoping every
day to hear of a little rise in the steer market from Omaha or
Chicago, hanging around the radio or the telephone until the
market reports came through. Or getting the bad news by

the old range grapevine after they had to give up the radio and the telephone. The boom had never come for them.

In the meantime old Charlie Goodnight had had a heart attack early in December of 1929 and on the morning of the twelfth he died, in his ninety-fourth year, one more proof that hardship, insecurity, danger, violence, swift changes of fortune, towering rages, bitter partisanship, and disappointments did not shorten human life. He was a pioneer of cattle and trails, a friend to the Indians, fighting their cause in Washington, giving the Taos Indians a foundation herd from his buffaloes when he was not much better off, financially, than they. He appreciated their integrity, their honor, their affection for their earth. These things he understood. He was planning a son-of-a-gun stew for Christmas, it was said, but he died before he could enjoy it.

"I wish I could find words to express the trueness, the bravery, the hardihood, the sense of honor, the loyalty to their trust and to each other," he once wrote of his Texas cowboys. There must have been many who contrasted this to John Clay's tirade against cowboys. But Goodnight knew. His life had often depended upon them.

By 1932 it seemed there was nobody left with the money to buy meat at any price and once more fat beeves put on the market didn't pay the freight and the commission. The Matador's good steers had climbed to an average of $66.41 a head by 1929, contrasted to the $120.03 of 1918. In 1930 they dropped to $39.83, in 1933 to $23.23. As seems inevitable, drouth came with the depression. When the ground winds of 1934 struck there was no grass cover and the black blizzards of spring, always lurking in the Panhandle regions, rose in their great, dark walls and moved up across the cow country almost on the trail over which Goodnight had once pushed his herds. They stripped the top soil and dropped it into gullies, into russian-thistled fence corners and across roadways, leaving little except dust pneumonia for man and beast.

The streams and wells were dry, the grass gone in much of the cow country, the good stock of the ranchers gaunted so their bones wore through the skin on hip and spine. And still some argued and protested against what was called the New Deal Roundup, the second Roosevelt Roundup that many had seen, only this was in stock. Yet the overloaded, drouth-gaunted range and the vanishing demand for beef were not matters visible only to the political eye. Finally, the summer of 1934, the biggest, strangest, and most heartbreaking cattle deal of all time was made through the controversial emergency stock-buying program, the Federal Surplus Relief Corporation. Although this was largely the conception of Congressman Marvin Jones of Texas, chairman of the House Committee on Agriculture, it was denounced as a Yankee work of the devil.

The stock the helpless cattlemen agreed to sell was divided into three categories: those for grass in other regions, the hopelessly starved or aged, to be killed on the spot, and that still in some meat. The latter, of eating quality, were slaughtered, the meat sent to relief larders for the hungry. Texas cattle were sold to the government at the rate of 30,000 a day, tears streaming down the leathery faces of the cattlemen as they watched their herds go, many carefully bred up and now swept into ignominy. Some refused to sell and had to see most of their stock die slowly—stumbling bags of bones that had perhaps been fine, sleek Shorthorns or Angus, or the hard-ranging Herefords, now finally dropping like old dried-up carcasses to the gray prairie. Eight million head were bought in all, at an average of $13 each. The ranches had already been going until the mortgage moratorium took effect.

Fortunately none of the early dedicated men lived to see this, and finally the rains did come again and another, a much more extensive war. With it came the Roosevelt-sponsored ceilings that were so strenuously opposed by many cattlemen, although they were making more money than ever before. So long denied a fair price for their meat, they wanted unhampered inflation but only in beef, not in what they must buy. As soon as the war was over they got the OPA killed and instead of going up, beef went down and shot up again for a while during the Korean action. Then came 1949 with its blizzards chasing each other like calves playing over the green spring range, a range now buried under weeks of drifting snow. A few cattle were saved by the hay lift—feed dropped from planes to storm-stranded cattle. But it was so very little for the millions of range stock, and once more many ranchers reached the warmth of spring cleaned out, cleaned out of much more expensive stock than any of 1887.

In 1951 ordinary beef brought $30 a hundred on the hoof, choice up to $36. By now the Matador, too, had struck oil, the stock booming on Wall Street with the news. Perhaps because of the general financial situation in Great Britain, or through pure canniness, the Scottish owners sold the ranch for an announced $19,000,000. So the finest of the foreign ranches, born of the beef boom of the eighties, was sold in the boom of 1950, and cut up.

In 1955 Omaha became the world's largest livestock market and meat-packing center, with Nebraska the leading beef state of the Union, Cherry County, out in the sandhills where Texans like Jim Dahlman punched cows in 1878, where Richards set his great Spade Ranch, the leading beef county of all the forty-eight states.

Omaha, Nebraska spread over the breaks and flats of the muddy Missouri, was started into the world's meat marketing and packing through rancher discontent with the packinghouse trust and the railroad freight rates. Back in the beef bonanza days of 1883 Alex Swan, the largest rancher of Wyoming, with six others, mostly of ranching experience, such men as Paxton, Creighton, and John McShane, whose mother was a Creighton, set up the Union Stock Yards of Omaha and donated an estimated $2,300,000 worth of land, buildings, and capital stock to attract meat packers. They drew in five, hoping to assure competition that way, and eventually these increased to seventeen, including such early firms as Armour, Cudahy, Swift, and Wilson, the Big Four who slaughter all kinds of livestock at their Omaha plants.

The stockyards at Omaha grew steadily enough to 1943. That year Harry B. Coffee became president. He was born out at the edge of Wyoming, the nephew of old C. F. Coffee, called Colonel or Chalk Eye, who came up on the trail with a Snyder herd in 1871. Colonel ranched in the region, keeping to the more open country for elbow room and inclined to the adventuresome in other ways, too. It was said he rode a wild buffalo at Ogallala once. It was under the nephew, that the swift expansion of Omaha as a livestock market took place. After all, running the world's largest Union Stock Yards can't be so very different from riding a buffalo bull on the prairie out near the wild trail town of Ogallala. Nor was this all done without some humor from the very start. In the center of the great spread of pens stands the eleven-story Livestock Exchange Building, like three great red bricks set on end in the form of a square-cornered U. Here the members throw a yearly dinner for themselves and their ladies, with the music of bawling cattle coming up soft from far below—the annual banquet of the Stock Yards 400 Club.

There is an ironic commentary on the mangement of the railroads here in Omaha. In 1955, 91 per cent of all cattle arriving at the Union Stock Yards came by truck, 99 per cent of the hogs and 49 per cent of the sheep, while 45,000 truckloads of livestock left the yards. If the cowmen of 1884 were interested in revenge for the monopolistic freight rates they were fighting then, here it is, at the world's beef market.

During World War II meat brought so much on the black market that rustling boomed beyond anything since the great bonanza times and never since law came to the West. In 1943-45 a steer butchered in some arroyo or coulee or canyon brought real money at markets selling without ration points. Some ranchers took up the practice themselves, getting two, even four and five times as much as the legal ceiling price. After the Korean War was over and prices dropped, the cowhands out of work kept on rustling, aided by the great cattle haulers rumbling over the roads. Down in Oklahoma a gang got away with 200 head in 1954. They stuffed the branded hides into old auto tires and burned them in piles, the stink of the rubber to hide the smell of burning skin and hair. Late in 1956 a South Dakota rancher was convicted of the state's biggest rustler haul: 233 head from a neighbor's herd of 269, leaving him thirty-six. The thief admitted he trucked the stock to market in big haulers and sold them under their own brand, which the neighbor had neglected to renew. Flack, the thief, had the brand recorded in his own name and got $18,000 for the lot.

But ordinary rustling declined fast after 1952—beef no longer worth the risk for the low return. When meat started down, some of the ranchers, particularly in the drouth regions of Texas, did some panic selling. Cows worth $300 a short time before went for $100. Many who could hold their stock were unable to believe that a president born in Texas would let the state's great product keep dropping in price when everything else climbed like a Panhandle thunderhead.

Once more holding their stock didn't help, only overgrazed the dried-out range with the increasing herds, spreading from the 53,000,000 head of 1951 to 63,000,000 in 1955, with a drouth such as Texas and much of the country north of there had not seen since the nineties, and in many regions not then. Finally Congress voted drouth relief to help buy feed to tide the needy cattlemen over, the relief to be distributed by the Department of Agriculture. Soon there were complaints and rumblings—not against federal intercession but that the relief was going to the big bugs able to buy feed, not to the little rancher whose cattle died around him, whose ranch went under the sheriff's hammer as in 1933 and no moratorium ahead to save him.

Eventually the investigators came. Turned out that

Richard Kleberg of the King Ranch, with money for race horses and with oil wells spouting, had received $32,585 in 1954 for drouth relief, just before he died, leaving the world's greatest ranch, estimated at $7,000,000, to his heirs. But his take from the relief fund was really piddling compared to what the Robbins Ranch got—$400,000 since 1954 to the time of the investigation. Besides, Robbins had not contributed to the upbuilding of the cattle business for one hundred years as the King Ranch had. Robbins was a New York investment banker for a while, still a director of the Santa Fe Railroad and of several other extensive ventures. When asked by the Department of Agriculture what he did with the $400,000, what he bought with it, he refused to tell them. It must have been something pretty substantial on a 60,000-acre ranch, over $6.66 an acre, compared to the very minor sum to Kleberg for the nearly 1,000,000 acres of the King. Such favoritism to an upstart would have embittered Richard Kleberg, who, as congressman back in 1938, complained loudly against the government's interference with natural economic laws, such as drouths and famines, and opposed every appropriation to help the farmer and the stockman except the one for the eradication of the old enemy of the King herds—the cow tick.

In the midst of this time came the political conventions of 1956, one at the Cow Palace in San Francisco, the other at the amphitheater of the Chicago stockyards. But all the cattle held from the Rio Grande to Canada finally had to be sold and beef dropped to $14.50 a hundred, with that thunderhead of prices on everything the cowman had to buy still going up into 1958. Once more there was a blizzard and the dispatch from Amarillo, Texas, to the *New York Times*, March 31, 1957, started "The grimmest spring round-up in years is taking place on the rangelands of the Texas and Oklahoma panhandles and in the Northeastern New Mexico." Five hundred fine cattle lost here out of 2,500, 300 there, with "fifty dead jackrabbits" standing poised as though to break and run for safety when the snow left. It struck up North, too, with whole trains buried for days, the herds drifting and gone. Only a low cattle population, perhaps the lowest since the days of the open range, saved the ranchers from another Big Die-Up. But spring brought the rains so the bluebonnets of Texas once more were like flowing swaths of fallen sky upon the prairie. There were floods, too, great ones, and record-breaking rainfall, in some places the highest in seventy, eighty years, the grass green and fine all the way across the Marias. Yet many cattlemen with no bank stock, no oil wells, no money in General Motors, were very hard pressed. But to those others cattle losses were convenient deductions.

Many must have wondered why they were ranchmen at all, as so many had before them, clear back to 1867. But then they probably went out to look at the cows, shining, sleek, and fat. Next year would be a mighty fine one.

# CHAPTER II

# RITUAL AND RESTORATION

THE five-way corral gate, the squeeze chute, and the stable-bred herd sire have just about retired the roper and the cutting horse from all except a few show places not concerned with the poundage run off or the extra hands on the pay roll. Even some of the smaller outfits have put on jeeps and light planes to round up the stock and hunt out strays that show little tendency to wander, with their heavy bodies and short legs, the balanced rations before them winter and summer, and medicated rubbing posts and insecticide oilers to keep flies and other insects off, water always in easy reach, as well as medicated salt.

Where once the Longhorns quit the country at the sight of anyone afoot, particularly a woman with blowing skirts, the later grade Herefords came running to see what this strange walking creature might be, a fine sweep of white faces charging up, sending the tenderfoot racing for the nearest wire fence, certain it had been a run for life. But if the walker had stood his ground, the cattle would have veered suddenly away, every whitefaced, horn-bearing head gone and only red rumps visible, fleeing. Now even the bulls are tame, particularly the placid Hereford sires who may come sidling up in any western pasture to have their bulging ribs scratched and the itchy places back of the drooping horns. All these changes in breed and coddling care brought a realization by 1927 that the foundation stock, the Longhorn, had vanished, the blood existing only in crosses. Then the United States Government tried to locate Longhorns for two official herds, one in the Wichita Mountain Wild Life Refuge in Oklahoma, the other at the Niobrara Game Reserve in Nebraska. They combed the Texas border and started the Wichita herd with twenty cows and three bulls. Several showed Brahman blood but this has apparently been bred out of the offsprings. Selected bulls have been brought in from Mexico to strengthen the strain, and by 1957 the two herds totaled around 500 head. However, as Goodnight wrote Frank Dobie, the climate in the Wichita Mountains would grow a shorter, thicker horn, with the bodies of the cattle also more compact. The greatest length of steer horn was generally developed in fairly low brush country, perhaps west of the Guadalupe River and often under rigorous circumstances. So far none in the tame herds have the fine, wild spread of horn or the generally wild look of the early photographs. Presumably the life is a little soft.

Another and more daring restoration is that attempted in Munich, Germany. By selecting domestic cattle with attributes found in drawings and sculpture of the urus, the wild ancestor of the present domestic cattle, including the Longhorn, the start was made. In one variety used the bull was black, the cow chestnut, the horns powerful, the legs longish, the back straight. These were crossed with cattle from the Hungarian plains, the Scottish highlands, and Corsica, the latter with the ringed nose, a stripe down the back, and a high crown of coarse hair, such as the urus, the aurochs, had, and from these a "present-day aurochs" has been created.

But long before any restoration was attempted the great changes that made a pretty tame business of ranching brought a reluctance to let the romance and the old seasonal routines die, particularly as they were recalled through the

sunset haze of time that gilded the dust, made gallant the
drudgery and the endurance of stinging blizzard and saddle
wolf. Out of this and the long and very deep relation of man
to the cow came the great American circus, the rodeo, which
has grown into the third American sport in number of spectators, outranked only by basketball and baseball. Both of
these get their followers from the very wide participation by
the young—baseball on the sand lot or the cow lot, milk-cow
lot, diamond, basketball from the schools.

In almost every competition of the rodeo the cow or
the means of handling, controlling, the cow as the rancher
used the term, is involved. In the center is the bulldogging,
now called steer wrassling, but the idea is still the same—the
supreme test of man against the lord of, say, the Chamber of
the Bulls at Lascaux.

Even the word *rodeo,* Spanish for a surround, a
roundup, once separated the initiates, the people of the
cow country from all the rest by the shift in accent to the
first syllable in the good old untutored Anglo-Saxon way. But
the rodeo as a contest did not start in Spanish America or in
Spain. Much of it reaches back to early religious dances and
combats, back into mythology. Midway through the Bronze
Age, perhaps four thousand years ago, there was rugged bull
grappling in the arena before the palace of Minos, king of
Crete. Scenes from this have been preserved in frescoes, bas-
reliefs, and statuettes showing the steps in the sport. The
challenger was posted into position, the bull released, and
when he charged, the grappler clutched the points of the
horns to swing lightly, feet first, upward on the force of the
bull's furious toss. With this momentum the grappler
turned himself into a back somersault as he released the
horns and landed standing on the bull, looking backward.
There, if he was an accomplished grappler, he struck a mo-
mentary pose for the applause and then leapt gracefully to
the ground behind the animal. It was proper and not unusual for women or even girls to join the ranks of the professionals in this acrobatic, ritualistic sport. There was also

the twisting of the bull's head by the horns to make him manageable.

In Thessaly riders chased the bulls around the arena and then brought them down by jumping upon them, grabbing the horns and twisting them in the Minoan fashion, much as the modern bulldogger does. It was only far in time and not in spirit from the Thessalian bull throwing to the capture of good young Longhorns about to escape into the brush of Texas by leaping upon them and twisting them down, to be tied with the piggin string and left to grow cramped and subdued enough to follow the decoys to the pens.

From the fourteenth through the sixteenth century the English put on bull baitings by specially bred dogs with pushed-out underjaws. Such a dog couldn't be choked off or shaken loose from his hold on the bull's nose no matter how powerful and swift the thrusts and lunges or how high he was swung, or how hard. There was bull running, too, the bull turned loose by the butcher and chased by the townsfolk until both were worn out. Then the animal was slaughtered.

In the Texas region of the 1770's the bulls of Espiritu Santo and Rosario Missions were prized mostly for the "Days of the Bulls," with bull tailing, bull roping, and riding. Even the occasional castration was left until the animal was grown for the sport of catching him on the prairie. In Spanish California, before the big Kill-Off, the bulls were sometimes run by horsebackers at full speed, each man spurring and maneuvering to get the bull by the tail to throw him, as later some of the brush poppers of Texas did to capture the wilier of the Longhorns, particularly some fine young bull for the ranch herd or a sleek young cow of good bone and meat. In Brazil the bull that showed special fight during cattle work might be surrounded by dozens of men grabbing at him anywhere, and brought down. Then, with the conqueror's boot on his neck, he was given long-winded and oratorical hell in a speech. If the bull got up and away, it just meant another speech.

The Indian was driven from his romantic hunting life to sit morosely on some reservation, the buffaloes killed off, and the law overtook the lawless. Wild West shows began to sell their romantic versions of the vanished era to the east, and the come-lately westerners, with spurious Indian fights, buffalo runs, and stagecoach robberies. As ranching turned toward bookkeeping, with planned breeding and the gasoline-powered hay sled not far off, cowboy shows were put on the road, although there were some cowboys in the Wild West shows that got so much spread in the magazines and newspapers and so little money.

Back in the spring of 1883, at the height of the beef bonanza, A. B. Grady of Lockhart, Texas, had organized a company of cowboys to put on exhibitions of Texas cowboy life: roping and tying wild stock and bronc busting and handling. They bought silver-banded Mexican hats, fringed leather jackets, Angora chaps, and great-roweled Mexican spurs. Their horses, all paints, carried Mexican saddles, the stirrups covered by huge silver and fringe-trimmed tapaderos. Gaudy and handsome, Grady's Cowboys helped set the style for all the show and dude cowboys to come. They advertised themselves as record breakers at roping and tying down wild steers, but at the show at San Antonio the local boys took the shine off Grady's professionals by beating their time. Grady's boys were fine, the local newspapers suggested, patronizingly, for the large eastern cities.

The same year along in June there was an argument at Pecos, Texas, about who was the best bronc rider and fastest roper in the region. Although the talk got hot as the rusty stove in the general store in a blue norther, nothing was settled. A contest was arranged for the Fourth of July, out on flat ground near the courthouse. There was no entrance fee, no ticket picker, no grandstand, no chute. The steers were turned out in the open for the ropers. The broncs were snubbed or tied down until the rider was in the saddle, then he was let up, the blind jerked away, with the circle of riders around to hold him from running off over the prairie and into some arroyo or over a cut bank. If he broke out, and took off in a blind run, fast-mounted hazers went after him, to turn him back or pull the rider from the the saddle and "let him go to hell."

Such riding and roping contests were being held all over the range country, often made up at the moment, just because some riders happened to get together, or rivals from neighboring ranches, the spontaneous "ridings" out on some flat, or some pole corral in Texas or Colorado, Kansas or Dakota.

Three years later Albuquerque put on a cowboy tournament described in the *New York Herald,* the drawing card twelve wild Texas steers released one at a time out upon the open prairie, the cowboy, rope up, spurring after him to bring him down and hogtie him, the prize for the best time a $75 saddle. Afterward there was wild bronc riding, too.

The idea of the cowboy tournaments spread and with them dust, excitement, and broken bones. At Montrose, Colorado, in 1887 a bronc bucked into the terrified audience, trampling a woman. This kind of publicity helped bring the crowds out. At Denver the same month a tournament drew an estimated 8,000 spectators to fill the grandstand, spread over the grounds, and gather twenty deep around the corrals. Some couldn't see but all could whoop and yell.

Inside, the broncs and Longhorn steers kept running around the corral walls, trying to get a nose over, for where the nose went the rest could follow. With the contestant flipping his loop back and forth in the dust, ready, the manager pointed out a horse in the wild-eyed, wild-maned circling herd to the man. Then he was to rope the bronc, dig in his heels to choke him down, saddle him, get on and bust him to a standstill, for which he got a box of cigars and a chance at the prize. One cowboy drew a ready-made outlaw that kicked, struck, and bit, and was so hard-winded it was almost impossible to choke him, the cowboy getting madder and madder as the crowd hooted him. Brutal with fury, he whipped the horse to a frenzy but still unwilling to be saddled. After an hour he was ordered to give up and turn the horse back into the herd, give another man a chance.

One cowboy who had great influence on the rodeo during those formative years was Bill Pickett, the Texas Negro who was credited with originating bulldogging, all unaware that there were some very substantial developments in the sport, beginning back in prehistoric times. Bill Pickett took after the released steer in the usual way, spurring up alongside, and taking a grand flying leap to grab the horns, twist them over toward him and, with the critter's nose pointing up, Bill bent forward, sank his strong teeth into the animal's tender lip, let loose of the horns and jerked himself backward. The steer flopped neatly over on his side, bulldogged. Pickett became very popular as the only cowboy bulldogger. Later he joined Miller Brothers' 101 Ranch Wild West Show and was the star of their outfit at the Jamestown Exposition, 1907, and at the New York Stampede of 1916. Jim Dahlman of the race horses, mayor of Omaha by then, and former President Theodore Roosevelt of the old Maltese Cross, the man who pushed the cattleman land-fraud cases, were honored guests to watch the bull biter work.

Ironically, Pickett died of a skull fracture, but from a sorrel horse, one that pawed him down and was on him like a cat, much as an old-time sorrel mustang mare might. Even so Bill Pickett didn't die immediately, although his head was a pulp.

Texas also furnished the rodeo with the man that many consider the greatest bronc rider of all times—Samuel Thomas Privett. He was born in Erath County, Texas, back in 1864. Redheaded Booger Red was riding at twelve, orphaned at fifteen, and went into rodeo bronc busting back when there was no time limit on the riding. It ended when a man was off or the horse gave up, standing head down, finished, or lit out to run. While other champions often went in for flossy saddles and other fixings, Booger's favorite bucking saddle was a plain hull or tree. His last public appearance was at Fort Worth in 1925. There, going on sixty-one, he rode a bucking horse on exhibition, and died two weeks later, normally.

There have also been noted women in the rodeo field, although they usually drifted into the more fixed routine of the Wild West performers, trick riders, queens of the rodeo, and so on. But at seventeen Lucille Mulhall, daughter of Colonel Zack Mulhall, was a steer roper and better at it than most men. She busted them so hard they seldom got up before she could tie them. When Theodore Roosevelt visited Oklahoma she roped a coyote for him. In 1904 she was with her father's Wild West Show at the World's Fair in St. Louis and in 1905 in New York's Madison Square Garden with Will Rogers and Tom Mix in the outfit. The Mulhall girl roped horses, too, and could ride a mean bronc. With Homer Wilson she staged the first indoor rodeo at the Southwestern Exposition and Fat Stock Show at Fort Worth. This was the real start of big-time rodeo in the region. Lucille Mulhall died in 1940, at fifty-six, in an auto crash, and was buried the day after Christmas on the last pitiful acres of the once great Mulhall ranch.

Depressions were always hard on the Wild West shows because they had a pay roll to meet. In the 1930's they just about vanished. The rodeo, made up of contestants who depend for their existence on prize money, could survive and did.

The first real impetus to the rodeo as a complete show came out of Wyoming. As early as 1872, with the Sioux still lords of all the Powder River country and the Black Hills, the rising Crazy Horse just growing into the war leader to stop General Crook, Cheyenne already had steer riding the Fourth of July. A few months later there was bronc busting right on the open streets, the crowd falling back as the horses bucked this way and that, endangering the windows, too, and the barking dogs.

The first rodeo in Wyoming was apparently around the early 1880's. The Two Bar Cattle Company, with 160,000 cattle and 200 riders, claiming a region approximately across the Territory, put it on. The Scottish and English owners came out to Cheyenne, about 150 of them. Alex Swan met them there. With carriages, wagons, saddle horses, and camp equipment, they headed out to Laramie Plains. A great wild west show and barbecue was laid out for them on the prairie, with Indians, too, for color. Each man on the pay roll trotted out his specialty. There was horse racing, bronc busting, an Indian and cowboy tug of war, bareback riding of wild horses and steers, and a bullfight of sorts. In this fight a little Mexican stepped on the charging bull's head, was tossed into the air, and came down on the animal's back, slid off the rump, and grabbed the tail, to run along behind, fanning the bull at every jump with his sombrero as rodeo clowns were to do for years and years.

One of the cowboys, Butch Cassidy, known as Parker then, later the notorious outlaw, put on a fine bit of fancy pistol shooting. There was a bronc race—twenty-five men on horses that had never been ridden before. Mounted, the blindfolded broncs in a rough sort of row, the best that could be managed, the blinds were jerked away for the start on the 200-yard course. There was bucking and squealing, some going farther backward than ahead, but half an hour later one of the men made it, still with a horse under him.

After a second night under the stars, this one of deep sleep, the visitors started back to Cheyenne, some of them, particularly the very blond, badly gnat-eaten, their eyes and ears red and puffed up like dough. But it was all a great success, and, as the spokesman who thanked Swan at breakfast had said, was worth coming 6,000 miles to see.

From then on there were small rodeos through Wyoming and the adjoining territory as there were over the rest of the cow country. In 1897 the editor-publisher of the *Cheyenne Sun-Leader*, Colonel E. A. Slack, who had seen the Greeley, Colorado, Potato Day, whooped it up for a Cheyenne

Frontier Day. He got it the twenty-third of that September, with blast of cannon and ringing of bells, everything from mule and sheep bells to a big one hauled in by the railroad. Even the blacksmiths whanged their anvils, and the Union Pacific shop whistles tooted. So Cheyenne's first Frontier Day opened to 3,000 spectators. Out of that beginning sprouted a dozen others, then hundreds all over the country. In the meantime the test of man against the wild, unconquered horse in a fight to a finish has been cut down to ten seconds, the horses mostly what the contemputous old cowmen call "pullman ponies." The tips of the Brahman's horns have been cut off, too, but there is still danger enough for an occasional blood offering in these ceremonials to the cow of the old range days, and before. In 1957, by July 5, the great hump-shouldered Brahmans had thrown twenty-three of their twenty-seven riders in two weeks of rodeos around the country. At Prescott, Arizona, which claims to have the oldest Frontier Days Rodeo, started seventy years ago, one of the riders got his mouth full of blood and teeth when his bull butted him in the face. Another was thrown by his bull as they came out of the chute and was tromped mortally, to the moaning and horrified cries of the spectators and the unconsciously increased interest in the contests. The more serious business of the rodeo clown is to lure the animal from any thrown man and then run for his barrel, the bull probably hard after him. Sometimes the little man in the baggy old pants doesn't make it.

Great reputations have been built for ropers and riders and for bucking horses in these rodeo years. It is still true that:

> There ain't no horse what can't be rode,
> There ain't no man what can't be throwed.

Perhaps Midnight was really the king of all the buckers, as his admirers claim. He probably spilled more cowboys than any other horse in the world, and earned the monument over his grave. There are outlaw mares, too. Miss Klamath, who died in 1955, tallied up the greatest buck-off record of recent years. She had been ridden and used as a pack horse on a ranch in Oregon before she decided to sink her nose and rid herself of man or pack. Her owner refused $10,000 for the Miss the year before she died. Current top buckers are not for sale at any price and their publicity is managed as carefully as a Hollywood starlet's sometimes is. Buckers are getting mighty scarce these stable-bred days.

But the first of the great rodeo bucking horses of international reputation, and to many still the greatest, was Steamboat. He came from the Two Bar Ranch where, almost twenty years before, the big rodeo had been put on for the visiting Scotsmen and the English. By 1903 Steamboat was bucking off all the ranch hands and professional bronc peelers as fast as they could crawl on and yell, "Jerk 'er!" to the man with the blindfold. In 1905 Steamboat was entered at Cheyenne and came away unconquered, unridden. Apparently nobody rode him until 1908, when Dick Stanley stayed with him at the Frontier Days, the horse past his bucking prime. In 1913 Steamboat, a really old horse now, was ridden again. The next year he died of an injury received in the Salt Lake City Rodeo, still bucking. He had never quit and was as surely a dedicated horse as the bulldogger Pickett and the bronc rider Privett were dedicated men, dedicated to the great memorial ceremony to the bygone power and glory of the cow.

From late spring deep into October is the season of the rodeo, the contestants moving from the larger western ones: Cheyenne, Pendleton, Calgary, Fort Worth, Prescott, Belle Fourche, and so on into the smaller fields, splitting up, a few to each state fair, and to the littler ones, counties, small towns, competing against local boys, and corn and hog exhibits, and pumpkins and preserves, with perhaps a rodeo queen and some Indian dances by the Boy Scouts in the dust before the little wooden grandstand in the evenings. But the rodeo people are working their way eastward, drawn to New York and Madison Square Garden for late September and the big prize money. Perhaps 200 cowboys and cowgirls will gather there, with the rodeo clowns, the current western moving-picture and TV stars, and perhaps some old standbys like the Lone Ranger and Lassie. There, before many, many thousands of partisans they re-enact their formal rituals, the bronc riding, bareback and saddled, the calf roping, wild-horse race, Brahman bull riding, and so on, always with the steer wrestling, wrassling, still the center of the events. But more and more there are pretty girls in few clothes, the girls of the arena, lightly draped, going through this formal ritual or that one, perhaps riding pure-white horses in a flying charge, almost a stampede, to applause that rocks the Garden.

But the cowmen are not there, no more than their kind would have been dancing around the golden calf at the foot of Sinai when Moses was late coming off the mountain, in the arena before Minos, or even in the great caverned ceremonial Hall of the Bulls. As always those who actually work with the cattle are out looking after the meat of the people. Perhaps some of the cowmen are thinking a little about their own shows, those of the state fairs, just past, where some of their calves might have gone in a Calf Scramble, or were shown by Four-H Club winners. One might have been a boy in jeans proudly showing his champion Hereford, or Angus or Shorthorn. Perhaps it was a girl, with her steer on display in some great hotel lobby while the evening-dressed crowd milled past, some glancing at the sight of the girl on a campstool calmly knitting a school sweater beside her great blocky young Angus who chewed his cud as calmly inside the velvet-roped little enclosure, his feet in the convenient hay.   ·

Perhaps the cowman out there on the Great Plains is thinking a lot about his own livestock shows, Fort Worth, or Denver, or Chicago, as he takes the fall buyers out to his sleek grass-fat stock and prepares for the forty-foot haulers. They will come in long rows, more orderly than the wild strings of Longhorns trailing themselves to Abilene or Dodge or Ogallala. As the cowman works he keeps an ear out for the market reports and later for blizzard warnings. In the meantime there is branding and dehorning of the young stuff, and weaning time, with the voice of the cow loud on every wind.

And as for thousands of years past he knows that they'll all make it somehow, if they can make it to grass.

# NOTES

On Some Controversial Points and Incidents

(The published material on man and his cattle in the Great Plains region is vast. Much more lie₀ unpublished but open to the researcher in the various historical repositories and particularly in the National Archives and related federal accumulations, such as the records of army posts and military divisions, the Department of the Interior, including Indian Affairs, the Congress and its investigations and hearings, the federal courts, the Department of Agriculture, and so on. Personal accumulations may also grow too voluminous for listing during a lifetime of research, interviews and writing concentrated upon one region. Often, too, the sources are confidential. In my childhood I knew men who came to the Niobrara River with Chisum's Jinglebob herd fresh from the Lincoln County War, some of them excellent cowmen, others hideouts. Few who were connected with the man-burning Olive gang liked to have this widely known. Although perhaps a dozen men from the Johnson County War lived in the sandhills around us, several were traveling under various names and the survivors are still unwilling to be connected with their stories, as are many others over the cow country, for various and sometimes good reasons.)

(Sources from bibliography listed by authors only.)

BOOK ONE

Chapter I. Much on the character of Longhorns from stories told by Jim Dahlman, A. R. Modisett, Tom Milligan and other old trail drivers in northwest Nebraska, and from Dobie's *The Longhorns*.

Chapter II. Wheel in America: Kluckhohn, Clyde, "Suppose Columbus Had Stayed at Home." *Saturday Review*. Sept. 22, 1956.

BOOK TWO

Chapter I. Olives: J. W. Snyder Papers, Library, University of Texas; Moore, Lee, *Letters from Old Friends and Members of the Wyoming Stock Growers Association*, pam., Cheyenne, 1923; Benschoter;

Foght; Taylorsville (Tex.) *Times,* Feb. 10, 1879; Appeal for Change of Venue, State of Nebraska vs I. P. Olive, (etc.), Indictment for Murder, 5th Jud. Dist., Adams Co., including depositions from everyone known to be involved, Nebraska State Historical Society.

Chapter III. Killing of Pierce: Beatrice (Nebr.) *Express,* Aug. 28, 1873, and Streeter, Floyd Benjamin, *The Kaw,* New York. 1941.

Chapter IV. Olives: See Chapter I above, also Butcher; Jenkins; and *Daily State Journal* (Lincoln, Nebr.), Dec. 1878 through Dec. 1880.

BOOK THREE

Chapter I. *Comancheros:* Files of Mackenzie Expedition, Sept.-Dec. 1874, Dept. of Texas, War Records, National Archives, for crushing defeat of Indians who supplied them.

Olive trial: See Notes above.

Chapter III. Montana man burners: When the "Cattle King" bill failed in 1884, even Granville Stuart, formerly a voice for moderation against the anger of Roosevelt and De Mores, was ready for direct action. He helped organize the Stranglers against the so-called horse thieves of the badlands. After some scattered killings, they made a dawn attack, July 8, on the old Missouri River woodyard at Bates Point, below the Musselshell, and burned the cabin to the ground with, some said, five smoking bodies inside. Of the men who escaped several were hanged later, the total dead estimated from 19 to 75. There was angry protest and some complaint that the aim was to scare out the rush of settlers. James Fergus, a neighboring cattleman, finally said the attack was not "by bands of lawless cowboys but was the result of a general understanding among all the large cattle ranges of Montana." There was a story that the Stranglers made a breed boy play his fiddle for them all evening and then strung him up next morning. In 1924 an old Montanan told this author, "You run with horse thieves, them days, you hung with them."

Chapter IV. Print Olive killed: *Border Ruffian,* Coolidge, Kans., Omaha (Nebr.) *Bee,* Aug. 18, 1886, and others.

Bill Olive Killed: Rister, *No Man's Land.*

## BOOK FOUR

Chapters I to III. Rebellion against Wyoming Stock Growers Association roundup rule: Lincoln County, Nebr., ranchers swore out warrants against members of the roundup and deputized cowboys to serve them if the Association men showed up—Capt. Luther H. North; A. R. Modisett, of Modisetts Ranch in the sandhills; Bratt's *Trails of Yesterday;* also from ranchers up around Black Hills in a rebellion of their own.

Wyoming: Sources on cattleman conflicts, 1888-1893, from bibliography: Baber; Baker; Canton; Clay; David; Frink (*Cow Country*); Hall; Jackson, of Frink, Jackson and Spring; Krakel, Mercer; Mokler; Osgood; Ricketts; Trenholm; Whitcomb; Brayer; Jackson ("Wyoming Stock Growers Association"). Additional sources: Bard, Floyd C., letter in *True West*, July-Aug., 1957; Brock, J. Elmer, "Who Dry-gulched the Hoe Foreman?", Denver, *Westerners Brand Book*, 1953; Sheldon, A. E., "A Nebraska Episode of the Wyoming Cattle War," *Proceedings and Collections*, Nebraska State Historical Society, Vol. V, sec. sr., 1902. There is much manuscript and interview material in private hands, usually not open to researchers.

Chapter V. End of free grass: sources from bibliography: Bye; Clay; Hall; Holden (*Spur Ranch*); Krakel; Osgood; Riordan ("Frontier Kingdom"); Sandoz (*Old Jules*); Sheldon; Trenholm; U. S. Congress ("Report on Public Lands Com."); Webb (*Texas Rangers*). Additional sources: Carpenter, Mrs. Martha, *Cherry County, Nebraska, Cattle Fight,* in author's files; Downing, Mrs. Harry (widow of Jason H. Cole), *Account of Cole Tragedy,* ms written for author; Holden, W. C., "The Problem of Stealing on the Spur Ranch," West Texas Historical Association *Year Book,* Vol. VIII; Hooper, Pat, letters to author; Lemmon, G. E., autobiographical ms in author's files; Modisett, A. R., *Recollections,* ms in author's files; Morse, Ruth, article on Sen. D. J. Cole, son of Jason H. Cole, *Nebraska Cattleman,* Apr., 1951; Rasch, P. J., "The Horrel War," New Mexican Historical *Review,* XXXI; Petersen, Marquard: copies of letters and documents of dealings with Richard and Comstock, including the homesteading and the sale of the Spade Ranch site. Presented to the author by Mr. Petersen.

# BIBLIOGRAPHY

Some representative selections for the general reader.

## BOOKS

Abbott, E. C. (Teddy Blue) and Helena Huntington Smith. *We Pointed Them North.* New York: Farrar and Rinehart. 1939.

Baber, D. F. as told by Bill Walker. *The Longest Rope, the Truth About the Johnson County Cattle War.* Caldwell: Caxton. 1940.

Baker, E. D. "A Rustler's Account of the 'Johnson County War'," Chicago, *The Westerners Brand Book, 1945-46.* 1947.

Barnes, W. C. *Winter Grazing Grounds and Forest Ranges.* Chicago. 1913.

Barrows, John R. *Ubet.* Caldwell: Caxton. 1934.

Bataille, Georges. *Lascaux, or the Birth of Art.* Switzerland: Skira. n.d.

Baughman, Theodore. *The Oklahoma Scout.* Chicago: Homewood. 188-.

Bell, James A. *A Log of the Texas-California Cattle Trail, 1854.* (ed. J. Evetts Haley), priv. pub. 1932.

Benschoter, Geo. E. *Book of Facts, Concerning the Early Settlement of Sherman County.* pam. Loup City, Nebr. About 1897.

Blanchard, Leola Howard. *Conquest of Southwest Kansas.* Wichita. 1931.

Bolton, Herbert Eugene. *Athanase de Mézières and the Louisiana-Texas Frontier, 1768-1780.* 2 vols. Cleveland: Arthur H. Clark. 1914.

Bratt, John. *Trails of Yesterday.* Lincoln and Chicago. 1921.

Brisbin, James S. *Beef Bonanza: or How to Get Rich on the Plains.* Philadelphia. 1881.

Bronson, Edgar Beecher. *Reminiscences of a Ranchman.* New York: McClure. 1908.

Brown, Dee, with Schmitt, Martin F. *Trail Driving Days.* New York: Scribners. 1952.

Burdick, Usher L. *Marquis De Mores at War in the Badlands.* pam. Fargo, N. Dak. 1929.

Burns, Robert Homer; Gillespie, Andrew Springs and Richardson, Willing Gay. *Wyoming's Pioneer Ranches, by Three Native Sons of the Laramie Plains.* Laramie: Top-of-the-World Press. 1955.

Burton, Harley True. *A History of the JA Ranch.* Austin. 1928.

Butcher, S. D. *Pioneer History of Custer County and Short Sketches of Early Days in Nebraska*. Broken Bow, Nebr. 1901.

Bye, John O. *Back Trailing in the Heart of the Short Grass Country*. Everett, Wash.: Alexander Printing Co., 1956.

Canton, Frank M. *Frontier Trails, the Autobiography of Frank M. Canton*. ed. Edward Everett Dale. Boston: Houghton Mifflin. 1930.

Carey, Fred. *Mayor Jim* (Jim Dahlman). Omaha: Omaha Printing Co. 1930.

Castaneda, C. E. *The Finding of Texas*. Vol. 1 of *Our Catholic Heritage in Texas*. 1518-1936. 2 vols. Austin: Von Boeckmann-Jones. 1936.

Clancy, Foghorn. *My Fifty Years in Rodeo, Living with Cowboys, Horses and Danger*. San Antonio: Naylor. 1952.

Clay, John. *My Life on the Range*. Chicago. priv. pub. 1924.

Collins, Hubert E. *Warpath & Cattle Trail*. New York: Morrow. 1928.

Cook, James H. *Fifty Years on the Old Frontier*. New Haven: Yale. 1923.

Crawford, Lewis F. *Badlands and Broncho Trails. Adventures of Ben Arnold Connor*. Bismarck. 1926.

Dale, Edward Everett. *The Range Cattle Industry*. Norman. 1930.

David, Robert B. *Malcolm Campbell, Sheriff*. Casper, Wyo. 1932.

Day, A. Grove. *Coronado's Quest*. Berkeley and Los Angeles: Univ. of California Press. 1940.

Dobie, J. Frank. *The Longhorns*. Boston: Little Brown. 1941.

———. "Trail Driving a Hundred Years Ago." Denver, *The Westerners Brand Book*, 1952.

———. *A Vaquero of the Brush Country*. Dallas. 1920.

Emmett, Chris. *Shanghai Pierce: a Fair Likeness*. Norman: Univ. of Oklahoma Press. 1953.

Foght, H. W. *Trail of the Loup*. 1906.

French, Wm. *Some Recollections of a Western Ranchman*. London. 1927.

Frewen, Moreton. *Milton Mowbray and Other Memories*. London. 1924.

Frink, Maurice. *Cow Country Cavalcade: Eighty Years of the Wyoming Stock Growers Association*. Denver: Old West Publishing Co. 1954.

Frink, Maurice; Jackson, W. Turrentine & Spring, Agnes Wright. *When Grass Was King*. Boulder: Univ. of Colorado Press. 1956.

Gard, Wayne. *The Chisholm Trail*. Norman: Univ. of Oklahoma Press. 1954.

Goodwyn, Frank. *Life on the King Ranch*. New York: Crowell. 1951.

Guernsey, Charles A. *Wyoming Cowboy Days.* New York: Putnam's. 1930.

Hagedorn, Herman. *Roosevelt in the Badlands.* Boston. 1921.

Haley, J. Evetts. *Charles Goodnight, Cowman and Plainsman.* Boston: Houghton Mifflin. 1936.

——. *The XIT Ranch of Texas.* Chicago: Lakeside Press. 1929.

Hall, Bert L. ed. *Roundup Years, Old Muddy to Black Hills.* Pierre. 1954.

Hastings, Frank S. *A Ranchman's Recollections.* Chicago. 1921.

Hibbard, Benjamin H. *A History of the Public Land Policies.* New York. 1924.

Holden, William Curry. *Alkali Trails, or Social and Economic Movements of the Texas Frontier, 1846-1900.* Dallas. 1930.

——. *Rollie Burns, an Account of the Ranching Industry on the South Plains.* Dallas. 1932.

——. *The Spur Ranch, a Study of the Inclosed Ranch Phase of the Cattle Industry in Texas.* Boston: Christopher. 1934.

Howard, Joseph Kinsey. *Montana, High, Wide and Handsome.* New Haven: Yale. 1943.

Horgan, Paul. *Great River, the Rio Grande in North American History.* 2 vols. New York: Rinehart. 1954.

Huidekoper, A. C. *My Experience and Investment in the Bad Lands of Dakota and Some of the Men I Met There.* pam. Baltimore: Wirth Bros. 1947.

Huidekoper, Wallis. *The Land of the Dakotahs.* Helena: Montana Stockgrowers Association. 1949.

Hunt, Frazier. *Cap Mossman, Last of the Great Cowmen.* New York: Hastings House. 1951.

Hunter, J. Marvin, (comp. and ed.) *The Trail Drivers of Texas.* 2 vols. Bandera, Tex. 1923.

James, Will. *Lone Cowboy: My Life Story.* New York: Scribners. 1930.

Jenkins, A. O. *Olive's Last Roundup.* Loup City, Nebr. 1930.

Krakel, Dean F. *The Saga of Tom Horn, the Story of a Cattlemen's War.* Laramie: Laramie Printing. 1954.

Lang, Lincoln A. *Ranching with Roosevelt.* Philadelphia. 1926.

Lockhart, John W. *Sixty Years on the Brazos.* Los Angeles, priv. 1930.

Henry, Stuart. *Conquering the Great Plains.* New York. 1930.

Lea, Tom. *The King Ranch.* 2 vols. Boston: Little Brown. 1957.

Lomax, John A., and Lomax, Alan. *Cowboy Songs and Other Frontier Ballads.* 1938.

Lydekker, Richard. *The Ox and Its Kindred.* London. 1912.

McCarty, John L. *Maverick Town, the Story of Old Tascosa.* Norman. 1946.

McCarty, "Col." Wm. C. *A Few Practical Remarks about Texas.* Colonization pam. New York. 1871.

McCracken, Harold. *The Charles M. Russell Book.* Garden City: Doubleday. 1957.

McCoy, Joseph A. *Historic Sketches of the Cattle Trade of the West and the Southwest.* Kansas City. 1874.

Madison, Virginia. *The Big Bend Country of Texas.* Albuquerque: Univ. of New Mexico Press. 1955.

Mattison, Ray H. *Ranching in the Dakota Bad Lands.* pam. Bismarck: State Historical Society of North Dakota. 1952.

————. *Roosevelt's Dakota Ranches.* pam. Bismarck: *Tribune.* n.d.

Mercer, A. S. *The Banditti of the Plains, or the Cattlemen's Invasion of Wyoming in 1892.* priv. pub. 1894.

Milligan, E. W. "John Wesley Iliff," Denver, *The Westerners Brand Book.* 1950.

Mokler, Alfred James. *History of Natrona County, Wyoming, 1888-1922.* Chicago. 1923.

Nordyke, Lewis. *Cattle Empire; the Fabulous Story of the 3,000,000-Acre XIT.* New York: Morrow. 1949.

————. *Great Roundup; the Story of Texas and Southwestern Cowmen.* New York: Morrow. 1955.

O'Connor, Richard. *Bat Masterson.* New York: Doubleday. 1957.

Osgood, Ernest S. *The Day of the Cattleman.* Minneapolis. 1929.

Parsons, John E. *The First Winchester.* New York: Morrow. 1955.

Peake, Ora Brooks. *The Colorado Range Cattle Industry.* Glendale. 1937.

Pelzer, Louis. *The Cattlemen's Frontier.* Glendale. 1936.

Pence, Mary Lou and Homsher, Lola M. *The Ghost Towns of Wyoming.* New York: Hastings House. 1956.

Powell, John Wesley. *Report on the Lands of the Arid Regions of the United States.* Washington. 1879.

Pulling, Hazel Adele. "History of the Range Cattle Industry of Dakota," South Dakota Historical *Collections.* Vol. XX. 1940.

Raht, Carlysle Graham. *The Romance of Davis Mountains and the Big Bend Country.* El Paso. 1919.

Raines, William McLeod, and Barnes, Will C. *Cattle.* New York. 1930.

Richardson, R. N. *The Comanche Barrier to South Plains Settlement.* Glendale. 1933.

Ricketts, W. P. *Fifty Years in the Saddle.* Sheridan, Wyo. 1942.

Rister, Carl Coke. *No Man's Land.* Norman. 1948.

————. *The Southwestern Frontier, 1865-1881.* Cleveland. 1928.

Robbers Roost Historical Society, *Pioneering on the Cheyenne River.* Lusk, Wyo.: *Herald.* 1947.

Rollins, P. A. *The Cowboy.* New York. 1922.

Rollinson, John K. *Wyoming Cattle Trails.* Caldwell: Caxton. 1948.
Roosevelt, Theodore. *Hunting Trips of a Ranchman.* New York. 1885.
Russell, Charles M. *Good Medicine.* New York. 1936.
Sandoz, Mari. *The Buffalo Hunters.* New York: Hastings House. 1954.
———. *Cheyenne Autumn.* New York: McGraw-Hill. 1952.
———. *Old Jules.* 20th Anniv. ed. New York: Hastings House. 1955.
Sheldon, Addison E. *Land Systems and Land Policies of Nebraska.* Lincoln: Nebraska State Historical Society Publications, Vol. XXII. 1936.
Siringo, Charles A. *A Texas Cowboy.* new ed. New York: Sloane. 1950.
Sonnichsen, C. L. *I'll Die before I'll Run; the Story of the Great Feuds of Texas.* New York: Harpers. 1951.
Sowell, A. J. *Rangers and Pioneers of Texas.* San Antonio. 1884.
Spring, Agnes Wright. *70 Years of the Cow Country, Panoramic History of the Wyoming Stock Growers Association.* Cheyenne. 1942.
Streeter, Floyd Benjamin. *Prairie Trails and Cow Towns.* Boston. 1936.
Stuart, Granville. *Forty Years on the Frontier.* 2 vols. Cleveland. 1925.
Tait, J. S. *The Cattle-fields of the Far West.* pam. Edinburgh. 1884.
Towne, Charles Wayland, and Wentworth, Edward Norris. *Cattle and Men.* Norman: Univ. of Oklahoma Press. 1955.
———. *Shepherd's Empire.* Norman. 1945.
Trenholm, Virginia Cole. *Footprints on the Frontier.* Douglas, Wyo. 1945.
Treadwell, Edward F. *The Cattle King.* New York. 1931.


*U. S. CONGRESS:*

Documents and Correspondence Relating to Leases of Indian Lands *** for Cattle Grazing *** 1884. *Sen. Ex. Doc. No. 54.* 48th Cong. 1st Sess.
Range and Ranch Cattle Traffic, by Joseph Nimmo. *House Ex. Doc. No. 267.* 48th Cong. 2nd Sess. 1884-5.
Report of Public Lands Commission. 1905. *Sen. Doc. No. 189.* 58th Cong. 3rd Sess.
Vestal, Stanley. *Queen of Cowtowns, Dodge City.* New York: Harpers. 1952.
Webb, Walter Prescott. *The Great Plains.* New York. 1931.
———. *The Texas Rangers, a Century of Frontier Defense.* Boston. 1935.
Whitcomb, E. W. "Reminiscences of a Pioneer," First *Biennial Report* of the State Historian of the State of Wyoming. 1920.
Wright, Robert M. *Dodge City, the Cowboy Capital and the Great Southwest,* etc. Wichita. 1913.

*PERIODICALS*

Aeschbacher, W. P. "Development of Cattle Raising in the Sandhills,"
   *Nebraska History*, XXVIII, no. 1.
Brayer, Herbert O. "The Influence of British Capital on the Western
   Range Cattle Industry." Denver, *Westerners Brand Book*, IV,
   no. 5.
Clay, John. "The Passing of Conrad Kohrs," *Breeders Gazette*, Dec. 2,
   1920.
Eaton, J. C. "Early Ranching in the Mouse River Valley," *Bar North*,
   June 1956.
Fletcher, Robt. S. "Organization of the Range Cattle Business in Eastern
   Montana," *Bulletin 265*, Mont. Agricultural Experiment Station,
   June 1932.
———. "That Hard Winter in Montana, 1886-1887," *Agricultural His-*
   *tory*, IV, Oct. 1930.
Goplen, Arnold O. "The Career of Marquis De Mores in the Badlands
   of North Dakota," *North Dakota History*, XIII, Nos. 1-2.
Hall, J. N. "Days of the Cattlemen in Northeastern Colorado," *Colo-*
   *rado Magazine*, May 1930.
Hinton, Harwood P., Jr. "John Simpson Chisum, 1877-1884," *New*
   *Mexico Historical Review*, XXXI, July 1956.
Jackson, W. Turrentine. "The Wyoming Stock Growers Association:
   Political Power in Wyoming Territory, 1873-1890," *Mississippi*
   *Valley Historical Review*, XXX, Mar. 1947.
Kennedy, Michael, "Judith Basin Top Hand, Reminiscences of Wm. C.
   Burnett, an Early Montana Cattleman," *Montana Magazine of*
   *History*, Spring 1953.
Kohrs, Conrad. "A Veteran's Experience in the Western Cattle Trade,"
   *Breeders Gazette*, Dec. 18, 1912.
Kuhn, Bertha M. "The W Bar Ranch on the Missouri Slope," *Collec-*
   *tions*, the State Historical Society, North Dakota, V, 1923.
Larson, T. A. "The Winter of 1886-87 in Wyoming," *Annals of Wyo-*
   *ming*, Jan. 1942.
McMechen, Edgar C. "John Hittson, Cattle King," *Colorado Magazine*,
   Sept. 1934.
Malin, James C. "Soil, Animal and Plant Relations of the Grassland,
   Historically Reconsidered," *Scientific Monthly*, LXXVI, no. 4.
Oliphant, J. Orin, "Eastward Movement of Cattle from the Oregon
   Country," *Agricultural History*, XX, No. 1.
Records, Ralph H. "Wildlife on the T-5 and Spade Ranches," *Chron-*
   *icles of Oklahoma*, XXI, Sept. 1943.
Riordan, Marguerite, "Frontier Kingdom," (Bartlett Richards) *The*
   *Nebraska Cattleman*, Nov. 1950 to Mar. 1951.

————. "Murdo Mackenzie, Ranch King," *The Westerner,* Oct. 1943 to Mar. 1944.

Schmidt, L. B. "The Westward Movement of the Corn-growing Industry in the United States," *Iowa Jr. of History and Politics,* XXI, no. 1.

Welsh, Donald H. "Cosmopolitan Cattle King, Pierre Wibaux and the W Bar Ranch," *Montana, the Magazine of Western History,* Spring 1955.

# INDEX

511